COMPUTERS AND COGNITION:
WHY MINDS ARE NOT MACHINES

STUDIES IN COGNITIVE SYSTEMS

VOLUME 25

COMPUTERS AND COGNITION:
WHY MINDS ARE NOT MACHINES

by

JAMES H. FETZER

University of Minnesota, Duluth, U.S.A.

KLUWER ACADEMIC PUBLISHERS
DORDRECHT / BOSTON / LONDON

A C.I.P. Catalogue record for this book is available from the Library of Congress.

OCLC# 44885371   BF
311
. F423
2001

ISBN 0-7923-6615-8

Published by Kluwer Academic Publishers,
P.O. Box 17, 3300 AA Dordrecht, The Netherlands.

Sold and distributed in North, Central and South America
by Kluwer Academic Publishers,
101 Philip Drive, Norwell, MA 02061, U.S.A.

In all other countries, sold and distributed
by Kluwer Academic Publishers,
P.O. Box 322, 3300 AH Dordrecht, The Netherlands.

Printed on acid-free paper

02-0102-200 ts

First published 2001, Reprinted 2002

Printed in the Netherlands.

To

Janice E. Morgan

CONTENTS

CONTENTS

EPILOGUE

SERIES PREFACE

This series will include monographs and collections of studies devoted to the investigation and exploration of knowledge, information, and data-processsing systems of all kinds, no matter whether human, (other) animal, or machine. Its scope is intended to span the full range of interests from classical problems in the philosophy of mind and philosophical psychology through issues in cognitive psychology and sociobiology (concerning the mental capabilitiess of other species) to ideas related to artificial intelligence and to computer science. While primary emphasis will be placed upon theoretical, conceptual, and epistemological aspects of these problems and domains, empirical, experimental, and methodological studies will also appear from time to time.

The domination of cognitive science by the computational conception of mind has been so complete that some theoreticians have even gone so far as to define "cognitive science" as the study of computational models of mind. The arguments presented in this volume clearly demonstate—definitively, in my judgment—that that paradigm is indefensible, not just in its details, but in its general conception. Minds are not digital machines and people are not computers. The conception of minds as semiotic systems appears to explain the phenomena—of consciousness, cognition, and thought—far more adequately than its predecessor ever could. The scope and limits of digital machines are delineated here. Others must judge if the time has come for a new paradigm of the mind.

J. H. F.

FOREWORD

Contemporary research in artificial intelligence and cognitive science has been dominated by the conception that minds either are computers or at least operate on the basis of the same principles that govern digital machines. This view has been elaborated and defended by many familar figures within these fields, including Allen Newell and Herbert Simon, John Haugeland, Jerry Fodor and Zenon Pylyshyn, Margaret Boden, Daniel Dennett, David J. Chalmers, Philip Johnson-Laird, Steven Pinker and scores unnamed, who have committed themselves to its defense. If general agreement were the measure of truth, it would be difficult to deny that computationalism, thus understood, appears to be true.

Indeed, even most of those who disagree with the computational conception tend to accept some of its elements. The alternative known as connectionism, for example, which has been endorsed by David Rumelhart, Paul Churchland, and Paul Smolensky, among others, retains the conception of cognition as *computation across representations*, even while it rejects the contention that computationalism has properly understood the nature of representations themselves. The difference between them turns out to be that connectionists hold that representations are distributed as patterns of activation across sets of neural nodes, where cognition is now taken as *computation across distributed representations*.

Even granting the difference between nodular and distributed forms of representations, computationalists and connectionists can agree on many aspects of cognition. The classic formulation of the computational conception, for example, has been advanced by John Haugeland, who has suggested *that thinking is reasoning, that reasoning is reckoning, that reckoning is computation, that computation is cognition, and that the boundaries of computability define the boundaries of thought*. As long as the differences between nodular and distributed representations are acknowledged, there are no reasons—no evident reasons, at least—why a connectionist should not adopt these computationalist contentions.

In order to establish whether minds are or operate on the basis of the same principles that govern computing machines, however, it is necessary to accomplish
three tasks. First, discover the principles that govern computing machines. Second,
discover the principles that govern human minds. And, third, compare them to ascertain whether they are similar or the same. That much should be obvious. But
while leading computationalists have shown considerable ingenuity in elaborating
and defending the conception of minds as computers, they have not always been
attentive to the study of thought processes themselves. Their underlying attitude
has been that no theoretical alternative is possible.

Part I: *Semiotic Systems*.

The essays collected here are intended to demonstrate that this attitude is no
longer justified. The conception of *minds as semiotic (or "sign-using") systems*
should lay this myth to rest, once and for all. According to this approach, which
builds on the theory of signs advanced by Charles S. Peirce (1839–1914), *minds* are
the kinds of things that are able to use signs, where *signs* are things that stand for
other things (in some respect or other). Since there are at least three different ways
in which things can stand for other things, there turn out to be at least three different
kinds of minds, which use different kinds of signs.

"Semiotic systems" as *systems that can use signs* ("minds"), of course, differ
from "semiotic systems" as *systems of signs of kinds that semiotic systems can use*
("signs"). The meaning of a sign for a system is understood on the basis of its
effects on (actual or potential) behavior, which requires a dispositional conception
of meaning that is non-behavioristic, non-extensional, and non-reductionistic. The
semiotic conception thus satisfies Fodor's condition that a theory of cognition ought
to connect the intensional properties of mental states with their causal influence on
behavior. It would be a blunder to dismiss the semiotic account merely on the basis
of mistaken preconceptions about dispositions.

Thus, the three essays that appear in Part I provide an introduction to the theory
of semiotic systems that includes a discussion of the theory of signs and of the
kinds of minds that are distinguishable on that basis. Since there are at least three
kinds of signs—namely, iconic, indexical, and symbolic—which have the ability to
use things as signs on the basis of their relations of resemblance, of cause-or-effect,
or of habitual association to other things, there also appear to be at least three *kinds
of minds*—namely, iconic, indexical, and symbolic—which have the ability to use

signs of those kinds. And there appear to be two higher kinds of mentality, known as transformational mentality and as metamentality.

The conception of cognition as computation across representations, of course, would be severely undermined if what computers can compute does not count as "representations", at least for those machines, where a distinction has to be drawn between "signs" that are significant for *the users of* machines and "signs" that are significant *for use by* those machines. There is nothing surprising about the idea that inputs and outputs are significant for the users of machines, which are designed to fulfill the expectations we impose upon them. The question that matters is whether those inputs and outputs are meaningful for those machines.

Thus, the papers in Part I concern one of the most important issues at stake here. The arguments presented there—in relation to definitions and definability, the physical symbol system hypothesis, and syntactical and semantical theories of language— are intended to establish the existence of what I shall call *the static difference* between them, which emanates from the capacity of digital machines to process marks as opposed to the ability of semiotic systems to process signs:

THE STATIC DIFFERENCE

ARGUMENT 1: Computers are mark-manipulating systems, minds are not.

Premise 1 Computers manipulate marks on the basis of their shapes, sizes, and relative locations.

Premise 2: These shapes, sizes, and relative locations exert causal influence upon computers, but do not stand for anything for those systems.

Premise 3: Minds operate by utilizing signs that stand for other things in some respect or other for them as sign-using (or "semiotic") systems.

_____

Conclusion 1: Computers are not semiotic (sign-using) systems.

_____

Conclusion 2: Computers are not the possessors of minds.

Thus, even if minds effected transitions between thoughts as the computational conception commends, the conception of minds as computational systems and as semiotic systems would continue to distinguish between them, as Part I explains.

Part II: *Computers and Cognition.*

If some computationalists have displayed the tendency to take for granted that minds operate on the basis of the same principles that govern computing machines, a matter that requires both empirical investigation and conceptual clarification for its vindication, others have been more cautious. Nevertheless, the dominant paradigm still appears to be vulnerable to detailed explorations of the nature of thought processes, on the one hand, and of the nature of computational procedures, on the other. The studies presented here strongly suggest—in my view, prove conclusively—that the principles that govern thought processes differ from those that control computational procedures. While Part I focuses on representations, Part II focuses on the nature of computation itself.

The core question is whether thinking is computing or whether computing is thinking. Since computing depends upon programs, and programs, in turn, depend upon algorithms, the answer hinges upon the existence and ubiquity of *mental algorithms*. Suppose, for example, that certain kinds of thinking—such as dreams, daydreams, and even ordinarily thought processes as well as perception and memory—are *not* controlled by algorithmic procedures. Then even if particular kinds of problem solving (such as the evaluation of proofs in logic and mathematics, for example) *are* controlled by algorithmic procedures, it would remain the case that computing is at best one special kind of thinking.

Thus, the papers in Part II concern another of the most important issues at stake here. The arguments presented there—in relation to exacting comparisons between the properties of algorithms and of programs as causal implementations of algorithms, and of the nature of thought processes and of computational procedures—are intended to establish the existence of what I shall call *the dynamic difference* between them, which arises because computers process information by means of algorithms, while minds, by contrast, are non-algorithmic systems:

THE DYNAMIC DIFFERENCE

ARGUMENT 2:	Computers are governed by algorithms, but minds are not.
Premise 1:	Computers are governed by programs, which are causal models of algorithms.
Premise 2:	Algorithms are effective decision procedures for arriving at definite solutions to problems in a finite number of steps.
Premise 3:	Most human thought processes, including dreams, daydreams, and ordinary thinking, are not procedures for arriving at solutions to problems in a finite number of steps.

Conclusion 1:	Most human thought processes are not governed by programs as causal models of algorithms.

Conclusion 2:	Minds are not computers.

Indeed, the conception of cognition that emerges from these analyses is that *cognition is a causal process involving the use of signs*. The computational conception appears to be no more than an overgeneralization based upon a special kind of thinking that is not characteristic of thought processes. Thinking is *not* reducible to reasoning, reasoning is *not* reducible to reckoning, reckoning is *not* reducible to computation, computation is *not* cognition, and the boundaries of computability do *not* define the boundaries of thought. Ironically, even computers themselves are best understood as special kinds of signs, where their own significance presupposes the existence of interpretations, interpreters, or minds.

The computational conception, according to which cognition is computation across representation, thus appears to be fatally flawed. First, as the papers in Part I have displayed, the kinds of representations that computers compute are not signs that are suitable for cognition. Second, as the papers in Part II have established, even if the kinds of representations that computers compute were suitable for cognition, computing is at best a special kind of thinking that does not adequately represent the character of cognition. Neither the nature of representations as the objects of cognition (thought) nor the nature of transitions between them (transitions between thoughts) are computational in character.

The Process of Paradigm Change.

As Thomas Kuhn has explained, abandoning an entrenched paradigm is as much a psychological process as it is a scientific procedure. The existence of anomalies of the kinds that the static difference and the dynamic difference display are more than sufficient to conclusively demonstrate the untenability of the computational paradigm—from a logical point of view. Were the existence of objective evidence enough to overthrow a paradigm, therefore, then the computational account would be abandoned forthwith! Scientists, even cognitive scientists, however, have commitments they may be reluctant to abandon, especially if that might imply their past time and effort has been devoted to advancing misconceptions regarding consciousness and cognition.

Moreover, as Kuhn also explained, scientists, including cognitive scientists, tend to abandon an old paradigm and embrace a new paradigm only when it has become apparent that the anomalies that burden the old paradigm cannot be resolved within the framework it provides and it has also become apparent that the new paradigm has the capacity to resolve them. Contemporary enthusiasm for the old (computational) paradigm continues virtually unabated, which suggests that it may be some time before the new (semiotic) paradigm takes its place. But there should be no doubt that the conditions for a paradigm change continue to abound. That this too shall come to pass appears to be as inevitable as were the triumph of Copernicus over Ptolemy or of Newton over Copernicus!

Among the most important vestages of hope for the old paradigm, moreover, are lingering misconceptions about the extent to which human thought and human behavior can be successfully modeled employing computational procedures. There is a tendency to confound the difference between mere *simulations* (where the same outputs are derived from the same inputs), *replications* (where the same outputs are derived from the same inputs by means of the same processes or procedures), and *emulations* (where the same outputs are derived from the same inputs by means of the same procedures by systems composed of the same or similar stuff). Computer models can successively approximate human thought and behavior without thereby also becoming thinking things.

SIMULATIONS

ARGUMENT 3: Digital machines can nevertheless simulate thought processes and other diverse forms of human behavior.

Premise 1: Computer programmers and those who design the systems that they control can increase their performance capabilities, making them better and better simulations.

Premise 2: Their performance capabilities may be closer and closer approximations to the performance capabilities of human beings without turning them into thinking things.

Premise 3 Indeed, the static and the dynamic differences that distinguish computer performance from human performance preclude those systems from being thinking things.

Conclusion: Although the performance capabilities of digital machines can become better and better approximations of human behavior, they are still not thinking things.

The theory that minds are machines, like many other controversial claims, thus trades on an ambiguity. There is a sense in which minds are "machines", namely: the sense in which anything that performs work is a *machine*—even if the energy it would require is no than a single peanut can supply—because the mind performs "work" in the form of mental labor. There is a second sense in which minds are not "machines", however: the sense in which the class of machines relevent to this thesis consists of *digital* machines—the contention of such immense popularity— because the mind does not operate on the principles that govern digital machines. The theory therefore equivocates between a claim that is true but trivial (that minds are machines) and a claim that is significant but false (that minds are digital machines). It thus secures its specious plausibility.

When attention turns from digital computers to connectionist machines for which distributed representations are subject to computational manipulation, however, the situation requires qualification. Although classic connectionist conceptions (of cognition as computation across distributed representations) do not equate to thinking things, as connectionist systems become more and more brain-like, they have the potential to become more and more mind-like as well. In particular, were the development of connectionist systems to reach the point of implementing neural networks that function in ways incorporating the static and the dynamic modes of operation under consideration here, then neo-connectionist cognitive scientists would have developed artificial thinking things. Indeed, none of the arguments presented here is meant to deny that human brains are neural networks of a special kind called "semiotic systems".

Part III: *Computer Epistemology.*

Indeed, the differences between digital machines and thinking things are explored with respect to the problem of simulation in the Prologue, which examines the epistemic problem of ascertaining whether or not a modeling system simulates, replicates, or emulates a thinking thing. This discussion takes the classic Turing Test in which two systems are compared in relation to their respective capabilities for yielding similar outputs given similar inputs as its point of departure, but also considers stronger versions in forms known as the "Total Turing Test" and the "Total Total Turing Test" as alternatives that might qualify as suitable successors to Turing's conception in establishing empirical evidence that would warrant inferences to the existence of thinking things.

The papers in Part III focus on digital machines and the nature of computers as complex causal systems even apart from any questions of their existence as thinking things. Here the crucial question is the extent to which we can count on the reliability of systems that are controlled by computers when they execute programs. At least three alternatives are explored, including the use of formal methods, the construction of prototypes, and reliance upon program testing. Indeed, reliance upon formal methods to guarantee the performance of computer systems raises especially fascinating issues in both ontology and epistemology.

The papers presented here have a rather rich and fascinating history that began with the appearance of "Program Verification: The Very Idea", a study of the role of formal methods in computer science, which triggered an extended and intense debate within the computer science community. It eventually generated articles and discussion in three journals—*Communications of the Association for Computing Machinery*, *Notices of the American Mathematical Society*, and *Minds and Machines*—as well as contributions to encyclopedias of computer science and technology, a story that is reviewed in the last piece reprinted there.

The Epilogue, finally, investigates the boundaries of what, in principle, can be known about the performance of computer systems in a world that is increasingly dependent upon them. Like those that undertake a sustained examination of the theoretical potential of the scope and limits of formal methods in software engineering, each of these papers and this entire book approach the study of computer science from the perspective of the theory of knowledge and are intended as contributions to a new discipline of *the philosophy of computer science*, which explores crucial issues that demand our attention and that must be understood, not simply for theoretical reasons of the kind that motivate most philosophical inquiry, but also for practical reasons of the kind that matter in everyday life.

Much of the message conveyed in this work concerns the ability of computers to perform mental labor on our behalf even though these machines are incapable of thought. Disabusing ourselves of false beliefs about the nature of computers and the nature of mind, of course, should be welcomed rather than condemned. When we understand both the strengths and weaknesses of ourselves and our machines, we can better serve our purposes by employing them in ways that benefit us without incurring risks we are unwilling to run. Even if minds are not special kinds of computing machines and even if computational procedures are not cognitive processes, we can derive immense benefit from what they can do for us. The adaptive advantages they confer upon us, however, have to be adequately understood to insure we do not incur risks we do not comprehend.

James H. Fetzer

Department of Philosophy
University of Minnesota
Duluth, MN 55812

4 July 2000

ACKNOWLEDGMENTS

1. "Minds and Machines: Behaviorism, Dualism, and Beyond", *Stanford Humanities Review* **4** (1995), pp. 251–165. By permission of Güven Güzeldere.

2. "Primitive Concepts: Habits, Conventions, and Laws", appeared in J. H. Fetzer, D. Shatz, and G. Schlesinger, eds., *Definitions and Definability: Philosophical Perspectives* (Dordrecht, The Netherlands: Kluwer Academic Publishers, 1991), pp. 51–68. By permission of Kluwer Academic Publishers.

3. "Signs and Minds: An Introduction to the Theory of Semiotic Systems" J. H. Fetzer, ed., *Aspects of Artificial Intelligence* (Dordrecht, The Netherlands, 1988), pp. 133–161. By permission of Kluwer Academic Publishers.

4. "Language and Mentality: Computational, Representational, and Dispositional Conceptions", *Behaviorism* **17** (1989), pp. 21–39. By permission of The Cambridge Center for Behavioral Studies.

5. "Mental Algorithms: Are Minds Computational Systems?", *Pragmatics & Cognition* **2** (1994), pp. 1–29. By permission of John Benjamins Publishing Company.

6. "What Makes Connectionism Different? A Critical Review of *Philosophy and Connectionist Theory*", *Pragmatics & Cognition* **2** (1994), pp. 327–348. By permission of John Benjamins Publishing Company.

7. "People are Not Computers: (Most) Thought Processes are Not Computational Procedures", *Journal of Experimental and Theoretical Artificial Intelligence* **10** (1998), pp. 371–391. By permission of Taylor & Francis, http://www.tandf.co.uk/journals.

8. "Program Verification: The Very Idea", *Communications of the ACM* **31** (1988), pp. 1048–1063. By permission of The Association of Computing Machinery.

9. "Philosophical Aspects of Program Verification", *Minds and Machines* **1** (1991), pp. 197–216. By permission of Kluwer Academic Publishers.

10. "Philosophy and Computer Science: Reflections on the Program Verification Debate", in T. Bynum and J. H. Moor, eds., *The Digital Phoenix: How Computers are Changing Philosophy* (Oxford, UK: Basil Blackwell, 1998), pp. 253–273. By permission of Blackwell Publishers Ltd.

11. "Computer Reliability and Public Policy: Limits of Knowledge of Computer-Based Systems", *Social Philosophy and Policy* **13** (1996), pp. 229–266. By permission of the editors.

PROLOGUE

CHAPTER 1

MINDS AND MACHINES

Behaviorism, Dualism and Beyond

DUALISM AND BEHAVIORISM

There are two great traditions in the philosophy of mind that continue to exercise their influence in the age of computing machines. These are the *dualistic* tradition associated especially with the name of René Descartes and the *behavioristic* tradition associated with B.F. Skinner. Dualism is strongly anti-reductionistic, insofar as mentality is taken be different than and not reducible to behavior. Behaviorism, by contrast, is strongly reductionistic, taking mentalistic language to be at best no more than an abbreviated mode for the description of behavior and at worst just scientifically insignificant gibberish.

The most important elements distinguishing dualism from behaviorism concern *ontic* (ontological) theses about the nature of minds and *epistemic* (epistemological) theses about how minds can be known. Descartes, for example, maintained that minds are thinking things (the kinds of things that can think), where access to knowledge about minds is available by means of introspection (envisioned as a kind of inner observation). Skinner, however, maintained that the concept of mind was dispensable in the scientific study of behavior, which only relies upon observation and experimentation.

In one form or another, these traditions continue to exert their influence within the study of the mind, where the work of Alan Turing, for example, seems to fall within the behavioristic tradition, while that of Stevan Harnad appears to fall within the dualistic tradition instead. The position that I am elaborating here, however, suggests that neither behaviorism nor dualism—in their classic or contemporary guises—can solve the problem of the nature of the mind, which requires an alternative approach that regards behavior as evidence for the existence of non-reductive, semiotic modes of mentality.

THE TURING TEST

Contemporary discussions of the nature of the mind are usually dominated by what is known as *the computational conception*, which identifies mentality with the execution of programs: humans and machines are supposed to operate in similar ways. Perhaps the most important representative of this position is Alan Turing, who introduced the Turing Test (or "TT") as a means for determining whether the abilities of machines were comparable to those of human beings.[1]   Turing's position has been enormously influential within *cognitive science*, which is dominated by the computer model of the mind.

Although the Turing Test has acquired the status of common knowledge among students of artificial intelligence and cognitive science, its character is not so widely known within the intellectual community at large. Turing adapted a party game, known as *the imitation game*, for the purpose of establishing evidence of the existence of intelligence or mentality in the case of inanimate machines. In the imitation game, a man and a woman might compete to induce a contestant to guess which is female, based solely upon answers given to questions (permitting the male, but not the female, to lie).

The game had to be arranged in such a way that the physical properties of the participants—their shapes, sizes, and voices, for example—would not give them away. Then if the contestant correctly identified their sex, he or she would win, but otherwise not. (Alternatively, if the contestant correctly identified their sex, then the woman as opposed to the contestant would win.) Turing's alternative conception was to adapt the test to pit an inanimate machine against a human being, where the property under consideration is no longer the participants' sex but their intelligence or mentality.

TT BEHAVIORISM

The TT could be carried out in several different ways. For example, it can be conducted by covertly substituting a machine for the male participant in the course of an ongoing play of the imitation game. Here the success of a machine in inducing the contestant to treat it as human would be taken as evidence of its intelligence or ingenuity. Alternatively, the game might be overtly advertised as pitting a human being against an inanimate machine, where the contestant knew the nature of the challenge. In the first instance, but not in the second, the contestant in the test would be "blind".

Turing's approach appears to fall within the tradition of behaviorism, moreover, not simply because he proposed a behavioral test for the existence of machine mentality but also because passing the TT is supposed to be *sufficient* to justify ascriptions of mentality. Answering the questions in such a way as to induce the contestant to mistakenly guess that it was human, for example, is viewed as a sufficient condition—as strong enough evidence—to justify the conclusion that the machine possesses mentality. If it passes the TT, then it possesses a mind, according to this conception.

In this sense, the ascription of mentality functions as an abbreviated mode of language for the description of behavior, where attributing this property is not merely scientifically insignificant gibberish. The behavioristic tradition within which the TT properly falls, therefore, is not the radical form that Skinner advocates but a milder version. There are such things as minds, whose existence can be discovered by the TT. Precisely what it is the TT actually tests, however, may or may not be conspicuous, since the idea of answering questions can be interpreted in various ways.

THE CHINESE ROOM

In order to conceal the identity of the TT participants, you may recall, arrangements have to be made to conceal their shapes, sizes, voices, and so forth by relying upon a medium of communication that does not give the game away. The precise form in which "answers" are provided to "questions", therefore, depends upon the specific arrangements that have been made, but typically would be conveyed by means of written (typed) messages. These "answers" must conform to the rules of grammar of the same language used to pose those "questions" or else could give away the game.

Merely providing "answers" that conform to the grammatical rules of the language in which those "questions" are posed, however, may or may not provide evidence of mentality. As John Searle has observed, if a non-Chinese speaker were to rely upon a set of instructions, written in English, that directed him to send certain sets of Chinese characters out in response to certain other sets of Chinese characters being sent in (when situated in an otherwise isolated location, for example), that person might seem to his correspondents to understand Chinese, even though by hypothesis he does not.[2]

Searle's example—known as "the Chinese Room"—implies that conforming to the rules of grammar of a language does not automatically infuse the sentences that are thereby generated with meaning. A fundamental distinction needs to be drawn between *syntax* and *semantics*, where syntax in relation to a language concerns how its words may be combined to create new words, phrases or sentences, for example, while semantics relative to that language concerns the meanings that those words, phrases or sentences may be used to convey. Syntax processing alone does not appear sufficient for mentality.

THE SYMBOL GROUNDING PROBLEM

The Chinese Room has provoked an enormous variety of responses, the most sensitive of which attempt to cope with the problem Searle has identified rather than dispute it. Stevan Harnad, for example, has explored its character and ramifications in a series of articles, which emphasize the importance of infusing otherwise purely syntactical strings with semantic content, if they are to be meaningful symbols rather than meaningless marks, as a suitable theory of the mind requires.[3] The necessity to locate a suitable mechanism for imparting meaning to symbols he calls *the symbol grounding problem*.

Harnad has elaborated upon the significance of the Chinese Room for the theory of mind by observing that a Chinese-Chinese dictionary may succeed in relating some Chinese symbols to other Chinese symbols, but that such a resource would be woefully inadequate for anyone who actually wanted to learn Chinese. The symbols that appear in that dictionary, after all, would be nothing more than entries that relate some meaningless marks to other meaningless marks for those who know no Chinese. The symbol grounding problem must be successfully resolved for those symbols to be meaningful.

The difficulty can be formulated more generally for any language whatever by observing that the words that occur in that language are either defined or undefined ("primitive"). The defined words, in principle, could be.replaced by those words by means of which they are defined and, in turn, *those* by others by means of which *they* are defined where, at some point in this process, nothing but strings of primitives specifying the meaning of non-primitive symbols should remain. If we cannot understand primitive symbols, surely we cannot understand symbols defined by means of them.

THE LINGUISTIC APPROACH

At least two avenues are available for approaching the symbol grounding problem, one of which is linguistic, the other not. The linguistic solution depends upon the existence of another language—*a base language*, we might call it—relative to which a second language might be learned. Anyone who already knows English, for example, might overcome the symbol grounding problem by learning to relate specific Chinese characters to corresponding

English words, phrases and expressions. The meaning of Chinese symbols might then be discovered by the process of translating them into English.

The problem with this approach, however, is that it leaves in its wake the residual problem of accounting for the meaning of the symbols which occur in English! If the words that occur in English are likewise meaningless marks, then the process of translation that was intended to solve the symbol grounding problem may merely succeed in relating one set of meaningless marks to another. The appeal to a base language to explain the meaning of another language through a process of translation holds no promise if we cannot account for the meaning of symbols in the base language itself!

If there were no non-linguistic means for understanding the meaning of symbols, of course, the symbol grounding problem might represent an ultimate dilemma, namely: that we cannot understand some language without already understanding some other language, which implies that we cannot understand any language unless we already understand a language! There could be an escape from this dilemma, however, if there were a base language that did not have to be learned because it is innate, inborn and unlearned, a language that might be described as "the language of thought".

THE LANGUAGE OF THOUGHT

The hypothesis that all neurologically normal human beings are born with an innate, species-specific *language of thought* has been advanced by one of the leading figures in cognitive science today, Jerry Fodor.[4] Fodor holds that every member of the species *Homo sapiens* who is not brain damaged, mentally retarded or otherwise neurologically impaired benefits from the possession of a set of semantic primitives as part of our genetic psychological endowment. It is this innate language which thereby provides an unlearned base language relative to which other languages might be learned.

In order for this unlearned base language to provide a foundation for the introduction of any word that might emerge during the course of human existence, the innate stock of primitives must be adequate to the description of any future development in art, history, science or technology. Otherwise, because this approach is committed to the principle that a language can be learned only in relation to another language, it would turn out to be impossible to introduce or to understand the meaning of words for those thoughts that the human mind was not disposed to understand.

There is a striking parallel to Plato's theory of *knowledge as recollection*, according to which everyone knows everything there is to know before they are born, which the trauma of birth causes us to forget. When life experiences trigger our recollections, we remember things we knew already but had forgotten.[5] Moreover, since everyone has the same stock of semantic primitives, our propects for successful translation from any language to another are unlimited. No one can ever mean anything that anyone else cannot understand relative to the base language they share.

THE NON-LINGUISTIC APPROACH

It has been said that there is no position so absurd that some philosopher has not held it. In the present instance, that generalization extends to at least one cognitive scientist. Surely there are more adequate theories than Plato's to account for the acquisition of learning, including the notion that we can *learn from experience* even without the benefit of knowing everything there is to know before birth. Surely linguists have ample evidence that *successful translations* between different languages are by no means always possible. Fodor's theory seems to be merely an intellectual fantasy.

Far more plausible accounts can be generated by abandoning the presumption that one language can only be understood by means of another. After all, if words can ever be understood other-than-linguistically, then the dilemma might be resolved without resorting to such an innate stock of semantic primitives, which is so complete that it includes concepts sufficient to accommodate any development—no matter how surprising or unexpected it might be—in art, history, science or technology, including impressionism, totalitarianism, electromagnetism, and color television.

Consider, for example, the alternative proposed by Ludwig Wittgenstein, who suggested that, rather than asking for the meaning of words, we should consider how they are used.[6] From the perspective of what has gone before, the immense appeal of Wittgenstein's position should be evident. Surely the words that are used in one language might have no counterparts in another language, due to differences in customs, traditions and practices. And surely there is no need to fantasize that the meaning words can have is determined by our species' genetic heritage.

THE TOTAL TURING TEST

When we consider the Turing Test from this point of view, it appears obvious that similar uses of language under similar conditions may be important evidence of similarity of meaning. Yet the Chinese Room has already displayed the possibility that syntactic behavior may be an inadequate foundation for drawing inferences about semantic meanings. What Harnad suggests to overcome the yawning chasm between mere syntax processing and cognitively meaningful language is to incorporate the TT within a strengthened conception of the Total Turing Test ("TTT").

Harnad's position reflects the realization that non-verbal behavior is at least as important as verbal behavior in determining what we mean by the words we use. He therefore appeals to the capacity to identify, classify, sort and label objects and properties of things, especially though not solely on the basis of their sensory projections. Thus, our capacity to categorize, for example, depends upon our ability to isolate features of the ways that things appear that are invariant across various contexts and which provide a usually reliable, but not therefore infallible, basis for their identification.[7]

In order to provide a more adequate foundation for determining what a human being or an inanimate machine may mean by the syntactical marks that it manipulates, therefore, Harnad introduces the TTT as a test of non-symbolic as well as of symbolic behavior, where symbols can be grounded by means of the verbal and non-verbal behavior that the system displays. When two systems exhibit similar behavior in identifying, classifying, sorting, and labeling objects and properties of things, that provides powerful evidence that those systems mean the same thing by the marks they use.

TTT DUALISM

Upon initial consideration, Harnad's position appears to be an extension and refinement of Turing's position, which strongly suggests that Harnad, like Turing, falls within the behavioristic tradition. After all, Harnad uses both verbal and non-verbal behavior as evidential criteria for determining semantic meaning. If he *defined* meaning by means of the verbal and non-verbal behavior that systems actually display, his position would fall within the behavioristic tradition. The way in which behavior functions as evidence on his account, however, places it in the dualistic tradition instead.

Harnad, like Descartes before him, identifies mentality not simply with the ability to think (cognition equals thinking) but also with the notion that thinking is always conscious (cognition equals conscious thinking). Because an inanimate machine—a "robot", let us say—might display verbal and non-verbal behavior that is arbitrarily similar to that of a human being—a real "thinking thing"—and still not possess mentality, there exists what Harnad, like Descartes before him, envisions as being an unbridgeable gulf between our easily accessible public behavior and our permanently private minds:

Just as immunity to Searle's [Chinese Room] argument cannot guarantee mentality, so groundedness cannot do so either. It only immunizes against the objection that the connection between the symbol and what the symbol is about is only in the mind of the [external] interpreter. A TTT-indistinguishable system could still fail to have a mind; there may still be no meaning in there. Unfortunately, that is an ontic state of affairs that is forever epistemically inaccessible to us: We cannot be any the wiser.[8]

There is yet another respect in which Harnad's position parallels that of Descartes, because they both accept introspection as providing privileged access to mental states, as Larry Hauser has remarked.[9] Since introspection offers access to our mental states but not to those of anyone else, we can only be certain that we ourselves have minds. Indeed, when certainty is taken to be necessary for knowledge, as Descartes understood it, no one can ever possess knowledge of the mental states of anyone else—which is why "the problem of other minds" cannot possibly be resolved.

THE TT VS. THE TTT

At least two properties distinguish the TT and the TTT in relation to the problem of other minds. The first is that, in the tradition of behaviorism, the TT functions as a *sufficient condition* for ascriptions of mentality, because passing the TT is viewed as enough evidence to justify the inference that anything that actually passes the test has a mind. The TTT, in the tradition of dualism, functions as a *necessary condition* for ascriptions of mentality instead, since failing to pass the TTT is viewed as enough evidence to justify the inference that anything that fails the test does not have a mind.

The second is that, in consonance with the computational conception, the TT compliments the approach within cognitive science that identifies minds with *the capacity to manipulate symbols*, where "symbols" are given a purely syntactical characterization. Systems of this kind are variously referred to as "symbol systems" and as "automated formal systems".[10] It is its syntactical character, of course, that makes the account vulnerable to the Chinese Room. The TTT, by comparsion, compliments the tradition within Cartesian philosophy that instead identifies minds with *conscious thinking things*.

The difference between the TT as a sufficient condition and the TTT as a necessary condition is an epistemic difference, while that between the conception of minds as symbol systems and as thinking things is an ontic difference. Given these differences, the manipulation of syntax should be viewed as *direct evidence* of mentality for the computational conception, but only as *indirect evidence* of mentality for the Cartesian. In fact, Harnad goes even further and maintains, "There is in fact *no evidence* for me that anyone else but me has a mind"[11], which is a rather surprising claim.

HAUSER'S OBJECTION

If there really were *no evidence for me* that anything else besides myself has a mind, however, the point of the TTT would be obscure. Surely if the TTT is to perform its intended function, it must supply some evidence of the presence or absence of mentality, since it would otherwise be meaningless in relation to the central question. Moreover, as Hauser observes, Harnad maintains that our linguistic capacities must be grounded in our robotic capacities, which would seem to imply that robotic capacities are a necessary condition for linguistic capacities; but that cannot be correct.[12]

Hauser's argument is that, if linguistic capacities presupposed robotic capacities, then any test of linguistic capacities, such as the TT, would also automatically test for robotic capacities, in which case the TTT would not improve upon the TT, after all. What Harnad presumably intends to claim is that, *for a system in which the manipulation of symbols is a cognitively meaningful activity*, linguistic capacities presuppose robotic capacities. On this account, the TTT tests for behaviorial indicators of the meanings that should be assigned to the symbols the manipulation of which the TT tests.

Harnad's position, as I understand it, is that there are infinitely many assignments of meaning (or "interpretations") that might be imposed upon any piece of syntax, no matter how complex. The function of the TTT is to *rule out* interpretations that are not compatible with the verbal and non-verbal behavior of that syntax-processing system. While the TTT cannot definitely *rule in* any single interpretation of the meaning of that syntax, it can definitely rule out those interpretations that are incompatible with the verbal and non-verbal behavior that that system happens to display.

AN EPISTEMIC PROBLEM

This understanding of Harnad's position makes sense of the TTT as a necessary condition for possessing mentality, but it undermines his contention that the possession of mentality or not is *an ontic state of affairs that is forever epistemically inaccessible to us,* where "we cannot be any the wiser". Surely passing more and more elaborate versions of the TTT would provide more and more evidence about the meaning that should be assigned to the syntax processed by a system, even if it cannot do so conclusively. That presumably is the purpose and importance of the TTT.

It may be worth noting, however, that a system could possess a mind even though it never passed the TTT, namely: *when it is never subjected to the TTT.* A system that is never placed under the kind of scrutiny that the TTT imposes (by observing and comparing its behavior with those of others)—such as a lone survivor of a shipwreck stranded on a deserted island—would not for that reason alone be shorn of his mentality. Instead, the TTT must be understood *hypothetically* as concerned with the kind of behavior that would be displayed, if that system were subject to the TTT.

Even more importantly, the Cartesian conception of minds as *thinking things* (even as *conscious* thinking things) really does not help us understand the nature of mentality, unless we already possess an appropriate conception of the nature of thinking things, on the one hand, and of the nature of consciousness, on the other. The most glaring inadequacy of Harnad's position is not the epistemic standing of the TTT (indeed, even the TT should be viewed as providing merely inconclusive inductive evidence)[13], but his failure to explain the ontic nature of conscious thought.

THE ONTIC PROBLEM

In case anyone doubts that the failure to explain the ontic nature of conscious thought almost completely undermines the theoretical signifi-cance of Harnad's position, then consider the following questions: What is that of which Harnad, like Descartes before him, claims to possess certain knowledge by means of introspection? What are we claiming for ourselves (even if we can *only* claim it for ourselves) when we maintain that we have minds? that we are thinking things? that we are capable of conscious thought? Exactly what are hypotheses like these supposed to mean?

There are, after all, three great problems that define the subject that is known as the philosophy of mind, namely, those of the nature of mind, the mind/body problem, and the problem of other minds. Surely neither the mind/body problem (of how the mind is related to the body) nor the problem of other minds (whether anyone besides ourselves has a mind) can be resolved in the absence of a solution to the problem of the nature of mind. Otherwise, we do not know precisely what kind of property it is that is supposed to be related to our bodies or possessed by someone else.

From this point of view, the TT might be said to fare somewhat better than the TTT, since the TT, as an element of the computational conception, compliments an answer to the problem of the nature of mind that is clear and intelligible, whether or not it is also adequate. The TTT, as a feature of the Cartesian conception, surely bears the burden of explaining the nature of thought and the nature of consciousness. Otherwise, that account itself might turn out to be no more than another instance of one meaningless string of marks being related to another meaningless string of marks.

THE NO-THEORY THEORY

The only response that Harnad seems prepared to provide to questions of this kind is "a full description of the internal structures and processes that succeeded in making the robot pass the TTT".[14] When a system succeeds in passing the TTT and we want to know why that occurred—that is, what it was about that system by virtue of which it passed that test—Harnad's reply is to propose that we take it apart and study its causal components. This may come as bitter medicine for all of those who think that there is or has to be a solution to this problem, but that is the answer he supplies.

There are at least two reasons why a response of this kind really won't do. The first is specific to any Cartesian account with the ingredients that Harnad combines. If we can never know whether or not anything else has a mind, how can we ever know whether we ourselves have a mind? If we were completely dissected and our internal organs were wholly displayed, would we be any closer to understanding the nature of the mind than we were before? What we want is an account of the distinctive differences between systems with minds and those without them, which is another thing.

Indeed, the very idea that a complete description of its "internal structures and processes" could possibly explain why something passed the TTT implies that minds and bodies interact without explaining how, which is an underlying problem that any Cartesian account invariably encounters. Without knowing more about the mind and its mode of operation, how can we possibly discover how minds can interact with bodies to produce behavior? Harnad's emphasis upon the problem of other minds thus conceals the absence of a theory concerning the relationship between bodies and minds.

KINDS OF SIMILARITY

The second is general and confronts any theory of mind, Cartesian or not. A distinction has to be drawn between (a) systems that display the same output when given the same input, (b) systems that display the same outputs when given the same inputs by processing them in similar ways, and (c) systems that not only display the same outputs when given the same inputs by processing them in similar ways but are made of similar "stuff". Systems standing in these relations reflect relations of *simulation*, *replication* and *emulation*, respectively, which are stronger and stronger in kind.[15]

If one system was made of "flesh and blood" while the other was made of electronic components, for example, no matter how similar they may be in their input/output behavior and in their modes of operation, they could not stand in a relationship of emulation. If one system arrives at answers to questions by multiplication and another by means of repeated addition, no matter how similar they may be in the answers they provide to questions, they could not stand in a relationship of replication. If they provide different answers to questions, then likewise for a relation of simulation.

From this point of view, it should be evident that the reason why the Chinese Room succeeds is because simulations do not establish sufficient conditions for replications. It should also be evident, relative to Harnad's conception, that descriptions of the internal structures and processes that succeeded in making a robot pass the TTT depend on the kind of stuff of which such things are made. That would be relevant if the issues at stake were matters of emulation, but what we want to know is whether we and they are performing the same mental functions as a matter of replication.

THE TTTT

What Harnad has done is to suggest an answer at the level of emulation in response to a question raised about the level of replication. This is a very difficult position for him to defend, however, especially given his attitude toward what he calls the Total Total Turing Test (or "TTTT"). This test goes beyond linguistic and robotic performance to the level of molecular neurology. If the TT depends upon linguistic indistinguishability and the TTT depends upon lingustic and behavioral indistinguishability as well, the TTTT further depends upon neurophysiological (or "bodily") indistinguishability.

Harnad suspects that the TTTT may be unnecessary to determine whether or not a system possesses mentality and considers passing the TTTT to be helpful "only inasmuch as it [gives] hints to accelerate our progress toward passing the TTT".[16] The problem that Harnad confronts, however, is that he really has no theory of mentality beyond the full description of the internal structures and processes that enable a robot to pass the TTT. What we need to have, however, is not a full description of the *structures* that enabled a robot to pass the TTT but a full explanation of the *functions*.

That the absence of any other account of the nature of the mind hobbles Harnad's approach becomes painfully apparent when consideration is given to the comparative character of the TT, the TTT, and even the TTTT. All of these tests succeed (to whatever extend they do succeed) only by assuming that *the systems employed for comparison possess the property for which those tests are supposed to test*. If two machines were TTTT indistinguishable, that would not show that they had minds. And even if a robot and a human were TTTT distinguishable, that would not show that they did not.

SIGNS AND MINDS

What we need is a theory of the mind that preserves the virtues of accounts of both kinds without retaining their vices. Behaviorism appears appealing to the extent to which it renders hypotheses about mentality accessible to observational and experimental tests without denying its existence altogether. Dualism appears appealing to the extent to which it denies that mentality can be reduced to behavior so long as hypotheses about behavior can be subjected to observational and experimental tests. What we want, in other words, is a non-reductionistic conception that relates minds with behavior.

An account of this kind can be elaborated on the basis of a dispositional conception that characterizes minds as *sign-using (or "semiotic") systems*.[17] The foundation for this account is the theory of signs advanced by Charles S. Peirce, one of the greatest of all philosophers, who introduced the notion of *a sign* as a something that stands for something else (in some respect or other) for somebody. By inverting and generalizing this conception, *minds* can be taken to be the kinds of things for which a thing can stand for something else (in some respect or other) for a human, other animal or machine.

In Peirce's view, signs not only stand for other things—typically, things in the world around us—but create in the mind of a sign user another sign, equal to or more developed than the original. This sign can be identified with the tendencies of that system to behave one way or another when conscious of that sign, where *consciousness* involves both the ability to use signs of that kind and the capacity to exercise that ability. *Cognition* then occurs as the effect of a causal interaction between a sign within a suitable proximity and the "context" of other properties of that system that affect its behavior.

THREE KINDS OF MINDS

Peirce distinguished three kinds of signs on the basis of the ways in which those signs are able to stand for other things, which he called their "ground". *Icons* (such as photographs, sculptures, and paintings) are signs that stand for other things because they resemble those other things. *Indices* (such as smoke in relation to fire, elevated temperature and red spots in relation to measles) are signs that are causes or effects of those other things. *Symbols* (such as the words which occur in English or Chinese), by comparison, are signs that are merely habitually associated with that for which they stand.

A stop sign at a traffic intersection affords an illustrative example. For a qualified driver who is familiar with signs of that kind, the appearance of a thing of that kind within a suitable proximity (when the driver's vision is not impaired, the sign itself is not obscured by trees and bushes, and so on) tends to bring about in the mind of that sign user another sign, namely, the disposition to slow down and come to a complete halt and proceed through the intersection when it is safe to do so (provided that his wife is not going into labor in the back seat, the driver is not a felon fleeing the police, etc.).

The distinction between three kinds of signs invites a distinction between three kinds of minds, where minds of Type I can utilize icons, minds of Type II can utilize indices, and minds of Type III can utilize symbols, where each type is successively stronger in presupposing the ability to use signs of any lower kind. This is an attractive conception from the evolutionary point of view, since it suggests the possibility that lower species may possess lower types of mentality and higher species higher, in contrast to the language of thought hypothesis, for example, which does not harmonize with evolution.[18]

THE PROBLEM OF PRIMITIVES

If thinking can occur through the use of icons and indices as well as symbols, however, then the distinction between syntax and semantics ought to apply to them as well as to symbols. Indeed, iconic signs can be combined in ways that make them resemble different things, as when different parts of a face are changed to create replicas of different faces, a technique well-known to law-enforcement communities. And indexical signs can be combined in ways that make them resemble different causes and effects, as when directors and actors rely upon "special effects" for the purpose of creating motion pictures.

This, in turn, implies that primitive icons and primitive indices as well as primitive symbols require "grounding" in our (mental and other) dispositions. Harnad's "symbol grounding problem" is better envisioned as *the problem of primitives*, at least to the extent to which the meaning of new (or molecular) signs created by combining old (atomic or molecular) signs depends upon or presupposes that those old (atomic or molecular) signs already possess meaning. An adequate theory of meaning thus requires understanding interactions between signs, what they stand for and sign users, which makes it *pragmatic*.

From this point of view, both the TT and the TTT provide relevant kinds of evidence for the meanings that systems happen to attach to signs, where similar (verbal and robotic) behavior under similar (internal and external) conditions serves to confirm some hypotheses and to disconfirm others. As a sufficient condition for the presence of mentality, however, the semiotic approach supports *the capacity to make a mistake*, which involves taking something to stand for something other than that for which it stands, which in turn implies the capacity to take something to stand for something else. [19]

BODIES AND MINDS

The conception of minds as semiotic systems compliments *the connnectionist conception*, which views the brain as a neural network of numerous neurons capable of activation. Each node is connected to other nodes where, depending upon its level of activation, it can bring about increases or decreases in the levels of activation of those other nodes. What is remarkable about this approach is that specific patterns of neural activation can function as causal antecedents of behavior for the systems of which they are component parts, where some of these causal roles may be genetic, while others are learned.

This suggests that the "signs" that are created in the mind of a sign user in the presence of a sign of a suitable kind might be identified with specific patterns of activation. Harnad has objected that a semiotic theory of the kind I have in mind implies the existence of a homuncular module that interprets the meaning of those signs—*as a mind within a mind*—thereby generating an infinite regress of minds within minds without explaining the mode of operation of any "mind".[20]   Harnad is mistaken in two different ways, however, each of which is interesting and important enough to deserve elaboration.

Harnad's first mistake is to overlook the possibility that dispositions for specific behaviors within specific contexts might accompany the presence of specific patterns of neural activation in systems of specific kinds, not in the sense that they are identical with ("indistinguishable from") those patterns of activation but rather that they are *functions* ("causal roles") that accompany those *structures* ("bodily states") for systems of specific kinds. These connections should not be understood as logical connections by way of definitions but rather as nomological relations by way of natural laws. [21]

CONSCIOUSNESS AND COGNITION

If specific patterns of neural activation are connected to specific dispositions toward behavior (within specific contexts) for various kinds of systems, then the semiotic conception would appear to have the potential to solve the mind/body problem. The advantage that it enjoys in relation to dualistic conceptions is that it provides the foundation for understanding *the nature of thought* as a semiotic activity in which something stands for something else in some respect or other for a system. This account thereby supplies a framework for investigating various kinds of thoughts, etc.

Harnad's second mistake is to ignore the conceptions of consciousness and of cognition that accompany the conception of minds as semiotic systems. *Consciousness* on this account qualifies as a completely causal conception: if a system has the ability to use signs (of a certain kind) and is not incapacitated from exercising that ability (because it is brain damaged, intoxicated, or otherwise impaired), then it is conscious (with respect to signs of that kind). Consciousness in this sense does not presuppose any capacity for articulation nor presume the presence of any self-concept.[22]

Cognition on this account likewise qualifies as a completely causal conception: when a system is conscious (relative to signs of a certain kind), then the occurrence of signs (of that kind) within an appropriate causal proximity would lead—invariably or probabilistically—to the occurrence of cognition. Depending upon the complete set of causally relevant properties of that system, the occurrence of cognition would bring about some internal or external changes in the system, which, when they involve the production of sounds or movement by that system, influence its behavior.

OTHER MINDS

If "consciousness" or "cognition" were left as primitives within an account of this kind, then that would pose a serious objection. The accounts of the nature of consciousness and cognition presented here, however, strongly support the conception of minds as semiotic systems. Indeed, perhaps the fundamental advantage of this dispositional approach over its dualistic alternative is that it supplies an account of what it means to be "a thinking thing" (namely, a semiotic system) and of what it means to be a "conscious thinking thing" (namely, a semiotic system that can exercise its abilities).

It also supplies a framework for pursuing the problem of other minds. The evidence that distinguishes systems that have minds from those that do not arises within the context of what is known as *inference to the best explanation*.[23] This principle requires selecting that hypothesis among the available alternatives which, if true, would provide the best explanation of the available evidence. When the behavior of a system is sufficiently non-complex as to be explainable without attributing mentality to that system, then it should not be attributed, nor should stronger forms if lesser will do.

The *E. coli* bacterium, for example, swims toward at least twelve specific chemotactic substances and away from at least eight others.[24] This counts as (surprising) evidence that *E. coli* might possess iconic mentality, but it could not support inferences to any stronger types. Vervet monkeys, however, make three distinctive alarm calls that cause them to run up trees in response to leopard alarms, to hide under the brush in respose to eagle alarms, and to look down and approach in response to snake calls.[25] Behavior of this complexity tends to support inferences to higher modes of mentality.

BEYOND BEHAVIORISM AND DUALISM

The arguments presented here have had several objectives. One has been to suggest that, when properly understood, Turing and Harnad are seen to fall into very different traditions. The behavioristic tradition (of Turing) embraces a reductionistic conception of mentalistic language as no more than an abbreviated mode for the description of behavior, the presence of which might be tested by the TT. The dualistic tradition (of Harnad), by comparison, embraces the non-reductive conception of minds as conscious thinking things, the presence of which might be tested by the TTT.

Although the TT is intended to function as sufficient evidence and the TTT as necessary evidence for the ascription of mentality, neither affords a suitable conception of mentality. The TT provides a test of the capacity of one system to simulate another, which is too weak to capture the difference between minded and mindless systems. The TTT, as Harnad admits, also provides no guarantee of mentality, where the best that he can do is a full description of the internal structures and processes that enable a robot to pass it, treating the problem of replication at the level of emulation.

Neither approach promise to resolve the problem, which appears to require an alternative conception that draws upon them. The theory of minds as semiotic systems identifies mentality with semiotic ability and meaning with dispositional tendencies rather than with behavior. It thus preserves the non-reductive character of dualism while going beyond it by accounting for the nature of consciousness and cognition. It retains the testability of behaviorism while rising above it by appealing to inference to the best explanation. The outcome is a completely causal theory of signs and minds.

NOTES

[1] Turing (1950).
[2] Searle (1984).
[3] Harnad (1990), (1991), (1992), and (1993a), for example.
[4] Fodor (1975), p. 80.
[5] Fetzer (1989), p. 30.
[6] Wittgenstein (1953).
[7] Harnad (1992), p. 81.
[8] Harnad (1993b), p. 30.
[9] Hauser (1993), p. 220.
[10] Newell and Simon (1976) and Haugeland (1981), (1985).
[11] Harnad (1991), p. 45.
[12] Hauser (1993), p. 227.
[13] As Hauser (1993), p. 225, indeed, has also observed.
[14] Harnad (1993c), p. 36.
[15] Fetzer (1990), pp. 17-18.
[16] Harnad (1993c), p. 36; see also Harnad (1991), p. 53.

[17] Fetzer (1988), (1989), (1990), and (1991), for example.
[18] I am indebted to William Bechtel for this observation.
[19] Fetzer (1988), (1990), (1991), and (1992), for example.
[20] Harnad (1993c), p. 36.
[21] Fetzer (1991), Ch. 5.
[22] Fetzer (1991), p. 78..
[23] Fetzer (1991), p. 32.
[24] Bonner (1980), p. 63.
[25] Slater (1985), p. 155.

REFERENCES

Bonner, J. T. (1980), *The Evolution of Culture in Animals* (Princeton, NJ: Princeton University Press, 1980).

Fetzer, J. H. (1988), "Signs and Minds: An Introduction to the Theory of Semiotic Systems", in J. H. Fetzer, ed., *Aspects of Artificial Intelligence* (Dordrecht, The Netherlands: Kluwer Academic Publishers, 1988), pp. 133-161.

Fetzer, J. H. (1989), "Language and Mentality: Computational, Representational, and Dispositional Conceptions", *Behaviorism* 17 (1989), pp. 31-39.

Fetzer, J. H. (1990), *Artificial Intelligence: Its Scope and Limits* (Dordrecht, The Netherlands: Kluwer Academic Publishers, 1990).

Fetzer, J. H. (1991), *Philosophy and Cognitive Science* (New York: Paragon House, 1991).

Fetzer, J. H. (1992), "Connectionism and Cognition: Why Fodor and Pylyshyn are Wrong", in A. Clark and R. Lutz, eds., *Connectionism in Context* (Heidelberg, Germany: Springer-Verlag, 1992), pp. 37-56.

Fetzer, J. H. (1993), "The TTT is Not the Final Word", *THINK* 2 (1993), pp. 34-36.

Fodor, J. (1975), *The Language of Thought*. Cambridge, MA: The MIT Press, 1975.

Harnad, S. (1990), "The Symbol Grounding Problem", *Physica D* 42 (1990), pp. 335-346

Harnad, S. (1991), "Other Bodies, Other Minds: A Machine Reincarnation of an Old Philosophical Problem", *Minds and Machines* 1 (1991), pp. 43-54.

Harnad, S. (1992), "Connecting Object to Symbol in Modeling Cognition", in A. Clark and R. Lutz, eds., *Connectionism in Context* (Heidelberg, Germany: Springer-Verlag, 1992), pp. 75-90.

Harnad, S. (1993a), "Grounding Symbols in the Analog World with Neural Nets: A Hybrid Model", *THINK* 2 (1993), pp. 12-20.

Harnad S. (1993b), "Harnad's Response" (to Eric Dietrich), *THINK* 2 (1993), pp. 29-30.

Harnad, S. (1993c), "Harnad's Response" (to James Fetzer), *THINK* 2 (1993), p. 36.

Haugeland, J. (1981), *"Semantic Engines: An Introduction to Mind Design"*, in J. Haugeland, ed., *Mind Design* (Cambridge, MA: The MIT Press, 1981), pp. 1-34.

Haugeland, J. (1985), *Artificial Intelligence: The Very Idea* (Cambridge, MA: The MIT Press, 1985).

Hauser, L. (1993), "Reaping the Whirlwind: Reply to Harnad's Other Bodies, Other Minds", *Minds and Machines* 3 (1993), pp. 219-237.

Newell, A. and H. Simon (1976), "Computer Science as Empirical Enquiry: Symbols and Search", reprinted in J. Haugeland, ed., *Mind Design* (Cambridge, MA: The MIT Press, 1981), pp. 35-66.

Searle, J. (1984), *Minds, Brains and Science* (Cambridge, MA: Harvard University Press, 1984).

Slater, P. J. B. (1975), *An Introduction to Ethology* (Cambridge, UK: The University of Cambridge Press).

Turing, A. M. (1950), "Computing Machinery and Intelligence", in E. Feigenbaum and J. Feldman, eds., *Computers and Thought* (New York: McGraw-Hill, 1963), pp. 11-35.

Wittgenstein, L. (1953), *Philosophical Investigations*. Translated by G. E. M. Anscombe. Oxford, UK: Oxford University Press, 1953.

PART I

SEMIOTIC SYSTEMS

CHAPTER 2

PRIMITIVE CONCEPTS
Habits, Conventions, and Laws

Perhaps no aspect of the theory of definitions has become more familiar to students of this subject than that there are really only two ways in which every word that occurs within a language could be defined. The first — that of definitional circularity — arises when the words that occur in a language *L* are permitted to be defined by means of other words, which are ultimately defined by means of those original words themselves. The second — that of definitional regress — arises when new words are allowed to be introduced to define the meaning of old words, and new words for those, *ad infinitum*.

On first consideration, the prospect of languages affected by circular or by regressive definitions may look like a relatively minor inconvenience of slight consequence to understanding the nature of language. The dictionary for an ordinary language, such as English — *Webster's New World Dictionary* (1988), for example — appears to succeed in providing useful definitions for the terms that it contains in spite of resorting to definitional circularity. If there is a problem here, therefore, then it needs to be made apparent, because there seem to be no problems in practice with dictionary definitions.

The problems arising here might or might not be practical, but they are important problems, especially with respect to understanding the nature of definitions and definability. Ask yourself, for example, how you could possibly know the meaning of a defined term without knowing the meaning of those terms by means of which it is defined. Presumably, you might know the meaning of a word on the basis of such a definition or you might know its meaning apart from any such definition. Yet it is not obvious how you could possibly know the meaning of a word without knowing its definition.

Even though it may not be obvious, that it must be possible to know the meaning of some words without knowing their definitions is not difficult to establish. It might be the case, after all, that one meaningless sequence of marks was "defined" by means of another meaningless sequence of marks without rendering either sequence meaningful.

Suppose "ab" were defined by means of "cd", "cd" by means of "ef", *ad infinitum*. In a case of this kind, these "words" would have meaning only if at least one member of that sequence had meaning. These could be defined, yet still meaningless, words.

If definitions are ever successful, therefore, it must be because at least some words can be understood without the mediation of other words. The success of definition, in other words, appears to depend crucially upon the possibility of understanding the meaning of words that are not defined by means of other words. So, if the vocabulary of a language L consists of its defined words and its undefined (or "primitive") words, then it appears as though understanding any of its defined words depends upon understanding its undefined words. But how is it possible to understand primitives?

This essay has the purpose of exploring several different ways in which it might be possible for words to have meaning for the users of a language, even when they are undefined. There seem to be at least three hypotheses:

($h1$) their meaning is determined by natural laws;
($h2$) their meaning is determined by personal habits; or,
($h3$) their meaning is determined by social conventions.

The problem, however, cannot be solved merely by accounting for the meaning of words. Different words can have the same meaning even though they were never so defined. The solution requires appeals to primitive concepts.

Sections 1 and 2 focus on the relationship between words and meaning where it becomes increasingly evident that an adequate theory of the meaning of primitive words depends upon an analysis of personal habits, tendencies, and dispositions. Section 3 explores several examples. Sections 4 and 5, however, shift attention to the relationship between meaning and reference, where the role of social convention in promoting communication and cooperation within communities becomes central. Sections 6 and 7 finally consider some relationships between social conventions and natural laws.

While the fundamental unit of meaning for a language user z appears to be a function of that user's linguistic habits, tendencies, or dispositions (see Fetzer 1989 and 1991), the fundamental unit of meaning for a community of language users Z is a function of those users' shared linguistic habits, tendencies, or dispositions. The success of efforts to ensure that different members of any such community share the same linguistic habits, tendencies, or dispositions, however, appears to depend upon the existence of natural laws of various different kinds, which are presupposed by linguistic conventions.

1. MEANING OF PRIMITIVES AS DETERMINED BY NATURAL LAWS

The most conspicuous advocate of hypothesis (*h1*) continues to be Jerry Fodor, who has advanced a theory now known as "the language of thought" in several publications (Fodor 1975 and 1987, for example). According to this conception, every (neurologically normal) human brain is born with an innate set of psychological primitives. In order to learn a natural language such as English, therefore, a person *z* must discover how to "match up" the words that occur within that natural language and the concepts that occur within the language of thought. The only problem is to pair them up right.

Fodor acknowledges that more than one word in a natural language can have the same meaning as a concept in the language of thought. Moreover, this is indispensable to the adequacy of his theory, since otherwise it would imply that only *one* natural language could be successfully "paired up" with the language of thought. If that were the case, then every (neurologically normal) human being would have to speak the same natural language, as a matter of natural law. Fodor's theory is thus compatible with the existence of a variety of different natural languages, which otherwise would refute it.

Since this approach affords a solution to the problem of accounting for the meaning of the primitive words that occur within a language, it clearly has something to recommend it. If every (neurologically normal) human brain *were* born with an innate set of psychological primitives, that *would* supply an explanation of how it is possible to learn a natural language. Indeed, Fodor maintains that it is only possible to learn a natural language on the basis of an unlearned innate language, "the language of thought" itself.

The key to Fodor's position, therefore, is the assumption that learning a language involves learning the truth conditions for the sentences that can occur in that language: ". . . learning (a language) *L* involves learning that *Px is true if and only if x is G* for all substitution instances. But notice that learning that could be learning *P* (learning what *P* means) only for an organism that already understands *G*"

(Fodor 1975, p. 80). Fodor takes for granted that the kind of understanding that such an organism must possess has to be *linguistic*. It is for this reason that what is innate must be a language.

What Fodor appears to overlook is the possibility that a person z might possess *non-linguistic* understanding of the G-phenomenon which P turns out to represent in L. For, if that were the case, then z might perfectly well possess one kind of understanding that is sufficient for learning P (learning what P means) without also having to possess some other kind. Those who have raised children, for example, have often noticed how typically they display patterns of behavior (playing with blocks, singing a song, drawing with crayons) before they acquire the ability to name or describe them.

Since Fodor concedes that experience and ingenuity are required in the process of matching up primitives in the language of thought with those in a natural language, the possibility remains that the "experience and ingenuity" that are required might afford a suitable foundation for a child to acquire a natural language — even in the absence of a language of thought! Indeed, to the extent to which economy, simplicity, and elegance provide criteria for preferring one theory to another in relation to a common domain, a theory that dispenses with the language of thought ought to be preferred.

The criteria of economy, simplicity, and elegance, of course, afford a relevant standard of relative preferability only when competing theories provide similar degrees of systematic power with respect to the phenomena of interest. This argument, therefore, depends upon establishing that such an alternative to Fodor's theory provides as much or more explanatory power with respect to the acquisition of language. The theory that the meaning of primitive concepts depends, not upon laws of nature, but upon habits that might vary from person to person, appears to provide a preferable theory.

From this point of view, it should be observed that, while Fodor's theory does afford a solution to the problem of accounting for the meaning of the primitive words that occur within a natural language, it does not provide a solution to the problem of accounting for the meaning of the primitive concepts that occur within the language of thought itself. Thus, a theory that accounted for both the meaning of primitive concepts and for the meaning of primitive words would thereby have demonstrated its superiority over Fodor's conception. An account of this kind is supplied by hypothesis (*h2*).

2. MEANING OF PRIMITIVES AS DETERMINED BY PERSONAL HABITS I

An adequate analysis of the nature of language ought to be approached from the perspective of the theory of signs (or "semiotic") advanced by C. S. Peirce, where natural languages qualify as exhibiting one of three basic kinds of signs (icons, indices, and symbols). Moreover, the theory of signs provides a foundation for a theory of mind, according to which "minds" are semiotic (or "sign-using") systems, some with the ability to use icons, some with the ability to use indices, and some with the ability to use symbols (cf. Fetzer 1988 and 1990). For now these important matters will be ignored.

The fundamental conception that ties these ideas together is that of the content of a concept, which Peirce accounted for in terms of its causal role:

> . . . the most perfect account of a concept that words can convey will be a description of the habit which that concept is calculated to produce. But how otherwise can a habit be described than by a description of the kind of action to which it gives rise, with a specification of the conditions and of the motive? (Peirce 1906, p. 286).

Thus, from this point of view, the theory of meaning presupposes the theory of action, where meanings are characterized in terms of their causal function in affecting the behavior of semiotic systems of various distinctive varieties.

Let us assume that human beings are influenced by their motives, their beliefs, their ethics, their abilities, their capabilities, and their opportunities (where "opportunities" concern how things are as opposed to how we think things are, i.e., they are related to various features of our beliefs, including their truth and their completeness in relation to the activities in which we happen to be engaged). People thus qualify as motive-belief-ethics-ability-capability-and-opportunity types of systems in comparison with other kinds of systems, including digital machines (cf. Fetzer 1989, 1990, and 1991).

People are *conscious* with respect to the use of symbols when they have both the ability to use symbols of that kind and also are not inhibited from the exercise of that ability, so that the presence of those symbols within a suitable causal proximity would lead — invariably or probabilistically — to an occurrence of cognition. Since an instance of *cognition* arises as an effect of causal interaction between the awareness of that sign and a person's other internal states (insofar as they make a difference to its significance for that person), the meaning of a sign cannot be fixed independent of those factors.

When a human being encounters specific words (sentences, etc.), the influence of those words (sentences, etc.) on that person's behavior depends upon their motives, beliefs, etc., specific values of which define a "context". Different persons are therefore in the same context (with respect to the use of specific symbols on specific occasions) only when their other motives, beliefs, ethics, abilities, and capabilities are the same. Then the meaning of a symbol is the same for different persons when their tendencies to behave in the same ways in its presence are the same across every similar context.

The appropriate standard of similarity of meaning, therefore, is not that different persons actually exhibit the same behavior in the various contexts in which they find themselves, but rather that the strength of their tendencies to display the same behavior would be the same were they or had they been in similar contexts. The relevant measure of similarity of meaning for specific words is not actual behavior but dispositions toward behavior. Even when different persons never find themselves in similar contexts and, as a result, never do display the same behavior, their meaning can be the same.

This account diverges from Fodor's conception of a language of thought, insofar as every (neurologically normal) human brain is born, not with an innate set of psychological primitives, but with predispositions toward the acquisition of semiotic abilities. States of mind are assumed to be properties of states of brains, where those brain states are "meaningful" because of the influence which they exert on human behavior. Some brain states may be meaningful for every (neurologically normal) human brain, while others acquire their meaning under the influence of environmental factors.

Since there are semiotic abilities of various (species-specific) different kinds, this approach affords a framework for understanding the nature of mentality for other species as well as for inanimate machines (if such a thing is possible), without presuming that minds must always be human. Some species are predisposed toward the use of icons, others toward the use of indices, and others toward the use of symbols, where these abilities can be variously acquired on the basis of type/token recognition, classical conditioning, operant conditioning, and so forth (Fetzer 1990 and 1991).

3. MEANING OF PRIMITIVES AS DETERMINED BY PERSONAL HABITS II

To isolate the content of an instance of cognition that induces the state of belief $B1$, for example, a specific context would hold constant some set of values for other beliefs $Bm, Bn, \ldots$, motives $M1, M2, \ldots$, ethics $E1, E2, \ldots$, abilities $A1, A2, \ldots$, capabilities $C1, C2, \ldots$, and opportunities $O1, O2, \ldots$, whose presence or absence makes a difference to the (internal or external) behavior that people tend to display in the presence of that belief. The meaning of that specific belief $B1$ would then be the possibly infinite totality of tendencies for behavior across every context. (Cf. the Appendix.)

Consider, for example, the following case involving the use of language, which exemplifies the use of the same words with the same meaning, yet where the response behavior differs for two persons in different contexts:

EXAMPLE (A): A middle-aged man is crossing the street when someone cries out, "Watch out!" He looks around and sees a truck coming up the wrong side of the street, so he moves out of the way in order to avoid injury.

EXAMPLE (B): A middle-aged man is crossing the street when someone cries out, "Watch out!" He looks around but his vision is poor and he does not see the truck coming up the wrong side of the street. So he is injured.

Presumably the person described by (B) would have displayed the same behavior as the person described by (A), had he not been incapacitated.

Consider, for example, another case that involves the use of language, which exemplifies the use of different words that have similar meaning, where the response behavior is the same for people in the same context:

EXAMPLE (C): Bill has been working for his father for $5.00 per hour. When his dad says, "I'll pay you half as much to wash the car", he starts looking for the bucket and a sponge.

EXAMPLE (D): Bill has been working for his father for $5.00 per hour. When his dad says, "I'll pay you $2.50 per hour to wash the car", he starts looking for the bucket and a sponge.

Once again, presumably, anyone in Bill's context would have been willing to work at that rate of pay, where how it was described would not matter.

These are easy cases, of course, yet they illustrate the principles that are involved. Similar uses of language with similar meanings tend to produce similar behavior in similar contexts. A far more difficult case, which was posed by W. V. O. Quine (1960), is also one that ought to be familiar:

EXAMPLE (E): A native sees a white patch of fur hop by in the bushes and shouts, "Gavagai!" He repeats this each time he sees a white patch of fur hop by, and he chases after them.

A foreign translator observing this scene might find it difficult to discern exactly what the native meant, where Quine suggests three possibilities:

(a) "gavagai" means a whole enduring rabbit;

(b) "gavagai" means undetached rabbit-parts; or,

(c) "gavagai" means a stage in the history of a rabbit.

The difficulty in sorting out which of these the native might have meant has been widely supposed to support "the indeterminacy of translation".

From the perspective of the theory elaborated here, several questions must be raised. The first is whether or not these three different possible translations are significantly different or not. Different words, we already know, can be used to convey similar meanings, as (C) and (D) make clear. If these are merely three different ways of saying the same thing, then they do not represent three alternative meanings but rather three ways to convey a single meaning. If there is a difference between them, it can be made explicit by means of dispositional differences in similar contexts.

And, indeed, there would appear to be differences of this kind within the English language, where different responses might be given to similar questions as a function of differences in meaning. If there is a particular duration to a "stage" in the history of a rabbit, for example, then it would be possible to count the number of those stages that transpire during an interval of time. So there might be several "stages" where there is only one enduring rabbit. But if there were no dispositional difference, then there would be no meaning difference. They would mean the same thing.

That these meanings might differ in English, however, does not imply that they must have counterparts in every other language. Quine seems to beg the question in taking for granted that distinctions that might be meaningful in one language provide a relevant background for interpreting another. Moreover, either there are dispositional differences across different contexts or there are not. If there are, then presumably they should emerge in relation to a native language as readily as they would in relation to English. But there might be no such distinctions here at all.

4. MEANING OF PRIMITIVES AS DETERMINED BY SOCIAL CONVENTIONS

The conception of dispositions that is thereby presupposed differs from those advanced by Gilbert Ryle (1949), by B. F. Skinner (1953), and by W. V. O. Quine (1960), because those accounts were excessively behavioristic, extensionalistic, and reductionistic. They therefore fell prey to various difficulties, including some highly plausible objections advanced by Fodor and by Donald Davidson, which do not confound the present account (cf. Fetzer 1989, pp. 32—35). Even more important within the current context is that nothing about this approach precludes the possibility of private languages.

That this is the case becomes apparent from various perspectives. The meaning of the primitive words that make up a language for a specific user depends upon their causal role in affecting that user's behavior. The same words would possess the same meaning for different language users, therefore, only when they stand for the same concept and thereby exercise the same causal influence within the same contexts. But what can guarantee that the strength of those dispositions that they happen to possess in the presence of those undefined words must be the same from one to another?

Even if every (neurologically normal) human brain possesses the same predispositions to acquire the same language under the same environmental circumstances (including, for example, having English-speaking parents, attending an English grammar school, etc.), that surely affords no grounds for assuming that different children have actually been raised in ways sufficiently similar to establish that sameness of meaning. The interests of a community, however, may certainly be advanced by taking steps that will insure that different members of that community speak the same language.

Indeed, from an evolutionary perspective, it should be obvious that human communities stand to benefit when its members speak the same language. The purpose of a human community, from a biological point of view, is to promote the survival and reproduction of its members. The prospects for the survival and reproduction of its members, however, tends to be advanced by cooperation between its members. And the prospects for cooperation between those members tends to be advanced when they speak the same language, insofar as successful communication promotes cooperation.

From this vantage point, one of the most basic words in the English language is "help". When uttered with force, as in the exclamation, "Help!", it can be used to cry out for assistance. Were a word of this kind not a part of the linguistic fluency of the members of such a community, they would be incapacitated from summoning aid or from providing help when it was needed. Analogously, other basic words in the English language appear to include "fire", "food", and (notably) "yes" and "no". Even primitive human communities depend upon a shared language for their continued survival.

It should therefore be evident that social conventions fulfill a different role with respect to language than do personal habits. The purpose of social conventions appears to be to insure a suitable degree of uniformity of linguistic usage among the members of a community, where the usage of its individual members is determined by their personal habits. Thus, the evidence at hand indicates that social conventions have a secondary role to play with respect to the nature of meaning, but that they may still have a primary role to play in relation to promoting the uniformity of meaning.

If these reflections are well-founded, then several conclusions suggest themselves. The particular, in relation to the hypotheses that we are exploring,

($h1$) the meaning of primitives is determined by natural laws;
($h2$) the meaning of primitives is determined by personal habits; or,
($h3$) the meaning of primitives is determined by social conventions;

it now appears to be the case that ($h1$) is false but ($h2$) is true. Since (*h2*) and (*h3*) are intended to be mutually exclusive, the apparent truth of (*h2*) entails the evident falsity of (*h3*) for understanding the nature of meaning.

Nevertheless, a certain ambiguity appears to affect these alternatives. For, even though it may be true that the meaning of primitive concepts is determined by personal habits (because meanings are fixed by means of causal influence upon behavior), it may also be true that which particular words are absorbed into those personal habits tends to be determined by social conventions. The customs, traditions, and practices that characterize specific communities, after all, profoundly affect the habits that are acquired by the members of those communities and thereby influence meanings.

5. RELATIONS BETWEEN SOCIAL CONVENTIONS AND NATURAL LAWS

Indeed, not only are social conventions profoundly important as determinants of the personal habits that are acquired by the members of a certain community, but the habits that are adopted and the conventions that prevail are profoundly affected by natural laws. The natural laws which make a difference here, moreover, appear to be of at least two distinctive kinds, namely: those that are involved in the acquisition of habits under the influence of environmental and genetic factors, on the one hand, and those that are presupposed by the existence of conventions, on the other.

That laws relating the acquisition of specific habits to specific genetic and environmental factors should be required to understand the nature of conventions is hardly a surprise. These are laws concerning the kinds of ways in which human behavior can be shaped, including classical conditioning, operant conditioning, and the like. They relate (neurologically normal) human brains of physically normal children with the acquisition of specific abilities, such as the ability to use English, under the influence of specific environmental factors, such as having English-speaking parents.

What other kinds of laws, after all, could possibly make a difference to the acquisition of conventions? The answer to this question concerns every natural law whose operation is presupposed by the establishment of a convention. Consider, for example, the distinctive aroma of garlic. Almost nothing else smells exactly like it, which makes it exceedingly difficult to describe. The expression, "the aroma of garlic", therefore, seems to function as a primitive expression in English, where the meaning of that expression — the concept of the aroma of garlic — is its causal role in affecting behavior.

Several different kinds of laws are involved in even this uncomplicated illustration. One is that this distinctive aroma is characteristically emitted by things of a specific kind, namely: instances of garlic, which is a bulbous herb (*Allium sativum*) of the lily family. Thus, laws of the first kind relate the possession of a certain specific aroma (the aroma of garlic) to instances of things of a specific kind (garlic). Laws of a second kind relate the presence of that specific aroma (the aroma of garlic) to the occurrence of a certain smell (the smell of garlic) for human beings under suitable conditions.

The aroma of garlic qualifies as a permanent property of garlic, in the sense that nothing could lose that aroma and remain an instance of garlic, even though the possession of this property is not one of those properties that things of this kind have by definition (such as being a bulbous herb). The smell of garlic, by comparison, arises from an interaction between a thing that exudes an aroma and a thing that has the ability to detect that aroma and is not incapacitated from exercising that ability. That it has a distinctive aroma does not require that garlic ever happens to be smelled.

The use of signs of the three kinds identified by Peirce can also be exlaborated on the basis of this example. Icons are signs that stand for that for which they stand by virtue of relations of resemblance between those signs and that for which they stand. One instance of the aroma of garlic (of the size of garlic, of the shape of garlic, etc.) therefore stands for any other, although occasionally an instance of that aroma might be so pungent (or of that size so gargantuan, or of that shape so peculiar, etc.) that they qualify as "abnormal" (and thus become the subject of humor, etc.).

Indices, by contrast, are signs that stand for other things by virtue of being either causes of or effects of those other things for which they stand. The presence of garlic thus stands for the presence of the aroma of garlic, and the aroma of garlic stands for the presence of garlic. Since there can be more than one cause of certain effects (such as the taste of garlic or impressions of garlic left in the wet sand, etc.) and some effects are probabilistic rather than deterministic, some stand-for relations are uncertain rather than certain signs of the presence of those other things.

Symbols, finally, are signs that stand for that for which they stand, not because of any natural relation of resemblance or of cause-and-effect, but merely on the basis of an habitual association. In the present instance, of course, the use of the words "garlic" and "aroma" are examples of signs we habitually associate with things of those kinds. Because we happen to use these specific words as standard usage within our language community, it turns out that these words are habitually associated with these things not only by us but by other users of the same language as a social convention.

6. RELATIONS BETWEEN KINDS OF SIGNS AND TYPES OF MINDS

The use of signs always involves a triadic relation between a sign, that for which it stands, and a sign user. Thus, although icons and indices are "natural" signs in the sense that the relations by virtue of which they can stand for other things are there in nature, whether we notice them or not, we are able to use those signs only if we have the ability to detect their presence and are not incapacitated from exercising that ability. With respect to symbols, moreover, we have to acquire the associations that we create between those signs and what they stand for by means of habits.

Without the existence of something that has the capacity to use signs of that kind and is not incapacitated from exercising that ability, therefore, nothing would ever stand for anything at all for anyone (or thing). Since those things that have the ability to use signs are minds (or semiotic systems), it appears appropriate to distinguish different minds of different types on the basis of the kinds of signs they can use. Minds of Type I, for example, can utilize icons. Minds of Type II can utilize indices. Minds of Type III can utilize symbols (Fetzer 1988 and 1990).

The presence of signs of a certain kind will bring about an instance of cognition in minds with the ability to utilize signs of that kind that are not incapacitated from exercising that ability. The smell of garlic can cause a human mind to infer the presence of garlic, and the sight of garlic can be used to infer the presence of the aroma of garlic. Such inferences are by no means infallible, however, since the smell of garlic, for example, may have been produced by some unusual combination of chemicals that brings about a similar aroma rather than by the real thing.

Indeed, were there no laws that relate one property (such as garlic) to another (such as the aroma of garlic), on the one hand, or that relate the acquisition of habits of one kind (such as the ability to use English) to genetic and environmental factors (including having parents who speak English), on the other, it would be difficult, if not impossible, for conventions to be sustained. Natural laws provide universal, inviolable, and unchangeable relations between phenomena of various kinds upon which social conventions can be established. These laws are essential to their existence.

The nasal cavity behind the human nose, for example, is lined with mucosa containing receptor cells which contain microscopic hairs known as *cilia*. When they are stimulated in different ways, these receptor cells send nerve impulses to the olfactory centers of the human brain (Ackerman 1990). The patterns of neural activation that occur cause different sensations to be experienced in the human body, as an effect of the kind of stimulation that has occurred. Depending on matters of context, that pattern of activation then tends to affect the behavior a person displays.

The specific kinds of stimulation that these receptor cells experience, moreover, are brought about by the causal influence of distinct aromas. Different aromas tend to produce different smells as sensations that are experienced in a human being, when such a person has the ability to detect the presence of that aroma and he is not incapacitated from the exercise of that ability. Someone who is suffering from a bad cold complete with sinus congestion, for example, would be unable to experience the smell of garlic, even were he entirely enveloped by the aroma of garlic.

If there were no laws relating the presence of garlic to the aroma of garlic, or relating the aroma of garlic to the smell of garlic, or relating the smell of garlic to human behavior (in relation to various contexts), the word "garlic" and the phrase "the aroma of garlic" would have no constancy of meaning. The presence of garlic would be attended by various different aromas on different occasions, which, in turn, might bring about some assortment of smells that varied from one to another time. The aroma of garlic might produce the smell of cinnamon instead.

From this perspective, therefore, it is fascinating to observe that, although meaning is a function of personal habits and sameness of meaning is promoted by social conventions, our success in sustaining conventions provides indirect — but nevertheless very strong — evidence for our belief in the existence of an external world. The best explanation available for our capacity to nurture and maintain customs, traditions, and practices within a community through substantial intervals of time may even be the hypothesis of an external world governed by natural laws.

7. RELATIONS BETWEEN SOCIAL CONVENTIONS AND EPISTEMIC OBJECTIVITY

Because the meaning of primitives is a function of their causal role in affecting behavior, it is tempting to conclude that Wittgenstein was right in maintaining that we should look for the use of words rather than ask for their meaning. The uses to which words are put, however, obviously depend upon contexts. Strictly speaking, therefore, it is crucial to distinguish between *public usage* and *private meaning*, where the public use of words provides evidence for, but does not thereby define, the private meaning that their users attach to them. The relationship is more subtle.

As J. L. Austin (1962) has emphasized, people use language for many different purposes: to amuse, to deceive, to mislead, to entertain, to seduce, to impress, to confound, and so forth. His distinction between the specific words that are used on a specific occasion (as a locutionary act), the specific meaning that was thereby conveyed (as an illocutionary act), and the specified effect that was thereby attained (as a perlocutionary act), warrants contemplation. The words used on a specific occasion might be a matter of choice, but the meaning that they convey has a public aspect.

When a young woman suggested to a young man that he should not do certain things, she may have used certain words to issue a warning ("We are going too far, Harold!") and thereby have preserved her virtue (since he did not want to offend her), but still feel a little disappointed (because she had hoped that he might be more insistent). Had he perceived her real intention (her desire to preserve the appearance of virtue without foregoing the pleasures of vice), he might have known what to do (without disappointing her). Her public usage thus concealed her true feelings.

From the point of view of the theory of knowledge, therefore, what someone means by the words they use on a specific occasion could be very difficult, if not impossible, to discover, in the absence of any real ability to "read one's mind". Hypotheses about the causal role that is fulfilled by specific words for specific human beings exhibit the epistemic interdependence of motive-belief-ethics-ability-capability-and-opportunity ascriptions, in the sense that testing a specific hypothesis about one of their values requires assigning values to all (Fetzer 1989).

Without doubt, those cases in which we have reason to believe that we can succeed in understanding what others mean by what they say are those in which we know those others well. Cases of this kind ought to include parents and children, husbands and wives, doctors and their patients, for example, provided, of course, that those parents, spouses, and doctors are perceptive observers of other persons. The surprises life can bring to parties who think they know other parties well still include affairs, divorces, and suicides that were entirely unforseen.

Nevertheless, the analysis of meaning that has been indicated here supports not only our belief in the existence of an external world but also the existence of an objective conception of truth. The word "truth" no doubt, needs to be applied to our beliefs, even when we are unable to explain their meaning by means of other words, precisely because they are couched in primitive words. For if no conception of truth were forthcoming from this approach, that would be a serious shortcoming.

Once again, the argument involves an inference to the best explanation. For when we happen to succeed in attaining our objectives, the best explanation for our success may be that the world possesses some of the properties that our beliefs ascribe to it, where those beliefs are, in specific respects, appropriate to guide our actions. From this point of view, therefore, it seems plausible to assume that beliefs are true when they are appropriate to guide our actions and that "truth" itself can perhaps be best understood as appropriate belief (Fetzer 1990).

During the course of this inquiry, distinctions have been drawn between laws, conventions, and habits as possible determinants of meaning. The theory elaborated here defends the view that habits are the fundamental units of meaning for language users z while conventions, understood as shared habits, are the fundamental units of meaning for a community of language users Z. The existence of natural laws, moreover, appears to play a crucial role in ensuring that different members of a community can share the same habits, tendencies, and dispositions.

Department of Philosophy
University of Minnesota, Duluth

APPENDIX

A more formal construction employing subjunctive ($\ldots \Rightarrow$ ___) and causal ($\ldots = n \Rightarrow$ ___) conditionals for a specific mental state (such as the belief $B1$) in relation to various contexts $C1, C2, \ldots$, therefore — where n may assume the deterministic value u or any probabilistic value p — would require the use of a possibly infinite set of conditionals (S) such as follows:

(S) $[B1zt \Rightarrow (C1zt = n1 \Rightarrow R1zt^*)] \And [B1zt \Rightarrow (C2zt = n2 \Rightarrow R2zt^*)] \And \ldots,$

which would be read, "if z were in state $B1$ at time t, then being in state $C1$ at t would bring about (with strength $n1$) response behavior of kind $R1$ at time t^*; and if z were in state $B1$ at time t, then being in state $C2$ at t would bring about (with strength $n2$) response behavior of kind $R2$ at time t^*; and so forth — where time t^* occurs at some specific interval after time t.

Alternatively, the difference between having belief $B1$ rather than $B2$, for z at t can be elaborated by holding each such context constant and by varying those beliefs in order to bring out their different consequences:

(S*) $[C1zt \Rightarrow (B1zt = n1 \Rightarrow R1zt^*)] \And [C1zt \Rightarrow (B2zt = n2 \Rightarrow R2zt^*)] \And \ldots.$

which would be read, "if z were in state $C1$ at time t, then being in state $B1$ at t would bring about (with strength $n1$) response behavior of kind $R1$ at time t^*; and if z were in state $C1$ at time t, then being in state $B2$ at t would bring about (with strength $n2$) response behavior of kind $R2$ at time t^*; and so forth — where time t^* occurs at some specific interval after time t.

Each of these conjuncts is s scientific conditional, where scientific conditionals are instantiations of lawlike sentences, which on this approach are trivially derivable from them by universal generalization, regardless of whether "z" is interpreted as an ambituous name or as in individual constant. The first of the conjuncts that collectively constitute the set 9S),

(SC) $[B1zt \Rightarrow (C1zt = n1 \Rightarrow R1zt^*)],$

thus entails the corresponding (universally quantified) lawlike sentence,

(LS) $(z)(t)[B1zt \Rightarrow (C1zt = n1 \Rightarrow R1zt^*)],$

which, of course, asserts that, "for all z and all t, if z were in state $B1$ at time t, then being in state $C1$ at t would bring about (with strength $n1$) response behavior of kind $R1$ at time t^*". (See Fetzer 1981, pp. 53—54).

Insofar as similar formulations (involving subjunctive and causal conditionals) are applicable for the formalization of lawlike sentences generally, perhaps it ought to be emphasized that the specifically mentalistic aspects of beliefs, for example, arises from their semiotic significance for a system at a time. In other words, while there are many kinds of lawful and causal relations, only some of those lawful and causal relations properly qualify as *semiotic*. The difference between "causal systems" and "semiotic systems", therefore, arises because semiotic systems are causal systems of certain special kinds. Those who desire to pursue this issue may want to consider Fetzer (1988, 1989, 1990, and 1991).

REFERENCES

Ackerman, D. (1990), *A Natural History of the Senses* (New York, NY: Random House).

Austin, J. L. (1962), *How to Do Things with Words* (Oxford, UK: Oxford University Press).

Fetzer, J. H. (1981), *Scientific Knowledge* (Dordrecht, The Netherlands: D. Reidel Publishing Company).

Fetzer, J. H. (1988), 'Signs and Minds: An Introduction to the Theory of Semiotic Systems' in J. H. Fetzer, ed., *Aspects of Artificial Intelligence* (Dordrecht, The Netherlands: Kluwer Academic Publishers), pp. 133—161.

Fetzer, J. H. (1989), 'Language and Mentality: Computational, Representational, and Dispositional Conceptions', *Behaviorism* **17**, pp. 21—39.

Fetzer, J. H. (1990), *Artificial Intelligence: Its Scope and Limits* (Dordrecht, The Netherlands: Kluwer Academic Publishers).

Fetzer, J. H. (1991), *Philosophy and Cognitive Science* (New York, NY: Paragon House Publishers).

Fodor, J. (1975), *The Language of Thought* (Cambridge, MA: MIT Press).

Fodor, J. (1987), *Psychosemantics* (Cambridge, MA: MIT Press).

Peirce, C. S. (1906), 'Pragmatism in Retrospect: A Last Formulation', in J. Buchler, ed., *Philosophical Writings of Peirce* (New York, NY: Dover Publications, 1955), pp. 269—289.

Ryle, G. (1949), *The Concept of Mind* (London, UK: Hutchinson Publishers).

Quine, W. V. O. (1960), *Word and Object* (Cambridge, MA: The MIT Press).

Skinner, B. F. (1953), *Science and Human Behavior* (New York, NY: The Macmillan Company).

Webster's New World Dictionary (1988), 3rd College Edition (New York, NY: Simon & Schuster).

CHAPTER 3

SIGNS AND MINDS
An Introduction to the Theory
of Semiotic Systems*

Perhaps no other view concerning the theoretical foundations of artificial intelligence has been as widely accepted or as broadly influential as the physical symbol system conception advanced by Newell and Simon (1976), where symbol systems are machines — possibly human — that process symbolic structures through time. From this point of view, artificial intelligence deals with the development and evolution of physical systems that employ symbols to represent and to utilize information or knowledge, a position often either explicitly endorsed or tacitly assumed by authors and scholars at work within this field (*cf.* Nii *et al.*, 1982 and Buchanan 1985). Indeed, this perspective has been said to be "the heart of research in artificial intelligence" (Rich 1983, p. 3), a view that appears to be representative of its standing within the community at large.

The tenability of this conception, of course, obviously depends upon the notions of system, of physical system, and of symbol system that it reflects. For example, Newell and Simon (1976) tend to assume that symbols may be used to designate "any expression whatsoever", where these expressions can be created and modified in arbitrary ways. Without attempting to deny the benefits that surely are derivable from adopting their analysis, it may be worthwhile to consider the possibility that this approach could be perceived as part of another more encompassing position, relative to which physical symbol systems might qualify as, say, one among several different sorts of systems possessing the capacity to represent and to utilize knowledge or information. If such a framework could be constructed, it might not only serve to more precisely delineate the boundaries of their conception but contribute toward the goal of illuminating the theoretical foundations of artificial intelligence as well.

Not the least important question to consider, moreover, is what an ideal framework of this kind ought to be able to provide. In particular, as their "physical symbol system hypothesis" — the conjecture that physical symbol systems satisfy the necessary and sufficient conditions for "intelligent action" (Newell and Simon, 1976) — itself suggests, the conception of physical symbol systems is intended to clarify the relationship between symbol processing and deliberate behavior, in some appropriate sense. Indeed, it would seem to be a reasonable expectation that an ideal framework of this kind ought to have the capacity to shed light on the general character of the causal connections that obtain between mental activity and behavioral tendencies to whatever extent they occur as causes or as effects of the production and the utilization of symbols (or of their counterparts within a more encompassing conception).

The purpose of this paper, therefore, is to explore this possibility by examining the issues involved here from the point of view of a theory of mind based upon the theory of signs (or "semiotic theory") proposed by Charles S. Peirce (1839-1914). According to the account that I shall elaborate, minds ought to be viewed as *semiotic systems*, among which symbolic systems (in a sense that is not quite the same as that of Newell and Simon) are only one among three basic kinds. As semiotic systems, minds are sign-using systems that have the capacity to create or to utilize signs, where this capability may be either naturally produced or artificially contrived. The result is a conception of mental activity that promises to clarify and illuminate the similarities and the differences between semiotic systems of various kinds — no matter whether human, (other) animal or machine — and thereby avail its support for the foundations of artificial intelligence, while contributing toward understanding mankind's place within the causal structure of the world.

1. PEIRCE'S THEORY OF SIGNS

It is not uncommon to suppose that there is a fundamental relationship between thought and language, as when it is presumed that all thinking takes place in language. But it seems to me that there is a deeper view that cuts into this problem in a way in which the conception of an intimate connection between thought and language cannot. This is a view about the nature of mind that arises from reflection upon the theory of signs (or "semiotic theory") advanced by Peirce. The most fundamental concept Peirce elaborated is that of a sign as a something that stands for something (else) in some respect or other for somebody. He distinguished between three principal areas of semiotic inquiry, namely, the study of the relations signs bear to other signs; the study of the relations signs bear to that for which they stand; and, the study of the relations that obtain between signs, what they stand for, and sign users. While Peirce referred to these dimensions of semiotic as "pure grammar", "logic proper", and "pure rhetoric", they are more familiar under the designations of "syntax", "semantics", and "pragmatics", respectively, terms that were introduced by Morris (1938) and have become standard.

Within the domain of semantics, Peirce identified three ways in which a sign might stand for that for which it stands, thereby generating a classification of three kinds of signs. All signs that stand for that for which they stand by virtue of a relation of resemblance between those signs themselves and that for which they stand are known as "icons". Statues, portraits and photographs are icons in this sense, when they create in the mind of a sign user another — equivalent or more developed — sign that stands in the same relation to that for which they stand as do the original signs creating them. Any signs that stand for that for which they stand by virtue of being either causes or effects of that for which they stand are known as "indices". Dark clouds that suggest rain, red spots that indicate measles, ashes that remain from a fire are typical indices in this sense. Those signs that stand for that for which they stand either by virtue of conventional agreements or by virtue of habitual associations between those signs and that for which they stand are known as "symbols". Most of the words that occur in ordinary language, such as "chair" and "horse"— which neither resemble nor are either causes or effects of that for which they stand — are symbols in this technical sense. (Compare Peirce, 1955, esp. pp. 97—155 and pp. 274—289; and Peirce, 1985.)

There is great utility in the employment of symbols by the members of a sign-using community, of course, since, as Newell and Simon (1976) recognize, purely as a matter of conventional agreement, almost anything could be used to stand for almost anything else under circumstances fixed by the practices that might govern the use of those signs within that community of sign users. Thus, the kinds of ways in which icons and indices can stand for that for which they stand may be thought of as natural modes, insofar as relations of resemblance and of cause-and-effect are there in nature, whether we notice them or not; whereas conventional or habitual associations or agreements are there only if we create them. Nevertheless, it would be a mistake to make too much of this distinction, because things may be alike or unalike in infinitely many ways, where two things qualify as of a common kind if they share common properties from a certain point of view, which may or may not be easily ascertainable.

The most important conception underlying this reflection is that of the difference between types and tokens, where "types" consist of specifications of kinds of things, while "tokens" occur as their instances. The color blue for example, when appropriately specified (by means of color charts, in terms of angstrom units, or whatever), can have any number of instances, including bowling balls and tennis shoes, where each such instance qualifies as a token of that type. Similar considerations obtain for sizes, shapes, weights, and all the rest: any property (or pattern) that can have distinct instances may be characterized as a kind (or type), where the instances of that kind (type) qualify as its tokens. The necessary and sufficient conditions for a token to qualify as a token of a certain type, moreover, are typically referred to as the intension (or "meaning") of that type, while the class of all things that satisfy those conditions is typically referred to as its extension (or "reference"). The distinction applies to icons, to indices and to symbols alike, where identifying things as tokens of a type presumes a point of view, which may or may not involve more than the adoption of a certain semiotic framework.

The importance of perspective can be exemplified. My feather pillow and your iron frying-pan both weight less than 7 tons, are not located on top of Mt. Everest, and do not look like Lyndon Johnson. Paintings by Rubens, Modigliani, and Picasso clearly tend to suggest that relations of resemblance presuppose a point of view. A plastic model of the battleship *Missouri* may be like the "Big Mo" with respect to the relative placement of its turrets and bulwarks, yet fail to reflect other properties — including the mobility and firepower — of the real thing, where whether a specific set of similarities ought to qualify as resemblance depends upon and varies with the adoption of some perspective. And, indeed, even events are described as "causes" and as "effects" in relation to implicit commitments to laws or to theories. Relations of resemblance and causation have to be recognized to be utilized, where the specification of a complex type can be a rather complex procedure.

In thinking about the nature of mind, it seems plausible that Peirce's theory of signs might provide us with clues. In particular, reflecting upon the conception of a sign as a something that stands for something (else) in some respect or other for somebody, it appears to be a presumption to assume that those somethings for which something can stand for something (else) in some respect or other must be "some-bodies": would it not be better to suppose, in a non-question-begging way, that these are "somethings", without taking for granted that the kind of thing that these somethings are has to be human? In reasoning about the kind of thing that these somethings might be, therefore, the possibility arises that those somethings for which something can stand for something (else) might themselves be viewed as "minds". (Morris, 1938, p. 1, suggests that (human) mentality and the use of signs are closely connected). The conception that I shall elaborate, therefore, is that minds are things that are capable of utilizing signs ("sign users"), where semiotic systems in this sense are causal systems of a special kind.

2. ABSTRACT SYSTEMS AND PHYSICAL SYSTEMS

In defense of this position, I intend to explain, first, what it means to be a system, what it means to be a causal system, what it means to be the special kind of causal system that is a semiotic system; and, second, what, if anything, makes this approach more appropriate than the Newell and Simon conception, especially with respect to the field of artificial intelligence. The arguments that follow suggests that Newell and Simon's account harbors an important equivocation, insofar as it fails to define the difference between a set of symbols that is significant *for a user of a machine* — in which case, there is a semiotic relationship between the symbols, what they stand for, and the symbol user, where the user is not identical with the machine — and a set of symbols that is significant *for use by a machine* — in which case, a semiotic relationship obtains between the symbols, what they stand for, and the symbol user, where the user is identical with the machine. The critical difference between symbol systems and semiotic systems emerges at this point.

Let us begin by considering the nature of systems in general. A system may be defined as a collection of things — numbers and operators, sticks and stones, whatever — that instantiates a fixed arrangement. This means that a set of parts becomes a system of a certain kind by instantiating some set of specific relations — logical, causal, whatever — between those parts. Such a system may be functional or non-functional with respect to specified inputs and outputs, where the difference depends on whether that system responds to an input or not. In particular, for a fixed input — such as assigning seven as the value of a variable, resting a twelve-pound weight on its top, whatever — a specific system will tend to produce a specific output (which need not be unique to its output class) — such as yielding four-teen as an answer, collapsing in a heap, whatever — where differences in outputs (or in output classes) under the same inputs can serve to distinguish between systems of different kinds, but only as a sufficient and not as a necessary condition (*cf.* the distinction of deterministic and indeterministic systems below).

For a system to be a causal system means that it is a system of things within space/time between which causal relations obtain; an abstract system, by comparison, is a system of things not in space/time between which logical relations alone can obtain. This conception of a causal system bears strong resemblance to Newell and Simon's conception of a physical system, which is a system governed by the laws of nature. Indeed, to the extent to which the laws of nature include non-causal as well as causal laws, both of these conceptions should be interpreted broadly (though not therefore reductionistically, since the non-occur-rence of emergent properties — possibly including at least some mental phenomena — is not a feature of the intended interpretation of causal systems; *cf.* Fetzer, 1981, 1986a). Since systems of neither kind are restricted to inanimate as opposed to animate systems, let us assume that their "physical systems" and my "causal systems" are by and large ("roughly") the same, without pretending to have conclusively estab-lished their identity.

Within the class of causal (or of physical) systems, moreover, two subclasses require differentiation. Causal systems whose relevant pro-perties are only incompletely specified may be referred to as "open", while systems whose relevant properties are completely specified are regarded as "closed". Then a distinction may be drawn between two kinds of closed causal systems, namely, those for which, given the same input, the same output invariably occurs (without exception), and those for which, given the same input, one or another output within the same class of outputs invariably occurs (without exception). Systems of the first kind, accordingly, are deterministic causal systems, while those of the second kind are indeterministic causal systems. Whether or not Newell and Simon would be willing to acknowledge this distinction, I cannot say for certain; but because it is well-founded and its introduc-tion begs no crucial questions, I shall suppose they would.

This difference, incidentally, is not the same as that in computational theory between deterministic and non-deterministic finite automata, such as parsing schemata, which represent paths from grammatical rules (normally called "productions") to well-formed formulae (typically "terminal strings") for which more than one production sequence is possible, where human choice influences the path selected (Cohen, 1986, pp. 142—145). While Newell and Simon acknowledge this distinction, strictly speaking, the systems to which it applies are special kinds of "open" rather than "closed" causal systems. The conception of abstract systems also merits more discussion, where purely formal systems — the systems of the natural numbers, of the real numbers, and the like — are presumptive examples thereof. While abstract systems in this sense are not in space/time and cannot exercise any causal influence upon the course of events during the world's history, this result does not imply that, say, inscriptions of numerals — as their representatives within space/time — cannot exercise causal influence as well. Indeed, since chalkmarks on blackboards affect the production of pencilmarks in notebooks, where some of these chalkmarks happen to be numerals, such a thesis would be difficult to defend.

For a causal system to be a semiotic system, of course, it has to be a system for which something can stand for something (else) in some respect or other, where such a something (sign) can affect the (actual or potential) behavior of that system. In order to allow for the occurrence of dreams, of daydreams, and of other mental states as potential outcomes (responses or effects) of possible inputs (stimuli or trials) — or as potential causes (inputs or stimuli) of possible outcomes (responses or effects) — and thereby circumvent the arbitrary exclusion of internal (or private) as well as external (or public) responses to internal as well as to external signs, behavior itself requires a remarkably broad and encompassing interpretation. A conception that accommodates this possibility is that of behavior as any internal or external effect of any internal or external cause. Indeed, from this point of view, it should be apparent that that something affects the behavior of a causal system does not mean that it has to be a sign for that system, which poses a major problem for the semiotic approach — distinguishing semiotic causal systems from other kinds of causal systems.

3. CAUSAL SYSTEMS AND SEMIOTIC SYSTEMS

To appreciate the dimensions of this difficulty, consider that if the capacity for the (actual or potential) behavior of a system to be affected by something were enough for that system to qualify as semiotic, the class of semiotic systems would be coextensive with the class of causal systems, since they would have all and only the same members. If even one member of the class of causal systems should not qualify as a member of the class of semiotic systems, however, then such an identification cannot be sustained. Insofar as my coffee cup, your reading glasses and numberless other things — including sticks and stones — are systems whose (actual and potential) behavior can be influenced by innumerable causal factors, yet surely should not qualify as semiotic systems, something more had better be involved: that something can affect the behavior of a causal system is not enough.

That a system's behavior can be affected by something is necessary, of course, but in addition that something must be functioning as a sign for that system: that that sign stands for that for which it stands for that system must make a difference to (the actual or potential behavior of) that system, where this difference can be specified in terms of the various ways that such a system would behave, were such a sign to stand for something other than that for which it stands for that system (or, would have behaved, had such a sign stood for something other than that for that system). Were what a red light at an intersection stands for to change to what a green light at an intersection stands for (and conversely) for specific causal systems, including little old ladies but also fleeing felons, then that those signs now stand for things other than that for which they previously stood ought to have corresponding behavioral manifestations, which could be internal or external in kind.

Little old ladies who are not unable to see, for example, should now slow down and come to a complete stop at intersections when green lights appear and release the break and accelerate when red lights appear. Felons fleeing with the police in hot pursuit, by contrast, may still speed through, but they worry about it a bit more, which, within the present context, qualifies as a behavioral manifestation. Strictly speaking, changes in external behavior (with respect to outcome classes) are sufficient but not necessary, whereas changes in internal behavior (with respect to outcome classes) are necessary and sufficient. Thus, a more exact formulation of the principle in question would state that, *for any specific system, a sign S stands for something for that system rather than for something else if and only if the strength of the tendencies for that system to manifest behavior of some specific kind in the presence of S —*

no matter whether publicly displayed or not — differs from case to case, where otherwise what it stands for remains the same.

This principle implies that a change that effects no change is no change at all (with respect to the significance of a sign for a system), which tends to occur when some token is exchanged for another token of the same type. Once again, however, considerations of perspective may have to be factored in, since one dime (silver) need not stand for the same thing as another dime (silver and copper) for the same system when they are tokens of some of the same types, but not of others. Although this result appears agreeable enough, the principle of significance being proposed does not seem to be particularly practical, since access to strengths of tendencies for behavior that may or may not be displayed is empirically testable, in principle, but only indirectly measureable, in practice (*cf.* Fetzer, 1981, 1986a). As it happens, this theoretical yardstick can be supplemented by a more intuitive standard of its kind.

The measure that I have proposed, of course, affords an account of what it means for a sign to change its meaning (what it stands for) for a system, where the differences involved here may be subtle, minute and all but imperceptible. For defining "sign", it would suffer from circularity in accounting for what it means for a sign to change its meaning while relying upon the concept of a sign itself: it does not provide a definition of what it is to be a sign or of what it is to be a semiotic system as such, but of what it is for a sign to change its meaning for a semiotic system. This difficulty, however, can be at least partially offset by appealing to (what I take to be) a general criterion for a system to be a semiotic system (for a thing to be a mind), namely, *the capacity to make a mistake*; for, in order to make a mistake, something must take something to stand for something other than that for which it stands, a reliable evidential indicator that something has the capacity to take something to stand for something in some respect or other, which is the right result.

We should all find it reassuring to discover that the capacity to make a mistake — to mis-take something for other than that for which it stands — appears to afford conclusive evidence that something has a mind. That something must have the capacity to make a mistake, however, does not mean that it must actually make them as well, since the concept of a divine mind that never makes mistakes — no matter whether as a matter of logical necessity or as a matter of lawful necessity for minds of that kind — is not inconsistent (Fetzer, 1986b). The difference between mistakes and malfunctions, moreover, deserves to be emphasized, where *mistakes* are made by systems while remaining systems of the same kind, while *malfunctions* transform a system of one kind into a system of another. That a system makes a mistake is not meant to imply that its output classes, relative to its input classes, have been revised, but rather that, say, a faulty inference has occurred, the false has been taken for the true, something has been misclassified, and so on, which readily occurs with perceptual and inductive reasoning (Fetzer, 1981).

4. THE VARIETIES OF SEMIOTIC SYSTEMS

The semiotic analysis of minds as semiotic systems invites the introduction of at least three different kinds (or types) of minds, where systems of Type I can utilize icons, systems of Type II can utilize icons and indices, and systems of Type III can utilize icons, indices, and symbols. Thus, if the conception of minds as semiotic systems is right-headed, at least in general, it would seem reasonable to conjecture that there are distinctive behavioral (psychological) criteria for semiotic. systems of these different types; in other words, if this approach is approximately correct, then it should not be overly difficult to discover that links can be forged with pyschological (behavioral) distinctions that relate to the categories thereby generated. In particular, there appear to be kinds of learning (conditioning, whatever) distinctive to each of these three types of systems, where semiotic systems of Type I display type/token recognition, those of Type II display classical conditioning, and those of Type III display instrumental conditioning, where behavior of these kinds appears to be indicative that a system is one of such a type. Let us begin, therefore, by considering examples of semiotic systems of all three kinds and subsequently return to the symbol system hypothesis.

Non-human animals provide useful examples of semiotic systems that display classical conditioning, for example, as systems of Type II which have the capacity to utilize indices as signs, where indices are things that stand for that for which they stand by virtue of being either causes or effects of that for which they stand. Pavlov's famous experiments with dogs are illustrative here. Pavlov observed that dogs tend to salivate at the appearance of their food in the expectation of being fed; and that, if a certain stimulus, such as a bell, was regularly sounded at the same time its food was brought in, a dog soon salivated at such a bell's sound whether its food came with it or not. From the semiotic perspective, food itself functions as an (unconditioned) sign for dogs, namely, as a sign standing to the satiation of their hunger as causes stand to effects. Thus, when the sound of a bell functions as a (conditioned) sign for dogs, it similarly serves as a sign standing to the satiation of their hunger as cause stands to its effects. In the case of the (unconditioned) food stimulus, of course, the stimulus actually is a cause of hunger satiation, while in the case of the (conditioned) bell stimulus, it is not; but that does not undermine this example, since it shows that dogs sometimes make mistakes.

Analogously, Skinner's familiar experiments with pigeons provide an apt illustration of semiotic systems of Type III that have the capacity to utilize symbols as signs, where symbols are things that stand for that for which they stand by virtue of a conventional agreement or of an habitual association between the sign and that for which it stands. Skinner found that pigeons kept in cages equipped with bars that would emit a pellet if pressed rapidly learned to depress the bar whenever they wanted some food. He also discovered that if, say, a system of lights was installed, such that a bar-press would now release a pellet only if a green light was on, they would soon refrain from pressing the bar, even when they were hungry, unless the green light was on. Once again, of course, the pigeon might have its expectations disappointed by pressing a bar when the apparatus has been changed (or the lab assistant forgot to set a switch, whatever), which shows that pigeons are no smarter than dogs in avoiding mistakes.

Classical conditioning and operant conditioning, of course, are rather different kinds of learning. The connection between a light and the availability of food, like that between the sound of the bell and the satiation of hunger, was artificially contrived. The occurrence of the bell stimulus, of course, causes the dog to salivate, whether it wants to or not, whereas the occurrence of a green light does not cause a pigeon to press the bar, whether it wants to or not, but rather establishes a conventional signal for the pigeon that, if it were to perform a bar press now, a pellet would be emitted. It could be argued that the bell stimulus has now become a sufficient condition for the dog to salivate, while the light stimulus has become a sufficient condition for the pigeon not to press the bar. But Skinner's experiments, unlike those of Pavlov, involve reinforcing behavior after it has been performed, because of which the pigeons learn means/ends relations over which they have some control.

An intriguing example of type/token recognition that displays what appears to be behavior characteristic of semiotic systems of Type I, at last, was described in a recent newspaper article entitled, 'Fake Owls Chase Away Pests' (*St. Petersburg Times*, 27 January 1986), as follows:

Birds may fly over the rainbow, but until 10 days ago, many of them chose to roost on top of a billboard that hangs over Bill Allen's used car lot on Drew Street in Clearwater. Allen said he tried everything he could think of to scare away the birds, but still they came — sometimes as many as 100 at a time. He said an employee had to wash the used cars at Royal Auto Sales every day to clean off the birds' droppings. About a month ago, Allen said, he called the billboard's owner for help fighting the birds. Shortly afterward, Allen said, two viny owl "look alikes" were put on the corners of the billboard. "I haven't had a bird land up there since", he said.

The birds, in other words, took the sizes and shapes of the viny owls to be instances of the sizes and shapes of real owls, treating the fake owls as though they were the real thing. Once again, therefore, we can infer that these systems have the capacity to take something to stand for something (else) in some respect or other on the basis of the criterion that they have the capacity to make a mistake, which has been illustrated by Pavlov's dogs, by Skinner's pigeons, and by Allen's birds alike. While there do seem to be criteria distinctive of each of these three types of semiotic systems, in other words, these more specific criteria themselves are consistent with and illuminate that more general semiotic criterion.

These reflections thus afford a foundation for pursuing a comparison of the semiotic approach with the account supported by the symbol system conception. Indeed, the fundamental difference that we are about to discover is that Newell and Simon appear to be preoccupied exclusively with systems of Type III (or their counterparts), which, if true, establishes a sufficient condition for denying that semiotic systems and symbol systems are the same — even while affirming that they are both physical systems (of one or another of the same general kind). The intriguing issues that arise here, therefore, concern (a) whether there is any significant difference between semiotic systems of Type III and physical symbol systems and (b) whether there are any significant reasons for preferring one or the other of these accounts with respect to the foundations of artificial intelligence.

5. SYMBOL SYSTEMS AND CAUSAL SYSTEMS

The distinction between types and tokens ought to be clear enough by now to consider the difference between Newell and Simon's physical symbol systems and semiotic systems of Type III. The capacity to utilize indices seems to carry with it the capacity to utilize icons, since recognizing instances of causes as events of the same kind with respect to some class of effects entails drawing distinctions on the basis of resemblance relations. Similarly, the capacity to utilize symbols seems to carry with it the ability to utilize indices, at least to the extent to which the use of specific symbols on specific occasions can affect the behavior of a semiotic system for which they are significant signs. Insofar as these considerations suggest that a physical symbol system ought to be a powerful kind of semiotic system with the capacity to utilize icons, indices and symbols as well, it may come as some surprise that I want to deny that Newell and Simon's conception supports such a conclusion at all. For, it appears to be the case that, appearances to the contrary notwithstanding, physical symbol systems in the sense of Newell and Simon (1976) do not qualify as semiotic systems.

Since I take it to be obvious that physical symbol systems are causal systems in the appropriate sense, the burden of my position falls upon the distinction between systems for which something functions as a sign for a user of that system and systems for which something functions as a sign for that system itself. According to Newell and Simon (1976), in particular:

A physical symbol system consists of a set of entities, called symbols, which are physical patterns that can occur as components of another type of entity called an expression (or symbol structure). Thus a symbol structure is composed of a number of instances (or tokens) of symbols related in some physical way (such as one token being next to another).

Notice, especially, that symbol structures (or "expressions") are composed of sequences of symbols (or "tokens"), where "physical symbol systems", in this sense, process expressions, which they refer to as "symbol structures". The question that I want to raise, therefore, is whether or not these "symbol structures" function as signs in Peirce's sense — and, if so, for whom.

At first glance, this passage might seem to support the conception of physical symbol systems as semiotic systems, since Newell and Simon appeal to tokens and tokens appear to be instances of different types. Their conceptions of expression and of interpretation, moreover, are relevant here:

Two notions are central to this structure of expressions, symbols, and objects: designation and interpretation.

Designation. An expression designates an object if, given the expression, the system can either affect the object itself or behave in ways depending on the object.

In either case, access to the object via the expression has been obtained, which is the essence of designation.

Interpretation. The system can interpret an expression if the expression designates a process and if, given the expression, the system can carry out the process.

Interpretation implies a special form of dependent action: given an expression, the system can perform the indicated process, which is to say, it can evoke and execute its own processes from expressions that designate them. (Newell and Simon, 1976, pp. 40-41.)

An appropriate illustration of "interpretation" in this sense would appear to be computer commands, whereby a suitably programmed machine can evoke and execute its own internal processes when given "expressions" that designate them. Notice, however, that portable typewriters (pocket calculators, and so forth) would seem to qualify as "physical symbol systems" in Newell and Simon's sense — since combinations of letters from their keyboards (of numerals from their interface, and so on) appear to be examples of "expressions" that designate a process whereby various shapes can be typed upon a page (strings of numerals can be manipulated, . . .). Other considerations, however, suggest that the sorts of systems that are intended to be good examples of symbol systems are general-purpose digital computers rather than simple systems of these kinds.

A consistent interpretation of Newell and Simon's conception depends upon an analysis of "symbols" as members of an alphabet/character set (such as "a", "b", "c", and so on), where "expressions" are sequences of the members of such a set. The term that they employ which corresponds most closely to that of "symbol" in Peirce's technical sense, therefore, is not "symbol" itself but rather "expression". Indeed, that "symbols" in Newell and Simon's sense cannot be "symbols" in Peirce's technical sense follows from the fact that most of the members of a character set do not stand for anything at all — other than that their inclusion within such a set renders them permissible members of the character sequences that constitute (well-formed) expressions. A more descriptive name for systems of this kind, therefore, might be that of "expression processing" ("string manipulating") systems; but so long as Newell and Simon's systems are not confused with semiotic systems, there is no reason to dispute the use of a name that has already become well-entrenched.

An important consequence of this account, moreover, is that words like "chair" and "horse", which occur in ordinary language, are good examples of symbols in Peirce's sense, yet do not satisfy Newell and Simon's conception of expressions. These words stand for that for which they stand without in any fashion offering the least hint that the humans (machines, whatever) for which such things are signs can either affect such objects or behave in ways that depend upon those objects: the capacity to describe horses and chairs does not entail the ability to ride or to train them, to build or to refinish them, or otherwise manipulate them. These symbols can function as significant signs whether or not Newell and Simon's conditions are satisfied, a proof of which follows from examples such as "elf" and "werewolf", signs that function as symbols in Peirce's sense, yet could not possibly fulfill Newell and Simon's conception because they stand for non-existent objects, which can neither affect nor be affected by causal relations in space/time. Thus, "symbol systems" in Newell and Simon's sense (of string manipulating systems) do not qualify as systems that utilize symbols in Peirce's sense.

6. SYMBOL SYSTEMS AND SEMIOTIC SYSTEMS

This result tends to reflect the fact that Newell and Simon's conception of physical symbol system depends upon at least these two assumptions:

(a)   expressions $=_{df}$ sequences of characters (strings of symbols); and,
(b)   symbols $=_{df}$ elements of expressions (tokens of character types);

where these "character types" are those specified by some set of characters (ASCII, EBCDIC, whatever). This construction receives further support from other remarks they make during the course of their analysis of completeness and closure as properties of systems of this kind, insofar as they maintain:

(i)   there exist expressions that designate every process of which such
       a system (machine) is capable; and,
(ii)   there exist processes for creating any expression and for modify-
       ing any expression in arbitrary ways;

which helps to elucidate the sense in which a system can affect an
object itself or behave in ways depending on that object, namely, when
that object itself is either a computer command or a string of characters
from such a set. (A rather similar conception can be found in Newell,
1973, esp. pp. 27—28.)

Conditions (i) and (ii), I believe, are intended to support the restriction of symbol systems to general purpose digital computers, even
though they can only be satisfied relative to some (presupposed) set of
symbols, no matter how arbitrarily selected. Whether or not these
conditions actually have their intended effect, however, appears to be
subject to debate. Although programming languages vary somewhat on
this issue, such practices as the overloading of operators, the multiple
definition of identifiers and the like are ordinarily supposed to be
important to avoid in order to secure the formal syntax of languages
that are suitable for employment with computers, which tends to
restrict the extent to which they can be arbitrarily composed. Moreover,
since typewriters and calculators seem to have unlimited capacities to
process any number of expressions that can be formulated within their
respective sets of symbols, it could be argued that they are not excluded
by these constraints, which is a striking result (insofar as few would be
inclined to claim that a typewriter "has a mind of its own").

No doubt, symbol systems in Newell and Simon's sense typically
behave in ways that depend upon certain members of the class of
expressions, since they are causal systems that respond to particular
computer commands for which they have been "programmed" (in a
sense that takes in hardware as well as software considerations). Since
computer commands function as input causes in relation to output
effects (for suitably programmed machines), it should be obvious that
Newell and Simon's conception entails the result that physical symbol
systems are causal systems. For the reasons outlined above, however, it
should be equally apparent that their conception does not entail that
these causal systems are semiotic systems of Type III. Indeed, if
expressions were symbols in Peirce's technical sense, then they would
have to have intensions and extensions; but it seems plain that strings of

symbols from a character set, however well-formed, need not have these properties.

Indeed, the most telling considerations of all emerge from inquiring for whom Newell and Simon's "symbols" and "expressions" are supposed to be significant (apart from the special class of computer commands, where, in fact, it remains to be ascertained whether or not those commands function as signs for those systems). Consider, for example, the following cases;

INPUT	(FOR SYSTEM)	OUTPUT
finger (pushes)	button (causing)	printout of file
match (lights)	fuse (causing)	explosion of device
child (notices)	cloud (causing)	expectation of storm

When a finger pushes a button that activates a process, say, leading to a printout, no doubt an input for a causal system has brought about an output. When a match lights a fuse, say, leading to an explosion, that an input for a causal system has brought about an output is not in doubt. And when a child notices a cloud, say, leading to some such expectation, no doubt an input for a causal system has brought about an output. Yet, surely only the last of these cases is suggestive of the possibility that something stands for something (else) for that system, where that particular thing is a meaningful token for that system (with an intensional dimension) and where that system might be making (or have made) a mistake.

If these considerations are correct, then we have discovered, first, that the class of causal systems is not coextensive with the class of semiotic systems. Coffee cups and matches, for example, are particular cases of systems in space/time that stand in causal relations to other things, yet surely do not qualify as sign-using systems. Since two words, phrases or expressions mean the same thing only if their extensions are the same, causal systems and semiotic systems are not the same thing. We have also discovered, second, that the meaning of "symbol system" is not the same as that of "semiotic system of Type III". General-purpose digital computers are causal systems that process expressions, yet do not therefore need to be systems for which signs function as signs. Since two words, phrases, or expressions mean the same thing only if their intensions are the same, symbol systems and semiotic systems of Type III are not the same things.

From the perspective of the semiotic approach, in other words, the conception of physical symbol systems encounters the distinction between sets of symbols that are significant for users of machines — in which case there is a semiotic relationship between those signs, what they stand for and those sign users, where the users are not identical with the machines themselves — and sets of symbols that are significant for use by machines — in which case there is a semiotic relationship between those signs, what they stand for and those sign users, where these users are identical with the machines themselves. Without any doubt, the symbols and expressions with which programmers program machines are significant signs for those programmers; and without any doubt, the capacity to execute such commands qualifies those commands as causal inputs with respect to causal outputs. That is not enough for these machines to be semiotic systems of Type III.

If these considerations are correct, then there is a fundamental difference between causal systems and semiotic systems, on the one hand, and between symbol systems and semiotic systems of Type III, on the other. Of course, important questions remain, including ascertaining whether or not there are good reasons to prefer one or another conception, which will depend in large measure upon their respective capacities to clarify, if not to resolve, troublesome issues within this domain. Moreover, there appear to be several unexamined alternatives with respect to the interpretation of Newell and Simon's conception, since other arguments might be advanced to establish that symbol systems properly qualify either as semiotic systems of Type I or of Type II — or that special kinds of symbol systems properly qualify as semiotic systems of Type III, which would seem to be an important possibility that has not yet been explored. For the discovery that some symbol systems are not semiotic systems of Type III no more proves that special kinds of symbol systems cannot be semiotic systems of Type III than the discovery that some causal systems are not semiotic systems proves that special kinds of causal systems cannot be semiotic systems.

7. THE SYMBOL-SYSTEM AND THE SEMIOTIC-SYSTEM HYPOTHESES

The conception of semiotic systems, no less than the conception of symbol systems, can be evaluated (at least, in part) by the contribution they make toward illuminating the relationship between the use of signs, on the one hand, and the manipulation of symbols, on the other, in relation to deliberate behavior. Both accounts, in other words, may be viewed as offering characterizations of "mental activity" in some appropriate sense, where these accounts are intended to afford a basis for understanding "intelligent" (or "deliberate") behavior. Indeed, the respective theoretical hypotheses that they represent ought to be formulated as follows:

(h_1) *The Symbol-System Hypothesis*: a symbol system has the necessary and sufficient means (or capacity) for general intelligent action; and,

(h_2) *The Semiotic-System Hypothesis*: a semiotic system has the necessary and sufficient means (or capacity) for general intelligent action;

where these hypotheses are to be entertained as empirical generalizations (or as lawlike claims) whose truth or falsity cannot be ascertained merely by reflection upon their meaning within a certain language framework alone.

Because these hypotheses propose necessary and sufficient conditions, they could be shown to be false if either (a) systems that display "intelligent" (or "deliberate") behavior are not symbol (or semiotic) systems; or (b) systems that are symbol (or semiotic) systems do not display "intelligent" (or "deliberate") behavior. Moreover, since they are intended to be empirical hypotheses (*cf.* Newell and Simon, 1976, esp. p. 42 and p. 46), these formulations ought to be understood as satisfied by systems that display appropriate behavior without assuming (i) that behavior that involves the processing or the manipulation of a string of tokens from a character set is therefore either "intelligent" or "deliberate" (since otherwise the symbol-system hypotheses must be true as a function of its meaning); and, without assuming (ii) that behavior that is "intelligent" or "deliberate" must therefore be successful in attaining its aims, objectives, or goals, where a system that displays behavior of this kind cannot make a mistake (since otherwise the semiotic-system hypothesis must be false as a function of its meaning). With respect to the hypotheses (h_1) and (h_2), therefore, "intelligent action" and "deliberate behavior" are synonymous expressions.

A certain degree of vagueness inevitably attends an investigation of this kind to the extent to which the notions upon which it depends, such as "deliberate behavior" and "intelligent action", are not fully defined. Nevertheless, an evaluation of the relative strengths and weaknesses of these hypotheses can result from considering classes of cases that fall within the extensions of "symbol system" and of "semiotic system", when properly understood. In particular, it seems obvious that the examples of type/token recognition, of classical conditioning, and of instrumental conditioning considered above are instances of semiotic systems of Type I, II, and III that do not qualify as symbol systems in Newell and Simon's sense. This should come as no surprise, since Newell and Simon did not intend that their conception should apply with such broad scope; but it evidently entails that hypothesis (h_1) must be empirically false.

Indeed, while this evidence amply supports the conclusion that the semiotic-system approach has applicability to dogs, to pigeons, and to (other) birds that the symbol-system approach lacks, the importance that ought to attend this realization may or may not be immediately apparent. Consider, after all, that a similar argument could be made on behalf of the alternative conception, namely, that — depending upon the resolution of various issues previously identified — the symbol-system approach has applicability to typewriters, to calculators, and to (other) machines that the semiotic-system approach lacks, which may be of even greater importance if the objects of primary interest are machines. For if digital computers, for example, have to be symbol systems but do not have to be semiotic systems, that they might also qualify as semiotic systems does not necessarily have to be a matter of immense theoretical significance.

Nevertheless, to the extent to which these respective conceptions are supposed to have the capacity to shed light on the general character of the causal connections that obtain between mental activity and behavioral tendencies — that is, to the extent to which frameworks such as these ought to be evaluated in relation to hypotheses such as (h_1) and (h_2) — the evidence that has been presented would appear to support the conclusion that the semiotic-system approach clarifies connections between mental activity as semiotic activity and behavioral tendencies as deliberate behavior — connections which, by virtue of its restricted range of applicability, the symbol-system approach cannot accommodate. By combining distinctions between different kinds (or types) of mental activity together with psychological criteria concerning the sorts of capacities distinctive of systems of these different types (or kinds), the semiotic approach provides a powerful combination of (explanatory and predictive) principles, an account that, at least with respect to non-human animals, the symbol-system approach cannot begin to rival.

This difference, however, surely qualifies as an advantage of an approach only so long as it is being entertained as an approach to a certain specific class of problems, such as explaining and predicting the deliberate behavior (the "intelligent actions") of non-human animals. To whatever extent Newell and Simon did not intend to account for the intelligent actions (the "deliberate behavior") of non-human animals, it may be said, the incapacity of their conception to accommodate explanations and predictions should not be held against them. The strict interpretation of this position would lead to the conclusions that (a) any theory should be evaluated exclusively in terms of its success or failure at achieving its intended aims, goals or objectives, where (b) unintended consequences should be viewed as, at most, of secondary importance, no matter how striking their character or significant their potential. Relative to this standard, the incapacity to accommodate non-human animals not only cannot count against Newell and Simon's conception but instead ought to support it.

8. WHAT ABOUT HUMANS AND MACHINES?

A more interesting — and less implausible — position would be for Newell and Simon to abandon their commitment to the symbol system hypothesis and restrict the scope of their analysis to the thesis that, after all, general-purpose digital computers *are* symbol systems, where it really does not matter whether or not they have captured the nature of mental activity in humans or in (other) animals. There is a sense in which this attitude is almost precisely right, so long as the possibility that they may have captured no sense of mental activity is itself left open. Newell and Simon's conception, in other words, may be completely adequate for digital computers but remain completely inadequate for other things — unless, of course, the precise processes that characterize symbol systems were the same processes that characterize, say, human or non-human systems that process knowledge or information, a position that is not consistent with the results we have discovered.

Notice, in particular, that the following theses regarding the relationship between symbol systems and semiotic systems are compatible:

(t_1) general-purpose digital computers are symbol systems; and,
(t_2) animals — human and non-human alike — are semiotic systems;

where, even if not one digital computer heretofore constructed qualifies as a semiotic system, that some digital computer yet to be built might later qualify as a semiotic system remains an open question. Indeed, whether information or knowledge processing in humans and in (other) animals is like that in symbol systems or that in semiotic systems appears to be the fundamental question at the foundations of artificial intelligence.

Strictly speaking, after all, to be a symbol system in Newell and Simon's sense is neither necessary nor sufficient to be a semiotic system in the Peircean sense. Recall, in particular, that their account of designation presupposes the existence of that which is designated, since otherwise that system could neither affect nor be affected by that thing; yet it is no part of the notion of an icon or a symbol, for example, that the things thereby signified should be open to causal influence by a semiotic system. Moreover — and most importantly — nothing about their conception warrants the conclusion that symbol systems in their sense even have the capacity to utilize signs in Peirce's sense at all, even though — as I readily concede — there is no reason to deny that they are causal systems.

Artificial intelligence is often taken to be an attempt to develop causal processes that perform mental operations. Sometimes such a view has been advanced in terms of formal systems, where "intelligent beings are . . . automatic formal systems with interpretations under which they consistently make sense" (Haugeland, 1981, p. 31). This conception exerts considerable appeal, since it offers the promise of reconciling a domain about which a great deal is known — formal systems — with one about which a great deal is not known — intelligent beings. This theory suffers from profound ambiguity, however, since it fails to distinguish between systems that make sense to themselves and those that make sense for others. Causal models of mental processes, after all, might either effect connections between inputs and outputs so that, for a system of a certain specific type, those models yield outputs for certain classes of inputs that correspond to those exemplified by the systems that they model; or else effect those connections between inputs and outputs and, in addition, process these connections by means of processes that correspond to those that are exemplified by those systems that they model.

This distinction, which is not an unfamiliar one, can be expressed by differentiating between "simulation" and "replication", where, say,

(a)   causal models that simulate mental processes capture connections between inputs and outputs that correspond to those of the systems that they represent; while,

(b)   causal models that replicate mental processes not only capture these connections between inputs and outputs but do so by means of processes that correspond to those of the systems they represent;

where, if theses (t_1) and (t_2) are true, then it might be said that symbol systems simulate mental processes that semiotic systems replicate — precisely because semiotic systems have minds that symbol systems lack. There are those, such as Haugeland (1985), of course, who are inclined to believe that symbol systems replicate mental activity in humans too because human mental activity, properly understood, has the properties of symbol systems too. But this claim appears to be plausible only if there is no real difference between systems for which signs function as signs for those systems themselves and systems for which signs function as signs for the users of those systems, which is the issue in dispute.

Another perspective on this matter can be secured by considering the conception of systems that possess the capacity to represent and to utilize information or knowledge. The instances of semiotic systems of Types I, II, and III that we have examined seem to fulfill this desideratum, in the sense that, for Pavlov's dogs, for Skinner's pigeons, and for Allen's birds, there are clear senses in which these causal systems are behaving in accordance with their beliefs, that is, with something that might be properly characterized as "information" or as "knowledge". Indeed, the approach represented here affords the opportunity to relate genes to bodies to minds to behavior, since phenotypes develop from genotypes under the influence of environmental factors, where phenotypes of different kinds may be described as predisposed toward the utilization of different kinds of signs, which in turn tends toward the acquisition and the utilization of distinct ranges of behavioral tendencies, which have their own distinctive strengths (Fetzer, 1985, 1986b). This in itself offers significant incentives for adopting the semiotic approach.

Yet it could still be the case that digital computers (pocket calculators and the like) cannot be subsumed under the semiotic framework precisely because (t_1) and (t_2) are both true. After all, nothing that has gone before alters obvious differences between systems of these various different kinds, which are created or produced by distinctive kinds of causal processes. The behavior of machine systems is (highly) artificially determined or engineered, while that of human systems is (highly) culturally determined or engineered, and that of (other) animal systems is (highly) genetically determined or engineered. Systems of all three kinds exhibit different kinds of causal capabilities: they differ with respect to their ranges of inputs/stimuli/trials, with respect to their ranges of output/responses/outcomes, and with respect to their higher-order causal capabilities, where humans (among animals) appear superior. Even if theses (t_1) and (t_2) were true, what difference would it make?

9. WHAT DIFFERENCE DOES IT MAKE?

From the point of view of the discipline of artificial intelligence, whether computing machines do what they do the same way that humans and (other) animals do what they do only matters in relation to whether the enterprise is that of simulating or of replicating the mental processes of semiotic systems. If the objective is simulation, it is surely unnecessary to develop the capacity to manufacture semiotic systems; but if the objective is replication, there is no other way, since this aim can not otherwise be attained. Yet it seems to be worth asking whether the replication of the mental processes of human beings would be worth the time, expense, and effort that would be involved in building them. After all, we already know how to reproduce causal systems that possess the mental processes of human beings in ways that are cheaper, faster, and lots more fun. Indeed, when consideration is given to the limited and fallible memories, the emotional and distorted reasoning and the inconsistent attitudes and beliefs that tend to distinguish causal systems of this kind, it is hard to imagine why anyone would want to build them: there are no interpretations "under which they consistently make sense".

A completely different line could be advanced by defenders of the faith, however, who might insist that the distinction I have drawn between symbol systems and semiotic systems cannot be sustained, because the conception of semiotic systems itself is circular and therefore unacceptable. If this contention were correct, the replication approach might be said to have been vindicated by default in the absence of any serious alternatives. The basis for this objection could be rooted in a careful reading of the account that I have given for semiotic systems of Type I, since, within the domain of semantics, icons are supposed to stand for that for which they stand "when they create in the mind of a sign user another — equivalent or more developed — sign that stands in the same relation to that for which they stand as do the original signs creating them". This Peircean point, after all, employs the notion of mind in the definition of one of the kinds of signs — the most basic kind, if the use of indices involves the use of icons and the use of symbols involves the use of indices, but not conversely — which might be thought to undermine any theory of the nature of mind based on his theory of signs.

This complaint, I am afraid, is founded upon an illusion; for those signs in terms of which other signs are ultimately to be understood are unpacked by Peirce in terms of the habits, dispositions, or tendencies by means of which all signs are best understood: "the most perfect account of a concept that words can convey", he wrote, "will consist in a description of the habit which that concept is calculated to produce" (Peirce, 1955, p. 286). But this result itself could provide another avenue of defense by contending that systems of dispositions cannot be causal systems so that, a fortiori, semiotic systems cannot be special kinds of causal systems within a dispositional framework. Without intimating that the last word has been said with reference to this question, there appears to be no evidence in its support; but it would defeat the analysis that I have presented if this argument were correct.

The basic distinction between symbol systems and semiotic systems, of course, is that symbol systems may or may not be systems for which signs stand for something for those systems, while semiotic systems are, where I have employed the general criterion that semiotic systems are capable of making mistakes. A severe test of this conception, therefore, is raised by the problem of whether or not digital computers, in particular, are capable of making a mistake. If the allegations that the super-computers of the North American Defense Command (NORAD) located at Colorado Springs have reported the U.S. to be under ballistic missile attacks from the Soviet Union no less than 187 times are (even roughly) accurate, this dividing line may already have been crossed, since it appears as though all such reports thus far have been false. The systems most likely to fulfill this condition are ones for which a faulty inference can occur, the false can be mistaken for the true or things can be misclassified, which might not require systems more complex than those capable of playing chess (Haugeland, 1981, p. 18) — but this question, as we have discovered, is theoretically loaded.

Human beings, as semiotic systems, display certain higher-order causal capabilities that deserve to be acknowledged, since we appear to have a remarkable capacity for inferential reasoning that may or may not differ from that of (other) animals in kind but undoubtedly exceeds them in degree. In this respect, especially, however, human abilities are themselves surpassed by "reasoning machines", which are, in general, more precise, less emotional, and far faster in arriving at conclusions by means of deductive inference. The evolution and development of digital computers with inductive and perceptual capabilities, therefore, would seem to be the most likely source of systems that display the capacity to make mistakes. By this criterion, systems that have the capacity to make mistakes qualify as semiotic systems, even when they do not replicate processes of human systems.

A form of mentality that exceeds the use of symbols alone, more-over, appears to be the capacity to make assertions, to issue directives, to ask questions and to utter exclamations. At this juncture, I think, the theory of minds as semiotic systems intersects with the theory of languages as transformational grammars presented especially in the work of Noam Chomsky (Chomsky, 1965, and Chomsky, 1966, for example; *cf.* Chomsky, 1986 for his more recent views). Thus, this connection suggests that it might be desirable to identify a fourth grade of mentality, where semiotic systems of Type IV can utilize signs that are transformations of other signs, an evidential indicator of which may be taken to be the ability to ask questions, make assertions and the like. This conception indicates that the capacity for explicit formalization of propositional attitudes may represent a level of mentality distinct from the occurrence of propositional attitudes as such.

Humans, (other) animals, and machines, of course, also seem to differ with respect to other higher-order mental capabilities, such as in their attitudes toward and beliefs about the world, themselves and their methods. Indeed, I am inclined to believe that those features of mental activity that separate humans from (other) animals occur at just this juncture; for humans have a capacity to examine and to criticize their attitudes, their beliefs, and their methods that (other) animals do not enjoy. From this perspective, however, the semiotic approach seems to classify symbol systems as engaged in a species of activity that, if it were pursued by human beings, would occur at this level; for the activities of linguists, of logicians, and of critics in creating and in manipulating expressions and symbols certainly appear to be higher-order activities, indeed.

A fifth grade of mentality accordingly deserves to be acknowledged as a meta-mode of mentality that is distinguished by the use of signs to stand for other signs. While semiotic systems of Type I can utilize icons, of Type II indices, of Type III symbols and of Type IV transforms, semiotic systems of Type V are capable of using meta-signs as signs that stand for other signs (one variety of meta-signs, of course, being meta-languages). Thus, perhaps the crucial criterion of mentality of this degree is the capacity for criticism, of ourselves, our theories and our methods. While the conception of minds as semiotic systems has a deflationary effect in rendering the existence of mind at once more ubiquitous and less important than we have heretofore supposed, it does not therefore diminish the place of human minds as semiotic systems of a distinctive kind, nevertheless.

The introduction of semiotic systems of Type IV and of Type V, however, should not be allowed to obscure the three most fundamental species of mentality. Both transformational and critical capacities are presumably varieties of semiotic capability that fall within the scope of symbolic mentality. Indeed, as a conjecture, it appears to be plausible to suppose that each of these successively higher types of mentality presupposes the capacity for each of those below, where evolutionary considerations might be brought to bear upon the assessment of this hypothesis by attempting to evaluate the potential benefits for survival and reproduction relative to species and societies — that is, for social groups as well as for single individuals — that accompany this conception (cf. Fetzer, 1985 and especially 1986a).

There remains the further possibility that the distinction between symbol systems and semiotic systems marks the dividing line between computer science (narrowly defined) and artificial intelligence, which is not to deny that artificial intelligence falls within computer science (broadly defined). On this view, what is most important about artificial intelligence as an area of specialization within the field itself would be its ultimate objective of replicating semiotic systems. Indeed, while artificial intelligence can achieve at least some of its goals by building systems that simulate — and improve upon — the mental abilities that are displayed by human beings, it cannot secure its most treasured goals short of replication, if such a conception is correct. It therefore appears to be an ultimate irony that the ideal limit and final aim of artificial intelligence — whether by replicating human beings or by creating novel species — could turn out to be the development of systems capable of making mistakes.

NOTE

* The original version of this paper was presented at New College on 8 May 1984. Subsequent versions were presented at the University of Virginia, at the University of Georgia, and — most recently — at Reed College. I am indebted to Charles Dunlop, Bret Fetzer, Jack Kulas, Terry Rankin, and Ned Hall for instructive comments and criticism.

REFERENCES

Buchanan, B.: 1985, 'Expert Systems', *Journal of Automated Reasoning* 1, 28—35.

Chomsky, N.: 1965, *Aspects of the Theory of Syntax*. MIT Press. Cambridge, MA.

Chomsky, N.: 1966, *Cartesian Linguistics*. Harper & Row, New York.

Chomsky, N.: 1986, *Knowledge of Language: Its Nature, Origin, and Use*. Praeger Publishers, New York.

Cohen, D.: 1986, *Introduction to Computer Theory*. John Wiley & Sons, Inc., New York.

Fetzer, J. H.: 1981, *Scientific Knowledge*. D. Reidel, Dordrecht, Holland.

Fetzer, J. H.: 1985, 'Science and Sociobiology', in J. H. Fetzer (ed.), *Sociobiology and Epistemology* (D. Reidel, Dordrecht, Holland), pp. 217—246.

Fetzer, J. H.: 1986a, 'Methodological Individualism: Singular Causal Systems and Their Population Manifestations', *Synthese* **68**, pp. 99—128.

Fetzer, J. H.: 1986b, 'Mentality and Creativity', *Journal of Social and Biological Structures* (forthcoming).

Haugeland, J.: 1981, 'Semantic Engines: An Introduction to Mind Design', in J. Haugeland (ed.), *Mind Design* (MIT Press, Cambridge, MA.), pp. 1—34.

Haugeland, J.: 1985, *Artificial Intelligence: The Very Idea*. MIT Press, Cambridge, MA.

Morris, C. W.: 1938, *Foundations of the Theory of Signs*. University of Chicago Press, Chicago, IL.

Newell, A.: 1973, 'Artificial Intelligence and the Concept of Mind', in R. Schank and K. Colby (eds.), *Computer Models of Thought and Language* (W. H. Freeman and Company, San Francisco.), pp. 1—60.

Newell, A. and Simon, H.: 1976, 'Computer Science as Empirical Inquiry: Symbols and Search', reprinted in J. Haugeland (ed.), *Mind Design* (MIT Press, Cambridge, MA.), pp. 35—66.

Nii, H. P. *et al.*: 1982, 'Signal-to-Symbol Transformation: HASP/SIAP Case Study', *AI Magazine* **3**, pp. 23—35.

Peirce, C. S.: 1955, *Philosophical Writings of Peirce*, J. Buchler (ed.) (Dover Publications, New York.).

Peirce, C. S.: 1985, 'Logic as Semiotic: The Theory of Signs', reprinted in R. Innis (ed.), *Semiotics: An Introductory Anthology* (Indiana University Press, Bloomington IN) pp. 4—23.

Rich, E.: 1983, *Artificial Intelligence*. McGraw-Hill, New York.

Department of Philosophy and Humanities
University of Minnesota
Duluth, MN 55812

CHAPTER 4

LANGUAGE AND MENTALITY
Computational, Representational,
and Dispositional Conceptions*

> (A) cognitive theory seeks to connect the *intensional*
> properties of mental states with their *causal* properties
> *vis-à-vis* behavior. Which is, of course, exactly what a
> theory of the mind ought to do.
> Jerry Fodor

ABSTRACT. The purpose of this paper is to explore three alternative frameworks for understanding the nature of language and mentality, which accent syntactical, semantical, and pragmatical aspects of the phenomena with which they are concerned, respectively. Although the computational conception currently exerts considerable appeal, its defensibility appears to hing upon an extremely implausible theory of the relation of form to content. Similarly, while the representational approach has much to recommend it, its range is essentially restricted to those units of language that can be understood in terms of undefined units. Thus, the only alternative among these three that can account for the meaning of primitive units of language is one emphasizing the basic role of skills, habits, and tendencies in relating signs and dispositions.

There are several reasons why the nature of language and mentality is fundamental to research in artificial intelligence and to cognitive inquiry in general. One tends to be the assumption – better viewed as a *pre*sumption – that thinking takes place in language, which makes the nature of language fundamental to the nature of mental processes, if not to the nature of mind itself. Another is that computers operate by means of software composed by means of a language – not a natural language, to be sure, but a computer language, which is a special kind of artificial language suitable for conveying instructions to machines. And another is that debates continue to rage over whether or not machines can have minds, a question whose answer directly depends upon the nature of mentality itself and indirectly upon the nature of language – especially the nature of languages suitable for use by machines.

Below the surface of these difficulties, however, lies another problematic question, namely: is artificial intelligence *descriptive* or *normative*? For if artificial intelligence is supposed to utilize the methods that human beings themselves – descriptively – actually employ in problem solving, then there would appear to be a powerful motive for insuring that the languages used by machines are similar (in all relevant respects) to those used by humans. If artificial intelligence is *not* restricted to the methods that human beings actually employ but may utilize those that humans should use – normatively – whether or not they actually do, then whether computer languages are like or unlike natural languages at once appears to be a less pressing issue.

Most students of artificial intelligence tend to fall into two broad (but heterogeneous) camps. One camp maintains the 'strong' thesis that AI concerns how we do think. The other maintains the 'weak' thesis that AI concerns how we ought to think. And there are grounds to believe that the predominant view among research workers today is that the strong thesis is correct. Eugene Charniak and Drew McDermott, for example, envision AI as "the study of mental faculties through the use of computational models" [Charniak and McDermott (1985), p. 6]. An assumption that underlies this approach is that, at some level, the way in which the mind functions is the same as the way in which certain computational systems – digital computers, especially – also function. This assumption, however, is one that adherents of both camps might endorse, insofar as even normative approaches to AI presumably would need to satisfy this condition 'at *some* (suitable) level'.

As though to disabuse those who might mistake the conception that they endorse for a normative one, Charniak and McDermott go so far as to assert that, "The ultimate goal of AI research (which we are very far from achieving) is to build a person, or, more humbly, an animal" [Charniak and McDermott (1985), p. 7]. Although their position may be extreme in this respect, much of the impetus for AI and cognitive science research along these lines arises from the *symbol system hypothesis* advanced by Alan Newell and Herbert Simon, according to which the necessary and sufficient conditions for general intelligence are those possessed by *physical symbol systems*, which are physical systems (or 'causal systems') that have the capacity to processes/manipulate/... sequences of marks/signs/... from a designated vocabulary [cf. especially Newell and Simon (1976), pp. 40–42].

This general approach, moreover, has been reinforced by the proposition that, when mental processes are viewed as computational, minds themselves can be viewed as special kinds of formal systems. John Haugeland (1981), (1985), for example, has gone further in suggesting that mental activity can be adequately portrayed as the behavior of an *automated formal system*, a position that leads him to the conjecture, "Why not suppose that people *just are* computers (and send philosophy packing)?" [Haugeland (1981), p. 5]. Indeed, the prospect of reducing the philosophy of mind to problems of design in the construction and development of digital machines has excited a host of adherents across many fields and disciplines, including those of linguistics, of psychology and of philosophy as well as those of computer science and AI.

The tenability of this computational conception, of course, has not gone unchallenged. In fact, from a perfectly general perspective rooted in (what is known as) *semiotic* (or 'the theory of signs'), there are three fundamental aspects to systems of signs, generally, and to languages, specifically. These distinctions, which were introduced by Charles S. Peirce and subsequently refined by Charles Morris (1938) and Rudolf Carnap (1939), concern, first, the relations that signs bear to other signs (known as 'syntax'); second, the relations that signs bear to that for which they stand (known as 'semantics'); and, third, the relations that signs bear to other signs, to that for which they stand, and to sign users (known as 'pragmatics'). After all, if there are three dimensions of signs, how could any theory of language that focuses on only *one* be expected to provide an adequate account of language and mentality?

The purpose of this paper, pursuing this lead, is to explore three alternative frameworks for understanding the nature of language and mentality, which accent syntactical, semantical, and pragmatical dimensions of the phenomena with which they are concerned, respectively. Although the computational conception currently exercises considerable appeal, its defensibility seems to hing upon an extremely implausible theory of the relation of form to content. Similarly, while the representational approach has much to recommend it, its range is essentially restricted to those units of language that can be under-stood in terms of undefined units. Thus, the only alternative among these three that seems capable of accounting for the meaning of the primitive units of language emphasizes the role of skills, habits and tendencies relating signs and dispositions. And the same considerations provide a foundation for assessing conceptions of these kinds as 'models of the mind'.

Perhaps one cautionary note is in order before pursuing this objective. For the methodology to be employed here is analytical rather than historical, in the sense that the subject of investigation is the *problem space* – or, even better, the *solution space* – appropriate to these problems. I am less con-cerned with the detailed positions that have been held by the specific individuals – such as Haugeland, Fodor, Stich, and others – whose works are mentioned in passing than I am with the general features of the problems and solutions toward which they are directed. By emphasizing the predominantly syntactical, semantical, and pragmatical aspects of the alternatives con-sidered, their essential dimensions may be perceived more clearly and their relative plausibility may be assessed more accurately – a procedure not unlike relating surface phenomena to their deep structure.

1. THE COMPUTATIONAL CONCEPTION:
SYNTACTICAL MODELS OF THE MIND

Computational conceptions of language and of mind depend upon the assumption that languages and mental processes can be completely characterized by means of purely formal distinctions. In discussing the computational conception (or 'model') of language and of mind, for example, Fodor has observed that such an approach entails the thesis that "...mental processes have access only to formal (non-semantic) properties of the mental representations over which they are defined" [Fodor (1980), p. 307]. Thus,

...the computational theory of the mind requires that two thoughts can be distinct in content only if they can be identified with relations to formally distinct representations. More generally: fix the subject and the relation, and then mental states can be (type) distinct only if the representations which constitute their objects are formally distinct. [Fodor (1980), p. 310].

Notice that at least two issues are intimately intertwined in this passage, for Fodor is maintaining (a) that thoughts are distinct *only if* they can be "identified" with distinct representations, without explaining how it is (b) that specific thoughts can be identified with specific representations. As a necessary condition for thought identity, in other words, condition (b) must be capable of satisfaction as well as condition (a); otherwise, his account will be *purely* syntactical as an analysis of the relations between signs lacking significance.

Fodor, Stich and others too have examined possible ways in which specific 'thoughts' might be identified with specific 'representations' (in other words, how forms could be infused with content). The strongest versions of the computational conception, however, tend to eschew concern for matters of semantics, as Stich, for example, as emphasized:

On the matter of content or semantic properties, the STM [the Syntactic Theory of the Mind] is officially agnostic. It does not insist that syntactic state types have no content, nor does it insist that tokens of syntactic state types have no content. It is simply silent on the whole matter ... the STM is in effect claiming that psychological theories have *no need* to postulate content or other semantic properties, like truth conditions. [Stich (1983), p. 186].

In order to preserve the differences between the syntactical character of the computational conception and the semantical character of its representational counterpart, we shall defer our consideration of thesis (b) until Section 2.

Fodor is suggesting an exceptionally strong connection between the *form* of a thought and its *content*. The strongest version of such a position would appear to be that mental tokens (which might be sentences in a natural language, inscriptions in a mental language, or some other variety of types and tokens capable of formal discrimination) have the same content (or express the same thought, convey the same idea or otherwise impart the same information) *if and only if* they have the same form (where 'mental tokens', of course, are instances of mental types that might have content). Differences and similarities, formal or not, no doubt presuppose a point of view, which establishes a standard of 'sameness' for tokens with respect to whether or not they qualify as 'tokens of the same type'. Assuming that this condition can be satisfied by systems for which formal distinctions are fundamental, let us draw some examples from ordinary English as helpful illustrations.[1]

Any biconditional, of course, is logically equivalent to the conjunction of two conditionals. In this case, those two conditionals are (i) if mental tokens have the same form, then they have the same content; and (ii) if mental tokens have the same content, then they have the same form. Since Fodor has stipulated that contents differ only if they can be identified with different forms, evidently he subscribes to thesis (i), whose contrapositive maintains if mental tokens do not have the same content, then they do not have the same form. Although we have observed that Fodor does not elaborate how distinct thoughts are connected to distinct tokens, we shall assume that he intends that, say, similar surface grammars sometimes conceal differences in meaning that are disclosed by an investigation of their deep structures, which means that their parse trees, if they were parsed, would differ, etc.

Indeed, there seem to be at least three different ways in which tokens having the same form might be exhibited as possessing different content, each of which appears to be successively less and less syntactical in nature:

(1)   *the parsing criterion*, according to which tokens have the same content only if they have the same parse trees;

(2)   *the substitutional criterion*, according to which tokens have the same content only if they are mutually derivable by the substitution of definiens for definiendum; and,

(3)   *the functional role criterion*, according to which tokens have the same content only if they fulfill the same causal role in their effects upon behavior relative to all possible situations.

Each of these, no doubt, requires unpacking to be clearly understood. Since they accent syntactical, semantical, and behavioral dimensions of language and mentality, in turn, we shall consider them separately in the following, beginning with the parsing criterion in relation to the syntactical approach.

Distinctive versions of the computational conception might defend one of these conditionals but abandon the other, while retaining their computational character; indeed, that appears to be Fodor's own position here. But it is difficult to image how a position that abandoned *both* of these theses could still qualify as a 'computational' conception. Thus, in order to display the poverty of the computational approach, arguments will be advanced to show that both of these conditionals are *false*. Moreover, the reasons that they are false are surprisingly obvious, but none the less telling. The first of these conditionals falls prey to the problem of ambiguity, while the second succumbs to the problem of synonymy, as numerous examples display.

The first conditional claims that mental tokens have the same content if they have the same form. This thesis would be false if it were ever the case that some mental tokens have the same form, yet differ in their content. If ordinary sentences in the English language qualify as 'mental tokens', therefore, then examples involving ambiguous words – such as 'hot', 'fast', etc. – generate counterexamples whose status as ambiguous sentences is not likely to be challenged. Consider the following specific cases as illustrations:

Example (A): Imagine a very warm summer afternoon, as a group of guys are conversing about a shiny red convertible. One casually remarks,

    (a)   'That car is hot!'

Clearly, at least two meanings (contents) might be intended by remark (a), since it might be interpreted as a comment on the temperature of the car,

    (b)   'That car has heated to over 100 degrees Fahrenheit!'

but might be meant to convey its status as a recent and illegal acquisition:

    (c)   'The cops are out looking for that car everywhere!'

In this case, tokens of the same form, (a), could thus have different content.

Example (B): Sitting on the steps of the stadium, two girls are engaged in animated conversation. As a young man passes by, one says to the other,

    (d)   'John is fast!'

Once again, at least two meanings (contents) might be intended by remark (d), since the speaker might be commenting on John's prowess as a sprinter,

    (e)   'John can beat almost everyone else at the 100 yard dash!'

but it might also be intended as a characterization of his dating behavior,

    (f)   'John wants to go farther faster than anyone I have dated!'

Once again, therefore, tokens of the same form (d) could differ in meaning.

Initially, ambiguous tokens, such as these, might seem to pose no problem for the computational conception, since the parsing criterion could be employed to discriminate between them. Since the construction of a parse tree presumes the availability of a suitable grammar for this purpose [cf. Winograd (1983)], let us adopt the following very elementary grammer, *G*:

Grammar G:

                <sentence>   → <noun phrase><verb phrase>
                <noun phrase> → <proper noun>
                <noun phrase> → <determiner><proper noun>
                <verb phrase> → <copulative verb><adjective>

which, for this exercise, is all of the grammar that happens to be required.

It is important to observe, therefore, that the parse tree for example (a) turns out to have the following structure,

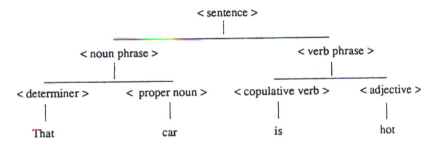

while the parse tree for example (d) has the following different structure,

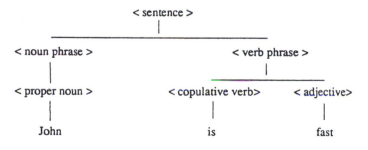

Thus, in terms of their parse trees, example (a) and example (d) clearly differ in their parse trees and thus differ in their form, which presumably provides *prima facie* evidence in support of the computational conception. But this is the case only if they also differ in their content. And we know that they differ in their content, because we have assumed they are in English!

The point is that, while it is indeed true that, relative to grammar *G*, the parse trees for sentences (a) and (d) are indeed different, that supports thesis (i), which asserts that tokens with different content have different forms, *only if* sentences (a) and (d) do have different content! We have taken for granted that the sentences, 'That car is hot!' and 'John is fast!', have different meanings and therefore ought to have different forms – provided thesis (i) is true. If, however, the object referred to by the noun phrases, 'that car' and 'John', were the same and the properties ascribed by the verb phrases, 'is hot' and 'is fast', were the same, then the results attained above would count as a counterexample *against* thesis (i) rather than as evidence *for* it! The effect obviously depends upon and varies with the relevant language.

Let us assume that all of these examples are well-founded, so there is no basis for denying that, in ordinary English, sentence (a) is often used to mean what is expressed by sentence (b) but also to mean what is expressed by sentence (c) – and, analogously, for sentence (d) in relation to sentences (e) and (f). Then these examples clearly establish that thesis (ii) is false, insofar as there are at least some sentences in English that have the same content but different forms, which would be impossible if mental tokens having the same content have to have the same form. It is evidently not the case that, if mental tokens differ in their form, then they differ in their content. This thesis of computationalism cannot cope with the problem of synonymy.

Now imagine an impoverished version of English, sub-English-4, say, in which the *only* words in the vocabulary happen to be those that are found in sentence (a) – or, alternatively, sub-English-3, those in sentence (d). Naturally, these are fanciful scenarios, since, for a variety of reasons, these are not likely to really be the *only* words in anyone's vocabulary. Nevertheless, they represent a class of cases of the relevant kind. Under these circumstances, would it not be possible that (a) could sometimes be used to mean (b) and sometimes to mean (c) or that (d) could sometimes be used to mean (e) and sometimes to mean (f)? Of course, it would not be possible to *articulate* the contemplated difference: would that mean *no* such difference could exist?

There are strong reasons for thinking it would not! Consider, after all, that some of the most frequently used exclamations in the English language vary in their meaning with the context of their use: 'Damn!', for example, is sometimes used as an expression of distress (discomfort or pain), but it also occurs as an expression of relief (happiness or joy). Here the same word is being used with very different content. Similarly, other criteria, such as the functional role criterion, could differentiate between different meanings for sentence (a): if the gang were to cease talking and scatter when a police car approached, that would tend to indicate that (a) was being used in sense (b); if they cracked an egg on the hood of the car when they wanted to eat it for a snack, that would tend to indicate that (a) was being used in sense (c); etc.

In cases of this kind, these differences in meaning (or content) would indeed exist, even though they could not be articulated *within those languages*. If these examples are acceptable, therefore, then it seems clear that thesis (i) is also false, insofar as at least some sentences in English (sub-English-4 or sub-English-3) have the same form but different contents, which would be impossible if mental tokens having the same form have to have the same content. This thesis of computationalism cannot cope with the problem of ambiguity. Appeals to dependence of meaning upon context, moreover, can be extended to larger classes of sentences through considering successively larger and larger units of discourse. But it should not be overlooked that successively larger and larger units of discourse remain vulnerable to problems of ambiguity, to problems of synonymy, and to problems of context.

There are no grounds at all to believe that longer and longer sentences (sequences of symbols, strings of marks) are necessarily or inevitably less and less ambiguous, as the computational conception would suggest. Sets of sentences constituting paragraphs and sets of paragraphs comprising documents (such as the *Constitution*) remain matters of great debate – even when attempts are made to understand them within their historical context! It would therefore be a mistake to imagine that appeals to 'context' would be more likely to support the computational conception than to undermine it. If these reflections are well-founded, therefore, then the computational conception does not appear to have a great deal to recommend it; for the twin theses that define that position are relatively clearly and decisively flawed.

2. THE REPRESENTATIONAL CONCEPTION: SEMANTICAL MODELS OF THE MIND

Hilary Putnam (1975) differentiates between psychological (or 'mental') states for which the ascription of that state (or 'token') does *not* presuppose "the existence of any individual other than the subject to whom that state is ascribed" (psychological states in *the narrow sense*) and the rest (psychological states in *the broad sense*) [Putnam (1975), p. 136]. As Fodor remarks, "Narrow psychological states are those individuated in light of the formality condition; viz. without reference to such semantic properties as truth and reference" [Fodor (1980), p. 331]. In view of the arguments presented in Section 1, it would not be unreasonable to wonder whether any account of the nature of language and of mind which, like computational accounts, restricts itself to psychological states in the narrow sense could possibly be adequate. In order to appreciate its appeal, therefore, it is crucial to consider precisely how a purely syntactical account can accommodate content.

Recall that computational conceptions not only require some strong relationship between the form of a token and its content but also need to explain how *any* specific content comes to be identified with *any* specific form. There appear to be at least three possible solutions to this problem, namely:

(4)   *by nature*, according to which the connection between tokens of a specific form and their specific content is a function of the laws of nature;

(5)   *by convention*, according to which the connection between tokens of a specific form and their specific content is a function of the practices, customs and traditions of a social group; and,

(6)   *by habituation*, according to which the connection between tokens of a specific form and their specific content is a function of the habits, skills and dispositions of individual token-users.

Indeed, the approach among these three that blends most harmoniously with syntactical models of the mind is the thesis that these relations are 'natural'.

Once mental tokens have been ascribed content by one or another of the modes indicated above, however, it becomes increasingly difficult to distinguish 'computational' from 'representational' conceptions. Stich, for example, has sought to separate 'strong' from 'weak' representational accounts:

Unlike the STM, however, the weak RTM [Representational Theory of the Mind] insists that these syntactic objects *must have content or semantic properties* ... The weak version claims only that every token mental state to which a cognitive theory applies has *some* content or *some* truth condition... The stronger version of the doctrine agrees with the weaker version in requiring all mental state tokens to have content or truth conditions. But it goes on to claim that these semantic features are correlated with the syntactic type of the token. [Stich (1983), p. 186].

Thus, (4), (5) and (6) reflect successively weaker and weaker modes of correlation between the syntactical type of a token and its semantical content.

A purely syntactical conception of language and mentality, presumably, would be an object of limited interest, since it would be unable to accommodate the ideas most fundamental to cognition and communication: content, information and belief. Indeed, even Haugeland (1981), who has championed the computational conception of minds as 'automated formal systems', has acknowledged the necessity for the formal tokens of those systems to possess semantic content: "Given an appropriate formal system *and interpretation*, the semantics takes care of itself" [Haugeland (1981), p. 24]. The problem that remains, therefore, is to explain how these correlations occur, without which the syntactical approach would simply fail to distinguish 'interpreted' from 'uninterpreted' formal systems [Hempel (1949a), (1949b)].

Fodor (1975) attempts to resolve this problem at a single stroke by introducing the notion of *the language of thought*, envisioned as an unlearned language that is both innate and species-specific. Among the most important theses upon which his position depends are (i) that learning a language presupposes the possession of a prior language; (ii) that learning a language cannot be a matter of acquiring dispositions; and (iii) that this innate language functions as a meta-language for learning other languages [Fodor (1975), pp. 64–79]. The key to Fodor's position is the assumption that learning a language requires learning the truth conditions for the sentences that can occur in that language: "... learning (a language) *L* involves learning that *Px is true if and only if x is G* for all substitution instances. But notice that learning that could be learning *P* (learning what *P* means) only for an organism that already understands *G*" [Fodor (1975), p. 80]. Having made this assumption, Fodor finds himself confronted by the unpalatable choice between the existence of an infinite hierarchy of meta-languages (for each meta-language in turn) and the existence of an unlearned language that serves as a base case.

Given exclusive commitment to truth condition semantics in the sense adumbrated here, Fodor suggests that learning a language is "literally a matter of making and confirming hypotheses about the truth conditions associated with its predicates" [Fodor (1975), p. 80], supporting the following claim:

Either it is false that learning *L* is learning its truth definition, or it is false that learning a truth definition for *L* involves projecting and confirming hypotheses about the truth conditions upon the predicates of L, or no one learns L unless he already knows some language different from L *but rich enough to express the extensions of the predicates of L.* [Fodor (1975), p. 82]

Notice that it is the commitment to truth functional semantics as an exclusive access to the meaning of a sentence in L combined with the theoretical necessity to block an infinite regress of meta-languages for meta-languages that anchors Fodor's position. No one, presumably, would want to deny that learning a language involves projecting and confirming hypotheses about the predicates of L; the question is, does this have to be done as Fodor suggests?

On its face, Fodor's position appears to be very difficult to swallow. Its general character parallel's Plato's theory of knowledge as recollection, which posits an Eternal Mind in which mortal minds participate before birth. Since the Eternal Mind is the respository of all knowledge and mortal minds participate in the Eternal Mind, all knowledge resides in every mortal mind before birth. Aware that not all mortal minds appear to be all-knowing, Plato contends that the trauma of birth induces forgetfulness in each of us, but that different experiences in life trigger off 'recollections' of that lost knowledge. An alternative to Plato's account, of course, would be the theory that knowledge is acquired through experience, so that the very 'experiences' in life that (for Plato) trigger off 'recollections' could be the mechanisms through which knowledge is actually acquired, an account that is far more elegant.

In an analogous fashion, Fodor posits a universal language of thought of which every (neurologically normal) human being is a possessor. In order to learn any ordinary language, it is necessary to discover (through experience) the truth conditions for each of the predicates in that language within the language of thought. The language of thought itself, moreover, must be infinitely rich and extraordinarily complex, since it must have the capacity to encompass each new predicate as it is introduced into its previously-impoverished ordinary language successor (in response to the discovery and growth of science and technology, for example). Since not all speakers of ordinary language display similar linguistic ability, evidently they simply have not exercised equal ingenuity in discovering the truth conditions that lie undiscovered in their mental language as an as-yet-unrealized resource.

Since experience and ingenuity as well as the language of thought are necessary conditions for learning an ordinary language on Fodor's account, an alternative would be the theory that languages can be learned through experience and ingenuity, so that the very 'experiences' in life that lead to projecting and confirming hypotheses about the predicates of L might occur even in the absence of a language of thought! For this to be possible, however, Fodor's argument must have at least one false premise; and, indeed, a little reflection suggests that Fodor may have begged the question in moving from the premise that learning P (learning what P means) can only occur for 'an organism that already understands G' to the conclusion that learning P (learning what P means) requires learning meta-linguistic truth conditions for P. For that conclusion would follow *only if* there were no other way for an organism to 'understand' the G-phenomenon that P happens to describe.

An alternative to Fodor's theory of learning a language, in other words, would be to take seriously that learning presupposes some sort of 'understanding', without assuming that the form of understanding involved here has to be *linguistic*. As infants and children, we frequently – even typically – learn to do things (suck a nipple, bounce a ball, smile a lot) without having any name or label for the habits, skills or activities thereby performed. It should not be especially surprising, therefore, that when (initially unfamiliar) words are associated with (already familiar) things, including patterns of behavior that we happen to have displayed, it does not demand extraordinary ingenuity or vast experience for a (neurologically normal) human being to learn forms of language that are appropriate to their age and past experience. The problem for Fodor is the same as the problem for Plato.

The same conclusion follows from a different starting point. One of the virtues of computational and of representational accounts would appear to be their capacity to exploit (what we shall refer to as) 'the inferential network' model of language and mentality. As Christopher Maloney observes,

Computationalism considers the mind to be an inferential system. That clearly presupposes the existence of structures over which the inferences are defined ... [and] the only things that seem physically fit to function as elements in material inferences are sentences. [Maloney (1988), p. 56]

Indeed, the meaning of a word or a sentence can be related to its place within a network of syntactical and of semantical relations, a paradigm of which is the standard conception of a *definition* as an entity consisting of two parts, a word, phrase or expression to be defined ('the definiendum') and the word phrase or expression by means of which it is defined ('its definiens'), where both the definiendum and the definiens are envisioned as *linguistic* entities.

The catch, of course, is that it is impossible for every word in a language to be defined on pain of either an infinite regress or definitional circularity, as everyone would acknowledge. Yet every defined term can be replaced in principle by some sequence of undefined terms with which it is synonymous. Thus, by the substitutional criterion, different mental tokens have the same content when they are mutually derivable by the exchange of definiens for definiendum. Even representational accounts, however, afford no solution to the problems of ambiguity and context that we have considered above.

Assuming that words like 'fast,' for example, are defined terms within the corresponding language, sentences like (d) and (e) or (d) and (f) could well be mutually derivable in harmony with the substitution criterion and presumably would possess the same content in accord with that standard. But even sentences like (f) remain ambiguous, since precisely 'where' John 'wants to go' might have social, sexual, or professional connotations, among others, depending upon context. The relations that obtain between the different elements that collectively comprise an 'inferential network' do not fix their content. The problem that therefore remains is accounting for the meaning of the undefined (or 'primitive') terms of that language. By positing a 'language of thought', of course, Fodor attempts to finesse this difficulty, which would resurrect itself *within the language of thought* were it not for the thesis that the meaning of these tokens has been fixed 'by nature'!

The question sounds funny on its face; yet I want to contend that this is the issue that poses the deepest concern for both computational and representational conceptions. The answer, after all, apparently consists of those habits, skills and practices by virtue of which the words we use are related to the world around us: we seldom think about defining words like 'wood', 'hammer', and 'nail', because we can use them – and can know how to use them – without the intervention of other linguistic forms. With respect to the primitive terms that occur in any ordinary language, we must discover how they are used rather than ask for their linguistic meaning, precisely as Wittgenstein proposed. From this point of view, therefore, knowledge of language is far more adequately envisioned as a skill than as a state (as a matter of 'knowing how' rather than of 'knowing that'), which itself may be the fundamental misconception lying at the foundation of these accounts.

A theory of language and mentality that could handle only uninterpreted formal systems, no doubt, would completely fail to satisfy the most elementary desiderata for theories of that kind. Yet it is important to notice a difference between at least two ways in which content could accompany a syntactical conception 'by nature'. A theory of the first type might assert the existence of laws of nature relating the sentential tokens that happen to occur in ordinary languages, such as English, German and French, to mental states with specific content. The very existence of ordinary languages with such very different grammars and vocabularies, however, suggests that an approach of this kind cannot possibly be correct. There do not appear to be any grounds for accepting any semantic theory with these general features.

A theory of the second type, however, might assert the existence of laws of nature relating mental states to specific content, while making connections between those mental states and the sentential tokens that occur in ordinary languages a matter of convention. An account of this kind, in effect, would posit a set of *linguistic primitives* for an ordinary language (consisting of the undefined words in its vocabulary) and a set of *psychological primitives* for a corresponding mental language (consisting of the tokens that are related to their content 'by nature') [cf. Fodor (1975), p. 124]. Obviously, Fodor's own account is of this general kind. A theory of yet a third type, however, might deny the existence of laws of nature of either kind, asserting instead that all of these connections are established either by conventions or else by habits. Only a theory of this kind offers the promise of resolving the difficulties that have been discussed above. But such an account, which emphasizes the role of individuals and of communities in establishing the significance of signs (as their users), could not appropriately qualify as a representational conception. Perhaps a pragmatical conception would provide a more promising approach.

3. THE DISPOSITIONAL CONCEPTION: PRAGMATICAL MODELS OF THE MIND

If these arguments are well-founded, then the dispositional conception appears to be right-headed on the whole, insofar as it provides an account that is completely compatible with the identification of the meaning of the primitives of a language with the linguistic habits that effect these connections between language and the world. Fodor's defense undoubtedly would be a thesis that we have merely mentioned in passing. For Fodor contends that learning a language cannot be a matter of acquiring dispositions: "If anything is clear", he maintains, "it is that understanding a word (predicate, sentence, language) isn't a matter of how one behaves or how one is disposed to behave" [Fodor (1975), p. 63]. And I would freely admit that some of the classic positions on the nature of dispositions, such as those of Ryle (1949), of Skinner (1957) and of Quine (1960), are unable to cope with his criticism.

These accounts suffer from a variety of maladies, which arise because the conceptions they present are behavioristic, reductionistic and extensional in kind. The nature of dispositions as they are understood here, by comparison, is non-behavioristic, non-reductionistic and non-extensional [Fetzer (1981), (1986)]. Nevertheless, the adequacy of the analysis that follows can be appraised in relation to Fodor's principal argument against dispositions:

Behavior, and behavioral dispositions, are determined by the interactions of a variety of psychological variables (what one believes, what one wants, what one remembers, what one is attending to, etc.). Hence, in general, any behavior whatever is compatible with understanding, or failing to understand, any predicate whatever. Pay me enough and I will stand on my head if you say 'Chair'. But I know what 'is a chair' means all the same. [Fodor (1975), p. 63]

For no dispositional conception of language and mentality should be adopted unless it can explain what is right and what is wrong with this position.

All of this would be so much 'smoke and mirrors', however, were it impossible to demonstrate the benefits that accrue from adopting a pragmatic point of view. Perhaps its most crucial features were recognized by Peirce, who accentuated the place of beliefs as causal elements affecting behavior.

Our beliefs guide our desires and shape our actions... The feeling of believing is a more or less sure indication of there being established in our nature some habit which will determine our actions... Belief does not make us act at once, but puts us into such a condition that we shall behave in some certain way, when the occasion arises. [Buchler (1955), pp. 9–10]

An analysis of this kind clearly falls within the broad tradition of functional conceptions of meaning and of mind, where the difference between this account and others of this general type is the specific role assigned to dispositions in understanding the nature of acts, in general, and of speech acts, in particular. While dispositional conceptions are functional accounts, in other words, not all functional accounts are dispositional conceptions – nor, indeed, do other dispositional accounts possess the special characteristics of this one.

Peirce defined a 'sign' as a something that stands for something (else) in some respect or other, where there are fundamental differences in the ways in which something can 'stand for' something (else). Thus, in particular, he distinguished between three different classes or varieties of signs as follows:

(7)   *icons*, which are signs that stand for other things by virtue of a relation of resemblance between those signs and that for which they stand;

(8)   *indices*, which are signs that stand for other things by virtue of being either causes or effects of those things for which they stand; and,

(9)   *symbols*, which are signs that stand for other things by virtue of conventional agreements or habitual relations between those signs and that for which they stand.

Photographs, paintings and statues, for example, are icons, while smoke and fires, symptoms and diseases, etc., are instances of indices. The words that make up ordinary languages, such as 'dog' and 'chair', by contrast, neither resemble nor are causes or effects of that for which, as symbols, they stand.

Another reason for disputing the thesis that thought requires language (in the sense that ordinary languages are languages), therefore, is that their vocabularies stand for that for which they stand because of conventional or habitual connections between those words and those things for which they stand, that is, they exemplify only *one* among at least three different types of ways that something can stand for something else. This, in turn, raises the intriguing possibility that there might be more than one type of mentality corresponding to more than one type of system of signs, where *semiotic systems* of Type I utilize icons, of Type II utilize icons and indices, and of Type III utilize icons, indices and symbols [Fetzer (1988a), (1988b)]. Moreover, there are grounds for thinking there may be grades of mentality that are higher than that of semiotic systems of Type III [Popper (1978), (1982)].

Nevertheless, the theory of signs provides a foundation for the theory of belief only if (what we shall call) 'a theory of cognition' ties them together. Thus, while signs provide modes of reference for objects and for properties, they lack the assertive character of beliefs, sentences, and propositions, i.e., they are neither true nor false. The connection between signs and beliefs for a semiotic system, therefore, appears to be a causal process that arises when a system becomes conscious of a sign in relation to its *other internal states*, including its pre-existing motives and beliefs. When such a system becomes conscious of something that functions as a sign for that system, its cognitive significance results from causal interaction between that sign and these internal states, which constitute its *context*. From this point of view, therefore, the content (or meaning) of a mental state (or token) cannot be fixed independently of consideration of the context provided by a semiotic system, apart from which even its constituent signs possess no significance.[2]

Since the term 'concept' would be useful to refer to the meaning of any mental token (whether sentence, sign, or belief), let us adopt it here. Thus, a complete account of the content of a concept for a specific semiotic system (if it were possible) would be provided by an inventory of all of the kinds of

behavior toward which that system would be disposed under all of the
different kinds of contexts within it might find itself. The conception of
'behavior' required by this construction, however, must be broad enough to
encompass mental effects among its manifestations, which occur, for
example, when someone 'changes their mind' [cf. Fetzer (1988b), p. 139].
When the content of a concept would be displayed in various ways under
infinitely varied conditions, then any merely finite description of its significance could never be more than partial and incomplete. The most suitable
approach toward understanding the content of a concept is in relation to its
causal role:

(Thus,) the most perfect account of a concept that words can convey will be a
description of the habit which that concept is calculated to produce. But how
otherwise can habit be described than by a description of the kind of action to which it
gives rise, with a specification of the conditions and of the motive? [Buchler (1955),
p. 286]

Indeed, it seems clear that, in the case of human semiotic systems, the range
of behavioral manifestations that a concept has for a system would have to
vary across (the complete sets of) motives, beliefs, ethics, abilities,
capabilities and opportunities that influence its behavior as a complex causal
system.

From this perspective, the theory of meaning presupposes the theory of
action. The theory of action that shall be adopted here takes it for granted that
human behavior and *human actions* are not identifiable, insofar as the class
of human actions is restricted to the class of human behaviors that are
brought about – possibly probabilistically – by the causal interaction of one's
own motives, beliefs, ethics, abilities and capabilities, where the success (or
failure) of those efforts tends to depend upon and vary with the opportunities
with which we are confronted (including, in particular, with whether or not
the world is as we believe it to be, i.e., as a function of their truth). Ultimately, of course, it may be important to distinguish more precisely
between these assorted types of factors, but let us assume they form a
complete set.

To illustrate the character of the account that I am endorsing, observe that
a marksman who wants to hit his target and believes that his target is present
and who does not rule out firing at this target on moral grounds can hit his
target only when his skills are equal to the task, his rifle and ammunition are
available and the target itself is within his vicinity [Fetzer (1986), p. 106].
When an individual happens to be neurologically impaired, physically

restrained, morally debauched, deliberately misinformed, etc., then the kinds of behavior that they tend to display under otherwise similar conditions varies from those that tend to be displayed by individuals who are not neurologically imparied, physically restrained, morally debauched, etc. The behavior someone displays on a specific occasion thus results from the complete set of relevant factors present on that occasion, where a factor is relevant if its presence or its absence on that occasion made a difference to the strength of the tendency for that person to display behavior of that kind.

Within the scope of this conception, the content (or the meaning) of a specific sign (or token) can be captured by identifying its causal role in influencing different kinds of behavior under different kinds of conditions, where those conditions (for human systems) tend to be complex. Thus, a few examples may serve to illustrate the conception recommended here:

Example (C): John has the misfortune to be confronted by a burglar in his own apartment. The burglar, whom John does not recognize, menaces him with a knife, so he escapes by climbing out the window, which is open.

Example (D): Mary has the misfortune to be confronted by a burglar in her own apartment. The burglar, whom Mary does not recognize, menaces her with a knife, but she has a broken leg and cannot climb out the window.

In appraising whether or not the same sign (the burglar with the knife) has the same content (or meaning) for John and for Mary, a comparison has to be drawn, not between their *actual* behavior (which was obviously different) but between their *dispositions toward behavior* (how they would have behaved, if they had the chance, relative to the same motives, beliefs, etc.), which requires intensional (subjunctive and counterfactual) rather than extensional (historical and indicative) formulations. If John and Mary would have behaved in the same ways across every complete set of relevant conditions when conscious of that sign (when these contexts were the same for both), then this sign would possess the same content (or meaning) for both, even though the behavior they actually displayed may have been different! In particular, if Mary would have escaped out the open window, if she had not had a broken leg; if John would have done whatever Mary actually did, had he found himself in her situation (including her abilities and capabilities); etc., then that sign would have had the same content for both of them.

What this implies is that Fodor is mistaken in thinking that there could be *no* behavioral constancy that would provide a foundation for a dispositional account. Fodor's mistake results from adopting an excessively behavioristic and extensional account of dispositions. "Pay me enough and I will stand on my head if you say, 'Chair'," says he. "But I know what 'is a chair' means all the same." Exactly! So too for everyone else whose motives and morals would inspire them to similar behavior – knowing what 'is a chair' means just as well! It also suggests the solution to a difficulty observed by Donald Davidson long ago, according to which the meaning of a token (sign) cannot be a disposition to use specific words in specific ways, *simplicitur*, if only because not everyone speaks English! Of course, he is right, except that our dispositional conception only requires that different speakers use similar words on similar occasions in similar contexts – *provided they have the same linguistic abilities*! Otherwise, no such similarity needs to follow.

Hence, if we want to isolate special kinds of causal factors, such as the content (or meaning) of specific beliefs B_1, B_2,..., then we can do so by holding constant those other beliefs B_m, B_n,..., motives, M_1, M_2,..., ethics E_1, E_2,..., abilities A_1, A_2,..., capabilities C_1, C_2,..., and opportunities O_1, O_2,..., whose presence or absence makes a difference to the (internal or external) behavior that would be displayed by that system, given the presence of B_i (where i ranges over 1,2,...). Then the content (or meaning) of a specific belief B_2, say, is the totality of tendencies that the system would possess in the presence of that belief, and the difference that having that belief rather than some other, say, B_1, is the difference between the totality of tendencies that that system would possess in the presence of B_1 and the totality of tendences that that system would possess in the presence of B_2!

For any specific semiotic system, therefore, a sign, S, stands for something x for that system rather than for something else y if, and only if, the strength of the tendencies for that system to manifest behavior of some specific kind when conscious of S – no matter whether publicly displayed or not – differs in at least one context; otherwise, there is no difference between x and y for that system. When two signs, S_1 and S_2, possess exactly the same meaning (as two tokens of exactly the same type), then the strength of the tendencies for that system to manifest behavior of various kinds when conscious of S_1 must be the same in every context as is the strength of its same tendencies when conscious of S_2. This account therefore allows – indeed, it requires – that 'sameness of meaning' be amenable to *degrees of similarity* that occur when two tokens are tokens of some of the same types but not of all. When comparisons of (what might be called) 'cognitive significance' in *its narrow sense* (encompassing differences in meaning other than purely linguistic ones, involving the specific words used, their precise sounds, etc.) are desired, that measure can be obtained, in principle, by subtracting all these purely linguistic behavioral phenomena from (what might be called) 'cognitive significance' in *its broad sense* (which encompasses all meaning). Indeed, these conceptions afford a foundation for resolving issues of ambiguity and of synonymy across the board within a dispositional framework.

Methodologically, at last, this conception exemplifies what Carl G. Hempel describes as, "the epistemic interdependence of belief and goal attributions" [Hempel (1962), Sec. 3.3] – or, better, "the epistemic interdependence of motive, belief, ethics, ability, capability and opportunity ascriptions". This means that, in order to subject an hypothesis about causal factors of any of these kinds to empirical test, it is necessary to make assumptions concerning the simultaneous values of each of the others. Fortunately, this result, which is not theoretically avoidable, is not theoretically objectionable. But if such a conception is even roughly right-headed in its approach, it provides a rather striking explanation for the inherent complexity of social and psychological phenomena. From this point of view, the complexity of the phenomena with which social science must contend in comparison to that with which natural science must contend becomes strikingly apparent – a remarkable outcome!

4. LANGUAGE AND MENTALITY: CONCLUDING REFLECTIONS

During the course of this investigation, we have undertaken an exploration of the solution space for the problem of discovering an adequate conception of the nature of language and mentality. Attention has been given to approaches of three distinct types, computational, representational, and dispositional conceptions, which accent syntactical, semantical and pragmatical aspects of the phenomena with which they are concerned, respectively. We have discovered that the computational conception, even when complemented by the parsing criterion, adopts an extremely implausible theory of the relation of form to content, which cannot contend with problems of ambiguity, with problems of synonymy, or with problems of context. We have also discovered that the representational conception, which benefits from an 'inferential network' approach and from the substitutional criterion, cannot resolve the underlying difficulty of fixing the meaning of primitive language.

These reflections have led to an exploration of the dispositional conception that, unlike its alternatives, appears to succeed where they have failed. In particular, by appreciating the role of habits, skills and dispositions in establishing connections between language and the world, the pragmatical approach has the capacity to deploy the functional role criterion in dispatching problems of ambiguity and of synonymy, while taking proper account of the place of context. It overcomes the *prima facie* case against dispositional conceptions by embracing an account of dispositions that is at once non-behavioristic, non-reductionistic and non-extensional, which enables it to overcome not only Fodor's complaints but Davidson's objection as well. Thus, an analysis of this kind, which unpacks the content (or meaning) of mental tokens by means of their causal role within an intensional framework, is not vulnerable to the criticisms that undermine different accounts, including Quine (1975).[3]

One of the most important consequences that attend this investigation, moreover, emanates from the crucial role of individual sign-users as semiotic systems. For the notion of an *idiolect* as the sign system utilized by a single sign-user turns out to be more fundamental theoretically than is that of a *dialect* (understood as a regional phenomenon) or that of a *language* (if understood as a social group phenomenon). Thus, there is nothing here that inhibits the prospects for the existence of 'private languages', in the sense of constellations of dispositions for speech and other behavior that reflect surface manifestations of possibly unique correlations of primitives to the world. Indeed, the results that have been uncovered here clearly suggest that convention has a secondary role to play by contrast with habituation, promoting communication by providing a social mechanism for resolving differences and for codifying practices concerning what does and does not qualify as 'standard usage' within particular language-using communities.

Another important consequence attends the realization that physical systems can be distinguished as systems of (shall we say) 'fundamentally different' kinds when the specific type of factors that make a difference to the behavior of those systems varies from case to case. Human beings, from this perspective, qualify as motive, belief, ethics, ability, capability and opportunity types of systems, since these reflect the range of causal factors that affect the behavior of systems of this kind. Digital computers, by comparison, seem to be electronic, magnetic, hardware, firmware, software and input types of systems, since these reflect the range of causal factors that affect the behavior of systems of that kind. The proper measure of similarity and difference, once again, of course, has to be subjunctive and counterfactual rather than historical and descriptive in relation to complete sets of relevant conditions that influence systems of these kinds.

Just as human beings and digital machines qualify as different types of physical systems, so too may they qualify as different sorts of semiotic systems. Indeed, if systems qualify as semiotic by virtue of establishing connections between the tokens they employ and the potential behavior they might display, then the semiotic abilities of humans and computers appear to be distinct. Human beings are fundamentally similar, from this point of view, when they are capable of acquiring and of manifesting all and only the same semiotic tendencies under the same causal conditions. Similarly, digital machines are fundamentally similar, from this point of view, when they are capable of performing all and only the same computations (calculations and operations) under the same causal conditions – which obviously includes the programs that they have the ability to run.

All fundamentally similar human beings and digital machines, however, need not actually acquire and manifest all and only the very same semiotic and computational tendencies, unless they are under the same causal conditions at all times – and, even then, not unless their predispositions to acquire and their tendencies to manifest those tendencies are deterministic rather than probabilistic. Thus, digital machines would be 'fundamentally similar' to human beings only if they were subject to the same range of factors, which is plainly not the case. Not the least of the benefits that follow from adopting the dispositional point of view, therefore, is that it provides an explanation for the deeply held intuition that human beings and digital machines really are 'fundamentally different' as types of knowledge, information and data processing causal systems.

While most students of artificial intelligence tend to believe that AI concerns how human beings do think rather than how they should think, the results of this investigation suggest another possibility. If, after all, human beings and digital machines *are* 'fundamentally different' as we have discovered above, then what grounds remain in support of the view that digital machines and human beings *can* process knowledge, information or data in similar ways? The great debate between the 'strong' and the 'weak' conceptions of AI, it appears, may rest upon a misconception, which would indeed be the case if systems of one kind (digital machines) are incapable of functioning in the same way as systems of the other kind (human beings). For, if this were the case, then it might not only be false that AI concerns how we do think but also false that AI concerns how we should think. If this were the case, then the proper conclusion to draw might be that AI strives to develop machines that can solve problems in ways that are not accessible to human beings, in which case it might be maintained that the aim of AI is the creation of new species of mentality.

NOTES

* This paper originated as an informal lecture entitled 'Cognitive Science and Epistemic Inquiry', which was delivered at the University of Georgia as the Keynote Address for the First Annual Southeastern Graduate Students' Philosophy Conference held on 11–12 April 1986. Special thanks to everyone responsible for the organization of that meeting, especially Terry L. Rankin. I have benefitted from the stimulating remarks of two anonymous referees and added some footnotes thanks to Charles E.M. Dunlop and to David Cole.

[1] One caveat. The argument might be made that the objections lodged in Section 1 do not affect the language of thought, precisely because in that language (or 'mentalese') our *thoughts* are always unambiguous. Even if this claim were correct, it would depend upon the nature of thought as a computational, representational or dispositional conception might unpack it. Fodor, however, suggests that the language of thought is 'very similar' to ordinary languages in all the relevant respects [Fodor (1975), p. 156].

This not only justifies the use of sentences from an ordinary language like English to exemplify the difficulties confronting his position but also hints that, if there *is* some unambiguous level of understanding, it is far more likely to be dispositional than to be like anything that Fodor has in mind. Only a pragmatical conception of language and mentality provides a theoretical foundation that might possibly explain why thought should seem to be so very different from the signs that we employ to express it.

[2] The use of the term 'conscious' may need some explanation here, since I do not thereby intend to preclude the potential influence of preconscious or of unconscious mental states. A sign-using system is *conscious* (with respect to signs of a certain kind) when it has both the ability to utilize signs of that kind and the capability to exercise that ability, where the presence of signs of that kind within the appropriate causal proximity would lead – invariably or probabilistically – to an occurrence of cognition [Fetzer (1990)].

[3] One of the principal motives for pursuing an analytical problem-space approach for this investigation is that some of the most influential figures working within this field have gradually evolved in their positions, Fodor especially. Fodor (1987), for example, yields a functional analysis within common-sense psychology; yet he persists in maintaining that "there has to be a *language of thought*" [Fodor (1987), pp. 135–154]. On this point, I believe he is completely mistaken. The only presupposition for learning a language appears to be species-specific *predispositions* [cf. Fetzer (1985)].

REFERENCES

Buchler, J.: 1955, *Philosophical Writings of Peirce*, New York: Dover Publications.

Carnap, R.: 1939, *Foundations of Logic and Mathematics*, Chicago, IL: University of Chicago Press.

Charniak, E. and McDermott, D.: 1985, *Introduction to Artificial Intelligence*, Reading, MA: Addison–Wesley.

Fetzer, J.H.: 1981, *Scientific Knowledge*, Dordrecht, Holland: D. Reidel.

Fetzer, J.H.: 1985, 'Science and Sociobiology', in Fetzer, J. (ed.), *Sociobiology and Epistemology*, Dordrecht, Holland: D. Reidel, pp. 217–246.

Fetzer, J.H.: 1986, 'Methodological Individualism: Singular Causal Systems and Their Population Manifestations', *Synthese* **68**, pp. 99–128.

Fetzer, J.H.: 1988a, 'Mentality and Creativity', *Journal of Social and Biological Structures* **11**, pp. 82–85.

Fetzer, J.H.: 1988b, 'Signs and Minds. An Introduction to the Theory of Semiotic Systems', in Fetzer, J. (ed.), *Aspects of Artificial Intelligence*, Dordrecht, The Netherlands: Kluwer Academic Publishers, pp. 133–161.

Fetzer, J.H.: 1990, *Artificial Intelligence: Its Scope and Limits*, Dordrecht, The Netherlands: Kluwer Academic Publishers.

Fodor, J.: 1975, *The Language of Thought*, Cambridge, MA: MIT Press.

Fodor, J.: 1980, 'Methodological Solipsism Considered as a Research Strategy in Cognitive Psychology'. Reprinted in Haugeland, J. (ed.), *Mind Design*, Cambridge, MA: MIT Press, pp. 307–338.

Fodor, J.: 1987, *Psychosemantics*, Cambridge, MA: MIT Press.

Haugeland, J.: 1981, 'Semantic Engines: An Introduction to *Mind Design*', in Haugeland, J. (ed.), *Mind Design*, Cambridge, MA: MIT Press, pp. 1–34.

Haugeland, J.: 1985, *Artificial Intelligence: The Very Idea*, Cambridge, MA: MIT Press.

Hempel, C.G.: 1949a, 'On the Nature of Mathematical Truth', in Feigl, H. and Sellars, W. (eds.) *Readings in Philosophical Analysis*, New York: Appleton-Century-Crofts, Inc., pp. 222–237.

Hempel, C.G.: 1949b, 'Geometry and Empirical Science', in Feigl, H. and Sellars, W. (eds), *Readings in Philosophical Analysis*, New York: Appleton-Century-Crofts, Inc., pp. 238–249.

Hempel, C.G.: 1962, 'Rational Action', reprinted in Care, N. and Landesman, C. (eds.), *Readings in the Theory of Action*, Bloomington, IN: Indiana University Press, pp. 281–305.

Maloney, C.: 1988, 'In Praise of Narrow Minds: The Frame Problem', in Fetzer, J. (ed.), *Aspects of Artificial Intelligence*, Dordrecht, The Netherlands: Kluwer Academic Publishers, pp. 55–80.

Morris, C.: 1938, *Foundations of the Theory of Signs*, Chicago, IL: University of Chicago Press.

Newell, A. and Simon, H. 1976, 'Computer Science as Empirical Inquiry: Symbols and Search', reprinted in Haugeland, J. (ed.), *Mind Design*, Cambridge, MA: MIT Press, pp. 35–66.

Popper, K.R.: 1978, 'Natural Selection and the Emergence of Mind', *Dialectica* **32**, 339–355.

Popper, K.R.: 1982, 'The Place of Mind in Nature', in Elvee, R. (ed.), *Mind in Nature*, San Francisco, CA: Harper & Row, Publishers, pp. 31–59.

Putnam, H.: 1975, 'The Meaning of "Meaning",' in Gunderson, K. (ed.), *Language, Mind and Knowledge*, Minneapolis, MN: University of Minnesota Press, pp. 131–193.

Quine, W.V.O.: 1960, *Word and Object*, Cambridge, MA: MIT Press.

Quine, W.V.O.: 1975, 'Mind and Verbal Dispositions', in Guttenplan, S. (ed.), *Mind and Language*, Oxford, UK: Oxford University Press, pp. 83–95.

Ryle, G.: 1949, *The Concept of Mind*, London, UK: Hutchinson.

Skinner, B.F.: 1957, *Verbal Behavior*, New York: Appleton-Century-Crofts, Inc.

Stich, S.: 1983, *From Folk Psychology to Cognitive Science*, Cambridge, MA: MIT Press.

Winograd, T.: 1983, *Language as a Cognitive Process*, Vol. I, Reading, MA: Addison-Wesley.

University of Minnesota, Duluth

PART II

COMPUTERS AND COGNITION

CHAPTER 5

MENTAL ALGORITHMS
Are Minds Computational Systems?

The idea that human thought requires the execution of mental algorithms provides a foundation for research programs in cognitive science, which are largely based upon the computational conception of language and mentality. Consideration is given to recent work by Penrose, Searle, and Cleland, who supply various grounds for disputing computationalism. These grounds in turn qualify as reasons for preferring a non-computational, semiotic approach, which can account for them as predictable manifestations of a more adquate conception. Thinking does not ordinarily require the execution of mental algo-rithms, which appears to be at best no more than one rather special kind of thinking.

The idea that human thought requires the execution of mental algorithms appears to provide a foundation for research programs in cognitive science, which are largely based upon the computational conception of language and mentality. Such an approach, which is widely embraced, presumes that the mind either is a computer or at least that, at some suitable level, it operates on the same principles as do computers. Computers, in turn, are envisioned as operating on the same principles as do Turing machines. This conception implies that the boundaries of computability thus define the boundaries of thought. If computing entails executing algorithms, then so does thinking.

A fairly pure version of this approach is found in John Haugeland (1981), while a more qualified version is advanced by Philip Johnson-Laird (1988). The primary difference between them is that Haugeland emphasizes the idea of computers as automatic formal systems, while Johnson-Laird emphasizes the role of programs in governing their behavior. If programs are properly understood as encodings of algorithms into forms suitable for execution by machines, which requires their formulation as elements of formal systems, however, their similarities may be more important than their differences.[1] It all depends on the nature of algorithms, programs, and formal systems.

Other philosophers who have explicitly focused their attention on this problem complex include Eric Dietrich (1990), Robert Cummins and Georg Schwarz (1991). Dietrich defends the thesis of "computationalism", which maintains that cognition is the computation of functions. Precisely which functions are "cognitive" depends upon which functions explain particular cognitive phenomena, but they are all assumed to be Turing-computable. Similarly, Cummins and Schwarz define "computationalism" as the thesis that cognitive systems are those that satisfy cognitive functions, which in turn implies that they execute algorithms that operate on representations.

The purpose of this paper is to explain why the computational conception cannot be sustained and why a semiotic approach appears to provide a more adequate conception. Consideration is given to important work by Roger Penrose (1989), John Searle (1992), and Carol Cleland (1993), who advance various grounds for disputing computationalism. These grounds, in turn, qualify as reasons for preferring the semiotic approach, which can account for them as predictable manifestations of a more adequate theory. Computability does not define the boundaries of thought. The execution of mental algorithms appears to be no more than one special kind of thinking.

1.   The computational conception

A useful summary of the computational conception can be derived from Haugeland (1981), who suggests that reasoning can be reduced to reckoning. If reckoning involves nothing more than the manipulation of marks in conformity with specific rules, moreover, then reasoning can be understood in terms of formal systems, which involve the manipulation of marks in conformity with specific rules, and minds themselves might be understood as automatic formal systems, where an "automatic formal system" is a device (such as a machine) that "automatically manipulates the tokens of some formal system according to the rules of that system" (Haugeland 1981: 10).

An automatic formal system, however, could be a purely formal system, whose marks do not stand for (or "represent") anything. In this sense, such a system would be purely syntactical. What turns a purely formal system into a cognitive system, therefore, is the existence of an "interpretation" in relation to which the well-formed formulae, axioms, and theorems of that formal system become meaningful and either true or false. Such systems (following Daniel Dennett) can be called "semantic engines", with the understanding that a semantic engine is an automatic formal system whose syntax has an interpretation by virtue of which its marks are representations.

The reason why, "given an interpreted formal system with true axioms and truth-preserving rules, if you take care of the syntax, *the semantics will take care of itself*" (Haugeland 1981: 23; original emphasis), as he puts it, however, is that the syntax of such a system has been deliberately constructed to reflect the relations that obtain between the entities that exist in some abstract or empirical domain. The role of soundness proofs is to insure that any theorems that are syntactically derivable in that system are semantical truths of the domain to which it is intended to apply, just as the role of completeness proofs is to ensure that every such semantic truth is syntactically derivable.

There therefore appears to be some sense in which Haugeland puts the syntactic cart before the semantic horse. Nevertheless, in his emphasis on reasoning as reckoning and on minds as automated formal systems, Haugeland embraces the computational conception. Moreover, when he suggests that thought itself "obeys (at least much of the time) various rules of inference and reason" (Haugeland 1981: 3), he tactily supports the additional contention that thinking itself is reducible to reasoning.[2] Thus, if thinking is reducible to reasoning and reasoning is reducible to reckoning, then perhaps the boundaries of computability *do* define the boundaries of thought.

2. What are algorithms?

Haugeland (1981), like Dietrich (1990), assumes the truth of the Church-Turing thesis, though they formulate its significance somewhat differently. Haugeland (1981: 13), for example, relates automatic formal systems to Turing machines, maintaining that any automatic formal system can be imitated by some Turing machine. Dietrich (1990: 152, n. 1) relates functions to those problems for which effective procedures exist, where there is an effective procedure to compute a function only if that function is Turing-computable. That whatever Turing machines can imitate are "automatic formal systems" and that whatever they can compute are "effective procedures" are taken for granted.

Algorithms are typically envisioned as *effective procedures*, which are rules or methods whose application to a problem within an appropriate domain leads invariably to a definite solution within a finite number of steps (Kleene 1967: Ch. V). Because algorithms have these properties, they are definite (you always get an answer), reliable (you always get a correct answer), and completable (you always get a correct answer in a finite interval of time). Any problem for which an effective procedure exists is known as *decidable* (or, when one does not exist, as *undecidable*). Determining the validity of arguments in sentence logic, for example, is a decidable problem.

Interestingly, in a discussion of this notion, Alonzo Church characterizes the notion of an "effective criterion" for the recognition of formulae, proofs, and proofs as a consequence of a set of formulae along the following lines:

> It shall be a matter of direct observation, and of following a fixed set of directions for concrete operations with symbols, to determine whether a given finite sequence of primitive symbols is a formula, or whether a given finite sequence of formulas is a proof, or is a proof as a consequence of a given set of formulas. If this requirement is not satisfied, it may be necessary — e.g. — given a particular finite sequence of formulas, to seek by some argument adapted to the special case to prove or disprove that it satisfies the conditions to be a *proof* (in the technical sense); i.e., the criterion for formal recognition of proofs then presupposes, in actual application, that we already know what a valid deduction is (in a sense which is stronger than that merely of the ability to follow concrete directions in a particular case) (Church 1959: 183; original emphasis).

There are at least two striking aspects to this passage: (i) Church allows for the possibility of methods other than following directions for determining the validity of arguments, for example; and (ii) the application of effective procedures is restricted to direct observation and operations with symbols.

When it is understood as relating algorithms to Turing-computability, the Church-Turing thesis says that an algorithm exists that can solve a problem if and only if a Turing machine can compute its solution. It thereby affords some precision to the notion of an algorithm, because Turing machines can be precisely characterized. A psychological version of this thesis, which we have found to be a feature of the computational conception, thus maintains that the boundaries of thought are determined by the boundaries of computability.

Because Turing machine computability applies to formal systems, the boundaries of thought and of computability are presumed to coincide.

3. Non-computational phenomena

The strongest possible version of the computational conception would therefore appear to incorporate the following claims: that all thinking is reasoning; that all reasoning is reckoning; that all reckoning is computation; and that the boundaries of computability are the boundaries of thought. Thus understood, the thesis is elegant and precise, but it also appears to suffer from at least one fatal flaw: it is (fairly obviously, I think) untrue! The boundaries of thought are vastly broader than those of reasoning, as the exercise of imagination and conjecture demonstrates. Dreams and daydreams are conspicuous examples of non-computational thought processes.[3]

The reasons why dreaming, for instance, does not qualify as computing may be characterized in relation to the concept of an effective procedure. Dreams are not properly envisioned as rules or methods whose application leads to a definite solution within a finite number of steps. Even when they are viewed as "psychic solutions" to emotional problems within a Freudian framework, they are indefinite (they do not always yield an answer), unreliable (they do not always yield a correct answer), and obviously incompletable (they do not always yield a correct answer in a finite interval of time).

Admittedly, some dreams may enable us to cope with problems more successfully than we would otherwise.[4] No doubt, dreams have a psychological role that can be beneficial, which may explain at least in part their evolutionary origins. But the Freudian framework appears to be the best-case scenario for dreams as computational phenomena. If they fail on this conception, there appears to be no more favorable framework. I certainly concede that dreams (daydreams, etc.) are amenable to causal explanations, even if they are frequently elusive. But that is far from enabling them to qualify as "computational phenomena". They are not effective procedures.

Admittedly, a refutation of this kind takes for granted that dreams, daydreams, and the exercise of imagination and conjecture really are examples of thought processes (or of "cognition") in some suitable sense. This in turn presupposes that we understand the nature of thought (or the meaning of "cognition") or else that we already know that these examples *are* examples of thought processes (or of "cognition") in that suitable sense. Otherwise, we run the risk of begging the question by taking for granted something that we ought to be establishing on independent grounds. For the time being, I shall simply assume these are acceptable examples and later return to this issue.

4. A "more modest" conception

If the strongest possible version of the computational conception cannot be sustained, then it might be desirable to consider the existence of weaker alternatives. Johnson-Laird (1988), for example, may offer such an account. While emphasizing the centrality of the notion of computability in the sense of the theory of computation (Johnson-Laird 1988: 9), he acknowledges that computers themselves have modest abilities. Although they operate on the basis of numerals, they have no ability to relate those numerals to the external world: "As to the meaning of their operations and results, the interpretation is left up to the people who use them" (Johnson-Laird 1988: 34).

His position thus appears to be substantially weaker than the computational conception identified with Haugeland (1981) and Dietrich (1990). Insofar as Johnson-Laird embraces the idea that the mind stands to the brain "in much the same way" as a program stands to a computer (Johnson-Laird 1988: 8), therefore, his conception of a program seems to be a broader and more encompassing notion than that of an algorithm, effective procedure or automatic formal system. Even Haugeland (1981), for example, admits that some programs operate on the basis of heuristics rather than of algorithms, where heuristics are usually reliable "rules of thumb" that are not effective.

In reference works on computer science, distinctions between "algorithms" and "heuristics" are commonly drawn. In *Barron's Dictionary of Computer Terms* (1986), for example, the word "heuristic" is used to refer to "a method of solving problems that involves intelligent trial and error. By contrast, an algorithmic solution method is a clearly specified procedure that is guaranteed to give the correct anwer" (Downing and Covington 1986: 117). In *Webster's NewWorld Dictionary of Computer Terms* (1988), moreover, "heuristic" is said to be "descriptive of an exploratory method of attacking a problem", while an "algorithm" is "a prescribed set of well-defined, unambiguous rules or processes for the solution of a problem in a finite number of steps".[5]

Johnson-Laird's conception appears to be more appealing as a foundation for comparing thinking to computing, not least of all because it would seem to enable certain otherwise apparently "non-computational" phenomena to qualify as possible candidates for heuristic processes. Dreams (daydreams, etc.), for example, within a Freudian framework, at least, *might* be described as "exploratory methods of attacking problems" that are not guaranteed to produce a correct solution to a problem in a finite interval of time. This consequence suggests that Johnson-Laird's "more modest" conception may provide benefits that remain unattainable with "less flexible" alternatives.

5. Programs vs. algorithms

Whether Johnson-Laird can separate his concept of "computability" from that of other theoreticians by appealing to the theory of computability, however, appears problematic. Daniel Cohen, for example, asserts that there is "no known definition for 'algorithm' either, as used in the most general sense by practicing mathematicians, except that if we believe Church's Thesis we can define algorithms as what TMs [Turing Machines] can do" (Cohen 1986: 790-791). He acknowledges the "unpleasant but unavoidable" possibility that some inputs to TMs may loop forever (Cohen 1986: 723) and that certain "algorithms" might be faulty, incomplete solutions (Cohen 1986: 791).

The kinds of cases that Johnson-Laird (1988) wants to emphasize appear to be asymmetrical decision procedures for which solutions are sometimes produced but sometimes not. In the case of theorem provers for predicate calculus, for example, the generation of a valid derivation "proves" an argument is valid, but the failure to generate a valid derivation, which may simply have not yet been discovered, does not "prove" its invalidity. A parallel case occurs in relation to scientific theories, which can be "falsified" by discovering falsifying evidence, where the failure to discover falsifying evidence, which may yet remain to be discovered, does not "prove" its lack of falsity.

Since programs that implement heuristics (for playing chess, checkers, and the like) or asymmetrical decision procedures are commonplace within computer science, Johnson-Laird's position supports a more general notion of a "program" as a set of instructions for a Turing machine, which returns a value for at least some inputs. It is therefore fascinating that an entry on "limits of computer power" reads (in part) as follows: "Computers can perform only tasks that can be reduced to mechanical procedures (algorithms)" (Downing and Covington 1986: 133). The significance of this claim clearly depends upon whether the stronger or the weaker conception is intended.

As a result, dreams and daydreams (conjectures and imagination) might remain candidates for "programs" even if they fail to satisfy the conditions required of "algorithms". Because dreams and daydreams (conjectures and imagination) are not effective decision procedures, they cannot qualify as algorithmic, but possibly they can be envisioned as non-algorithmic forms of reasoning that might still qualify as instances of "programs". The notions of heuristics and of asymmetrical decision procedures, after all, appear more promising for encompassing dreams and daydreams (conjectures and imagination) as computational phenomena than does the notion of an algorithm.

6.   Thinking vs. reasoning

More promising, perhaps, but not therefore more compelling. Heuristics and asymmetical decision procedures within the computational conception should be understood as "modes of reasoning" or as "methods of decision". The difference is that *modes of reasoning* involve advancing reasons on behalf of the acceptance or the rejection of specific beliefs, while *methods of decision* involve advancing reasons in support of adopting or rejecting specific decisions. Beliefs, in turn, concern what we take to be true or false, while decisions concern what actions we perform or else decline to perform. The differences between actions and beliefs are real but can also be subtle.[6]

The reason why "reasoning" is called by that name is because it involves having *reasons* (grounds or evidence) for accepting the truth or the falsity of *conclusions* (hypotheses or theories) or for adopting or rejecting various *decisions* (acts or behaviors). In its ordinary sense, therefore, "heuristics" are supposed to qualify as forms of reasoning that can be employed even when conclusive (decisive, deductive) forms of reasoning are unavailable. In playing games such as chess, for example, the range of available moves and combinations of moves is sufficiently large as to overwhelm the most powerful computers, which makes appealing to heuristics indispensable.

Even though heuristics are supposed to be inconclusive (non-decisive, non-deductive), that does not mean they are supposed to be unjustifiable. On the contrary, the expectable benefits of adopting one heuristic rather than another can be evaluated on the basis of their modes of justification. When heuristics are compared with respect to their relative frequencies of success in cases of that kind in the past, the heuristic with a higher relative success frequency ought to be preferred. And when they are based upon scientific laws, they can be used with corresponding degrees of confidence.[7]

While it may be more plausible to view dreams and daydreams (conjectures and imagination) as heuristic rather than as algorithmic, that does not make such a conception compelling. Indeed, even if reasoning qualifies as a kind of thinking and thinking as a kind of causal process, that does not imply, in turn, that dreams and daydreams (conjectures and imagination) *therefore* qualify as a kind of thinking that also involves reasoning. Mental activities of these kinds may sometimes be motivated by reasons, but reasons are not indispensable to these kinds of mental activities. It would therefore be mistaken to conclude that they are properly entertained as modes of reasoning.[8]

7.   Non-algorithmic procedures

Dietrich (1990) also distinguishes programs and algorithms. He regards all *programs* as procedures, where "procedures" that halt in a "yes" or "no" state after a finite amount of time rather than go into an infinite loop are also *algorithms*. Given this conception, while every program is a procedure, only some programs are algorithms, i.e., those that are effective procedures (Dietrich 1990: 152n). According to him, "computationalists" are only committed to the position that cognition requires the execution of procedures and not to the stronger claim that cognition requires the execution of algorithms, because some procedures might not produce definite answers.[9]

In order to distinguish the stronger from the weaker senses of this term, therefore, let us reserve the term "algorithm" for the stronger sense and use the term "program" for the weaker sense. This seems to be reasonable, especially since there are programs for heuristics and theorem provers, which do not implement algorithms in the sense of effective procedures. Thus, the issue of whether thinking requires the execution of mental algorithms can be further refined, since at least some kinds of human reasoning involve the use of heuristics and asymmetrical decision procedures rather than of algorithms. This establishes a second way in which thinking does not require algorithms.

Johnson-Laird (1988) still qualifies as a computationalist on this conception, which is clearly weaker than the notion with which we began this inquiry.

At this point we have established (a) that thinking does not require the execution of mental algorithms because imagination and conjecture (including dreams and daydreams) involve thought but do not require the execution of any algorithm, and (b) that some kinds of reasoning (including the use of heuristic procedures and asymmetrical decision methods) are kinds of reasoning that do not require the execution of any algorithm.[10] Thus, the question now is to what extent the computationalist position remains intact.

Roger Penrose, for example, suggests that thinking may be a quantum phenomenon and therefore qualify as non-algorithmic (Penrose 1989: 437-439). The basis for this objection is that algorithms are understood as functions that map single values within some domain onto single values in some range. If mental processes are algorithmic (functions), then they must be deterministic, in the sense that the same mental-state cause (completely specified) would invariably bring about the same mental-state effect or behavioral response. Since quantum phenomena are not deterministic, if mental phenomena are quantum processes, they are not (even partial) functions.

8.   Functions and partial functions

Computationalists commonly appeal to the notion of function to support their conception of cognition, as has been noted in passing. Dietrich (1990) and Cummins and Schwarz (1991), for example, both define "cognition" as the computation of functions. The term itself belongs to the vocabulary of mathematics. In his primer on functions, Ralph Boas contrasts the "working definition" of a function (where "y is a function of x if, when x is given, the value of y is determined" uniquely) with a more technical definition (where a function is identified with a class of ordered pairs, which map values in a domain E of values x onto those of a range F of values y) (Boas 1960: 65).

Dietrich (1990) and Cummins and Schwarz (1991) agree that the same function may be implemented in more than one way. As Dietrich remarks, "Computer scientists frequently distinguish between computing a function and executing a procedure because every procedure realizes exactly one function, but each function can be realized in several different procedures" (Dietrich 1990: 192n). He illustrates this with two multiplication procedures for the product function $2 * x$, where one procedure adds x to itself while the other multiplies x by 2. The properties of functions thus appear to correspond closely to and are perhaps identical with those of algorithms.

The conception of a program in the sense of Johnson-Laird (1988), however, would seem to correspond to that of a partial function rather than of a function, where a partial function is a partial mapping from a domain x to a range y which is unique for each value of x when a corresponding value of y happens to exist. In this sense, partial functions are incomplete classes of ordered pairs. This may accommodate the possibilities of heuristics and of asymmetrical procedures, but it still retains the uniqueness condition that for specific values of x, there exists at most one corresponding value of y.

What Penrose (1989) has in mind appears to be quite different, because the quantum phenomena he is considering involve the possibility of more than one possible value of y for specific values of x. Consider, for example, the case of radioactive decay, where during a specific interval of time, say, 3.05 minutes, an atom of polonium^{218} has a probability of 1/2 of undergoing decay. For the same value of x (polonium^{218} atom over 3.05 minute interval), more than one value of y (decay, non-decay) is possible. If mental phenomena are in at least some cases quantum processes, then they are sometimes neither functions (algorithms) nor partial functions (programs).[11]

9. Is thinking indeterministic?

Cummins and Schwarz (1991: 62) elaborate a general notion of computing for all kinds of functions, where "computing a function f is executing an algorithm that gives o as its output on input i just in case $f(i) = o$". The idea they elaborate is that "executing an algorithm" involves satisfying various steps "in the right order", which they describe as "disciplined step satisfaction". The generality of this approach thus emanates from the notion that a system satisfies steps in the right order because its causal structure requires it. A *computation* is an abstract causal process, "a causal process specified abstractly by an algorithm" (Cummins and Schwarz 1991: 63).[12]

Whatever else it may entail, their invocation of algorithms to specify the nature of computation implies that the causal systems that are modeled thereby are *deterministic* systems, in the sense that, for an inital state i of the system, there is at most one outcome state o, where o is a causal consequence of satisfying the function f. More than one outcome o under the same initial conditions i (assuming that complete sets of causally relevant factors are taken into account) would be incompatible with Cummins and Schwarz's (1991) appeal to functions, even though they are implemented causally. Computationalism is therefore threatened by indeterminism.

In this sense, *indeterminism* is probabilistic causation, where more than one outcome may occur under exactly the same causally relevant conditions. No factor whose presence or absence makes a difference to the occurrence of those possible outcomes is not taken into account. This is different from *nondeterminism* in computational theory, where incomplete computations require human intervention in order to arrive at an outcome. Thus, in relation to transition graphs, Cohen (1986: 143) explains: "The ultimate path through the machine is not determined by the input alone. Therefore, we say this machine is *non-deterministic*. Human choice becomes a factor in selecting the path; the machine does not make all its own determinations".

What makes mental indeterminism important is that some experience (of a sight, a sound or a smell, for example) might bring to mind more than one train of thought (such as thoughts of similar sights, sounds or smells; or of the causes or effects of those sights, sounds or smells; or thoughts about other things that are merely habitually related to or conventionally associated with sights, sounds or smells of such kinds). Our thinking appears to exemplify associations of all these varieties from time to time, where the occurrence of one kind of association rather than another under the same conditions seems to provide plausible examples of mental indeterminism.

10. Mental "hidden variables"

These may be plausible examples of mental indeterminism, but computationalists might hold out for "hidden variables" — in the form of additional causal factors — whose discovery would render them instances of mental determinism instead. Indeed, the history of modern physics provides ample precedent for adopting such an attitude, since physicists committed to the deterministic paradigm represented by classical mechanics found it very difficult — even psychologically impossible — to accept the transition to an indeterministic paradigm represented by quantum mechanics. Some argue that paradigm shifts eventually succeed only because scientists are mortal!

It should therefore hardly be surprising that parallel transitions from deterministic to indeterministic paradigms should encounter opposition in other domains of inquiry. Admittedly, whether or not psychological phenomena themselves are or are not indeterminstic is an empirical question that cannot be answered independently of experience. At least two kinds of considerations, however, appear to make a difference in assessing this possibility. The first is that the scope of quantum mechanics has gradually increased to encompass phenomena in chemistry and in biology as well as in physics, and there is no reason to think psychology will be an exception.

That is a higher-order argument from the history of science itself. Another argument derives from lower-order phenomena with which we are all acquainted. When we prefer one kind of ice cream to another, such as liking butter pecan twice as much as chocolate chip, we tend to order butter pecan about twice as often as we order chocolate chip. We do not simply never order the one we less prefer, but instead order it about half as often, under similar conditions.[13] As with scientific hypotheses in general, the evidence is both inconclusive and tentative, yet it supplies grounds in support of the testable conjecture that minds are probabilistic mechanisms.[14]

Penrose (1989) thus provides a third reason for doubting the adequacy of the computational conception, since ordinary thinking appears to display indeterministic cognition. A certain look, a friendly smile, a familiar scent can trigger enormously varied associations of thoughts under what appear to be the same relevant conditions. If such phenomena are indeed aspects of ordinary thinking, then we have discovered yet another reason to doubt the computational conception: (c) that associations of thoughts of this kind do not qualify as algorithms (functions) or as programs (partial functions), and therefore represent yet another species of non-computational thinking.

11. Mental processes are semantic

Searle (1992) takes a different tack, contending that, if mental processes are nothing more than algorithmic operations on formal systems, the computational conception is not strong enough to encompass the nature of thought, because thoughts have a semantical dimension (they are meaningful), while manipulations of formal systems are purely syntactical (they do not possess any inherent meaning). His position depends upon drawing a strong distinction between *syntax*, which concerns the relations that marks (or tokens or signs) bear to one another, and *semantics*, which concerns the relations between those marks and that for which they stand (or represent or signify).

This position has been challenged by those, such as William J. Rapaport (1988), who want to maintain that pure syntax can be sufficient for semantic meaning. Searle has sought to reinforce his position by adding the further thesis that, not only is semantics not inherent in syntax, but syntax is also not inherent in physics (Searle 1992: 207-212). Computationalists could contend, however, that, in some systems, at least, syntax *is* physical, namely, in the case of machines that are intentionally designed to operate on the basis of those marks, which is the case for digital computers. Thus, the views that Searle has advanced confront a variety of counterarguments.

A crucial distinction must be drawn between marks (or tokens or signs) that are significant for the *users* of a system and those that are significant for *use by* a system (Fetzer 1988a, 1990c, 1991, 1992). Causal systems *can* be designed to operate on the basis of the sizes, shapes, and relative locations of various marks without those marks having any meaning for those systems themselves. To this extent, Searle's critics seem to be right. When those marks are envisioned as *syntax*, however, they are viewed as the (actual or potential) bearers of meaning, which presupposes a point of view. In this sense, syntax *is* relative to an interpretation, interpreter or mind.[15]

When Searle maintains that the recognition of sizes, shapes, or relative locations as constituting marks that might be manipulated according to the rules of a formal system *presupposes* the existence of an interpretation, interpreter or mind, therefore, his position requires disambiguation. It is the potential to sustain an interpretation that qualifies marks as elements of a formal system, automatic or not. Thus, those who would defend computational conceptions of language and mentality are confronted not only by the distinction between interpreted and uninterpreted formal systems but also by the necessity to presume the possibility of an interpretation, interpreter or mind in order to define the elements of a formal system at all.[16]

Searle (1992) therefore agrees with Johnson-Laird (1988) in regarding computers as endowed with modest abilities, not only because they have no capacity to relate the marks that they manipulate to the external world but also because what qualifies as a mark that is suitable for manipulation has to be determined by those who design them. As a result, Searle advances a fourth reason for doubting the adequacy of the computational conception: (d) that even the possibility of marks as subject to manipulation presupposes the possibility of interpretations, interpreters or minds, which takes for granted what computational conceptions are intended to explain.

12. Some procedures are mundane

Cleland (1993) has recently proposed that the notion of an effective procedure is vastly broader than the notion of Turing computability and that, as a result, the Church-Turing thesis cannot be sustained. Her argument is that distinctions have to be drawn between various domains of application, especially between abstract numerical functions and mental or physical phenomena. She appeals to a class of "mundane functions", which includes recipes for cooking and directions for assembling devices, as examples of effective procedures that are not Turing computable. She thus implicitly draws a crucial distinction between abstract domains and causal or mental domains.

Cummins and Schwarz (1991) clearly acknowledge that some algorithms are defined in relation to a specific notation (the symbolic algorithms), while others may involve manipulating things rather than numerals. They assert:

> While executing an algorithm always involves following rules for manipulating things — tokens, we might call them, like tokens in a game (Haugeland 1986), the things manipulated are not always symbols. Indeed, the objects of computation needn't be representations of any sort. An algorithm for solving Rubic's Cube requires manipulation of the cube, not of symbols for the cube. Algorithms implemented on a computer typically manipulate symbols, but many common and useful algorithms do not. The most obvious examples are recipes and instruction manuals ("How to clean your steam iron") (Cummins and Schwarz 1991: 62).

The example of instructions for cleaning a steam iron would seem to make it especially apparent that there are effective procedures that do not qualify as Turing computable, which implies that the Church-Turing thesis not only cannot be proven to be true but, evidently, can be proven to be false.

Cleland's argument is both fascinating and ironic in relation to Cohen's discussion of the Church-Turing thesis, where he remarks, "Someday someone might find a task that humans agree is an alogrithm but that cannot be executed by a TM, but this has not yet happened. Nor is it likely to. People seem very happy with the Turing-Post-Church idea of what components are legal parts of algorithms" (Cohen 1986: 791). What Cleland has exposed is the difference between "symbolic" and "non-symbolic" procedures, a distinction that depends on the difference between purely symbolic solutions to problems and those that require acting in accordance with instructions.

The reason why the Church-Turing thesis appears to be true, therefore, is that its domain of application is implicitly confined to the class of numerical (or of symbolic) computations. You may recall Church's remark that the application of effective procedures is restricted to direct observation and operations with symbols. Direct observation is required because the marks that qualify as elements of formal systems have to be identifiable on the basis of their properties, including their shapes, sizes, and relative locations. These are the properties that render them eligible for manipulation. Cohen's position seems to reflect similar symbolic presuppositions.

13. Some procedures are non-symbolic

The deep (even profound) ambiguity we have encountered here arises from the difference between (purely) *symbolic procedures*, whose domains have values of the same general kind as do their ranges (from numerals to numerals, for example), and mundane procedures, whose domains may have values of very different kinds than do their ranges (from instructions to behavior, for example). What makes this distinction important with respect to the computational conception is (e) that the kind of activity involved in the execution of *mundane* procedures seems to involve thinking, yet reflects a class of effective procedures which does not qualify as Turing-computable.[17]

Perhaps the most important implication of Cleland's study is that it reinforces a fundamental distinction between abstract domains and causal or mental domains. Turing machines, after all, are abstract entities that have infinite memories, cannot malfunction, and never make mistakes. Physical computers, by comparison, are causal systems with limited memories and can malfunction, whether or not they are capable of making mistakes, an issue to which we are going to return (See Fetzer 1990c, 1991, and 1992). Human beings, of course, have limited memories, can malfunction, and are capable of making mistakes. They are not the same (Kleene 1967: 233).

It should come as no great surprise, therefore, that properties of things of one of these kinds may be wrongly supposed to be properties of another. When procedures are defined as sequences requiring disciplined step satisfaction, algorithms and heuristics can be characterized as procedures which are justified by means of different kinds of evidence. From this perspective, *algorithms* appear to be procedures for which deductive justification ("conclusive evidence") is available, while *heuristics* appear to be procedures for which inductive justification ("inconclusive evidence") is available. This may account for their varying degrees of reliability in application.[18]

The distinction between thinking and reasoning can then be accommodated by recognizing that *thinking* as such does not require any specific forms of justification. Indeed, as a causal process, it does not require any justification at all. By contrast, *reasoning* as such does require specific forms of justification. While reasoning qualifies as a causal process, it is a causal process that is expected to meet codified standards of acceptability. Precisely which standards those are, of course, depends upon whether the kind of reasoning under consideration happens to be deductive, inductive, or otherwise.[19] The principal difference between thinking and reasoning is one of justifiability.

14. Minds as semiotic systems

The theory of minds as *semiotic* (or sign-using) systems provides an alternative non-computational framework for investigating the nature of cognition. According to this conception, minds are things for which something can stand for something else in some respect or other (Fetzer 1988a, 1989, 1990c). The sign relation itself, originally elaborated by Charles S. Peirce, is triadic (or three-placed), since it involves a relation of *causation* between signs and sign users, a relation of *grounding* between signs and what they stand for, and an *interpretant* relation between signs, what they stand for, and sign users with respect to potential behavior in relation to those signs.

Among the most important dimensions of this theory is a distinction between different kinds of minds on the basis of the kinds of signs that they are able to utilize, such as *icons*, which resemble that for which they stand, *indices*, which are causes or effects of that for which they stand, and *symbols*, which are merely habitually (or conventionally) associated with that for which they stand. "Symbols" in this sense must be distinguished from "symbols" in the computational sense, which are merely syntactical marks. Even the use of icons already presupposes a point of view with respect to the specific ways in which one thing is intended to resemble another thing.

The semiotic approach generates even more grounds for supposing that the execution of mental algorithms is at best only a special kind of thinking. These include, for example, that *the same sign* may be variously viewed as an icon (because it brings to mind things that resemble that thing), as an index (because it brings to mind things that cause or are caused by things of that kind), or as a symbol (because it brings to mind other things that it can conventionally signify), and that *inductive reasoning* employing heuristics (or "rules of thumb"), which are usually reliable but by no means effective procedures, appears to be fundamental to our survival (Fetzer 1991: Ch. 7).

Meanings are pragmatical, because the kind of meaning that something can have may differ from one context to another, where *a context* includes the motives, beliefs, abilities, and capabilities that a sign-user brings to its encounters with signs. This approach can explain what it is to be conscious relative to a class of signs, where a system is conscious with respect to signs of that kind when it has the ability to utilize signs of that kind and is not inhibited from the exercise of that ability. It supports the conception of cognition as an effect that occurs as a causal consequence of causal interactions between sign-users and signs in suitable proximity (Fetzer 1989, 1990c, 1991).

15. Semiotic systems vs. input/output systems

The triadic relation between signs, what they stand for, and sign users can be diagrammed (see Figure 1). Observe that a sign S stands for something x (in some respect or other) for something z, where that something z might be human, (other) animal, or machine. A sign S must exist in order for it to function as a sign by entering into causal relations with sign users z, but that for which S stands need not exist at all. Thus, we can talk about the Fountain of Youth — and even search for it — whether or not it exists. We can make movies about werewolves — and distribute them widely — although they do not exist. We can dress up like Santa Claus — and amuse our children — even though Santa bears faint resemblance to any historical person.

From this perspective, there is a crucial difference between sign-using systems and other systems that, while they may function causally on the basis of marks of specific shapes, sizes, and relative locations, nevertheless do not qualify as semiotic systems. Ordinary digital computers are systems of this kind, because the marks by means of which they operate are meaningless for systems of that kind. While they may be meaningful for users of those systems, they are not meaningful for those systems themselves. The explanation for this difference is the absence of a grounding relationship between these marks and that for which they stand (see Figure 2).

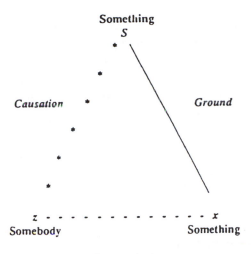

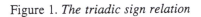

Figure 1. *The triadic sign relation*

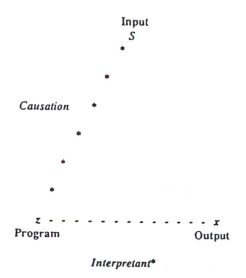

Figure 2. *The input/output relation*

It is this difference with respect to grounding in the case of the input/ output relation that distinguishes digital machines from systems that can use the triadic sign relation, like human beings (Fetzer 1990c). This is reflected by the use of the term "Interpretant" in Figure 1 and the use of the term "Interpretant*" in Figure 2. The use of "Interpretant" in Figure 1 is meant to indicate that the behavior of the system occurs (at least in part) because of the nature of the relationship (of resemblance, of cause-or-effect, or of habit or convention) between the sign and what it stands for. The use of "Interpretant*" in Figure 2 reflects the absence of any such relations.

Even when an input/output system happens to simulate the behavior of a semiotic system, therefore, its mode of functioning is fundamentally different. A distinction must therefore be drawn between the case in which two systems exhibit the same input/output behavior as one of *simulation*, the case in which those systems produce similar input/output behavior by similar processes as one of *replication*, and the case in which those systems not only produce the same input/output behavior by similar processes but are composed of the same materials as one of *emulation*. Figure 2 systems may simulate Figure 1 systems, but can never replicate them (Fetzer 1990c: ch.1).

16. The problem of robots

The distinction between semiotic systems and input/output systems can be tested in relation to robots, such as those that have been constructed at the MIT AI Laboratory.[20] One of them was a battery operated robot guided by a little computer, which needed to recharge its battery from time to time. To do this, it first went to a place where it could secure a small map, which it would scan and thereby discover where in the room it could go to be recharged. It then proceeded to that location and recharged. This was a very simple device, but the objection could be raised that it seems to be a system for which "something can stand for something else in some respect or other".

If this little robot really were a system for which "something can stand for something else in some respect or other", then it would properly qualify as a semiotic system and thereby as possessing a mind. No doubt, the robot behaved "as if" it had beliefs and desires, such as the *belief* that it could recharge its battery by going to a certain location and the *desire* that it wanted to recharge its battery. Systems that behave *as if* they have beliefs and desires, however, may or may not actually have them. Even though the robot is *described* as scanning a little map to discover where it could have its battery recharged, it is simply a small system that simulates that behavior.

In order for the robot to actually scan a map, for example, it would have to grasp the concept of a mapping relationship between a series of lines or marks and corresponding features of its environment. As a causal system that has been designed to exhibit behavior that simulates the behavior that someone actually *scanning a map* might display, however, it possesses the properties discussed in Section 11, namely: the robot is causally affected by the features of the map without them meaning anything for that system. It should be apparent that this little map does not *stand for* anything for this little robot, which has neither beliefs nor desires about charging its battery.

Simple robots such as this one, of course, can be succeeded by more complex robots that display more variable behavior. As Selmer Bringsjord (1992) has observed, there appears to be no end to the extent to which robots can be constructed that simulate more and more varieties of human behavior. Yet these robots are semiotic systems only if their behavior is brought about by virtue of the *grounding relations* (of resemblance, of cause-or-effect, and of habitual association) between signs and what they stand for by contrast to behavior that simulates them. No matter how successfully such robots might simulate behavior, that does not make those systems semiotic.

17. Penrose, Searle, and Cleland

The theory of minds as semiotic systems blends with the connectionist conception of the nature of the brain to provide an account that has the capacity to explain and predict the features of thinking that Penrose, Searle, and Cleland have observed. According to connectionism, the brain is a network of numerous neural nodes that are capable of activation. These nodes can be connected to other nodes where, depending upon their levels of activation, they may bring about increases or decreases in the levels of activation of those other nodes and create patterns of activation that can function as signs for the systems in which they occur (Fetzer 1990c, 1991, 1992, 1993b).

In the case of Penrose (1989), for example, the conception that he needs but does not have at hand is that of *probabilities as propensities*, which are probabilistic causal tendencies. Neural nodes may be envisioned as endowed with propensities to effect connections with other nodes (Fetzer 1991: 84). Indeed, the tendency to view something as an icon, as an index, or as a symbol can be appropriately understood as a probabilistic phenomenon, which makes it physically possible for more than one outcome to occur under exactly the same conditions. Thus, the same sign might be interpreted iconically, indexically, or symbolically, displaying indeterministic aspects of thinking.

In the case of Searle (1992), it follows from the semiotic conception that semantics is not inherent in syntax and that syntax is not inherent in physics. Semiotic systems are sign-using systems that transcend the merely syntax-processing capacities of computer systems by using marks (or "signs") that are meaningful for those systems. Among the most basic distinctions drawn by the semiotic approach is the difference between signs that are significant for the users of a system and signs that are significant for use by a system. Moreover, even the use of signs of the most basic kinds (that resemble what what they stand for) requires a mode of mentality (Fetzer 1991: Ch. 8).

In the case of Cleland (1993), finally, the distinction between "symbolic" and "mundane" procedures appears to be illuminating in attempting to distinguish abstract machines from semiotic systems (Fetzer 1988a and 1988b). Cleland seems to have identified a crucial aspect of the interpretation of the Church-Turing thesis as it may apply to mental processes, precisely because mental processes are not abstract properties of abstract machines but causal properties of human beings, who are governed not by abstract algorithms but by causal laws, which might be deterministic or indeterministic (Fetzer 1991). Semiotic systems are not properly understood as Turing machines.[21]

18. Thinking about thinking

The strongest version of the computational conception with which we began maintains that all thinking is reasoning, that all reasoning is reckoning, that all reckoning is computation, and that the boundaries of computability are the boundaries of thought. During the course of this investigation, however, we have found grounds for doubting this position. There are kinds of thinking, such as dreams and day-dreams, that do not qualify as reasoning. There are kinds of reasoning, such as heuristics and asymmetrical decision procedures, that do not qualify as algorithmic. And there are effective procedures, including recipes and instruction manuals, that are not Turing-computable.[22]

From this perspective, the computational conception, which inspires so much of cognitive science today, appears to be a stunning example of over-generalization. No one would want to deny that some of our reasoning involves the execution of mental algorithms. We sometimes prove that an argument in sentence logic is valid or calculate that operations on numerals are correct. But thinking involves vastly more than reasoning, and reasoning involves vastly more than executing algorithms. Indeed, to execute algorithms in the mode of a Turing machine requires abstracting formal syntax from semantic meaning, which appears unrepresentative of human thought.

The reduction of reasoning to reckoning and of reckoning to calculating, after all, represents a movement away from human thought processes and toward inanimate machine performance. As Stephen Kleene has observed,

> In performing the steps [involved in executing an algorithm], we have only to follow the instructions mechanically, like robots; no insight or ingenuity or invention is required of us. After any step, if we don't have the answer yet, the instructions will tell us what to do next. The instructions will enable us to recognize when the steps come to an end, and to read off from the resulting situation the answer to the question, "yes" or "no" (Kleene 1967: 223).

If all kinds of thought processes were nothing more than "disciplined step satisfaction", which could be executed by a machine, human beings would be no more than robots with respect to their mental activities (albeit perhaps robots of an especially interesting kind). Perhaps we deny that we are nothing but robots because our mental activities involve much more.

The semiotic conception of the mind affords a non-computational frame-work for understanding the nature of cognition. Our use of signs extends far beyond the mere execution of algorithms in its strong or weak senses. Our use of language, our powers of observation, our powers of deductive and of inductive reasoning, and our exercise of imagination and conjecture can be accommodated within the framework that it supplies. Indeed, the theory of semiotic systems implies that the capacity of making mistakes is a criterion for mentality, since the capacity to make mistakes presumes the ability to take something to stand for something else which is the right result (Fetzer 1988a: 141-142).

19. Are minds computers?

There are several defenses that computationalists might advance on behalf of their position, among which I have discussed the more promising. Perhaps the most important qualification that remains to be considered, however, is that computationalism could be viewed as positing sufficient rather than necessary conditions for the existence of mentality. Such an interpretation would allow the possibility that non-computational forms of thinking (such as dreams and daydreams as well as heuristics and asymmetrical decision procedures) exist, yet maintain that systems which have the capacity to manipulate syntax possess the capacity for thought.

A defense of this kind would concede that thinking does not *require* the execution of mental algorithms, but it would insist that any system which has the capacity to manipulate marks on the basis of their shapes, sizes and relative locations alone possesses mentality. The problem with this position, however, is that it trades on ambiguity. Marks that stand for something else for a system function as signs for such systems, which makes them semiotic. Human beings, after all, can also manipulate marks on the basis of their shapes, sizes and relative locations as well. The difference depends upon how these things are done (see Fetzer 1990c: Ch. 9).

A computationalist could insist that dreams and daydreams, properly understood, really are instances of disciplined step satisfaction (or of the execution of complete or partial functions) by observing that, even in the case of dreams and daydreams, a system simply shifts from a state S_1 at time t_1 to state S_2 at time t_2 in some specific sequence. Because there is always some specific sequence of shifting states, one could insist that any system that passes through those states is computing some particular function — the function f that takes input S_1 at t_1 and returns output S_2 at t_2.[23] This defense, however, trivializes computationalism by ignoring the difference between causal processes and computational procedures.

20. Some parting thoughts

In defining algorithms, Church (1959) and Kleene (1967), no less than Dietrich (1990) and Cummins and Schwarz (1991), tend to emphasize their mechanical character. As Kleene observes, "we have only to follow the instructions mechanically, like robots". The execution of an algorithm has to be performed just as a machine might perform it. Yet machines have the advantage of having been designed to perform exactly the operations that we intend for them to perform. Humans, by comparison, have to learn to execute exactly the operations that they are supposed to perform. Following instructions is not something that people are born knowing how to do.[24]

If humans, unlike machines, have to learn to execute algorithms, then perhaps the conception of mundane procedures has even broader scope than we have previously supposed. The distinction between "symbolic" and "mundane" procedures, after all, may not sufficiently emphasize the role of human effort in executing algorithms. Even Church (1959) notes that the application of algorithms involves direct observation as well as operations with symbols. If operations on symbols presuppose the identification of marks as suitable for manipulation, then the very idea of the execution of an algorithm seems to presuppose the presence of mentality.[25]

From this perspective, the computational conception appears to have arisen from the almost irresistible temptation to appeal to a domain about which a great deal is known (formal systems and computability theory) as a repository of answers to questions in a domain about which very little is known (the nature of mentality and cognition). The train of thought from *thinking as reasoning* and *reasoning as reckoning* to *reckoning as computation* and *computability as cognition* exerts tremendous attraction. It has motivated most of what passes for cognitive science today. Yet this view appears to represent a profound misconception in thinking about thinking.

Nothing here has touched on the significance of incompleteness proofs in higher-order logic established by Kurt Gödel, which have excited the interest of other scholars, including J. R. Lucas (1961) and Douglas Hofstadter (1979). My explanation for this seeming omission is that, so far as I can discern, the properties of formal systems have scant relevance to understanding the nature of cognition. Formal systems are useful in modeling reasoning, but reasoning is a special case of thinking. If we want to understand the nature of thinking, then we have to study thought and not just the properties of formal systems. The boundaries of thought far transcend mere computability.[26]

University of Minnesota, Duluth

Notes

1. The definition of a program as an algorithm encoded into a form suitable for execution by a machine is common in computer science, but within AI somewhat broader conceptions tend to be employed (see Section 4).

2. To be precise, his view strictly implies only that thinking is reducible to reckoning "at least much of the time"; but there can be scant doubt that what he conversationally implies is the notion that thinking is reasoning.

3. Strictly, dreams are or appear to be non-computational thought processes. There are senses in which every thought process might qualify as "computational", but they also appear to be trivial (see Section 19).

4. Even what qualifies as a "correct answer" to an emotional problem can be difficult to say. It may simply be something that "makes us feel better". Nightmares seem to qualify as counterexamples even to this conception.

5. Similar definitions of "algorithm" and of "heuristic" can be found in other sources, such as the *Dictionary of Computing* (1991), which under "effective computing" also identifies "algorithms" with effective procedures.

6. Decision-making typically entails acting as though an hypothesis were true, while accepting that an hypothesis is true typically entails acting as though it were true. For discussion, see Fetzer (1981: 234-238).

7. For discussion, see Fetzer (1990a) and (1990b) and also Hayes (1990).

8. Conjectures, for example, are sometimes advanced in a tentative and scientific fashion as potential solutions to outstanding problems; on other occasions, however, they involve no more than jumping to conclusions.

9. Even weaker positions would maintain that computation is sufficient but not necessary for cognition, in which case even the claim that cognition requires the execution of procedures may be too strong (see Section 19).

10. Of course, the execution of some specific heuristic may actually involve the execution of several subroutines (or "macros"), which are themselves algorithmic. In cases of this kind, thinking is not exclusively algorithmic.

11. Quantum mechanics is our most encompassing theory of matter, which is supported by wide-ranging evidence. The interpretation that I have in mind envisions quantum probabilities as single-case propensities by contrast with the subjectivistic Copenhagen interpretation (Fetzer 1983).

12. This is almost the opposite of the conception of Fetzer (1988b), in which a "program" is defined instead as a causal model of an algorithm that is suitable for execution by a machine. For more discussion, see Fetzer (1993a).

13. That various computer programs make use of "random number" generators, incidentally, may enable them to simulate quantum indeterminacy but cannot turn them into systems instantiating quantum indeterminacy.

14. Devising suitable tests to differentiate between probabilistic mentality and deterministic (possibly chaotic) mentality poses challenges, but evidence increases the longer we search for hidden variables without success.

15. This matter is pursued in Section 19. As Jahrens (1990) has observed, Rapaport's argument seems to beg the question by assuming that humans implement natural language "the same way it would be on a computer".

16. Thus, some causal systems may be formal systems, but others are not. As the following paragraph implies, causal systems properly qualify as computers by virtue of their potential to sustain various interpretations.

17. A computationalist could object, however, that computationalism is only responsible for explaining thinking and therefore is only responsible for explaining mundane procedures to the extent that they involve thinking.

18. Observe that the kind of (inductive) knowledge we can acquire about causal systems differs categorically from the kind of (deductive) knowledge we can acquire about purely formal systems (Fetzer 1988b, 1993a).

19. It could be argued, of course, that even bad (poor or invalid) reasoning still qualifies as *reasoning*, in which case some reasoning may turn out to be unjustified, after all. But the term, as I am using it, is normative.

20. This example was advanced by one of the anonymous referees. In an effort to do it justice, I am adhering closely to the referee's description.

21. To those who may be thinking, "But no one holds the position that minds *are* Turing machines", I would suggest that they consider various ongoing discussions over e-mail bulletin boards about the nature of cognition.

22. But they are not exclusively mental either, as was observed in note 17.

23. The possibility of maintaining that shifts between such states involve the execution of functions may lie behind the claim that anything can be taken to be a computational system, a computer, or even a mind.

24. People do have the capacity to simulate formal systems, as in the case of applying inference rules to construct formal proofs. But if we really were automatic formal systems, surely logic would be easier to teach.

25. While a non-semiotic causal system, such as a digital computer, might take an input S_1 at t_2 and return an output S_2 at t_3, the description of that process as "executing an algorithm" presupposes an interpretation, interpreter, or mind, which the machine, by hypothesis, does not have. See note 23 and also the discussion of this issue in Sections 11 and 19.

26. The author is indebted to David Cole and to Allen Long for their comments and criticism, which led to the endnotes and to the addition of Section 19, and to the anonymous journal referees for their very perceptive criticism.

References

Boas, R. 1960. *A Primer of Real Functions*. New York: John Wiley and Sons.

Bringsjord, S. 1992. *What Robots Can and Can't Be*. Dordrecht: Kluwer.

Church, A. 1959. "Logistic system". In D. Runes (ed), *Dictionary of Philosophy*. Ames, IO: Littlefield, Adams and Company, 182-183.

Cleland, C. 1993. "Is the Church-Turing Thesis True?". *Minds and Machines* 3(3): 283-312.

Cohen, D.I.A. 1986. *Introduction to Computer Theory*. New York: John Wiley and Sons.

Cummins, R. and G. Schwarz 1991. "Connectionism, Computation, and Cognition". In T. Horgan and J. Tienson (eds), *Connectionism and the Philosophy of Mind* (Studies in Cognitive Systems 9). Dordrecht: Kluwer, 60-73.

Dictionary of Computing. 1991. Oxford: Oxford University Press.

Dietrich, E. 1990. "Computationalism". *Social Epistemology* 4(2): 135-154.

Downing, D. and M. Covington 1986. *Barron's Dictionary of Computer Terms*. Woodbury, NY: Barron's Educational Series.

Fetzer, J.H. 1981. *Scientific Knowledge*. Dordrecht: D. Reidel.

Fetzer, J.H. 1983. "Probability and Objectivity in Deterministic and Indeterministic Situations". *Synthese* 57(3): 367-386.

Fetzer, J.H. 1988a. "Signs and Minds: An Introduction to the Theory of Semiotic Systems". In J. Fetzer (ed), *Aspects of Artificial Intelligence*. Dordrecht: Kluwer, 133-161.

Fetzer, J.H. 1988b. "Program Verification: The Very Idea". *Communications of the ACM* 31(9): 1048-1063.

Fetzer, J.H. 1989. "Language and mentality: Computational, representational, and dispositional conceptions". *Behaviorism* 17(1): 21-39.

Fetzer, J.H. 1990a. "The Frame Problem: Artificial Intelligence Meets David Hume". *International Journal of Expert Systems* 3(3): 219-232.

Fetzer, J.H. 1990b. "Artificial Intelligence Meets David Hume: A Response to Pat Hayes". *International Journal of Expert Systems* 3(3): 239-247.

Fetzer, J.H. 1990c. *Artificial Intelligence: Its Scope and Limits* (Studies in Cognitive Systems 4). Dordrecht: Kluwer.

Fetzer, J.H. 1991. *Philosophy and Cognitive Science*. New York: Paragon.

Fetzer, J.H. 1992. "Connectionism and Cognition: Why Fodor and Pylyshyn are Wrong". In A. Clark and R. Lutz (eds), *Connectionism in Context*. London: Springer Verlag, 37-56.

Fetzer, J.H. 1993a. "Program Verification". In A. Kent and J. Williams (eds), *Encyclopedia of Computer Science and Technology*, Vol. 28. New York: Marcel Dekker, 237-254.

Fetzer, J.H. 1993b. "Primitive Concepts: Habits, Conventions, and Laws". In J. Fetzer, D. Shatz, and G. Schlesinger (eds), *Definitions and Definability: Philosophical Perspectives*. Dordrecht: Kluwer, 51-68.

Haugeland, J. 1981. "Semantic Engines: An Introduction to Mind Design". In J. Hauglend (ed), *Mind Design*. Cambridge, MA: MIT Press, 1-34.

Haugeland, J. 1986. *Artificial Intelligence: The Very Idea*. Cambridge, MA: MIT Press.

Hayes, P. (1990). "Commentary on 'The Frame Problem: Artificial Intelligence Meets David Hume'". *International Journal of Expert Systems* 3(3): 233-238.

Hofstadter, D. 1979. *Gödel, Escher, Bach: An Eternal Golden Braid*. New York: Basic Books.

Jahrens, N. 1990. "Can Semantics be Syntactic?". *Synthese* 82(3): 309-328.

Johnson-Laird, P. 1988. *The Computer and the Mind*. Cambridge, MA: Harvard University Press.

Kleene, S.C. 1967. *Mathematical Logic*. New York: John Wiley and Sons.

Lucas, J.R. 1961. "Minds, Machines, and Gödel". *Philosophy* 36(2): 112-127.

Penrose, R. 1989. *The Emperor's New Mind*. New York: Oxford University Press.

Rapaport, W.J. 1988. "Syntactical Semantics: Foundations of Computational Natural Language Understanding". In J. Fetzer (ed), *Aspects of Artificial Intelligence* (Studies in Cognitive Systems 1). Dordrecht: Kluwer, 81-131.

Searle, J.R. 1992. *The Rediscovery of the Mind*. Cambridge, MA: MIT Press.

Webster's NewWorld Dictionary of Computer Terms, 3rd ed. 1988.New York: Prentice-Hall, Inc.

CHAPTER 6

WHAT MAKES CONNECTIONISM DIFFERENT?
A Critical Review of Philosophy and Connectionist Theory

W. Ramsey, S. Stich, and D. Rumelhart (eds), *Philosophy and Connectionist Theory*. Hillsdale, NJ: Lawrence Erlbaum Associates, xiii + 320 pp., 1991, ISBN 0-8058-0592-3 (hardback); 0-8058-0883-3 (paperback).

This anthology consists of twelve studies concerning the theoretical foundations of connectionism, which the series editor, David Rumelhart, characterizes in the "Series Foreword" as "brain-style computation". In the Preface, the three editors (including Rumelhart) contrast connectionism with Newell and Simon's conception of "physical symbol systems". This conception finds its philosophical counterpart in the theories of Chomsky (regarding syntax) and Fodor (regarding syntax and semantics), which underlie the language of thought hypothesis that humans have linguistic abilities among their innate genetic endowments, an approach which connectionistic conceptions reject.

Their difference on this point deserves comment. Since humans utilize natural languages, they clearly have the capacity to utilize them. The issue, therefore, is not whether humans are able to use natural languages but the best explanation for how it is that humans possess this capacity. Chomsky and Fodor contend that every neurologically normal human brain comes into the world with built-in syntactical and semantical tendencies (which are "[innate] linguistic abilities"). But connectionists contend that every neurologically normal human brain comes with built-in *capacities to acquire* syntactical and semantical tendencies ("[innate] linguistic capabilities") instead.

Any theory of the mind that could not explain the human ability to use language would thereby qualify as inadequate. That the physical symbol system and language of thought conception can satisfy this desideratum is not in doubt, but whether connectionism has this potential has been challenged, especially by Fodor and Pylyshyn (1988). While the papers in this volume fall into three broad categories — comparisons between connectionism and other styles of cognitive modeling (Part I); discussions of connectionist modes of representation (Part II); and philosophical implications of connectionism (Part III) — many display a concern with meeting the challenge thus posed.

1.   Connectionism and other styles of cognitive modeling

In Chapter 1, "Horses of a different color?", Margaret Boden suggests that both GOFAI ("good old-fashioned artificial intelligence") and connectionism have roots in earlier work, especially McCulloch and Pitts (1943). Their differences are often cast as those between competing "symbolic" and "subsymbolic" paradigms. Thus, if a distinction is drawn between "atomic" and "molecular" syntactical structures, where every molecular structure consists of some arrangement of atomic elements, then GOFAI assumes that semantic meanings have the same relation, where every meaningful molecular structure consists of some arrangement of meaningful atomic elements.

Connectionism adopts a neural network model of the brain for which the basic conception is one of patterns of activation that arise as a result of connections between neurons. On this approach, it is these patterns of activation rather than the individual nodes that possess meaning for the system, even though they are neural counterparts of GOFAI's atomic elements. In spite of this difference, Boden credits McCulloch and Pitts (1943) with having proven "that every function of propositional logic is realizable by some (fairly simple) net of all-or-none threshold units, and that every Turing-computable function can be computed by some such net" (p. 6).

The problem with these "proofs", she says, is that they take for granted *neat and tidy connections* and *constantly reliable thresholds*, which make them idealized rather than realistic models of brain function. Because McCulloch and Pitts were convinced that mental processes can be understood as computations — where all thought is (one or another kind of) computation — and implemented these logical functions by means of neural-counterpart *and*-gates, *or*-gates, and such, they "in effect, turned computers from mere number crunchers into general-purpose symbol-manipulating machines" (p. 9). Their work thus motivates research in both connectionism and GOFAI, which from this perspective seem to be the same entity in different guises.

While Boden wants to emphasize the similarities between two seemingly disparate movements, Daniel Dennett begins Chapter 2, "Mother nature versus the walking encyclopedia", by emphasizing the diversity of approaches within the superficially unified movement of connectionism itself. The objective of his discourse is to reaffirm "a few points that seem [to him] to be not only true and important but insufficiently appreciated" (p. 22). These concern the advantage of connectionism as a biologically plausible model, that connectionism is a member of a larger class of non-rule-following systems, and that connectionism may yet make room for language accquisition.

Dennett suggests that connectionist approaches are somehow "more biological" than classic symbol-system approaches, where he explains what he means in terms of *efficiency*, namely, that classic models are exceptionally efficient in the sense that, for example, functions call subfunctions, which in turn call subfunctions, where every component has a distinct role to fulfill. This kind of efficiency, however, does not typify the world of living things, in which natural selection works "bottom up" rather than "top down", trying out various coping strategies in the process of separating out the successful from the unsuccessful. And, indeed, nature does not appear to display the optimal adaptations thus implied by classic models of cognitive processing.

Moreover, connectionist systems appear to belong to a species that belongs to a larger genus of non-rule-following systems, where a distinction is drawn between systems that *operate by following rules* (including those that are designed to implement them) and systems that are *governed by natural laws* (especially ones that have evolved through a process of natural selection). Even though they can be described as-if-they-follow-rules, these systems cannot be adequately understood as rule-following systems, because the causal mechanisms that they instantiate have a different kind of history than those that typify the production of technological inventions.

While conceding that specific nodes of neural networks may "have no interpretation at all", Dennett believes that even with respect to those that appear to stand for specific notions — such as a DOG-node that seems to stand for *dog* — it is wrong to identify specific nodes with specific notions, because even the deletion of those nodes does not thereby delete those notions — the "graceful degradation" phenomenon (p. 24). Most importantly, he contends that the systematicity desideratum — according to which organisms that can think *that John loves the girl* should also be able to think *that the girl loves John* — advanced as a necessary condition of an adequate theory of cognition in humans and other animals, cannot be justified and should be abandoned.

Dennett's beautiful counterexample — of organisms that can think *that a lion wants to eat them* but cannot think *that they want to eat a lion* — sheds considerable light on this issue. He observes that human capacities for language and logic are higher-order abilities, which (as it might be expressed) only matter to certain forms of life. Our modes of thinking are relative to our ecological niches and may qualify as specialized adaptations. Indeed, his example also illustrates the more general point that the cognitive capacities of various species are matters of *psychology*, while the conditions imposed by the classic conception are rooted in principles of *logic* instead.

At this intersection, Dennett's points converge. The psychological mechanisms that various species have evolved, after all, are causal products of a lawful process of natural selection affecting biological organisms. While he concedes that Pinker and Prince (1988) and others "have shown that language cannot be *acquired* without the aid of pre-existing symbolic architectures", he suggests this may take the form of an immature linguistic competence rather than a full-blown symbolic architecture. Without committing himself to connectionism, therefore, he nonetheless rejects the views of Fodor and Pylyshyn about the character of cognition (cf. Fetzer 1991a).

2. Representation in connectionist models

In Chapter 3, "What is the 'D' in 'PDP'?", Tim van Gelder provides a survey of alternative conceptions of *distribution*. If connectionism provides a distinctive approach to cognition, he believes, then it almost certainly lies in this direction. Yet an alternative to the classic symbol-system conception must still "satisfy some demanding conditions", including that it be (i) demonstrably nonsymbolic in character, but (ii) sufficiently general, rich and abstract to support a broad conception of the mind, while (iii) possessing enough power to "effectively represent" the kinds of information essential to human cognitive performance. Hopefully, it should also elucidate the relations between mentality and neurology, between mind and brain (p. 34).

Observing that the notion of a distributed representation has yet to be adequately explicated, van Gelder begins by considering the conception advanced by Hinton, McClelland and Rumelhart (1986), where representations are supposed to be *distributed* if "[e]ach entity is represented by a pattern of activity distributed over many computing elements, and each computing element is involved in representing many different entities". The basic idea, presumably, is that varieties of different patterns of neural activation might overlap or include other patterns of neural activation involving at least some of the same neurons, where each neuron qualifies as a "computing element".

Van Gelder's objection to this conception is that it does not appear to distinguish what is distinctive about connectionism "from other cases that ... are not distributed in any interesting sense". He uses hand calculators, in which numerals are encoded as strings of bits, as a counterexample. And, indeed, any system based on the utilization of a set of (individually meaningless) alphanumeric characters to produce (collectively meaningful) words and sentences would appear to satisfy this conception, which means that even ordinary digital machines can be described as using "distributed representations". The difference at stake here thus remains to be uncovered.

An alternative approach emphasizes the notion of representations that are extended. In order to establish a standard of reference as a basis for measuring this property, van Gelder adopts "the benchmark of one computing unit to every item", relative to which a representation is *extended* if it uses many computing units for every item. Once again, however, the proposed distinction does not appear to generate the right class of cases. In a footnote, for example, he observes that single-bit storage locations in digital memories can be viewed as "extremely simple computing units, changing state according to their inputs, and outputting their states when accessed", a conception that also encompasses ordinary digital machines.

Van Gelder plausibly contends that what is crucial for the sense of extendedness that captures what is distinctive about distributed representations is that "no particular unit or location is crucial", citing Rosenfeld and Touretzky (1988), who define distributed representation schemes as those for which "each entity is represented by a pattern of activity over many units" (p. 38). The crucial factor here, however, appears to be the *qualitative similarity* of these units themselves, where a brain might be viewed as a massive arrangement of homogeneous cells. Thus, spatially (distributed) patterns of activation as opposed to specific microfeatures of (undistributed) individual units are the foundation for representation.

In exploring the question of when two representations have the same semantic character (that is, when two patterns have the same meaning), van Gelder expresses skepticism that there should be a general answer, largely due to the influence of pragmatical conditions "that have little or nothing to do with the intrinsic properties of the representations themselves" (p. 51). He also observes that representations that are extended in this sense are appropriate subjects for operations of *superposition*, in which one pattern of activation is imposed upon another. And he argues that distributed representations of this kind not only support psychological theorizing but also benefit the integration of neurology with cognition.

In Chapter 4, "Representational genera", John Haugeland differentiates between three broad varieties of representation, namely: those that are *language-like* (or "logical") in their character; those that are *image-like* (or "iconic") in their character; and those that are *distributed* (or "extended") in their character. He follows van Gelder by taking superpositionality as the feature that is most fundamental to connectionism. He presumes that these modes of representation are adequate only if they define *mutually exclusive* notions. Utilizing three counterexamples — a designer's floorplan, a philosophical theory, and ordinary holograms — he illustrates that these notions share instances and thus are not mutually exclusive.

The counterexamples demonstate that floorplans, for example, have properties characteristic of the compositional semantics associated with language-like representations, yet possess the isomorphic character that distinguishes iconic representations as well. They also demonstrate that a philosophical theory, known as *logical atomism*, which maintained that the logical structure of sentences reflects the ontological structure of the world, incorporates both language-like and image-like modes of representation. And they also demonstrate that ordinary holograms display properties of distribution and superposition distinctive of connectionism, while they also exhibit the isomorphic properties of iconic representations (p. 66).

Since these conceptions share instances in common, Haugeland is right in maintaining that they are not mutually exclusive. He is wrong, however, to take for granted that these notions *ought to be* mutually exclusive in the sense of having no common instances. The properties of superposition and distribution, for example, are characteristic of neural networks and of icons alike, but that does not establish any inadequacy in either approach. Alternative accounts of the same phenomena — physical, chemical, or otherwise — surely are expected to share instances in common, namely: the phenomena they are advanced to explain. There is nothing wrong or mistaken in that.

What Haugeland misunderstands is that genuine alternative theories provide *distinct explanations* for the phenomena, which can be tested (at least in part) by considering their respective scope and power. A theory that covers a broader range of phenomena should be preferred over one that covers a lesser range, provided they are similar with respect to other desiderata, such as the clarity and precision of the language in which they are expressed, their explanatory and predictive significance with respect to the phenomena, and the simplicity or "elegance" with which they attain that degree of systematic power. Theories that have instances in common are suspect only if such cases should not be subsumable by those theories.

How far Haugeland's assumption — which qualifies as a "blunder" — is off the mark can readily be demonstrated relative to Peirce's theory of signs, for which the same *instance of red* can be viewed as an icon (relative to other instances of that color, which it resembles), as an index (relative to the operation of a traffic signal, as its cause), or as a symbol (relative to applying the brakes and coming to a complete halt, as its conventional significance); yet these notions still distinguish three kinds of signs. They differ with respect to the way in which signs of these kinds are related to things of the kinds for which they stand, known as their *ground*.

Haugeland advances a set of three "outlandish theses", namely: first, that any iconic or distributed representation is translatable into an equivalent logical representation; second, that any logical or distributed representation is translatable into an equivalent image; third, that any iconic or logical representation is translatable into an equivalent distributed representation (pp. 66-67). He supplies (what he refers to as) "spurious justifications" on their behalf, which he does not mean to be serious. Indeed, it is easy to show they are not equivalent: abstract concepts, such as pi or the square-root of -1, for example, have logical but not iconic representations.

In fact, the notion of equivalence is highly ambiguous. A picture may be said to be worth a thousand words, but a photograph of Marilyn and a verbal description thereof are simply not the same. Haugeland wants to use these theses as the springboard for introducing a distinction between "representing" and "recording", but what he has in mind is rather obscure. Moreover, if one of his "outlandish theses" — say, that any logical or iconic representation is translatable into an equivalent distributed representation — could be shown to be true, while the converse could be shown to be false, that approach would thereby have demonstrated its superior scope of application. That would properly count as strong evidence in its favor.

Haugeland attempts to capture "the distinctive structure of the skeletal contents" of logical, of iconic, and of distributed representations. The contents of logical representations are supposed to be objects and their properties and relations (p. 77); of iconic representations, relations that obtain between dependent and independent "dimensions" (p. 79); and of distributed representations, connection weights that are often displayed by patterns of activation (p. 84). Whether or not Haugeland has misconceived the issues, distinguishing between connection weights and their intermittent displays seems to be entirely appropriate — and even fundamental — to grasping the character of neural networks (cf. Fetzer 1991b).

In Chapter 5, "The role of representation in connectionist explanations of cognitive capacities", Robert Cummins contends that whatever may distinguish connectionism from classic cognitive science, they both exemplify *the representationalist strategy*, according to which cognition involves computations over representations. Moreover, although it has been assumed that connectionist approaches differ fundamentally from "orthodox representationalism" with respect to its treatment of learning, on the one hand, and its lack of semantic structure, on the other, these allegations have no evident merit, where connectionism fares as well as orthodox approaches.

Cummins begins by elaborating the classic conception of *cognition* as computation over representations, using the process of addition as an example:

> To get a device to add, you have to get it to satisfy a function interpretable as addition. And that means you have to design it so that causing it to represent a pair of addends causes it to represent their sum (p. 93).

A system is cognitive, according to this conception, when its syntactical operations (by virtue of its design) sustain a systematic interpretation as semantically significant (by virtue of their meaning). Such an interpretation must not be arbitrary, however, but has to satisfy certain "epistemological constraints", which distinguish that specific domain of cognition.

Cummins thus characterizes cognitive systems as "inference engines", in the sense that

> ..... having a cognitive capacity is instantiating a function that relates propositional contents, that is, a function that takes propositional contents as arguments and values and relates them as premises to conclusions (p. 94).

He maintains in a footnote that rules of inference of systems of formal logic "have nothing to do with inferences as it is meant here". What he means requires interpretation. Presumably the canons of valid deductive reasoning (that speciffy what follows from what within propositional contexts) would be among the "epistemological constraints" that causal structures of cognitive systems satisfy under ideal conditions.

Cummins suggests that connectionist systems are subject to two kinds of semantic interpretation: *localist* approaches, which assign meaning to individual nodes; and *distributed* approaches, which assign meaning to patterns of activation among nodes. (Global approaches can be viewed as subsuming localist approaches, however, when those patterns consist of the activation of singular nodes.) He concurs with Fodor and Pylyshyn (1988) in their contention that "connectionists are representationalists", where cognition is simply *computation over distributed representations*. But that may or may not be a suitable inference to draw. It depends on the causal character of connectionist operations on those representations.

Cummins argues that orthodox representationalism and connectionism agree on PERFORMANCE, where both engage in computations over representations, and TRANSDUCTION, where both are committed to the existence of psycho-physical laws (relating states of the world to representational receptor states) and motor-theory laws (relating representational states to motor activities). Yet they may differ with respect to REPRESENTATION, where orthodox systems utilize data structures but connectionist systems use connection weights and activation patterns, and LEARNING, which, for orthodox systems, is the acquisition of new data structures or changes in old ones, but for connectionist systems, is the acquisition of new connection weights or changes in old ones (pp. 97-98).

Having lucidly displayed their similarities, Cummins focuses on their crucial difference with respect to REPRESENTATION. In an exceptionally valuable discussion, he explains that the foundation for the allegation by Fodor and Pylyshyn (1988) that connectionist systems lack the capacity for systematicity that distinguishes human thought processes hinges on whether or not connectionist systems have the capacity to identify and process representations on the basis of *logical forms*: "So the Fodor and Pylyshyn claim is that connectionist representations cannot have logical form" (p. 105). The foundation for this view seems to be the assumption that representations that have logical form are *therefore* not connectionist.

Cummins maintains that Fodor and Pylyshyn have offered some "bad reasons" in support of their position, while conceding that "the fact that there are bad reasons for thinking something does not mean it is not true". He responds by introducing a simple neural network that derives conjuncts from conjunctions, negations from negations of disjunctions, and such, in the style of McCulloch and Pitts (1943), as Boden reviewed it:

> Different patterns of activation in the input array correspond to different logical forms, and these lead to patterns of activation in the output array that themselves correspond to logical forms appropriate to those of the inputs (pp. 108-109).

The only response that Fodor and Pylyshyn seem to have left is to maintain that such a system must *therefore* be orthodox.

Cummins demonstrates that some logical representations are translatable into equivalent distributed representations and that embracing connectionism need not entail abandoning the conception of cognition as the computation of semantically structured representations (p. 114). The case for this conclusion, moreover, receives support from several other directions. One is that icons and indices as well as symbols possess syntactical structure, including part-whole and superpositional relations, for example, with corresponding kinds of semantic significance (Fetzer 1990: 80, 273-274). What is distinctive about symbols with respect to semantics is not that they can be interpreted but the way that they are interpreted.

Another is that Fodor and Pylyshyn neglect the apparent consideration that in the case of symbols, especially, syntactical systems are deliberately constructed in order to reflect the semantically relevant features of an intended domain, which might consist of abstract or of physical objects and their properties and relations. But other means can also be employed to stand for the semantically relevant features of various (natural or contrived) domains. There is nothing about "distributed representations" that precludes features of patterns of activation from possessing semantic significance or from functioning as semantically structured representations. The notion of "logical form" is broader than Fodor and Pylyshyn are willing to allow. Once this is acknowledged, their position looks implausible.

In Chapter 6, "In defense of explicit rules", Andy Clark raises the possibility that certain kinds of mental performance —involving a distinctive kind of *cognitive flexibility*, which is displayed by human subjects — may require not merely the capacity for systematicity distinctive of orthodox systems but perhaps even a flull-blown language of thought, suggesting

> ..... systems in which problem solutions are effective ... but not yet made in some sense *explicit* are intrinsically limited ... due to the inability of such systems to treat the problem solution as a structured object capable of being systematically amended (pp. 124-125).

He is therefore drawn toward the conclusion that the language of thought may be unavoidable.

Clark characterizes changes in weights of connectionist systems due to repeated exposure to instances of categories (instances of dogs in relation to the concept of *dog*, of specific voltages in relation to the behavior of *circuits*, and so on), where "[a] network stores its knowledge superpositionally across a single set of units and weights" (p. 116). Such systems thus possess connection weights that have been brought about by repeated exposure to instances as a process of conditioning, training, or learning, but do not — better, do not necessarily — have the ability to formulate the rules or relationships represented thereby in the form of "explicit rules".

While this kind of "emergent knowledge" may be adequate for many kinds of problem situations, Clark suggests that there are other kinds of problem situations for which it may be inadequate. These appear to be cases in which assumptions about situations that have been satisfied by cases encountered in the past are no longer satisfied. Suppose, for example, that a banker has been very successful in extending loans based on local data concerning income, marital status, address, and other variables. If the significance of address variables were to be reversed (where good addresses became bad and bad good), a system operating on the basis of explicit rules might cope with the problem thus generated (by reversing its pointers), but an emergent system would require massive retraining.

Clark interprets cases of this kind as evidence supporting reliance upon explicit representations of rules as well as of data. Indeed, he submits that a theoretical foundation for this conclusion is found in the theory of *representational redescription* advanced by developmental psychologist Karmiloff-Smith. According to this approach, there is an important difference between "basic mastery" of a problem domain (which might be successfully explained on the basis of emergent connectionism) and theorizing about that problem domain by means of "re-descriptions" (which appears to require something akin to the language of thought) (p. 121).

An example he offers to illustrate this distinction is learning to play the piano, where a piece is initially learned by playing in sequence, but where later the sequence might be violated by playing "variations on a theme". In order to encompass cases of various kinds, therefore, Clark is led to suppose "that the human mind deploys essentially connecitonist style representations but augments itself with the symbol structures of public language" (p. 120). He follows Karmiloff-Smith in advancing a general model of learning involving three phases, where "Phase 1" involves basic mastery, "Phase 2" redescriptions with sequential constraints, and "Phase 3" redescriptions allowing violation of sequential constraints.

Clark suggests that

> .... only the Phase 1 style representations are plausibly treated as connectionist representations, and ... the ascent to higher levels of redescription constitutes a progression between *classical* representational formalisms culminating perhaps in a full-blooded Fodorian language of thought (p. 124).

But even if certain classes of problem solving require the acquisition of cognitive resources of this kind, it would qualify as "a full-blooded Fodorian language of thought" only if those abilities were part of our innate genetic endowment and do not have to be learned. The contribution of symbol systems such as natural languages to problem solving, after all, is not at stake. The question is how to explain this ability.

In Chapter 7, "The concept of representation and the representation of concepts in connectionist models", Thomas Goschke and Dirk Koppelberg examine the thesis of the *compositionality of meaning*, according to which the meaning of complex representations is determined by the meaning of their atomic elements and their constituent structure. They recommend a correlational semantics for the internal states of neural networks relative to external states of the world in order to accommodate atomic meanings. They contend that the strong form of compositionality (for which meaning is completely determined thereby) seems to be false, but that a weak form of this thesis (for which meaning is partially determined thereby) is true.

The role of inner states (or "hidden units") enormously complicates the problem of semantic interpretation. Indeed, the authors acknowledge that "it may be impossible to detect dependencies between hidden units and input patterns that allow for easy interpretation" (p. 131). Suppose, for example, that (intentional) human behavior is an effect that is brought about by the causal interaction of a person's motives, beliefs, ethics, abilities, and capabilities (Fetzer 1990, 1991b). The specific use of language on specific occasions may be due to enormously varied combinations of these factors — linguistic ability being only one — which span the full range of human performance: amusing, deceiving, entreating, misleading, and so forth (Austin 1962). There seems to be no systematic way to relate linguistic outputs to linguistic and nonlinguistic inputs, moreover, without making assumptions about the simultaneous values of these variables (Fetzer 1990: 83-85).

For the most part, Goschke and Koppelberg focus upon whether or not the meaning of language is *context-sensitive* in various senses required to sustain the thesis of composiitonality of meaning. In their opinion, "people seem to use analogies and similarities between different contexts to infer the meaning of a given conceptual combination" (p. 146). They recommend the integration of correlational semantics with constraint satisfaction as a promising approach to connectionist representation, but evidence for contextual effects goes far beyond analogies and similarities, including irony, sarcasm, and humor. If meanings depend on pragmatic factors, however, then the compositionality of meaning essential to the language of thought is at best an idealized simplification and at worst a myth about cognition.

In Chapter 8, "Representation in perception and cognition", Gary Hatfield considers some alternatives to the identification of representations with symbols as syntactically defined elements of a language of thought. Certain philosopheres, for example, have suggested that "representation" should be understood as a "stands for" relation between representations and that which is represented (he identifies Dretske, Searle, and himself), while others have approached this problem from within a connectionist framework (Rumelhart and McClelland, for example, as well as Smolensky). Although those who employ the first approach tend to embed it within the context of belief-desire analyses of behavior, he wants to analyze the cognitive capacities that underlie behavior, such as vision, memory, learning, and linguistic capacities, by forming psychological models instead (p. 164).

The key to an aproach of this kind, no doubt, is the sense in which something is supposed to "stand for" something for any cognitive system. Hatfield attempts "to show how the 'stands for' notion of representation fits nicely with a task-analysis approach to cognition and a connectionist approach to psychological processes" (p. 182), but he takes for granted a causal conception built upon causal connections between representations and what they represent. An approach of this kind appears unpromising for understanding representations that stand for abstract objects, theoretical relations, non-observable properties or non-existent entities, none of which stand in obvious "causal relations" to their mental representations.

Ultimately, Hatfield accepts Fodor's critique of the disjunction problem, according to which causal theories of this kind appear to be unable to account for the *problem of error*: "we can represent a fly as being present when there is really only a moving black dot, even if both flies and black dots regularly cause our fly-representation to engage" (p. 191). Thus, he concedes that an analysis of the kind he recommends "may or may not be able to handle full-scale intentionality". The problem, however, appears to be the adoption of a hopelessly inadequate analysis of the "stands for" relation. An alternative approach, which is based upon Peirce's theory of signs, not only appears to be able to handle full-scale intentionality but posits *the capacity to make mistakes* as a general criterion of the mental within the context of a pragmatic account (cf. Fetzer 1990, 1991a, 1991b).

3.   Philosophical implications of connectionism

In Chapter 9, "Connectionism, eliminativism and folk psychology", William Ramsey, Stephen Stich, and Joseph Garon contend that, if connectionism is successful as a model of cognition, then that success will imply the elimination of folk psychology. The features that are supposed to generate this incompatibility have to do with *ontology*, that is, with the kinds of structures and processes that distinguish connectionist systems from folk-psychological systems. Their argument is that folk psychology presupposes an ontology of "*discrete, semantically interpretable* states that play a *causal* role in some cognitive episodes but not in others", which is incompatible with connectionist systems that only support "widely distributed and subsymbolic" encodings of information (p. 217).

They characterize "folk psychology" as what they take to be the common sense psychology of beliefs and desires, where *propositional attitudes* (relating persons and attitudes, such as wanting, wishing, hoping, etc.) serve as posits of this theory. That seems to be appropriate, but they then proceed to "load the dice" by associating folk psychology as a *theory of causal roles* with an *ontology of the brain* that appears to be gratuitous and question-begging. The thesis that beliefs are supposed to be "functionally discrete", especially, is sustained by observations such as that, according to folk psychology, persons can acquire beliefs (memories, thoughts, and so on) *one at a time* (p. 205). This may be true of ordinary modes of speech, but it requires significant reconstruction to yield their ontological interpretation.

Consider, for example, the case of a person who has just learned that his mother has died. That belief acquisition could be described as that of having added a single belief to his system of beliefs. But that is obviously *only* "in a manner of speaking". To know that your mother has died is also to know that it is no longer the case that your mother is alive, that the person you have frequently spoken with in the past will no longer be taking your calls, and so forth. An endless variety of logical and behavioral consequences attend the acquisition of this "single belief", which cannot by any stretch of the imagination be properly construed as implying an ontology of semantically interpretable states which are "ontologically discrete".

On my understanding, for example, folk psychology is a theory about semantically interpretable states that play a causal role in some cognitive episodes but not in others. This means that some of these states may not be relevant to the production of some behavior, while others are. Moreover, folk psychology reflects a strong distinction between *structures* and *functions*, where the causal roles assigned to these semantically interpretable states as aspects of psychology might be rooted in any variety of underlying brain states as aspects of neurology. Indeed, as I understand it, folk psychology is *ontologically neutral* apart from serving as the psychology of neurologically-normal human beings. The only neurology it implies is one that supplies structures for nomologically-related cognitive functions.

Indeed, insofar as folk psychology interprets cognitive states in terms of their causal roles, a determination of whether or not connectionist systems can provide neurological structures that are capable of sustaining these cognitive functions hangs on the characterization of those roles. A proper characterization of beliefs, for example, would be something like that of *cognitive states that direct behavior* and of motives, *cognitive states that energize behavior* or as "directive function variables" and "dynamogenic function variables", respectively, in the sense of Madsen (1959). If connection weights, patterns of activation, and such cannot support causal roles such as these — not necessarily on their own, but as parts of entire causal systems — then their conclusion follows, but otherwise not.

Moreover, it appears evident that appropriate formulations of folk psychology do take intentional behavior to be an effect that is brought about by the causal interaction of motives, beliefs, ethics, abilities, and capabilities (Fetzer 1990, 1991b). That makes behavior a complex outcome of (what might be described as) superimposed cognitive states, a conception that harmonizes well with superposition in neural networks. So far as I can see, none of the other arguments that Ramsey, Stich, and Garon advance salvages their position. By adopting the thesis of "functional discreteness" as an element of folk psychology, the authors not only misrepresented the complex (logical and behavioral) character of these cognitive states but imposed an unjustifiable ontological assumption they then attacked.

Chapter 10, "Concepts, connectionism, and the language of thought", by Martin Davies, likewise attempts to demonstrate an incompatibility between connectionism and common-sense psychology, which is associated with *the language of thought* hypothesis. Fodor's most basic argument for a language of thought, no doubt, is that understanding the predicates of a language, such as "P", presupposes "understanding" the G-phenomenon that "P" happens to describe (Fodor 1975: 82). What Fodor, Davies, and others overlook is that the kind of "understanding" involved here does not have to be *linguistic* (Fetzer 1989). Infants and children, for example, can learn to play with blocks, color with crayons or bounce a ball without knowing words used to describe those activities.

They can thus acquire corresponding concepts of what it is to play with blocks, to color with crayons, to bounce a ball, and so on, relative to which they may readily learn words that stand for those things and activities, without possessing prior knowledge of a language of thought. Neural networks, such as human brains, would appear to be capable of learning a language without possessing prior knowledge of a language, provided they have the capacity to acquire concepts to which corresponding predicates can be attached. The connectionist model thus presupposes only (innate) linguistic capabilities and not (innate) linguistic abilities. It presupposes the capacity to learn to use symbols but not a pre-existing symbolic architecture of the kind Davies endorses (p. 254).

Admittedly, the kind of linguistic competence that infants and children might thus acquire may seem to be partial and limited in comparison with the computational competence Fodor and Pylyshyn prescribe. That such an idealized conception could be embraced by connectionist thinkers has been observed by Cummins in a delicious piece of sarcasm:

> Indeed, Fodor and Pylyshyn rightly point out that there is no architectural reason why a connectionist should not adopt semantically structured representations (and hence enjoy whatever empirical glory accrues to being able to account for unbounded competencies and ubiquitous semantic systematicity) (p. 105).

For their conception is obviously far too strong to be satisfied by mere fallible and mortal human beings (Fetzer 1991a).

Davies wants to demonstrate that our common-sense conception of ourselves — *our self-concept* — reflects a commitment to the language of thought (p. 247). Even if that were true, however, it would not imply the truth of such an hypothesis. Suppose, for example, there are kinds of mentality, such as, say, *iconic, indexical, symbolic, transformational,* and *critical,* which are successively stronger and stronger in the sense that each higher level of mentality presupposes those below it (Fetzer 1988). It would not be surprising if human beings, who, under certain favorable conditions — as possessors of transformational mentality — are especially good at varieties of syntactical operations in the form of limited computational competence, say, might nevertheless think of themselves in the idealized fashion associated with the language of thought.

In Chapter 11, "Homuncular functionalism meets PDP", William Lycan considers possible relations between connectionist systems and a theory of mind — *homuncular functionalism* — of which he is the leading proponent. The analytical strategy motivating this position might be better described as *functional decomposition,* since it proceeds by decomposing higher functions into relatively lower functions until the operation of each such unit becomes more or less self-explanatory. Lycan's retention of the term 'homunculus' appears to be anachronistic and misleading when his approach is properly understood. Nevertheless, he offers several astute comments in the current debate on how connectionist systems are best understood.

Lycan accents the possibility of functional specialization as a feature of connectionist systems, where

> ..... it is reasonable to suppose that — especially in the brain —there are neural patterns that have specific functions at least at particular times, but are diffusely distributed from the observer's point of view (p. 270).

These functionally-specialized operations, moreover, do not require the existence of "modules" in any technical sense, such as that of Fodor, who imposes the condition of information encapsulation thereupon. This notion enhances the conception of brains as massive arrangements of homogeneous cells, which can also be extended to accommodate several different kinds of neurons that can combine to produce different causal capabilities, very much in the spirit of the atomic theory of matter.

Lycan challenges the critique of Ramsey, Stich, and Garon that propositional attitudes in the sense of folk psychology cannot be derived from connectionist systems. While acknowledging that there is a conception that coheres closely with homuncular functionalism — namely, "the view that beliefs and other attitudes are internal representations, stored and manipulated by organs whose function it is to store and manipulate" (p. 271) — his approach to this problem is refreshingly empirical. He discusses a specific connectionist system, NETtalk, "that after training audibly pronounces English words given written text" (p. 278). The existence of this system provides rather strong evidence that some connectionist systems have the capacity to acquire certain basic linguistic abilities.

Among the nice points that emerge from his discussion is the observation that NETtalk appears to

> ..... acquire phonological categories in the process of learning its job, and, we may say counterfactually, it would not have achieved its extraordinary accomplishment had it not acquired those categories (p. 278).

In this sense, Lycan is prepared to ascribe the acquisition of concepts to NETtalk. Moreover, the role of back-propagation in training this system proceeds on the basis of semantic considerations:

> As Jay Rosenberg has pointed out ... the back-propagation of error used to train up connectionist networks is conducted in semantic terms, for example, by misunderstanding or by correction (p. 280).

This point is vital to understanding how such systems learn to satisfy semantic constraints.

Lycan advances an "implementation thesis" according to which at least some connectionist systems exhibit

> ..... higher-level organization in terms of propositional representations. [He is] predicting that this will generally be true of systems *whose inputs, outputs and correction feedback are understood in semantical terms*, and probably also true of other language-linked capacities (p. 279).

He observes that even distributed patterns of activation can appropriately be envisioned as possessing causal powers, which means that there appears to be no conceptual difficulty in the hypothesis that connectionist systems can acquire semantically interpretable states that play a causal role in cognitive episodes. The acceptability of this hypothesis must be measured by the results of tests with suitable systems.

In Chapter 12, "Connectionism and three levels of nativism", finally, Ramsey and Stich distinguish between three positions —minimal nativism, anti-empiricism, and rationalism — that arise as distinct responses to the "poverty of the stimulus argument" advanced by Chomsky. According to this argument, "human beings must have a rich store of innate knowledge, because without such innate knowledge it would be impossible for children to learn a language on the basis of the data available to them" (p. 287). While various authors, including Chomsky, have taken this as "proof" that empiricist theories of knowledge and the mind are mistaken and that the only viable alternatives are rationalist conceptions, Ramsey and Stich suggest that the situation — especially given connectionism — is not that simple.

The first response to Chomsky's argument is one they call *minimal nativism*, which maintains that "the child approaches the task of language acquisition with an innate learning mechanism that is strongly biased in favor of certain grammars and against others" (p. 292). As a defense of rationalism, however, this position appears too weak as a bulwark against empiricism. They report Quine's remark that the empiricist "is knowingly and cheerfully up to his neck in innate mechanisms of learning readiness". This position thus apparently fails to capture any sense in which the poverty of the stimulus argument might defeat empiricism.

The second response is *anti-empiricism*, which not only contends that human beings are born with innate language-learning mechanisms with strong biases, "but also that these biases are not compatible with the account of mental mechanisms suggested by even a very generous characterization of the empiricist mind" (p. 296). The correct response from an empiricist perspective, no doubt, is that if human beings can be born with innate *language-learning* mechanisms, human beings can be born with innate *learning* mechanisms, including ones that would enable us to learn a language. Thus, even the anti-empiricist position does not secure its aim.

Chomsky, however, has a response to this reply, which involves taking this idea seriously. Consider that "learning mechanism" to be a competent scientist, who is fortified with methodological principles and whatever else a competent scientist has available. According to Chomsky, such a person could "think up" the right grammar, yet the available evidence would not permit her to identify it to the exclusion of every other alternative. Here, however, the argument proves too much. It not only reflects Quine's well-known thesis of the *underdetermination of theories* by evidence, which is a perfectly general result, but also assumes that there *is* a unique grammar excluding every other to be found! Yet the "right grammar" might not exist!

The possibility that we communicate successfully to whatever extent we do because we share overlapping (or "similar") rather than the same (or "identical") grammars and vocabularies has apparently been ignored. Surely it makes more sense to suppose that every human being learns a language (under suitable conditions), where the language learned may differ (in grammar or vocabulary) from one person to another. From this point of view, much of the purpose of public education — in maintaining a system of "grammar schools" — is to endeavor to insure that the citizens of the country share a common language, in large measure at least, in order to promote communication and cooperation between them (Fetzer 1991c).

The third response is *rationalism*, according to which "the innate language learning mechanism embodies biases or constraints that are specific to the task of language learning and of no use in other domains" (p. 307). Ramsey and Stich conclude that minimal nativism must be true and that anti-empiricism may be true, but that, if the only connectionist language acquisition models that capture how children learn languages appeal to "language-specific algorithms or architectures, then even rationalism will be sustained" (p. 308). Whether or not "rationalism" in this sense is true thus depends upon contingent features of connectionist systems with respect to their capacity to learn a language without already knowing one.

Concluding remarks

From my review of this volume, I conclude that proponents of connectionism should be greatly heartened in several very important respects. One is that the most influential arguments advanced against connectionism — from Chomsky's "poverty of the stimulus" and Fodor and Pylyshyn's "compositionality of meaning" to Pinker and Prince's "pre-existing symbolic architectures" to Ramsey and Stich's "minimal nativism" and "anti-empiricism" — are either unsound or unthreatening to the connectionist program. Even the thesis of "rationalism" can be sustained only if syntactical and semantical dispositions ("language abilities") cannot be acquired on the basis of innate pre-dispositions ("language capabilities").

Another — perhaps even more important — is that connectionism does indeed appear to represent an approach to understanding the nature of cognition that promises distinctive solutions to theoretical problems. If we consider connectionism as envisioning cognition as *computation over distributed representations* (as Cummins suggests), then no doubt what is most important about the program is its commitment to "distributed" representations. As we have discovered, representations may be "distributed" in several different senses, some of which are also properties of ordinary digital systems. But there nevertheless appear to be other senses in which connectionist systems are "distributed" and others not.

In the final analysis, however, the enduring contribution that may emerge from the study of connectionism may derive not from the distributed representations that they employ, but rather from *the causal character of connectionist operations* on those representations. The cognitive capacities of various species are matters of psychology, while the conditions imposed by the classic conception are rooted in principles of logic instead (as Dennett perceives). The differences between them are crucial. The classic conception is immersed in the conception of thinking as requiring the execution of mental algorithms (Fetzer 1994). Once we emancipate ourselves from the limitations inherent in this misconception, we will begin to derive the full benefits of causal conceptions of cognition.

University of Minnesota, Duluth

References

Austin, J.L. 1962. *How to Do Things with Words*. Oxford: Oxford University Press.

Fetzer, J.H. 1988. "Signs and minds: An introduction to the theory of semiotic systems". In J.H. Fetzer (ed), *Aspects of Artificial Intelligence*. Dordrecht: Kluwer Academic Publishers, 133-161.

Fetzer, J.H. 1989. "Language and mentality: Computational, representational, and dispositional conceptions". *Behaviorism* 17: 21-39.

Fetzer, J.H. 1990. *Artificial Intelligence: Its Scope and Limits*. Dordrecht: Kluwer Academic Publishers.

Fetzer, J.H. 1991a. "Connectionism and cognition: Why Fodor and Pylyshyn are wrong". In A. Clark and R. Lutz (eds), *Connectionism in Context*. London: Springer, 37-56.

Fetzer, J.H. 1991b. *Philosophy and Cognitive Science*. New York: Paragon House.

Fetzer, J.H. 1991c. "Primitive concepts: Habits, conventions, and laws". In J.H. Fetzer (ed), *Definitions and Definability*. Dordrecht: Kluwer Academic Publishers, 51-68.

Fetzer, J.H. 1994. "Mental algorithms: Are minds computational systems?". *Pragmatics & Cognition* 2: 1-29.

Fodor, J.A. 1975. *The Language of Thought*. New York: Thomas Crowell.

Fodor, J.A. and Pylyshyn, Z. 1988. "Connectionism and cognitive architecture: A critique".

Cognition 28: 3-71.

Hinton, G., McClelland, J., Rumelhart, D., and the PDP Research Group. 1986. *Parallel Distributed Processing*, vol. 1. Cambridge, MA: The MIT Press, 19-86, 77-109.

Madsen, K. 1959. *Theories of Motivation*. Copenhagen: Munksgaard.

McCulloch, W. and Pitts, W. 1943. "A logical calculus for the ideas immanent in nervous activity". *Bulletin of Mathematical Biophysics* 5: 115-133.

Pinker, S. and Prince, A. 1988. "On language and connectionism: Analysis of a parallel distributed processing model of language acquisition". *Cognition* 28: 73-193.

Rosenfeld, R. and Touretzky, D. 1988. "Coarse-coded symbol memories and their properties". *Complex Systems* 2: 463-484.

CHAPTER 7

PEOPLE ARE NOT COMPUTERS
(Most) Thought Processes are Not Computational Procedures

As a professional philosopher, of course, I have become accustomed to the truth that no position is so absurd that some philosopher has not held it. As a human being, of course, I have also had to personally cope with experiences in life that have involved formal systems and syntax processing. Sometimes our professional activities become detached from our life experiences to a degree that might astonish empirical scientists. Our enthusiasm for a theoretical position may even appear to be virtually independent of our experiences in life, which, were they only taken seriously, might completely undermine what we take as our best theories. The computational conception that dominates what is known as "cognitive science" provides a remarkable illustration of this point. Even if some of our thought processes are computational, most of them are not, which makes *our best theory* either trivial or false. We need something better.

A FEW OF (MY) LIFE'S EXPERIENCES

As a naive student in the fifth grade at La Habra Heights Elementary School more years ago than I care to imagine, my teacher threatened to keep me back from entering the sixth grade if I did not master my multiplication tables. Of course, they were not really "my" multiplication tables, since they belonged to everyone else at least as much at they did to me—*more*, actually, if my teacher was to be believed. Indeed, that was his point, namely: that I had not memorized them and therefore could not recite them by heart. Over the summer, I dutifully fulfilled my obligations as a student and as the offspring of my parents, who would have been acutely disappointed if their young son had failed the fifth grade. I memorized the tables—ones through nines—and when classes resumed, I sought him out to display my newly-acquired competence. He was, alas, voluntarily or involuntarily, no longer there. Which it was I never knew.

Many years later, as a student of philosophy at Princeton University, I had to complete one semester of symbolic logic. It was a course with two lectures and one review class a week. The professor was Carl G. Hempel and what he had to day—about barbers who shaved all and only those who did not shave themselves, for example—was fascinating and enjoyable. The class reviews, which were conducted by Paul Benacerraf, by contrast, were not. When it came to the construction and evaluation of proofs, I was (almost) completely lost. If there was ever a course I wanted to end, this was it. As luck had it, by the day of the final, I had been admitted to the infirmary with some (no doubt, minor) malady. But the idea of having logic hang over me for another semester was so dreadful that, as the appointed time drew near, I simply got dressed and took the final without checking out. I passed, but not by much.

Little did I then suspect that, as one of life's ironies, it would fall to me to instruct generations of eager young minds in the subtleties of symbolic logic. I explained to them things I, as an undergraduate, had not understood about sentential and predicate logic, such as that they were deliberately simplified models that are intended to capture only some, but not all, of the properties of ordinary language and everyday reasoning. The rules of inference for '. . . and ___' supplied a useful illustration, insofar as the temporal dimension that commonly accompanies the meaning of that notion was absent from the rules at our disposal. The conjunction, "Mary got married and had a baby", may not mean the same thing as the conjunction, "Mary had a baby and got married", in ordinary conversation, but it would be treated as an instance of '$p \mathrel{\&} q$' within the context of our calculus, where '$p \mathrel{\&} q$' and '$q \mathrel{\&} p$' were logically equivalent.

The material conditional, of course, posed more complex problems. While I was inclined to suggest that it was something akin to a lowest common denominator among various kinds of 'if . . . then ___' sentences that are encountered in daily life, I emphasized that it was not meant to capture the content of subjunctive, counterfactual or causal conditionals that may occur in other contexts, especially because what is described by the antecedent and what is described by the consequent of conditionals of these kinds are customarily related by a connection of some kind—whether definitional, analytical, or nomological—such that the mere falsity of the antecedent '. . . ' does not render sentences of any of those kinds true on that account alone, contrary to the material conditional. Indeed, it is better to view sentences of this kind as abbreviations for disjunctions of the form 'either not-. . . or ___' ('either not-p or q') to avoid confusion.

MODELS OF LOGIC AND LANGUAGE

Even more importantly, I explained that formal systems such as these are not intended to accurately reflect the properties of ordinary language or even of ordinary reasoning, but instead represent the deliberate constuction of sets of models that, to whatever degree they may succeed, are meant to clarify and illuminate particular and partial aspects of the phenomena within the modeled domain. Indeed, in view of the differences between the ordinary meanings of '. . . and ___' and of 'if . . . then ___', it should be apparent that symbolic logic is actually *a syntactical model of a semantical model* that is created by a process of abstraction from the pragmatical phenomena of the actual use of language by actual human beings, where the construction of that model essentially depends upon decisions concerning which properties of actual use should be retained and which should be ignored within the scope and limits of the model.

The process of model development thus involves two levels of abstraction, where the semantics of the language must be derived from the pragmatics of its context-dependent actual use and then the syntax of the language must be derived relative to the semantics and the pragmatics, thus understood. As a result, the vocabulary of the symbolic-logic model may be more spartan and less complete and the grammar more rigid and less complex than is the case for the pragmatic phenomena thereby modeled. The formation rules, which specify which strings of elements of the vocabulary qualify as grammatically well-formed formulae (or "sentences"), and the transformation rules, which specify what follows (deductively) from what, thus represent relatively high degrees of abstraction rather than any kind of direct correspondence to the vocabulary and grammar of the languages that they only partially describe.[1]

Thus, deductive rules of inference are acceptable if and only if, when applied to true premises, only true conclusions follow. For some sets of rules, such as sentential logic, it is possible to prove that an argument is syntactically valid if and only if its correponding conditional is a semantic tautology. The corresponding conditional is formed by taking (the conjunction of) the premises of an argument as the antecedent of a material conditional having the conclusion of that argument as its consequent. When this conditional is a tautology, there is no case in which its antecedent is true and its consequent is false together, which makes the corresponding argument valid, since there is no case in which it has both true premises and a false conclusion. For systems of this kind, the properties of syntactical derivability and of semantical entailment coincide, since there cannot be one without the other (Beth 1969).

Soundness and completeness, of course, are counterpart notions. Thus, in relation to axiomatic formulations, a formal system is said to be *sound* when every formula that can be derived by means of its syntactical rules is true of the (possibly abstract, including infinite) domain to which that set of formulae is intended to apply (its "intended interpretation") and is said to be *complete* when every formula that is true of the domain to which it is intended to apply is syntactically derivable as a theorem. While sentential logic has been shown to be both sound and complete, Gödel has demonstrated that any formal system that is more complex than monadic first-order predicate logic will be complete only if it is inconsistent and consistent only if it is incomplete. For formal systems modeling the syntax and the semantics of languages that include multiple quantifiers, relations and identity, completeness proofs are not to be expected.[2]

SYMBOL SYSTEMS VS. SEMIOTIC SYSTEMS

In the meanwhile, my research interests had turned in the direction of computer science and artificial intelligence, where I suspected that crucial distinctions were being overlooked, especially from the perspective of the theory of signs introduced by Charles S. Peirce (Hartshorne and Weiss 1960). Peirce proposed that something was *a sign* just in case it is a something that stands for something (else) in some respect or other for somebody. Peirce had also differentiated between three basic kinds of signs, depending upon the way in which signs of each kind stand for something else for somebody, where *icons* are things that resemble that for which they stand, *indices* are causes or effects of that for which they stand, and *symbols* are merely habitually or conventionally associated with that for which they stand, notions I presumed were indispensable to properly understand the nature of mentality.[3]

What I was discovering was that some of the most fundamental premises adopted in AI were fraught with ambiguity or traded upon equivocation, an especially striking instance of which was the physical symbol system hypothesis that Alan Newell and Herbert Simon had proposed, according to which being a *physical symbol system* (in their sense) is both necessary and sufficient for mentality (or, what they called, "general intelligent action"). The problem with their conception appeared to be that something could qualify as a "symbol" (in their sense) whether or not it stood for anything else for anyone at all (Newell and Simon 1976). Consequently, Newell and Simon's "symbols" might or might not be *signs* of the kind Peirce called "symbols", but could be merely meaningless marks that might be processed on the basis of their shapes, their sizes and their relative locations. They could be meaningful, but need not be.

This struck me as a matter of importance. By inverting and generalizing Peirce's theory of signs, I had arrived at the conception that the kind of thing that had the ability to use signs was the same kind of thing that possessed a mind, where *minds* are sign-using or "semiotic" systems (Fetzer 1988a, 1989). On this account, there are at least three kinds of minds, where minds of Type I can use icons, those of Type II can use icons and indices, and those of Type III can use icons, indices and symbols. But while minds of Type III display the ability to use symbols, a class of systems had now been declared to have the ability to use symbols that, on the semiotic conception, were not minds—namely, physical symbol systems, in Newell and Simon's sense—because the symbols that systems of these kinds were capable of using did not have to be meaningful for those systems, whether or not they were for their users.

Their conception thus defined (what might be called) "syntax processing" or "string manipulating" systems, where the meaningfulness of that syntax or of those strings was not thereby guaranteed. Newell and Simon thought they had captured the necessary and sufficient conditions for mentality, but they manifestly had not. If a system could be a physical symbol system (in their sense), yet not be processing meaningful marks, it might still have no semantic capacity essential to mentality. Consequently, it might not qualify as a semiotic system of Type III, which has the ability to use signs that are symbols (in Peirce's sense). Even without assuming that minds are semiotic systems, it was evident that their physical symbol systems were not minds. While the syntax processing capacity that Newell and Simon define might be necessary for the possession of mentality, it did not appear to be sufficient. [4]

ALGORITHMS AND PROGRAMS

The inspiration for the computational conception of language and mentality has always been a presumptive analogy between computers and minds, namely: that hardware is to software as bodies are to minds. This had been succinctly captured by John Haugeland's recommendation, "Why not suppose that people *just are* computers (and send philosophy packing)?" (Haugeland 1981, p. 5). What now became evident, however, was that the capacity to process syntax might not be sufficient for mentality. Haugeland appeared to concede this point by defining "computers" as *automatic formal systems*, which automatically manipulate the marks of formal systems according to the rules of those systems as self-contained, perfectly definite and finitely checkable systems, but where the meaningfulness of the marks subject to manipulation is a matter lying beyond their scope (Haugeland 1981, p. 10).

Upon initial consideration, Haugeland seemed to have formulated a conception going far beyond Newell and Simon's by imposing the requirement that the rules for mark manipulation should be self-contained, perfectly definite and finitely checkable, which Haugeland takes to define what makes a system "digital", but which perhaps more closely approximate "algorithmic". When algorithms are defined as *effective decision procedures*, for example, they have the properties of being completely reliable routines, procedures or processes that can be carried out in a finite number of steps to solve a problem, as S. C. Kleene (1967), among others, has observed. Newell and Simon's conception and Haugleland's converge at this point, however, in view of the consideration that the conduct of physical symbol systems is supposed to be governed by programs as implementations of algorithms for these machines.

Algorithms are available to solve a rather large class of problems, including, especially, problems of mathematics. But an important distinction must be drawn between "algorithms" and "programs", where *programs* implement algorithms in a form suitable for execution by machine. This requires that an algorithm be translated into a programming language (such as Pascal, LISP, or Prolog), where the corresponding program might be loaded into a computing machine and then compiled into machine language for execution. Ultimately, therefore, distinctions must be drawn between at least four different senses of "program", namely: (a) as algorithms, (b) as encodings of algorithms, (c) as encodings of algorithms that can be compiled or (d) as encodings of algorithms that can be compiled and executed by a machine (Fetzer 1988b, p. 1058). The sense appropriate to Newell and Simon and Haugeland thus corresponds to (d).

While Haugeland's assertions about his conception seem to be weaker than Newell and Simon's about their conception (since he acknowledges that marks manipulated in accordance with the encoding of an algorithm may or may not be meaningful), it should be evident that the underlying objection still obtains, namely: that the marks that are manipulated by means of programs might be meaningful for the *users of* that system—especially, presumably, for those who program them—but are not therefore meaningful for use by that system itself. It may sound appealing to suggest that people *just are* computers, but so long computers as are nothing more than syntax processing mechanisms as automated formal systems or even as physical symbol systems, the meaningfulness of the marks they process appears to derive from those who use and who design them. If people have minds but computers do not, people cannot *simply be* computers.

COMPUTATION IS NOT SUFFICIENT

According to (what is known as) *the thesis of strong AI*, computers actually possess mentality when they are executing programs. On the assumption that programs as encodings of algorithms are capable of providing solutions to the problems to which they are being applied, the executions of programs by computers are purposeful activities in relation to their users. But that no more implies that computers therefore have minds than the fact that having an unmowed lawn is a problem that can be solved by cutting it with a lawnmower, which is also a purposeful activity in relation to its user, implies that a lawnmower has a mind. Certainly, neither the physical symbol system conception nor the automated formal system conception satisfies conditions that might plausibly qualify as being enough for mentality. They have the ability to manipulate marks or to process syntax, but that is not sufficient to infuse those marks with meaning.

According to (what is known as) *the thesis of weak AI*, by comparison, computers are simply tools, devices or instruments that are or may be useful, helpful or valuable in the study of mentality but do not possess minds, even when they are executing programs. Indeed, from this perspective, automatic formal systems and physical symbol systems may be envisioned as physical counterparts that at least partially realize the logical properties of Turing machines in the form of complex causal systems of those very kinds. As long as these machines are constructed to appropriate specifications and subjected to appropriate empirical testing, including quality controls that ensure their reliability or trustworthiness, they need not possess the least inkling of the faintest whiff of the slightest trace of mentality at all. Perhaps automatic formal systems and physical symbol systems define "computational systems" rather than "minds".

Haugeland concedes as much when he maintains that automatic formal systems that consistently make sense—where the semantics follows the syntax, under an appropriate interpretation—are *semantic engines* and that *intelligent beings* are things of that kind (Haugeland 1981, p. 24 and p. 31). But it should be obvious by now that this formulation trades upon the same ambiguity as before, namely: that an automatic formal system might consistently make sense to the users of that system without consistently making sense—or making any sense at all—to that system itself. It should come as no surprise that formal systems that are constructed with an interpretation in mind consistently make sense—where the semantics follows the syntax, under some appropriate interpretation—when the syntax was intended to sustain that interpretation by the designers of that system. Only confusion arises from confounding interpretability with mentality.

Indeed, as most students of formal logic are aware, even the construction of simple arguments in sentential and in predicate logic assumes that marks and sequences of marks that occur more than once—that appear in both conclusions and premises, for example—must have the same meaning or stand for the same thing throughout the formulation of those arguments. Otherwise, fallacies of ambiguity arise, where conclusions that follow from premises on the basis of the syntactical rules of inference may have conclusions that are false even when their premises are true. If "John has lost his marbles" occurs in both places, for example, then it must be assigned the same interpretation, lest we infer from *John's loss of some small, round balls used in children's games* to *John's loss of mental capacity*. This semantical condition—the requirement of a uniform interpretation—must be satisfied, not only by semantic engines, but by every formal system that is consistent.

COMPUTATION IS NOT NECESSARY

Neither the conception of physical symbol systems nor the conception of automatic formal systems supports the thesis of strong AI rather than its alternative, where these conceptions properly apply. Even the conception of semantic engines does not appear to salvage the situation, since the properties that distinguish computers under that designation are precisely those we would expect them to have as formal systems that can be designed and constructed for the purpose of executing algorithms by means of machines. Neither conception is able to overcome the objection that causal systems with the capacity to manipulate marks or to process syntax—even on the basis of programs that have the capacity to solve problems—do not satisfy conditions sufficient to qualify them for possession of mentality. While the users and designers of these systems must be capable of interpreting them, we have found nothing that would enhance the credibility of the thesis of strong AI.[5]

A stronger blow against the computational conception, however, might be struck if it could be shown that the conditions it would impose are not merely *insufficient* for mentality, as we have already discovered, but are *unnecessary* for mentality, as well. The appropriate strategy in adopting this approach would be to discover some properties—preferably, of a general kind—that are satisfied by any kind of thought that properly qualifies as computational, yet are not always satisfied by thinking things. There appear to be such features. One of the more appealing features of formal proofs for most students, I have observed, is that they begin at a definite starting point—given *premises*—and end at a definite stopping point—the desired *conclusion*. Similarly, algorithms begin with a *problem*, which is given, and end with a *solution*, while programs begin with *input* and end with *output*. What goes on in between, of course, involves the application of rules, processes or procedures.

Moreover, the application of those rules, processes or procedures has the property that they are supposed to be *appropriate* to derive those conclusions from those premises (in the case of proofs), to obtain that solution for that problem (in the case of algorithms) and to generate that output from that input (in the case of programs). Not only are such rules, processes or procedures designed to produce results when they are applied, they are supposed to yield *the right result* (as valid proofs, correct solutions, or accurate outputs). And, of course, securing the right result has to be something that can be accomplished in a finite number of steps. Otherwise, the system would not satisfy the conditions either for being a semantic engine (as an automatic formal system that is self contained, perfectly definite, and finitely checkable) or for being algorithmic (as a completely reliable routine, process, or procedure that can be carried out in a finite number of steps to solve a problem).

On the assumption that nothing causal interferes with its physical operation, the execution of software by hardware has the effect of creating a system whose behavior conforms to special *normative* constraints defined by these properties. Indeed, that is precisely what we should expect of a computational system that has been designed to fulfil the requirements of an automatic formal system or of a physical symbol system. Computational systems thus appear to be properly envisioned as complex causal systems that are designed and constructed as syntax-processing or mark-manipulating systems, which conform to the restrictions imposed upon semantic engines or physical symbol systems. They have the ability to execute algorithms encoded into the form of programs by means of a programming language that enables them to function properly. They thus appear to be normatively-directed, problem-solving, syntax-processing causal systems.

DISCIPLINED STEP SATISFACTION

On the assumption that the kind of syntax-processing systems under consideration are classic (or "von Neumann") digital machines, there are many indications that regarding them as normatively-directed, problem-solving causal systems is appropriate within in this context. Robert Cummins and Georg Schwarz (1991), for example, define "computing" as the *execution of functions*, which entails the execution of algorithms:

"computing a function f is executing an algorithm that gives o as its output on input i just in case $f(i) = o$" (Cummins and Schwarz 1991, p. 62). Executing an algorithm, in turn, involves *disciplined step satisfaction* or satisfying various steps "in the right order". This conception thus presumes the existence of a beginning (input) and an end (output), where the application of an appropriate routine, process or procedure (algorithm) yields the right result in a finite number of steps. They are normatively directed, problem-solving systems.

Moreover, as Eric Dietrich has observed, the same function may be implemented in more than one way. Indeed, "Computer scientists frequently distinguish between *computing a function* and *executing a procedure* because every procedure realizes exactly one function, but the same function can be realized in several different procedures" (Dietrich 1990, p. 192, emphasis added). This distinction has great merit, not only because the same algorithm can be implemented in various different programs but also because "computing a function" appears to be a more abstract description than is that of "executing a procedure". Indeed, pure mathematics may perhaps be best understood as a domain of abstract entities between which only logical relations can obtain, while applied mathematics concerns a domain of physical entities between which causal relations can obtain (Fetzer 1988b). It might be helpful to entertain "functions" as abstract and "procedures" as causal.

The multiplication tables of my youth affords an appropriate illustration. My fifth-grade teacher was concerned because I had not learned multiplication and the functions thereby defined, such as that $0 \times 0 = 0$, that $8 \times 7 = 56$, that $8 \times 8 = 64$, and so on, which map values in a domain onto those of a corresponding range:[6]

Domain	Range
$< 0 , 0 >$	0
$< 0 , 1 >$	0
.. . .	. . .
$< 8 , 7 >$	56
$< 8 , 8 >$	64
. . .	. . .
$< 9 , 9 >$	81

Strictly speaking, I suppose, it would not have mattered to him whether I had internalized this function by means of addition (where the value of $< 8 , 8 >$, for example, is obtained by adding 8 to itself 8 times) or by some other procedure, as long as it gave the right results. What mattered was whether I had mastered multiplication by becoming a normatively-directed, problem-solving system of a special kind by implementing this set of functions as a set of mental procedures.

Dietrich (1990) and Cummins and Schwarz (1991) go much further, however, and define "cognition" as the computation of functions. On their view, *cognition* implies the execution of procedures, which, of course, can be causal counterparts of functions in an abstract domain. Thus, the kinds of things that are capable of cognition are the kinds of things that are capable of the computation of functions (abstractly described), which entails the capacity for the execution of procedures (implemented causally). If the capacity for cognition is the distinctive characteristic of things that have minds, then the kinds of things that are capable of the execution of procedures are also the kinds of things that have minds. Insofar as the execution of procedures entails disciplined step satisfaction, therefore, minds are a species of normatively-directed, problem-solving syntax-processing causal systems. So if our minds satisfy this conception, perhaps people just are computers, after all.[7]

HUMAN THOUGHT PROCESSES

It is fascinating to observe, therefore, that many kinds of thought processes of human beings as thinking things fail to satisfy these conditions. *Dreams and day-dreams*, for example, fail to satisfy them because they have no definite starting point and no definite stopping point: they begin and they end, but they have no given premises or conclusions. The sequence of events between their beginnings and their endings has a causal character that is neither normatively directed nor problem solving in kind. They do not have to satisfy appropriateness conditions, and there are no right results for them to yield. They may contribute to solving problems—emotional or otherwise—but when that occurs, it is incidental to rather than constitutive of thought processes of this kind (Fetzer 1994a). Some dreams and daydreams may be pleasant or enjoyable, while others may be frightening or even terrifying. But these thought processes are certainly not computational.

Perception appears to be another case of this kind. Properly understood, of course, the results of perception arise as a consequence of causal interaction between the perceiver and the perceived. As a human phenomenon, it involves at least the use of language to describe the contents of experience. The completeness, accuracy and detail with which experience can be described thus depends upon our ability to use language, but it also depends on our perceptual abilities and the circumstances under which perceptions are acquired. All of these factors vary tremendously from new-born infants to toddling tots to the elderly and the senile and from case to case. Even assuming that perceptual episodes have a beginning and an end, what transpires in between lacks the normative character of always yielding the right result. Perception is a fallible activity, which makes perception a second kind of non-computational thought process.[8]

Memory is yet another case. Since memories are retained as effects of the occurrence of past perceptions, there are at least two ways in which they can be faulty: our original perceptions may be mistaken or our retentions of those original perceptions may be wrong. The very idea of remembering something that never occurred may initially sound anomalous, but when you consider the influence of the multiple conditions that affect perception—including ones both internal and external to the perceiver, including attention span, state of awareness, and perceptual access—as well as the multiple conditions that affect memory—including physical age, temporal proximity to the original occurrence, and presence or absence of impairment—it should be obvious that there is no algorithm for remembering. There is no finite sequence of steps such that, if those steps are followed, then a specific memory will be recalled—not even hypnosis.

One underlying factor that may contribute to confusion about the scope and limits of computational procedures arises from failing to systematically differentiate causal processes that *implement the normative procedures that distinguish the execution of algorithms* from those that do not. Laws of nature that are causal rather than non-causal—no matter whether they are deterministic or probabilistic in kind—bring about changes in systems across time from state *S1* at time *t1* to state *S2* at time *t2*. There are no doubt causal laws of dreams and daydreams, perception and memory, just as there causal laws for physical, chemical and biological processes and systems. But special constraints must be satisfied by computational systems that do not have to be satisfied by other kinds of causal systems. Thought processes that do not invariably yield definite solutions to problems in a finite number of steps can still be non-computational properties of thinking things.

PHILOSOPHICAL ALTERNATIVES

What is most striking about dreams and daydreams, perception and memory within this context is that they are familiar phenomena from the life experience of human beings. When we reflect upon our experiences in life, it seems obvious that many if not most of our ordinary thought processes do not properly qualify as the execution of procedures. There are no algorithms for when to start looking and when to stop looking or even how to look such that, if only you follow this procedure, then your perceptions must be accurate and you cannot make a mistake. There are no algorithms for when to start remembering or for how to go about remembering. Saying to yourself, "Remember!", certainly will not do. The very idea of compelling yourself to remember is at least faintly ridiculous. The case of dreams and daydreams is even more compelling as an example of a causal process each of us experiences that is not a computational procedure.

The question might therefore be posed, "Why should the computational conception be taken seriously at all?", to which I conjecture there are at least three possible answers. One is that we may be uncertain about the nature of thought and of thought processes themselves. If dreams and daydreams, perception and memory are not processes involving thought, then they do not count as counter-examples to the computational conception. Indeed, if cognition turned out to be computation, then they would not be examples of cognition. Such a result, however, would surely strain the plausibility of the computational account severely. Not least of the benefits to be derived from adopting the conception of minds as semiotic systems is that any kind of sign-using system possesses mentality, no matter whether the signs such a system is processing are dreams or daydreams and no matter whether those processes conform to normative constraints or not.

A second possible reason for taking computationalism seriously may be that we have not adequately understood the properties that separate computational procedures specifically from causal processes generally. If changes in systems from state $S1$ at time $t1$ to state $S2$ at time $t2$ in accordance with causal laws always qualified as *disciplined step satisfaction*, for example, then the difference between computational procedures and causal processes remains obscure. Any causal process could be cognitive. Another benefit to be derived from adopting the semiotic conception of mentality, therefore, is that it can explain why causal processes in physics, chemistry and biology, for example, can involve changes in systems from state $S1$ at time $t1$ to state $S2$ at time $t2$ without displaying mentality on that account alone. Causal processes qualify as "cognitive" only when they involve the use of signs by a sign-using system. Most of them are not cognitive.[9]

A third reason for taking computationalism seriously may be the conjecture that, if some of our cognitive processes are computational procedures, perhaps all of our cognitive processes are computational procedures. Haugeland exemplifies this attitude when he suggests that thought "obeys (at least much of the time) various rules of inference and reason" (Haugeland 1981, p. 3) and covertly implies that thinking is reducible to reasoning. Indeed, if thinking is reducible to reasoning and reasoning is reducible to computing, then perhaps the boundaries of computation exhaust the boundaries of thought. Such an approach, however, not only runs the risk of *begging the question* by assuming that human reasoning is a computational process but the risk of *overgeneralization* by assuming that the kinds of routines, processes or procedures that operate in one domain of thought operate in every other. Computationalism thus appears to be founded on fallacies.[10]

WHAT IS COGNITIVE SCIENCE?

Perhaps the most striking effort to bolster the computational conception has been advanced by Barbara von Eckhardt (1993), who adopts the strategy of taking the central aim of cognitive science to be "the human adult's normal, typical cognition (ANTCOG for short)" (von Eckhardt 1993, p. 6). The ANTCOG approach thus excludes from consideration variations in cognitive capacities and abilities ranging from those of new-born infants and toddling tots to those of the elderly and senile. The domain of human cognition is taken to be capacities or abilities that are intentional or purposeful, pragmatically evaluable as more or less successful, coherent when they are successful, usually reliable, and productive in having potentially unrestricted applicability (von Eckhardt 1993, pp. 47-48). The effect of adopting these conditions is to constrict the range of pragmatical phenomena within the domain to which cognitive science is supposed to apply.

The rather flexible character of the properties that von Eckhardt adopts to define the properties of human cognition seems initially promising within the scope of its limited domain, where the course of science should decide whether typical, normal adult human cognition is computational or not. She diminishes the tenability of her own position, however, by adopting (what she refers to as) *two major substantive assumptions*, namely: that cognition is computational and that cognition involves representations (von Eckhardt 1993, p. 8). Her account of the general character of cognitive science thus implies that non-computational phenomena or non-representational phenomena cannot possibly be cognitive. The basic conception of von Eckhardt, therefore, is that cognition is computation across representations, which is true by stipulation. She thereby precludes the logical possibility that there might be non-computational cognitive phenomena.

From the perspective of the philosophy of science, von Eckhardt's work thus exemplifies the historical dilemma encountered by normal scientists, who have a paradigm in which they believe but are also confronted by anomalies. In this case, of course, the paradigm is defined by the conception that *cognition is computation across representations*. The anomalies are displayed by phenomena— such as dreams and daydreams, perception and memory—that appear to involve representations but also seem to be non-computational. Von Eckhardt's account entails that phenomena of this kind cannot possibly be cognitive, which appears to be a rather difficult position to defend. Those who take the phenomena seriously, after all, already have empirical evidence that falsifies the computational paradigm, while those who adhere to the paradigm have only a definitional stipulation to justify its dismissal. Surely the phenomena have to be taken seriously.

Von Eckhardt thus begs the question in taking for granted that cognition must be computational. This is difficult to understand, since she acknowledges that the concepts of computation and of representation "are (for the present, at least) quite open-ended and vague" (von Eckhardt 1993, p. 9). Indeed, her position is untenable in at least two respects. First, she appears to have succumbed to the almost irresistable temptation to identify the discipline itself (as a field of inquiry) with one of the theories that inspired it (the computational conception), a fatal defect in a work that pretends to define the field.[11] The second is that less open-ended and more precise concepts of computation—involving algorithms, functions and disciplined step satisfaction—imply that computational procedures always yield definite solutions to problems in a finite number of steps. Her "flexible" conception of the domain of cognition appears to be inconsistent with her substantive commitments.

THE PEIRCEAN FRAMEWORK

Ultimately, von Eckhardt also adopts the conception of computers as devices that are capable of accepting, storing, manipulating, and outputting data or information in accordance with a set of effective rules, characterizing minds—"if they are computers at all"—as automatic formal systems, very much as Haugeland envisions them (von Eckhardt 1993, p. 113). If she senses a tension in her implicit commitment to the twin theses that computers do not have minds, even though minds are computational systems and operate the same way computers operate, which apparently implies that even minds do not have minds, she does not reveal it. Indeed, occasionally she suggests the possibility that the computational model of the mind might be no more than a metaphor; other times, she hints that it has to be taken literally. But she also states that the seriousness with which it should be taken depends upon the level of theoretical detail that is available and desired.

A better definition of "cognitive science", of course, would be that of the science of cognition—whether in human beings, other animals, or even machines, if such a thing is possible—which appears to be the appropriate conception. The constraints that von Eckhardt imposes on the pragmatical phenomena of cognition combined with her substantive assumptions guarantee the emergence of a semantical model of cognition as computation over representations, *no matter what the phenomena*, which is unscientific. Indeed, dreams, daydreams, perception and memory appear to be typical cognitive experiences of even most normal adult human beings, which is evident from the perspective of Peirce's theory of signs. The images, events and words that are the stuff of dreams, daydreams, perception and memory are things that stand for other things in various respects for somebody, which qualifies them as "representatives" that are components of non-computational cognitive processes.

Even though von Eckhardt adopts Peirce's theory of signs in the guise of a theory of representations, a term that Peirce himself employed—which I applaud—her commitment to computationalism apparently precludes her from appreciating what the theory of signs has the potential to reveal about the nature of cognition. The triadic sign relation, for example, implies (1) the existence of a causal relation between a sign and a sign user; (2) a semantic relation between the sign and that for which it stands; and (3) a behavioral relation between the sign, its user and that for which it stands. The existence of a semantic (or "grounding") relation between signs and what they stand for is significant, first, because it offers an explanation for how a thing *can stand for something else* (by virtue of a relation of resemblance, of cause or effect, or of habitual association) and, second, because it also explains how something can stand for something else *in some respect or other* (by virtue of a relation of partial resemblance, of partial cause or effect, or of partial habitual association).[12]

More significantly within the present context, these considerations are able to explain the underlying difference between semiotic systems and symbol systems and automatic formal systems, where genuine mentality presupposes *the existence of a grounding relation* between signs and that for which they stand. If minds of Type I can use icons as signs that are grounded in resemblance relations, minds of Type II can use indices as signs that are grounded in cause and effect relations, and minds of Type III can use symbols as signs that are grounded in habitual or conventional associations, while symbol systems in Newell and Simon's sense and automatic formal systems in Haugeland's sense cannot, then this can account for their difference with respect to semantics and meaning. Semiotic systems have the ability to use things to stand for other things as signs for those systems, an ability that symbol systems and automatic formal systems do not possess. This property distinguishes between systems with minds and those without (Fetzer 1988a, 1990b, 1995; cf. Searle 1992).

SEMIOTIC SYSTEMS AND SYMBOL SYSTEMS

The differences between semiotic systems and symbol systems are not confined to the fact that symbol systems have the capacity to process syntax in the form of meaningless marks, while semiotic systems have the capacity to process signs that are meaningful for those systems. This might be described as a difference in *semantic content*: semiotic systems process signs that have semantic content for those systems themselves, but symbol systems manipulate marks that are meaningful, if they are meaningful at all, only for the users of those systems. There is, however, another difference at stake here, which is displayed by the fact that dreams, day-dreams, perception and memory are processes that do not involve the execution of procedures. This might be described as a difference in *causal processing*: symbol systems process marks by the execution of computational procedures, but semiotic systems also have the capacity to process signs by non-computational procedures.

The difference in content that exists because semiotic systems have an ability which symbol systems lack can be displayed by means of the following diagram:

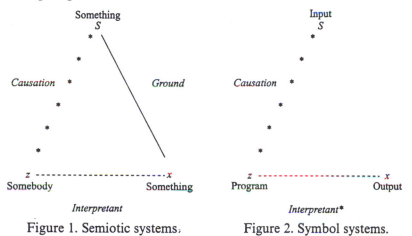

Figure 1. Semiotic systems.   Figure 2. Symbol systems.

Some of the differences between symbol systems and semiotic systems are obvious from these diagrams. A grounding relationship between signs and what they stand for for a sign-user does not appear in the symbol system diagram, precisely because the absence of such a relationship is the most important feature distinguishing between systems of these kinds. Indeed, even when something affects the behavior of another thing (as causes bring about effects or as stimuli bring about responses), unless that causal connection obtains because that thing functions as *a sign* relative to those effects—unless it functions as an icon, an index or a symbol for that system—that connection cannot be semiotic.[13]

"Interpretant" thus stands for a dispositional account of the meaning of a sign for a semiotic system, where the totality of ways in which that system would (invariably or probably) behave in the presence of that sign in relation to different (possibly infinite) specific contexts—including preexisting motives and beliefs but also other abilities and capabilities—*is the meaning of that sign* for such a system.[14] "Behavior" in this sense includes changing one's mind, where two systems, even when confronting the same sign with the same meaning for them both, would be expected to display the same behavior only when they were in the same context. When drivers approach an intersection and notice a red traffic light, they tend to apply the breaks and come to a complete halt until the light turns green, but possibly not when they are frantic husbands with wives in labor, felons who are fleeing the police, or driving emergency vehicles (Fetzer 1989, 1990b, 1991a, 1991b).

"Interpretant*", instead, stands for a dispositional account of input processing by a symbol system, which is the totality of computations that that system would perform, relative to a specific program—assuming that other components of that causal system function properly—which, however, is not a semiotic phenomenon.[15] Von Eckhardt embraces a conception of this kind, which she extends to (what she calls) *mental representations*, where "The interpretant of a mental representation R for some subject S consists of the set of all possible determinate computational processes contingent upon entertaining R in S" (von Eckhardt 1993, pp 297-298). By virtue of its restriction to computational consequences, however, this conception has the effect of delimiting the causal consequences of cognition to its logical consequences.[16] Human beings are complex semiotic causal systems rather than normatively directed, computational causal systems of the kind she has defined.[17]

CONSCIOUSNESS AND COGNITION

Other benefits of the semiotic approach may be less obvious. The theory also implies a conception of consciousness (relative to signs of specific kinds) according to which a system is *conscious* (relative to signs of specific kinds) when it (a) possesses the ability to use signs of that kind and (b) is not incapacitated from exercising that ability. When a system is anesthetized, intoxicated, blindfolded or otherwise impaired, it may be incapacitated from the exercise of some of its semiotic abilities. Moreover, when properly understood, *cognition* is an effect that is brought about by a causal interaction between the presence of signs of specific kinds (within suitable causal proximity) and a system that is conscious with respect to signs of that kind in relation to its *context*, consisting of its other internal states, including preexisting motives and beliefs. Cognition thus is not computation across representations but causal processing that involves signs.[18]

This approach also appears to resolve "Block's problem". Ned Block (1995a) has made a plausible case for drawing a distinction between *P-consciousness* (phenomenal-consciousness) and *A-consciousness* (access-consciousness), but he has been unable to locate their "real difference" (Block 1995b). However, Block's conception of P-consciousness appears to apply to the causal relationship between *possible* signs and semiotic systems, while his conception of A-consciousness appears to apply to the causal relationship between *actual* signs and semiotic systems. P-consciousness thus appears to be the experience of a (potentially semiotic) phenomenon, while A-consciousness is an interpretation of its significance. A semiotic system can have P-consciousness without A-consciousness whenever it is subjected to things that are not signs for that system. P-consciousness thus turns out to be necessary but not sufficient for cognition.[19]

The semiotic theory also compares favorably with that of minds as semantic engines. The difficulty confronting the conception of minds as automatic formal systems that consistently make sense—where the semantics follows the syntax, under an appropriate interpretation—has always been the source and character of that interpretation. The most popular candidates for that role among current alternatives have been *the language of thought hypothesis*, which posits a genetic species-specific semantics of in-born concepts, and *causal theories of meaning*, which effect an interpretation by means of reference.[20] The first supplies an internalist account for which meanings are innate, the second an externalist account for which meanings are acquired. Neither, however, appears to supply a viable alternative to the semiotic theory that languages, for example, are systems of signs that are gradually learned to describe innate or acquired concepts.

The language of thought hypothesis, for example, presumes that understanding a language presupposes understanding another language, which invites the introduction of *a base language*—the language of thought—relative to which any other language might be acquired. This account not only overlooks the prospect that language learning might be rooted in *non-linguistic* understanding instead, an approach the semiotic conception embraces, but also implies that unsuccessful translations between different languages must be a theoretical impossibility. Causal theories of meaning, moreover, presuppose the existence of causal chains that connect names and predicates to their referents, an assumption that might seem appealing for ordinary uses of familiar terms but which appears appalling for cases where causal chains cannot or do not exist: in relation to non-existent entities, abstract entities, theoretical relations, and non-observable properties. [21]

THE LAWS OF THOUGHT

Perhaps the most farreaching discovery that has emerged from the pursuit of the semiotic conception of mentality, however, concerns the nature of the laws of thought. While it appears unproblematical to maintain that perception and memory, for example, are semiotic activities governed by causal laws, the conception of cognition as an effect brought about by causal interaction between a sign user and a sign may appear inadequate in comparison with the computational conception of cognition as the execution of procedures, which are causal counterparts of functions in an abstract domain. The causal processes that relate signs to other signs and meaning and behavior for ordinary thought, however, which is neither normatively-governed nor problem-solving in kind, appear to be associationistic rather than computationalistic. They do not satisfy the conditions of disciplined step satisfaction but rather approximate the free association of ideas.

Consider, for example, the following panels drawn by the humorist B. Kliban, which are the first and second in a series entitled, "Cornish Game Clams: A False Start in Six Parts".[22] These appear to capture the ordinary thought processes of ordinary human beings. Panel I, for example, shows a fellow responding to the waiter's presentation by saying, "Ah! Cornish game clams, my favorite seafood!", where the meal itself was an icon that resembled other meals of a certain kind, which, in turn, caused the effect of bringing to his mind symbols by which food of that kind is described. His use of the phrase, "cornish game clams", in turn, is a cause that trigger's off another diner's recollection of related experiences as an effect, where he and Professor Jimbob were exploring an incredibly ancient temple. Thinking of this experience causes him to become pale, which functions as an index for his dining companion, who uses symbols to inquire about its cause, etc.

Panel II is, if anything, even more revealing. As he and Professor Jimbob proceed to the temple to rescue Lydia, he hears her cries for help, symbols functioning as causes intended to bring about an effect. Hearing her cries reminds him of similar sounds made by the brakes on his old convertible on the basis of a resemblance relation, which, in turn, was an effect brought about by that cause. Thinking about the car, he recalls

associated experiences indexically related to that car, including the night that Shirley's dress got sucked into the carburetor, where she is identified symbolically by her first name, which causes him to try to remember her last name, "Wozzle? Winkle? Workle?", which, successfully recalled, in turn, reminds him of her activities as associated effects thus brought to mind, which included singing at the Pancake House on Thusdays, for example, where one sign causes cognitive connections with other signs as a series of semiotic associations.

These panels (about which a great deal more could be said) thus provide vivid illustrations of the associative character of ordinary thought. In these cases, what we are observing are themselves iconic and symbolic representations of a series of semiotic associations, which displays an absence of the kind of disciplined step satisfaction characteristic of computational systems. These thought processes do not satisfy the computational conception and therefore properly count against it. It should also be observed that *the same thing*, such as the presentation of food, can function as an *icon* (by virtue of resembling other things of that kind), as an *index* (by virtue of being a cause of a future effect, for example), or as a *symbol* (by virtue of being habitually associated with things of other kinds). The cognitive effects of a sign within suitable causal proximity of a sign-using system that is conscious with respect to signs of that kind, therefore, appears heavily dependent upon context and may be either an indeterministic or a chaotic phenomenon.[23]

FURTHER CONSEQUENCES

The semiotic conception of the mind also supplies a criterion for mentality in the form of the capacity to make a mistake (Fetzer 1988a, 1990b, 1991a, 1996b). A system can make a mistake just in case it has the ability to take something as standing for something (else) in some respect or other, but does so wrongly (by taking one individual thing for another individual thing, a thing of one kind for a thing of another kind, the false for the true, and so forth). Insofar as the semiotic conception is intended to apply to systems that have minds, no matter whether they are human, other animal, or even machine (if such a thing is possible), it is indispensable that the very idea of mentality should not beg the question by implying the applicability or inapplicability of this conception to systems of any of these kinds on the basis of a mere stipulation. If other animals or computing machines are capable of making mistakes, then they are possessors of mentality.[24]

It should be observed, moreover, that misdescriptions, faulty inferences, and the like qualify as "mistakes" only if they are unintentional. If we distinguish between *standard cognitive situations* in which our intentions are truth-directed (in seeking to discover the truth, speak the truth, and so forth), then we tend to make mistakes when the available evidence does not support an appropriate inference—although, of course, even when sufficient evidence is available, we may still make mistakes when reasoning is inductive. A pragmatical condition—the requirement of total evidence—thus insists that, in arriving at conclusions, we must take into account all of the available relevant evidence. When we are in *non-standard cognitive situations*, however, where our intentions are not truth-directed (in desiring to mislead, to amuse, to insult, and so on), misdescriptions, miscalculations, and misdirections that otherwise would might or might not properly qualify as "mistakes".[25]

The realization that many if not most thought processes—including dreams and daydreams, perception and memory, and ordinary thinking—do not fulfil the conception of being normatively-governed, problem-solving causal activities does not mean that we never function in that capacity. As I and other students of symbolic logic have found, when *syntactical procedures* are adequately understood (within the context of constructing and evaluating formal proofs, for example), human beings seem to be capable of functioning (more or less) as though we were computational systems.[26] Indeed, as Carol Cleland (1993) has observed, there exists a class of *mundane procedures* that are often employed to achieve specific effects, such as recipes for cooking and instructions for assembling. When implemented under appropriate causal conditions, these step-by-step routines bring about their effects as an especially interesting class of non-syntactical but still effective procedures.[27]

It should have been apparent from the start, however, that the computational conception—according to which thinking is reducible to reasoning and reasoning is reducible to computing—casts a shallow net in relation to human cognitive abilities. The semiotic activities of human beings are barely tapped by deductive reasoning, where conclusions are drawn from premises and arguments are appraised. The use of declarative sentences that are true or false is not even representative of human linguistic abilities, which include the use of imperative sentences to issue directions and commands, exclamatory sentences to express emotions and attitudes, and interrogatory sentences to ask questions and make inquiries. Once we abandon a propositional paradigm and embrace a speech-act paradigm, where the diversity of human cognitive activities can be more adequately appraised, we may discover that the semiotic conception of minds is an even broader and more powerful theory.[27]

During the course of this inquiry, we have discovered that a wide variety of cognitive activities do not satisfy the constraints imposed by the computational conception. Even if human beings are capable of disciplined step satisfaction in formal reasoning and in mundane procedures, activities of this kind appear to be special cases that are not representative of most human cognition. If the theory is taken to assert that *all* human cognitive activities are computational, it is false; but taken to assert that only *some* human cognitive activities are computational, it is trivial. Even our own experiences in life strongly suggest the computational conception cannot be sustained. In abstracting from the pragmatical phenomena, its proponents have begged the question by assuming that procedures that may apply in one domain must apply in every other, where the theoretical model that they provide is neither sound nor complete. "Our best theory" is either trivial or false, where the conception of minds as semiotic systems offers something better.

NOTES

* Special thanks to Michael Costa for inviting me to organize a symposium on whether minds are computational systems for the annual meeting of the Southern Society for Philosophy and Psychology, Nashville, 4-7 April 1996, and to Selmer Bringsjord and William J. Rapaport for participating with me.

[1] One manifestation of this process of simplification is that the sentences that are the focus of elementary logic are only declarative and not imperative, exclamatory or interrogatory. All this was explained by Rudolf Carnap (Carnap 1939). A proper education ought to begin here. (See Section 15.)

[2] A lucid discussion of these issues may be found in Church (1959). Since ordinary languages abound with multiple quantifiers, relations and identity, it follows that they are not amenable to suitable formalization by means of systems for which completeness proofs might be expected to be available.

[3] During 1983-84, as MacArthur Visiting Professor at New College of the University of South Florida, one of my duties was to present a series of public lectures. In the third of these (Spring 1984), I advanced the conception of minds as sign-using (or "semiotic") systems (Fetzer 1988a, 1989, 1990b).

[4] If Newell and Simon have the right definition of their conception of the character of *physical symbol system*, then they are wrong in thinking that minds are systems of that kind. But they may have been successful, nevertheless, in advancing conditions appropriate to define *computational system*.

[5] Indeed, the description of a machine as "executing an algorithm" may be taken to imply that the machine understands that what it is doing is a thing of this kind, even though that may be true only relative to its users' own objectives. We can use them to solve problems, a point to which I shall return.

[6] Strictly speaking, the values in the domain could be specified in terms of sets of pairs of numbers rather than ordered pairs, since multiplication does not discriminate between which integer comes first and which comes second. In other cases, such as subtraction, it matters, so I have used ordered pairs.

[7] Provided, of course, that the procedures that are subjected to execution are *meaningful* for the systems that are executing them. In other words, the previous objection to Newell and Simon's and to Haugeland's conceptions remains, but the focus has turned to the *form* of computations rather than their *content*.

[8] This is not to deny that vision, as a causal process evolution has produced, has to be understood within the context of adaptive problems. As David Marr notes, "it is the problem of vision that is being attacked, not neural visual mechanisms" (Marr 1981, p. 141). But that does not make it an effective procedure.

[9] There is an important ambiguity here. What I am denying is that a causal process merely by virtue of being a causal process should qualify as cognitive. I am not denying that cognition is a causal process, nor am I denying that causal processes can serve as signs for sign-users and in that sense be "cognitive".

[10] Even if humans were to cope with logic proofs in the same way as do computers, that would not establish that other human cognitive activities—such as dreams, daydreams, perception, and memory—are governed by the same procedures. The evidence under consideration here suggests the opposite is true.

[11] I pointed out the seriousness of this problem in Fetzer (1991a), pp. xvi-xvii.

[12] For example, a partial symbolic or habitual association occurs when we refer to Scott as "the author of *Waverly*" and do not know him under other descriptions. These considerations illuminate the sometimes paradoxical properties of various intensional contexts, as I have elsewhere explained (Fetzer 1990b, pp. 202-203).

[13] Something must exist to function as a sign for a system, but it is not the case that that for which it stands must also exist. We can create signs that stand for non-existent kinds of things, such as *vampires* and *werewolves*, and for specific people who do not exist, such as *Santa Claus* or *Mary Poppins*. (Cf. Fetzer 1996b.)

[14] Fetzer (1989), (1990b), (1991a), and (1991b), for example. This approach, of course, is a pragmatic conception for which the meaning of a sign for a sign-user is the totality of ways in which the sign would influence actual or possible behavior. Its meaning is an internal state with potential external manifestations.

[15] A distinction can be drawn between "ordinary" and "connectionist" systems, where the latter concern consequences of computations across *distributed* representations, while the former concern consequences of computations across *ordinary* representations, as von Eckhardt (1993), pp. 292-293 and p. 297, has done.

[16] The limited inferential powers and partial knowledge of real human beings further undermines the notion that we are computational systems. At best, we appear to possess no more than some kind of limited computational competence as semiotic systems of Type IV (Fetzer 1988a, 1990b, 1992, 1994a, and 1995).

[17] Von Eckhardt suggests that what connects computations with the contents or the referents of representations is that they "depend on that referent or content". Although von Eckhardt implies that she has a solution for "the regress problem" (von Eckhardt 1993, p. 301)—the problem of accounting for the meaning of the undefined (or "primitive") elements of a system—that does not appear to be the case. She mentions Fetzer (1988a), but it might have been a good thing for her to have compared her account with Fetzer (1989), (1990b), (1991a) and (1991b).

[18] Nor is it computation across distributed representations. (See Fetzer 1994b.)

[19] Recall that consciousness (with respect to signs of a certain kind) implies (a) the ability to use signs of that kind and (b) the absence of incapacity to exercise that ability. But what about phenomena that do not function as signs for such a system? When that occurs, there can be P-consciousness of the phenomena without A-consciousness, where P-

consciousness might be better termed "sentience". In other words, there can be sentience without consciousness but not vice versa.

[20] The language of thought conception was introduced by Jerry Fodor (1975). An excellent collection of articles that explore causal theories of meaning and reference (influenced by Kripke, Donnellan, and Putnam) is Schwartz (1977).

[21] Some reasons for doubting the language of thought hypothesis are supplied by Fetzer (1989), (1990b), (1991a) and (1992). Discussions of causal theories of meaning include Fetzer (1991a), (1996b) and (forthcoming), which suggests that the problems extend to misconceptions in relation to possible-world semantics.

[22] Kliban (1982). By permission. This humorist has captured the nature of ordinary thought processes better than has any philosopher or any cognitive scientist.

[23] The possibility neurons may have propensities to activate connections with other neurons and that minds may be probabilistic causal systems is discussed in Fetzer (1991a) and related to Penrose (1989) in Fetzer (1994a). The thesis that computer systems may be chaotic systems is advanced in Fetzer (1996a).

[24] In order for something to be able to make a mistake, it must be able to take something to stand for something else, which is the definition of mentality. This criterion is therefore heavily theory-laden. Mistakes, moreover, must be distinguished from malfunctions (Fetzer 1988a, 1990b, 1991a, and especially 1992).

[25] Paul Coates (1997) has discussed meaning, mistakes and miscalculations.

[26] The ubiquitous applicability of the (semantical) requirement of a uniform interpretation and of the (pragmatical) requirement of total evidence, however, indicate that *evaluations of proofs* may not be reducible to (pure) syntax manipulation and that even *formal deductive reasoning* may be non-computational.

[27] Abstract (or symbolic) algorithms as effective procedures that involve only notational manipulations should be separated from mundane procedures as physical (or causal) effective procedures that involve causal manipulations. Laws of nature may *even be thought of* as nature's algorithms (cf. Fetzer 1990a, 1994a). [*Note added 2000*: Thinking doesn't make it so, of course, as I have also explained in relation to "the intentional stance" (Fetzer 1990b, pp. 14 – 15) and the conception of biological evolution as an "algorithmic process" (Fetzer forthcoming).]

[28] Broader and more powerful, first, as an account that applies to other animals and even machines, if such a thing is possible, as well as to human beings; second, as an account that provides a solution for the problem of primitives (see note 17); third, as an account that is adequate to explain the phenomena.

REFERENCES

Beth, E. W. (1969), "Semantic Entailment and Formal Derivability", in J. Hintikka, ed., *The Philosophy of Mathematics* (New York, NY: Oxford University Press, 1969), pp. 9-41.

Block, N. (1995a), "On a Confusion about a Function of Consciousness", *Behavioral and Brain Sciences* 18 (1995), pp. 227-247.

Block, N. (1995b), "How Many Concepts of Consciousness?", *Behavioral and Brain Sciences* 18 (1995), pp. 272-284.

Carnap, R. (1939), *Foundations of Logic and Mathematics*. International Encyclopedia of Unified Science, Volume 1, Number 3. Chicago, IL: University of Chicago Press, 1939.

Church, A. (1959), "Logic, formal", in D. Runes, ed., *Dictionary of Philosophy* (Ames, IO: Littlefield, Adams & Company, 1959), pp. 170-181

Cleland, C. (1993), "Is the Church-Turing Thesis True?", *Minds and Machines* 3 (1993), pp. 283-312.

Coates, P. (1997), "Meaning, Mistake and Miscalculation", *Minds and Machines* 7 (1997), pp. 171-197.

Cummins, R. and G. Schwarz (1991), "Connectionism, Computation and Cognition", in T. Horgan and J. Tienson, eds., *Connectionism and the Philosophy of Mind* (Dordrecht, The Netherlands: Kluwer Academic Publishers, 1991), pp. 60-73.

Dietrich, E. (1991), "Computationalism", *Social Epistemology* 4 (1991), pp. 135-154.

Fetzer, J. H. (1988a), "Signs and Minds: An Introduction to the Theory of Semiotic Systems", in J. H. Fetzer, ed., *Aspects of Artificial Intelligence* (Dordrecht, The Netherlands: Kluwer Academic Publishers, 1988), pp. 133-161.

Fetzer, J. H. (1988b), "Program Verification: The Very Idea", *Communications of the ACM* (September 1988), pp. 1048-1063.

Fetzer, J. H. (1989), "Language and Mentality: Computational, Representational, and Dispositional Conceptions", *Behaviorism* 17 (1989), pp. 21-39.

Fetzer, J. H. (1990a), "The Frame Problem: Artificial Intelligence Meets David Hume", *Expert Systems* 3 (1990), pp. 219-232.

Fetzer, J. H. (1990b), *Artificial Intelligence: Its Scope and Limits.* Dordrecht, The Netherlands: Kluwer Academic Publishers, 1990.

Fetzer, J. H. (1991a), *Philosophy and Cognitive Science.* New York, NY: Paragon House.

Fetzer, J. H. (1991b), "Primitive Concepts: Habits, Conventions, and Laws", in J. H. Fetzer, ed., *Definitions and Definability* (Dordecht, The Netherlands: Kluwer Academic Publishers, 1991), pp. 51-68.

Fetzer, J. H. (1992), "Connectionism and Cognition: Why Fodor and Pylyshyn are Wrong", in A. Clark and R. Lutz, eds., *Connectionism in Context* (London, UK: Springer-Verlag, 1992), pp. 37-56.

Fetzer, J. H. (1994a), "Mental Algorithms: Are Minds Computational Systems?", *Pragmatics and Cognition* 2 (1994), pp.1-29.

Fetzer, J. H. (1994b), "What Makes Connectionism Different? Discussion Review of W. Ramsey, S. Stich, and D. Rumelhart, eds., *Philosophy and Connectionist Theory*", *Pragmatics and Cognition* 2 (1994), pp. 327-348.

Fetzer, J. H. (1995), "Minds and Machines: Behaviorism, Dualism, and Beyond", *Stanford Humanities Review* 4 (1995), pp. 251-265.

Fetzer, J. H. (1996a), "Computer Reliability and Public Policy: Limits of Knowledge of Computer-Based Systems", *Philosophy and Public Policy* 13 (1996), pp. 229-266.

Fetzer, J. H. (1996b). *Philosophy and Cognitive Science*, 2nd ed. New York, NY: Paragon House.

Fetzer, J. H. (forthcoming), *Evolution and the Mind* (forthcoming).

Fodor, J. (1975), *The Language of Thought.* Cambridge, MA: The MIT Press.

Hartshorne, P. and P. Weiss (1960), *The Collected papers of Charles S. Peirce*, Vols. 1 and 2. Cambridge, MA: The Harvard University Press.

Haugeland, J. (1981), "Semantic Engines: An Introduction to *Mind Design*", in J. Haugeland, ed., *Mind Design* (Cambridge, MA: The MIT Press, 1981), pp. 1-34.

Kleene, S. C. (1967), *Mathematical Logic.* New York, NY: John Wiley & Sons.

Kliban, B. (1982), *Two Guys Fooling Around with the Moon.* New York, NY: Workman Publishing Company.

Marr, D. (1981), "Artificial Intelligence: A Personal View", in J. Haugeland, ed., *Mind Designs* (Cambridge, MA: The MIT Press, 1981), pp. 129-142.

Newell, A. and H. Simon (1976), "Computer Science as Empirical Inquiry: Symbols and Search", reprinted in J. Haugeland, ed., *Mind Design* (Cambridge, MA: The MIT Press, 1981), pp. 35-66.

Penrose, R. (1989), *The Emperor's New Mind*. New York, NY: Oxford University Press.

Schwartz, S., ed. (1977), *Naming, Necessity and Natural Kinds*. Ithaca, NY: Cornell University Press.

Searle, J. R. (1992), *The Rediscovery of the Mind*. Cambridge, MA: The MIT Press.

von Eckhardt, B. (1993), *What is Cognitive Science?* Cambridge, MA: The MIT Press.

PART III

COMPUTER EPISTEMOLOGY

CHAPTER 8

PROGRAM VERIFICATION: THE VERY IDEA

> I hold the opinion that the construction of
> computer programs is a mathematical activity
> like the solution of differential equations, that
> programs can be derived from their specifica-
> tions through mathematical insight, calculation,
> and proof, using algebraic laws as simple and
> elegant as those of elementary arithmetic.
>
> C. A. R. Hoare

There are those, such as Hoare [20], who maintain that computer
programming should strive to become more like mathematics. Others,
such as DeMillo, Lipton and Perlis [8], contend this suggestion is
mistaken because it rests upon a misconception. Their position emphasizes the crucial role of social processes in coming to accept the validity
of a proof or the truth of a theorem, no matter whether within purely
mathematical contexts or without: "We believe that, in the end, it is a
social process that determines whether mathematicians feel confident
about a theorem" [8, p. 271]. As they perceive it, the situation with
respect to program verification is worse insofar as no similar social
process occurs between program verifiers. The use of verification to
guarantee the performance of a program is therefore bound to fail.
Although Hoare's work receives scant attention in their paper, there
should be no doubt that his approach — and that of others, such as E.
W. Dijkstra [10], who share a similar point of view — is the intended
object of their criticism.

Their presentation has aroused enormous interest and considerable
controversy, ranging from unqualified agreement [expressed, for example, by Glazer [13]: "Such an article makes me delight in being . . . a
member of the human race"] to unqualified disagreement [expressed,
for example, by Maurer [28]: "The catalog of criticisms of the idea of
proving a program correct . . . deserves a catalog of responses . . ."].
Indeed, some of the most interesting reactions have come from those
whose position lies somewhere in between, such as van den Bos [37],
who maintains that,

Once one accepts the quasi-empiricism in mathematics, and by analogy in computer science, one can either become an adherent of the Popperian school of conjectures (theories) and refutations [32], or one may believe Kuhn [23], who claims that the fate of scientific theories is decided by a social forum . . .[1]

Perhaps better than any other commentor, van den Bos seems to have put his finger on what may well be the crucial issue raised by [8], namely: if program verification, like mathematical validation, could only occur as the result of a fallible social process, if it could occur at all, then what would distinguish programming procedures from other expert activities, such as judges deciding cases at law and referees reviewing articles for journals? If it is naive to presume that mathematical demonstrations, program verifications and the like are fundamentally distinct from these activities, on what basis can they be differentiated?

The purpose of this article is to investigate the arguments that DeMillo, Lipton and Perlis have presented in an effort to disentangle several issues that seem to have become intricately intertwined. In particular, their position, in part, rests upon a difference in social practice that could change if program verifiers were to modify their behavior. It also depends, in part, upon problems that arise from the complexity of the programs to be verified. There appear to be two quite different kinds of 'program complexity', however, only one of which succumbs to their arguments. Moreover, if program verifiers were to commence collaborating in their endeavors, the principal rationale underlying their position would tend to disappear. Indeed, while social processes are crucial in determining what theorems the mathematical community takes to be true and what proofs it takes to be valid, they do not thereby make them true or valid. The absence of similar social processes in determining which programs are correct, accordingly, does not affect which programs are correct. Nevertheless, there are reasons for doubting whether program verification can succeed as a generally applicable and completely reliable method for guaranteeing the performance of a program. Therefore, it looks as though DeMillo, Lipton and Perlis have offered some bad arguments for some positions that need further elaboration and deserve better support.

MATHEMATICS AS A FALLIBLE SOCIAL PROCESS

> Outsiders see mathematics as a cold, formal, logical, mechanical, monolithic process of sheer intellection; we argue that insofar as it is successful, mathematics is a social, informal, intuitive, organic, human process, a community project.
>
> DeMillo, Lipton and Perlis

The conception of mathematical procedure portrayed by DeMillo, Lipton and Perlis initially drew a distinction between *proofs* and *demonstrations*, where demonstrations are supposed to be long chains of formal logic, while proofs are not. The difference intended here, strictly speaking, appears to be between proofs and what are typically referred to as 'proof sketches', where proof sketches are incomplete (or 'partial') proofs. Indeed, proofs are normally defined in terms of demonstrations, where a proof of theorem T, say, occurs just in case theorem T can be shown to be the last member of a sequence of formulae where every member of that sequence is either given (as an axiom or as an assumption) or else derived from preceding members of that sequence (by relying upon the members of a specified set of rules of inference) [6, p. 182]. In fact, what is known as *mathematical induction* is a special case of the application of demonstrative procedures to infinite sequences, where these processes, which tend to rely upon recursive techniques, are completely deductive [2, p. 169].

Moreover, when DeMillo, Lipton and Perlis offer 'proof sketches' as the objects of mathematicians' attention rather than proofs, it becomes possible to make (good) sense of otherwise puzzling statements such as:

In mathematics, the aim is to increase one's confidence in the correctness of a theorem, and it's true that one of the devices mathematicians could in theory use to achieve this goal is a long chain of formal logic. But in fact they don't. What they use is a proof, a very different animal. Nor does the proof settle the matter; contrary to what its name suggests, a proof is only one step in the direction of confidence. [8, p. 271]

Thus, while a proof, strictly speaking, is a (not necessarily long) chain of formal logic that is no different than a demonstration, a proof sketch is "a very different animal", where a proof sketch, unlike a proof, may often be "only one step in the direction of confidence." Nevertheless, although these reflections offer an interpretation under which their statements appear to be true, it leaves open a larger question, namely: whether the aim of proofs in mathematics can be adequately characterized as that of "increasing one's confidence in the correctness of theorems" rather than as formal demonstrations.

In support of their depiction, DeMillo, Lipton and Perlis emphasize the tentative and fallible character of mathematical progress, where out of some 200,000 theorems said to be published each year, "A number of these are subsequently contradicted or otherwise disallowed, others are thrown into doubt and most are ignored" [8, p. 272]. Since numerous purported proofs are unable to withstand critical scrutiny, they suggest, the acceptability or believability of a specific mathematical result depends upon its reception and ultimate evaluation by the mathematical community. In this spirit, they describe what appears to be a typical sequence of activity within this arena, where, say, a proof begins as an idea in someone's mind, receives translation into a sketch, is discussed with colleagues and, if no substantial objections arise, is developed and submitted for publication, where, if it survives the criticism of other mathematicians, then it tends to be accepted [8, p. 273].

In this sense, the behavior of typical members of the mathematical community in the discovery and promotion of specific findings certainly assumes the dimensions of a social process involving more than one person interacting together to bring about a certain outcome. Although it may be difficult to imagine a Bertrand Russell or a David Hilbert rushing to his colleages for their approval of his findings, there would appear to be no good reasons to doubt that average mathematicians frequently behave in the manner described. Therefore, I would tend to agree that mathematicians' mistakes are typically discovered or corrected through casual interaction with other mathematicians. The restraints imposed by symbolic logic, after all, exert their influence only through their assimilation as habits of thought and as patterns of reasoning by specific members of a community of this kind: discoveries and corrections of mistakes usually occur when one mathematician gently nudges another "in the right direction." (Relevant discussions can be found in [4] and [24].)

To the extent to which DeMillo, Lipton and Perlis should be regarded as endorsing the view that review procedures exercised by colleagues and peers tend to improve the quality of papers that appear in mathematics journals, there seems to be little grounds for disagreement. For potential proofs are often strengthened, theorems altered to correspond to what is provable, and various arguments discovered to be deeply flawed through social interaction. Nevertheless, a community of mathematicians who are fast and sloppy referees is not especially difficult to imagine: where is the university whose faculty do not occasionally compose shoddy and inaccurate reviews — even for very good journals? After all, what makes (what we call) a *proof* a proof is its validity rather than its acceptance (by us) as valid, just as what makes a sentence true is what it asserts to be the case is the case, nor merely that it is believed (by us) and therefore referred to as *true*. Social processing, therefore, is neither necessary nor sufficient for a proof to be valid, as DeMillo, Lipton and Perlis implicitly concede [8, p. 272].

DEDUCTIVE VALIDITY AND PSYCHOLOGICAL CERTAINTY

> . . . a theorem either can or cannot be derived from a set of axioms. I don't believe that the correctness of a theorem is to be decided by a general election.
>
> L. Lamport

Confidence in the truth of a theorem (or in the validity of an argument), of course, appears to be a psychological property of a person-at-a-time: one and the same person at two different times can vary greatly in his confidence over the truth of the same theorem or the validity of the same argument, just as two different persons at the same time might vary greatly in their confidence that that same theorem is true or that that same argument is valid. Indeed, there is nothing inconsistent about scenarios in which, say, someone is completely confident that a specific formula is a theorem (when it happens to be false) or else completely uncertain whether a particular argument is valid (when it happens to be valid). No doubt, mathematicians are sometimes driven to discover demonstrations of theorems after they are already completely convinced of their truth. Demonstrations, in such cases, cannot increase the degree of confidence when that degree is already maximally strong. But that is not to deny they can still fulfill other — non-psychological — functions, such as providing objective evidence of the truth of one's subjective belief.

From the point of view of a traditional theory of knowledge, the role of demonstration becomes readily apparent; for the classical conception of knowledge characterizes 'knowledge' in terms of three necessary and sufficient conditions as warranted, true belief (for example [7, ch. 2]). Hence, an individual z who is in a state of belief with respect to a certain formula f, where z believes that f is a theorem, say, cannot be properly qualified as possessing knowledge that f is a theorem unless his belief can be supported by means of reasons, evidence, or warrants, which might be one or another of three different kinds, depending upon the nature of the objects that might be known. For results in logic and mathematics fall within the domain of deductive methodology and require demonstrations. Lawful and causal claims fall within the domain of empirical inquiries and require inductive warrants. Observational and experimental findings fall within the domain of perceptual investigations and acquire support on the basis of direct sense experience.[2]

With respect to deductions, the term *verification* can be used in two rather different senses. One of these occurs in pure mathematics and in pure logic, in which theorems of mathematics and of logic are subject to demonstration. These theorems characterize claims that are always true as a function of the meanings assigned to the specific symbols by means of which they are expressed. Theorem-schemata and theorems in this sense are subject to verfication by deriving them from no premises at all (within systems of natural deduction) or from primitive axioms (within axiomatic formal systems).[3] The other occurs in ordinary reasoning and in scientific contexts in general, whenever *conclusions* are shown to follow from specific sets of *premises*, where there is no presumption that these conclusions might be derived from no premises at all or that those premises should be true as a function of their meaning. Thus, within a system of natural deduction or an axiomatic formal system, the members of the class of consequences that can be derived from no premises at all or that follow from primitive axioms alone may be said to be *absolutely* verifiable. By contrast those members of the class of consequences that can only be derived relative to specific sets of premises whose truth is not absolutely verifiable, may be said to be *relatively* verifiable.[4]

The difference between absolute and relative verifiability, moreover, is extremely important for the theory of knowledge. For theorems that can be verified in the absolute sense cannot be false, so long as the rules are not changed or the axioms are not altered. But conclusions that are verified in the relative sense can still be false (even when the premises and the rules remain the same). The absolute verification of a theorem thus satisfies both necessary and sufficient conditions for its warranted acceptance as true, but the relative verification of a conclusion does not. Indeed, as an epistemic policy, the degree of confidence that anyone should invest in the conclusion of an argument should never exceed the degree of confidence that ought to be invested in its premises — even when it is valid! Unless the premises of an argument cannot be false — unless those premises themselves are absolutely verifiable — it is a mistake to assume the conclusion of a valid argument cannot be false. No more can appropriately be claimed than that its conclusion must be true if all its premises are true, which is the defining property of a valid demonstration.

CONSTRUCTING PROOFS AND VERIFYING PROGRAMS

> Formal proofs carry with them a certain objectivity. That a proof is formalizable, that the formal proofs have the structural properties that they do, explains in part why proofs are convincing to mathematicians.
>
> T. Tymoczko

The truth of the conclusion of a valid deductive argument, therefore, can never be more certain than the truth of its premises — unless its truth can be established on other grounds. While deductive reasoning preserves the truth (insofar as the conclusion of a valid argument cannot be false if its premises are true), the truth of those premises can be guaranteed, in general, only under those special circumstances that arise when they themselves are verifiable in the absolute sense. Otherwise, the truth of the premises of any argument has to be established on independent grounds, which might be deductive, inductive or perceptual. Yet none of these types of warrants provides an infallible foundation for any inference to the truth of the conclusions they support. Perhaps few of us would be inclined to think that our senses are infallible, i.e. that things must always be the way they appear to be. The occurrence of illusions, hallucinations and delusions disabuses us of that particular fantasy. The mistakes we make about reasoning are far more likely to occur concerning inductive and deductive arguments, whose features are frequently not clearly understood. We should not overlook that, apart from imagination and conjecture, which serve as sources of ideas but do not establish their truth, all of our states of knowledge — other than those of pure mathematics and logic — are ultimately dependent for their support upon direct and indirect connections to experience.

The features that distinguish (good) deductive arguments are the following:

(a) they are *demonstrative*, i.e. if their premises were true, their conclusions could not be false (without contradiction);

(b) they are *non-ampliative*, i.e. there is no information or content in their conclusions that is not already contained in their premises; and,

(c) they are *additive*, i.e. the addition of further information in the form of additional premises can neither strengthen nor weaken these arguments, which are already maximally strong.

Thus, the non-ampliative property of (good) deductive arguments can serve to explain both their demonstrative and additive characteristics. Demonstrative arguments, of course, are said to be 'valid', while valid arguments with true premises are said to be 'sound' (and cannot possibly have false conclusions).[5]

Compared to deductive arguments, (good) inductive arguments are (a) *non-demonstrative*, (b) *ampliative*, and (c) *non-additive*. Arguments satisfying appropriate inductive standards likewise should be said to be 'proper', while proper arguments with true premises may be said to be 'correct' (but can have conclusions that are false even when their premises are true). It should come as no surprise, therefore, that the purposes served by such different types of arguments are quite distinct, indeed. For inductive arguments are meant to be *knowledge-expanding*, while deductive arguments are meant to be *truth-preserving*. The ways in which inductive arguments expand our knowledge assume various forms. Reasoning from samples to populations, from the observed to the unobserved and from the past to the future always involves drawing inferences to conclusions that contain more information or content than do their premises. The most familiar instances of inductive reasoning we all employ in our daily lives concern the behavior of ordinary physical things — things that may or may not work right, fit properly, or function smoothly (such as electrical appliances, including microwave ovens and personal computers). When we interact with systems such as these, we invariably base our expectations upon our experience: we draw conclusions concerning their behavior in the future from their behavior in the past. All such reasoning is ampliative and — as we all too often discover to our dismay — is both non-demonstrative and non-additive.

The function of a program, of course, is to convey instructions to a computer. Most programs today are written in high-level programming languages, such as Pascal, LISP and Prolog, which simulate 'abstract machines', whose instructions can be more readily composed than can those of the machines that ultimately execute them. Thus, a source program written in a high-level language is translated into an equivalent low-level 'object program' written in machine language either directly, by an interpreter; or indirectly, by a compiler. The 'target machine' then executes the object program when instructed to do so. If programs are verifiable, therefore, then they must be subject to deductive procedures. Indeed, precisely this conception is advanced by [19, p. 576]:

Computer programming is an exact science in that all the properties of a program and all the consequences of executing it can, in principle, be found out from the text of the program itself by means of purely deductive reasoning.

Thus, if programs are absolutely verifiable, then there must exist some *program rules of inference* or *primitive program axioms* permitting inferences to be drawn concerning the performance that a machine will display when such a program is executed. If they are relatively verifiable, then there must be sets of premises concerning the text of such a program from which it is possible to derive conclusions concerning the performance that that machine will display when that program is executed. If these conditions cannot be satisfied, however, then the very idea of program verification will have been misconceived.

SOCIAL PROCESSES AND PROGRAM VERIFICATIONS

> We do not argue that strict logical deduction should be the only way that mathematics should be done, or even that it should come first; rather, it should come last, after the theorems to be proved, and their proofs, are well understood.
>
> W. D. Maurer

The critical dimension of deduction and induction, furthermore, is the justification of corresponding classes of rules as acceptable principles of inference. For, in their absence, it would be impossible to ascertain which, among all those arguments that — rightly or wrongly — are supposed to be valid or proper, actually are. Within this domain, "thinking doesn't make it so." The fact that a community of mathematicians happens to agree upon the validity of an argument or the truth of a theorem, alas, no more guarantees the validity of that argument or the truth of that theorem than agreement within a society of observers that the Earth is flat (for which a variety of mutually convincing arguments are advanced) could guarantee that that belief is true. In the absence of classes of rules of inference whose acceptability can be justified, in other words, validity and propriety are merely subjective properties of arguments insofar as specific persons happen to hold them in high esteem, where their standing may vary from person to person and from time to time.

Since computer programs, like mathematical proofs, are syntactical entities consisting of sequences of lines (strings of signs and the like), they both appear to be completely formalized entities for which completely formal procedures appear to be appropriate. Yet programs differ from theorems, at least to the extent to which programs are supposed to possess a semantic significance that theorems seem to lack. For the sequences of lines that compose a program are intended to stand for operations and procedures that can be performed by a machine, whereas the sequences of lines that constitute a proof do not.[6] Even if the social acceptability of a mathematical proof is neither necessary nor sufficient for its validity, the suggestion might be made that the existence of social processes of program verification may actually be even more important for the success of this endeavor than it is for validating proofs. The reason that could be advanced in support of this position is the opportunity that such practices would provide for more than one programmer to inspect a program for a suitable relationship between its syntax and its intended semantics, i.e. the behavior expected of the machine.

There are no reasons for believing that DeMillo, Lipton and Perlis are mistaken in their observation that the verification of programs is not a popular pastime [8]. The argument we are considering thus serves to reinforce the importance of this disparity in behavior between the members of the mathematical community and the members of the programming fraternity. Their position implicitly presumes that programmers are inherently unlikely to collaborate on the verification of programs, if only because it is such a tedious and complex activity. Suppose, however, that conditions within society were to change in certain direct and obvious ways, say that substantial financial rewards were offered for the best team efforts in verifying programs, with prizes of up to $10,000,000 awarded by Ed McMahon and guest appearances on *The Tonight Show*. Surely under circumstances of this kind, the past tendency of program verifiers to engage in solitary enterprise might be readily overcome, resulting in the emergence of a new wave in program verification, "the collaborative verification group," dedicated to mutual efforts by more than one programmer to verify particular programs. Surely under these conditions — which are not completely far-fetched in the context of modern times — a social process for the verification of programs could emerge within the computer science community that would be the counterpart to the social process for the validation of proofs in mathematics. Under these circumstances, there would not be any difference of this kind.

If this were to come about, then the primary assumption underlying the position of DeMillo, Lipton and Perlis would no longer apply. Regardless of what other differences might distinguish them, in this respect their social processing of theorems and of programs would be the same. If we refer to differences between subjects or activities that could not be overcome, no matter what efforts we might undertake, as differences 'in principle', and to those that could be overcome, by making appropriate efforts, as differences 'in practice', then it should be obvious that DeMillo, Lipton and Perlis have identified a difference in practice that is not also a difference in principle. What this means is that to the extent to which their position depends upon this difference, it represents no more than a contingent, *de facto* state-of-affairs that might be a mere transient stage in the development of program verification within the computer science community. If there is an 'in principle' difference between them, it must lie elsewhere, because divergence in social practice is a difference that could be overcome.

THE CONCEPTION OF PROBABILISTIC PROOFS

If proofs bear little resemblance to formal deductive reasoning, if they can stand for generations and then fall, if they can contain flaws that defy detection, if they can express

> only the probability of truth within certain
> error bounds — if they are, in fact, not able to
> prove theorems in the sense of guaranteeing
> them beyond probability and, if necessary,
> beyond insight, well, then, how does mathe-
> matics work?
>
>   DeMillo, Lipton and Perlis

When DeMillo, Lipton and Perlis [8, p. 273] advance the position that "a proof can, at best, only probably express truth," therefore, it is important to discover exactly what they mean, since proofs are deductive and accordingly enjoy the virtues of demonstrations. There are several alternatives. In the first place, this claim might reflect the differences that obtain between proofs and proof sketches, insofar as incomplete or partial proofs do not satisfy the same objective standards — and therefore need not convey the same subjective certainty — as do complete proofs. In the second place, it might reflect the fallibility of acceptance of the premises of such an argument — which could be valid yet have at least one false premise and therefore be unsound — because of which acceptance of its conclusion would be tempered with uncertainty as well. While both of these ideas find expression in their article, however, their principal contention appears to be of a rather different character altogether.

Thus, DeMillo, Lipton and Perlis distinguish between the 'classicists' and the 'probabilists', where classicists maintain that:

... when one believes mathematical statement A, one believes that in principle there is a correct, formal, valid, step by step, syntactically checkable deduction leading to A in a suitable logical calculus ...

which is a complete proof lying behind a proof sketch as the object of acceptance or of belief. Probabilists, by comparison, instead maintain that:

... since any very long proof can at best be viewed as only probably correct, why not state theorems probabilistically and give probabilistic proofs? The probabilistic proof may have the dual advantage of being technically easier than the classical, bivalent one, and may allow mathematicians to isolate the critical ideas that give rise to uncertainty in traditional, binary proofs.

Thus, in application to proofs or to proof sketches, there appear to be three elements to this position: first, that long proofs are difficult to follow; second, that probabilistic proofs are easier to follow; and, third, that probabilistic proofs may disclose the problematic aspects of ordinary proofs. Rabin's algorithm for testing probable prime numbers is offered as an illustration, where, "if you are willing to settle for a very good probability that N is prime (or not prime), then you can get it within a reasonable amount of time — and with (a) vanishingly small probability of error."

Their reference to "traditional, binary proofs" is important insofar as traditional proofs (in the classical sense) are supposed to be either valid or invalid: there is nothing 'probable' about them. Therefore, I take DeMillo, Lipton and Perlis to be endorsing an alternative conception, according to which arguments are amenable to various measures of strength (or corresponding 'degrees of conviction'), which might be represented by, say, some number between zero and one inclusively, with some of the properties associated with probabilities, likelihoods, or whatever [11, Part III]. A hypothetical scale could be constructed accordingly, such that degrees of partial support of measures zero and one for instance are distinguished from worthless fallacies (whose premises, for example. might be completely irrelevant to their conclusions), on the one hand. and from demonstrative arguments (the truth of whose premises guarantees the truth of their conclusions), on the other, as extreme cases not representing *partial* support (Figure 1).

From this perspective. the existence of even a 'vanishingly small' probability of error is essential to a probabilistic proof. If there were no probability of error at all a proof could not be probabilistic. Thus, if the commission of an error were either a necessity (as in the case of a fallacy of irrelevance) or an impossibility (as in the case of valid demon-

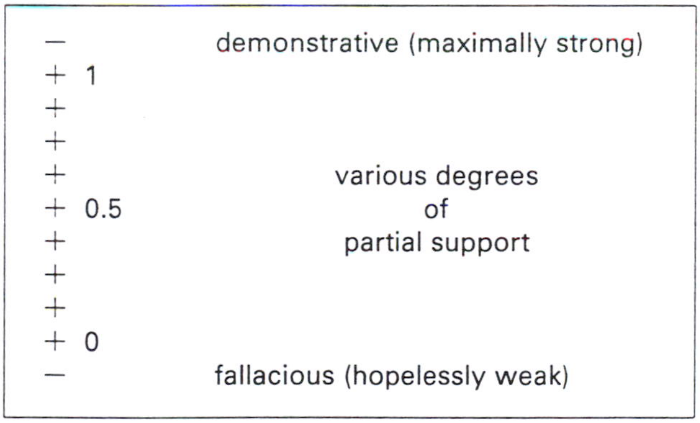

```
 —          demonstrative (maximally strong)
 + 1
 +
 +
 +              various degrees
 + 0.5               of
 +              partial support
 +
 +
 + 0
 —          fallacious (hopelessly weak)
```

Fig. 1. A measure of evidential support.

stration), then an argument would have to be other than probabilistic. Indeed, the existence of fallacies of irrelevance exemplifies an important point discussed above: fallacious arguments, though logically flawed, can nevertheless exert enormous persuasive appeal — otherwise, we would not have to learn how to detect and avoid them [29, Ch 10]. But, if this is the case, then DeMillo, Lipton and Perlis, when appropriately understood, are advocating a conception of mathematics according to which (a) classical proofs are practically impossible (so that demonstrations are not ordinarily available), yet (b) worthless fallacies are still unacceptable (so that our conclusions are nevertheless supported). This position strongly suggests the possibility that DeMillo, Lipton and Perlis should be viewed as advocating the conception of mathematics as a domain of inductive procedure.

When consideration is given to the distinguishing characteristics of inductive arguments, this interpretation seems to fit their position quite well. As stated earlier, inductive arguments are (a) nondemonstrative, (b) ampliative, and (c) nonadditive. This means (a) that their conclusions can be false even when their premises are true (permitting the possibility of error); (b) that their conclusions contain some information or content not already contained in their premises (otherwise they would not be nondemonstrative); and, (c) the addition of further evidence in the form of additional premises can either strengthen or weaken these arguments (whether that evidence is discovered days, months, years or centuries later). Thus, in accepting the primality of some very large number N probabilistically, for example, one goes beyond the content contained in the premises (which do not guarantee the truth of that conclusion) and runs a risk of error (which cannot be avoided with probabilistic reasoning). Yet one thereby possesses evidence in support of the truth of such a conclusion, so that its acceptance is warranted to some degree. After all, that might be the best we can do.

MATHEMATICAL PROOFS AND PROBABLE VERIFICATIONS

> Mathematical proofs increase our confidence in the truth of mathematical statements only after they have been subjected to the social mechanisms of the mathematical community. These same mechanisms doom the so-called proofs of software, the long formal verifications that correspond, not to the working

> mathematical proof, but to the imaginary
> logical structure that the mathematician con-
> jures up to describe his feeling of belief.
>
> DeMillo, Lipton and Perlis

Indeed, whether or not we can do better appears to be at the heart of the controversy surrounding this position. DeMillo, Lipton and Perlis, after all, do not explicitly deny the existence of classical bivalent proofs (although they recommend probabilistic proofs as more appropriate to their subject matter). Moreover, they implicitly concede the existence of classical bivalent proofs (insofar as the pursuit of probabilistic proofs may even lead to their discovery). They even go so far as to suggest the social processing of a probabilistic proof, like that of a traditional proof, can involve "enough internalization, enough transformation, enough generalization, enough use, . . ." that the mathematical community accepts it as correct: "The theorem is thought to be true in the classical sense — that is, in the sense that it could be demonstrated by formal, deductive logic, although for almost all theorems no such deduction ever took place or ever will" [8, pp. 273—274].

The force of their position appears to derive from the complexity that confronts those who would attempt to undertake mathematical proofs and program verifications. They report a formal demonstration of a conjecture by Ramanujan would require 2000 pages to formalize. They lament that Russell and Whitehead "in three enormous, taxing volumes, (failed) to get beyond the elementary facts of arithmetic." These specific examples may be subject to dispute: for Ramanujan's conjecture, precisely how is such a fanciful estimate supposed to be derived and verified? For Russell and Whitehead, is *Principia Mathematica* therefore supposed to be a failure? And yet their basic point ("The lower bounds on the length of formal demonstrations for mathematical theorems are immense and there is no reason to believe that such demonstrations for programs would be any shorter or clearer — quite the contrary") nevertheless merits serious consideration.

One of the most important ambiguities to arise within this context emerges at this juncture. While DeMillo, Lipton and Perlis [8, p. 278] suggest that the *scaling-up argument* (the contention that very complex programs and proofs can be broken down into much simpler programs and proofs for the purposes of verification and of demonstration) is the best the other side can produce, they want to deny it should be taken seriously insofar as it is supposed to depend upon an untenable assumption:

The scaling-up argument seems to be based on the fuzzy notion that the world of programming is like the world of Newtonian physics — made up of smooth, continuous functions. But, in fact, programs are jagged and full of holes and caverns. Every programmer knows that altering a line or sometimes even a bit can utterly destroy a program or mutilate it in ways that we do not understand and cannot predict.

Indeed, since this argument is supposed to be the best argument in defense of the verificationist position, what they call "the discontinuous nature of programming" is said to sound "the death knell for verification."

Maurer has strenuously objected to their complaints that the verification of one program can never be transferred to any other program ("even to a program only one single line different from the original") and that there are no grounds to suppose that the verification of a large program could be broken down into smaller parts ("there is no reason to believe that a big verification can be the sum of many small verifications") [28, p. 278]. In response, he has observed that, while the modification of a correct program can produce an incorrect one for which "no amount of verification can prove it correct" and while minute changes in correct programs can produce "wildly erratic behavior .... if only a single bit is changed," that does not affect the crucial result, namely: that proofs of the correctness of a program can be transferred to other programs, when those other programs are carefully controlled modifications of the original program, if not in whole then at least in part. Indeed, quite frequently, "if a program is broken up into a main program and n subroutines, we have $n + 1$ verifications to do, and that is all we have to do in proving program correctness."

CUMULATIVE COMPLEXITY AND PATCH-WORK COMPLEXITY

> ... verifications cannot be internalized, transformed, generalized, used, connected to other disciplines, and eventually incorporated into a community consciousness. They cannot acquire gradual credibility, as a mathematical theorem does; one either believes them blindly, as a pure act of faith, or not at all.
>
> DeMillo, Lipton and Perlis

DeMillo, Lipton and Perlis, however, cannot be quite so readily dismissed, for their contentions on behalf of their position are quite intriguing:

> No programmer would agree that large production systems are composed of nothing more than algorithms and small programs. Patches, *ad hoc* constructions. Band-Aids and tourniquets, bells and whistles, glue, spit and polish, signature code, blood-sweat-and-tears, and, of course, the kitchen sink — the colorful jargon of the practicing programmer seems to be saying something about the nature of the structures he works with; maybe theoreticians ought to be listening to him. [8, p. 277]

Thus, it appears to be because most real software tends to consist of a lot of error messages and user interfaces — *ad hoc*, informal structures that are by definition 'unverifiable' — that they want to view the verificationist position as so far removed from the realities of programming life. But I think the strong arguments advanced on both sides of this issue suggest that two different concepts may be intimately intertwined that should be unraveled, where these involve differing dimensions of the nature of program complexity.

Maurer's position, for example, tends to support the view of complexity according to which more complex programs consist of less complex programs interacting according to some specific arrangement, a conception that is quite compatible with the scaling-up argument that DeMillo, Lipton and Perlis are inclined to disparage. This conception of complexity might be described as:

(C1)   Cumulative Complexity $=_{df}$
       the complexity of larger programs arising when they consist of (relatively straightforward) arrangements of smaller programs;

as opposed to an alternative conception of complexity that is quite different:

(C2)   Patch-Work Complexity $=_{df}$
       the complexity of larger programs arising when they consist of complicated, *ad hoc*, peculiar arrangements of smaller programs;

where the verificationist attitude appears to be appropriate to cumulative complexity, but far less adequate (perhaps hopelessly inappropriate) for cases of patch-work complexity, while the anti-verificationist attitude appears to have the opposite virtues in relation to cases of both of these kinds, respectively. Thus, the differences that distinguish large from small programs in the case of cumulative complexity tend to be differences of degree, whereas the differences that distinguish cumulative from patch-work complexity are differences in kind.[7]

If this reconstruction of the situation is approximately correct, then the verificationist approach, in principle, would appear to apply to small programs and to large programs when they exemplify cumulative complexity. However, it would not apply — or, at best, only in part — to those that exhibit patch-work complexity. Moreover, the *in principle* qualification is important here, because DeMillo, Lipton and Perlis offer reasons to doubt that large programs are or ever will be subject to verification, even when they are not 'patch-work programs':

> The verification of even a puny program can run into dozens of pages, and there's not a light moment or a spark of wit on any of those pages. Nobody is going to run into a friend's office with a program verification. Nobody is going to sketch a verification out on a paper napkin. Nobody is going to buttonhole a colleague into listening to a verification. Nobody is ever going to read it. One can feel one's eyes glaze over at the very thought. [8, p. 276]

This enchanting passage is almost enough to beguile one into the belief that a program verification is among the most boring and insipid of all the world's objects. Yet even if that were true — even if it destroys all our prospects for a social process of program verification parallel to that found in mathematics — it would not establish the potential for their production as pointless and without value, if its purpose is properly understood.

Indeed, one of the most important insights that can be gleaned from reviewing this debate is an appreciation of the role of formal demonstrations in both mathematical and in programming contexts. For while it is perfectly appropriate for DeMillo, Lipton and Perlis to accentuate the historical truth that the vast majority of mathematical theorems and computer programs will never be subjected to the exquisite pleasures of formal validation or of program verification, it remains enormously important, as a theoretical possibility, that those theorems and programs could have been or could still be subjected to the critical scrutiny that such a thorough examination would provide. Indeed, from this point of view, the theoretical possibility of subjecting them to rigorous appraisal ought to be regarded as more important than its actual exercise. For it is this potentiality, whether or not it is actually exercised, that affords an objective foundation for the intersubjective evaluation of knowledge claims: z knows that something is the case only when z's belief that that is the case can be supported deductively, inductively, or whatever, not as something that has been done but as something that could be done were it required. This may be called 'an examiner's view' of knowledge [14, p. 319].[8]

THEOREMS, ALGORITHMS, AND PROGRAMS

> Lamport and Maurer display an amazing inability to distinguish between algorithms and programs.
>
> DeMillo, Lipton and Perlis

The argument that has gone before, however, depends upon an assumption that DeMillo, Lipton and Perlis seem to be unwilling to grant: the presumption that programs are like theorems from a certain point of view. That some analogy exists between theorems and programs is a tempting inference, not least of all given their own analogy with mathematics. In Table I we begin with the most seemingly obvious comparison one might make. Thus, from this perspective, proofs are to theorems as verifications are to programs — demonstrations of their truth or correctness.[9] (To avoid ambiguity, we will assume the correctness of a program means 'program correctness' rather than 'specification correctness', even though, in other contexts, specification correctness is important as well. Our concern here is whether or not a program satisfies a certain set of specifications instead of whether those specifications are something a user may want to change at any point.)

This analogy, however, might not be as satisfactory as it initially appears. If we consider that programs can be viewed as functions from

TABLE I
A plausible analogy

	Mathematics	Programming
Objects of Inquiry:	Theorems	Programs
Methods of Inquiry:	Proofs	Verifications

inputs to outputs, the features of mathematical proofs that serve as counterparts to inputs, outputs, and programs, respectively, are premises, conclusions, and rules of inference. Thus, in lieu of the plausible analogy with which we began, a more adequate conception emerges in Table II, where the acceptability of this analogy itself depends upon interpreting programs as well as rules of inference as functions (from a domain into a range). This analogy is still compatible with the first, however, so long as it is understood that rules of inference are used to derive theorems from premises, whereas programs are used to derive outputs from inputs. Thus, to the extent to which establishing that a certain theorem follows from certain premises (using certain rules of inference) is like establishing a certain output is generated by a certain input (by a certain program), proving a theorem is indeed like verifying a program.

TABLE II
A more likely analogy

	Mathematics	Programming
Domain:	Premises	Input
Function:	Rules of inference	Programs
Range:	Theorems	Output

In order to discern the deeper disanalogy between these activities, therefore, it is necessary to realize that while algorithms satisfy the conditions previously specified (of qualifying as functions from a domain to a range), programs need not do so. One reason, of course, emerges from considerations of complexity, especially when programs are patch-work complex programs, because programs of this kind have idiosyncratic features that make a difference to the performance of those programs, yet are not readily amenable to deductive procedures. The principal claim advanced by DeMillo, Lipton and Perlis (with respect to the issue here), is that patch-work complex programs have *ad hoc*, informal aspects such as error messages and user interfaces, that are unverifiable 'by definition' [8, p. 227]. In cases of this kind, presumably, no axioms relating these special features of specific programs to their performance when executed are available, making verification impossible.

A more general reason, however, arises from features of other programs that are obviously intended to bring about the performance of special tasks by the machines that execute them. Illustrations of such tasks include the input and output behavior that is supposed to result as a causal consequence of their execution. Thus, the IBM PC manual for Microsoft BASIC defines various 'I/O Statements' in the following fashion:[10]

(A)   **Statement:**   **Action:**
        BEEP   Beeps the speaker.
        CIRCLE (x, y) r Draws a circle with center x, y and radius r.
        COLOR b, p In graphics mode, sets background color and pallette of foreground colors.
        LOCATE row, col   Positions the cursor.
        PLAY   string   Plays music as specified by string.

Although these 'statement' commands are expected to produce their corresponding 'action' effects, it should not be especially surprising that prospects for their verification are problematic.

Advocates of program verification, however, might argue that commands like these are special cases. They are amenable to verification procedures; not in the sense of absolute verifiability, but rather in the sense of relative verifiability. The programs in which these commands appear could be subject to verification, provided special 'causal axioms' are available relating the execution of these commands to the performance of the corresponding tasks. The third reason, therefore, ought to be even more disturbing for advocates of program verification. For it should be evident that even the simplest and most commonplace program implicitly possesses precisely the same causal character. Consider, for example, the following program, simple, written in Pascal:

(B)   program simple (output);
        begin
            writeln ('2 + 2 =', 2 + 2);
        end

This program, of course, instructs the machine to write '2 + 2 =' on a line followed by its solution '4' on the same line. For either of these outcomes to occur, however, obviously depends upon various different causal factors, including the characteristics of the compiler, the processor, the printer, the paper and every other component whose specific features influence the execution of such a program.

Taking all together, these considerations support the theoretical necessity to distinguish programs as encodings of algorithms from the logical structures that they represent. A program, after all, is a particular implementation of an algorithm in a form that is suitable for execution by a machine. In this sense, program, unlike an algorithm, qualifies as a causal model of a logical structure of which a specific algorithm may be a specific instance. The consequences of this realization are enormous, insofar as causal models of logical structures need not have the same properties that characterize those logical structures themselves. Algorithms, rather than programs, thus appear to be the appropriate candidates for analogies with *pure mathematics*, while programs bear comparison with *applied mathematics*. Propositions in applied mathematics, unlike those in pure mathematics, run the risk of observational and experimental disconfirmation.

From this point of view, it becomes possible to appreciate why De-Millo, Lipton and Perlis accentuate the role of program testing as follows:

It seems to us that the only potential virtue of program proving [verification] lies in the hope of obtaining perfection. If one now claims that a proof of correctness can raise confidence, even though it is not perfect or that an incomplete proof can help one locate errors, that that claim must be verified! There is absolutely no objective evidence that program verification is as effective as, say, *ad hoc* theory testing in this regard.

If not for the presumption that programs are not algorithms in some fundamental respects, these remarks would be very difficult — if not impossible — to understand. But when the assumption is made that,

(D1)   algorithm = $_{df}$
        — a logical structure of the type function suitable for the
          derivation of outputs when given inputs;

(D2)   program = $_{df}$
        — a causal model of an algorithm obtained by implement-
          ing that function in a form that is suitable for execution
          by a machine;

it is no longer difficult to understand why they should object to the conception of program verification as an inappropriate and unjustifiable exportation of a deductive procedure applicable to theorems and to algorithms for the purpose of evaluating causal models that are executed by machine.[11]

ABSTRACT MACHINES VERSUS TARGET MACHINES

> I find digital computers of the present day to be very complicated and rather poorly defined. As a result, it is usually impractical to reason logically about their behavior. Sometimes, the only way of finding out what they will do is by experiment. Such experiments are certainly not mathematics. Unfortunately, they are not even science, because it is impossible to generalize from their results or to publish them for the benefit of other scientists.
>
> C. A. R. Hoare

The conception of computer programs as causal models and the difference between programs and algorithms deserve elaboration, especially insofar as there are various senses in which something might or might not qualify as a program or as a causal model. The concept of a program is highly ambiguous, since the term 'program' may be used to refer to (i) algorithms, (ii) encodings of algorithms, (iii) encodings of algorithms that can be compiled, or (iv) encodings of algorithms that can be compiled and executed by a machine. There are other program senses as well.[12] As an effective decision procedure, an algorithm is more abstract than is a program, insofar as the same algorithm might be implemented in different forms suitable for execution by various machines by using different languages. From this perspective, the senses of program defined by (ii), (iii) and (iv) provide conceptual benefits that the sense defined by (i) does not. Indeed, were 'program' defined by sense (i), programs could not fail to be verifiable.

The second sense is of special importance within this context, especially in view of the distinction between 'abstract machines' and 'target machines'. As noted earlier, source programs are written in high-level languages that simulate abstract machines, whose instructions can be more readily composed than can those of the target machines that ultimately execute them. It is entirely possible, in sense (ii), to envision the composition of a program as involving no more than the encoding of an algorithm in a programming language, no matter whether that program is now or ever will be executed by a machine or not. Indeed, it might be said that the composition of a program involves no more than the encoding of an algorithm in a programming language, even if that language cannot be executed by any machine at all. An instance of this state-of-affairs, moreover, is illustrated by the mini-language CORE, introduced by Marcotty and Ledgard [27] as a means for explaining the features characteristic of programming languages in general, without encountering the complexities involved in discussions of Pascal, LISP and so on. In cases of this kind, these languages may reflect properties of abstract machines for which there exist no actual target machine counterparts.

The crucial difference between programs in senses (i) and (ii) and programs in senses (iii) and (iv), therefore, is that (i) and (ii) can be satisfied merely by reference to abstract machines, whereas (iii) and (iv) require the existence of target machines. In the case of a mini-language like CORE, it might be argued that the abstract machine is the target machine. But this contention overlooks the difference at stake here because an abstract machine no more qualifies as a machine than an artificial flower qualifies as a flower. Compilers, interpreters, processors and the like are properly characterized as *physical things*, i.e. as systems in space/time for which causal relations obtain. Abstract machines are properly characterized as *abstract entities*, i.e. as systems not in space/time for which only logical relations obtain. It follows that, in sense (i) and (ii), the intended interpretations of programs are abstract machines that are not supposed to have physical machine counterparts. But in senses (iii) and (iv), the intended interpretations of programs are abstract machines that are supposed to have physical machine counterparts. And this difference is crucial: it corresponds to the intended difference between definitions (D1) and (D2).

On the basis of these distinctions, it should be evident that algorithms — and programs in senses (i) and (ii) — are subject to absolute verification by means of deductive procedures. This possibility occurs because the properties of abstract machines that have no physical machine counterparts can be established by definition, i.e. through stipulations or conventions, which might be formalized either by means of program rules of interference or by means of primitive program axioms. In this sense, the abstract machine under consideration simply *is* the abstract entities and relations thereby specified. By comparison, programs in senses (iii) and (iv) are merely subject to relative verification, at best, by means of deductive procedures. Their differences from algorithms arise precisely because, in these cases, the properties of the abstract machines they represent, in turn, stand for physical machines whose properties can only be established inductively. With programs, unlike algorithms, there are no 'program rules of inference' or 'primitive program axioms' whose truth is ascertainable by definition.

In either case, however, all these rules and axioms relate the occurrence of an input I to the occurrence of an output O, which can be written in the form of claims that input I causes output O more or less as follows:

(C) $I \ c \ O$;

thus, given this rule or axiom, the occurrence of output O may be inferred from the occurrence of input I together with a rule or axiom of that form:

(D)   From '$I \ c \ O$' and 'I' infer to 'O;'

thus, from axiom or rule '$I \ c \ O$' and input 'I', output 'O' validly follows. The difference between algorithms and programs, from this point of view, is that patterns of reasoning of form (D) are absolutely verifiable in the case of algorithms but are only relatively verifiable in the case of programs — a difference that reflects the fact that claims of form (C) can be established by deductive procedures as definitional stipulations with respect to algorithms, but can only be ascertained by inductive procedures, as lawful or causal generalizations, in the case of programs, thus understood.

THE VERY IDEA OF PROGRAM VERIFICATION

> When the correctness of a program, its compiler, and the hardware of the computer have all been established with mathematical certainty, it will be possible to place great reliance on the results of the program, and predict their properties with a confidence limited only by the reliability of the electronics.
>
> C. A. R. Hoare

When entertained from this point of view, the fundamental difficulty encountered in attempting to apply deductive methodology to the verification of programs does not appear to arise from either the idiosyncracy of various features of those programs or from the inclusion of instructions for special tasks to be performed. Both types of cases can be envisioned as matters that can be dealt with by introducing special rules and special axioms that correspond to either the *ad hoc* features of those patch-work complex programs or to the special behavior that is supposed to be exhibited in response to special commands. The specific inputs '*I*' and the specific outputs '*O*', after all, can be taken to cover these special kinds of cases. Let us therefore take this for granted in order to provide the strongest case possible for the verificationist position and thereby avoid any chance of being charged with having attacked a straw man.

As we discovered, the crucial problem confronting program verification is establishing the truth of claims of form (C) above, which might be done in two possible ways. The first is to interpret rules and axioms of form (C) as definitional truths concerning the abstract machine thereby defined. The other is to interpret rules and axioms of form (C) as empirical claims concerning the possible behavior of the target machine thereby described. Interpreted in the first way, the performance of an abstract machine can be conclusively verified, but it possesses no significance at all for the performance of any physical system. Interpreted in the second way, the performance of an abstract machine possesses significance for the performance of a physical system, but it cannot be conclusively verified. And the reason, by now, should be obvious; for programs are subject to 'relative' rather than 'absolute' verification, in relation to 'rules and axioms' in the form of lawful and causal generalizations as premises — empirical claims whose truth can never be established with certainty!

The very idea of program verification trades upon an equivocation. Interpreted in senses (i) and (ii), there is no special difficulty that arises in 'verifying' that output O follows from input I as a logical consequence of axioms of the form, I c O. Under such an interpretation, however, nothing follows from the verification of a 'program' concerning the performance of any physical machine. In this case, the absolute verification of an abstract machine is theoretically possible and is not particularly problematic. Interpreted in senses (iii) and (iv), however, that output O follows from input I as a logical consequence of axioms of the form, I c O, cannot be subject to absolute verification, precisely because the truth of these axioms depends upon the causal properties of physical systems, whose presence or absence is only ascertainable by means of inductive procedures. In this case, the absolute verification of an abstract machine is logically impossible because its intended interpretation is a target machine whose behavior might not be described by those axioms, whose truth can only be established by induction.

This conclusion strongly suggests the conception of programming as a mathematical activity requires qualification in order to be justified. For while it follows from the axioms for the theory of natural numbers that, say,

(E) $2 + 2 = 4$;

the application of that proposition — which may be true of the abstract domain to which its intended interpretation refers — for the purpose of describing the causal behavior of physical things like alcohol and water need not remain true:

(F)   2 units of water + 2 units or alcohol = 4 units of mixture.

For while the abstract proposition (E) is true, the empirical proposition (F) is false. The difference involved here is precisely that between *pure* mathematics and *applied* mathematics.[13] When the function of a program is merely to satisfy the constraints imposed by an abstract machine for which there is no intended interpretation with respect to any physical system, then the behavior of that system can be subject to conclusive absolute verification. This scenario makes Hoare's [20] four basic principles true because then:

(1) computers are mathematical machines;
(2) computer programs are mathematical expressions;
(3) a programming language is a mathematical theory; and
(4) programming is a mathematical activity.

But if the function of a program is to satisfy the constraints imposed by an abstract machine for which there is an intended interpretation with respect to a physical system, then the behavior of that system cannot be subject to conclusive absolute verification but requires instead empirical inductive investigation to support inconclusive relative verifications. In cases of this kind, Hoare's four principles are false and require displacement as follows:

(1′) computers are applied mathematical machines;
(2′) computer programs are applied mathematical expressions;
(3′) a programming language is an applied mathematical theory; and
(4′) programming is an applied mathematical activity;

where propositions in applied mathematics, unlike those in pure mathematics, run the risk of observational and experimental disconfirmation.

COMPUTER PROGRAMS AS APPLIED MATHEMATICS

> A geometrical theory in physical interpretation can never be validated with mathematical certainty, no matter how extensive the experimental tests to which it is subjected; like any other theory of empirical science, it can acquire only a more or less high degree of confirmation.
>
> C. G. Hempel

The differences between pure and applied mathematics are very great, indeed. As Einstein remarked, insofar as the laws of mathematics refer to reality, they are not certain; and insofar as they are certain, they do not refer to reality. DeMillo, Lipton and Perlis likewise want to maintain that, to the extent to which verification has a place in programming practice, it applies to the evaluation of algorithms; and to the extent to which programming practice goes beyond the evaluation of algorithms, it cannot rely upon verification. Indeed, from the perspective of the classical theory of knowledge, their position makes excellent sense; for the investigation of the properties of programs (thus understood) falls within the domain of inductive methodology, while the investigation of the properties of algorithms falls within the domain of deductive methodology. As we have discovered, these are not the same.

Since the behavior of algorithms can be known with certainty (within the limitations of deductive procedure), but the behavior of programs can only be known with uncertainty (within the limitations of inductive procedure), the degree of belief (or 'strength of conviction') to which specific algorithms and specific programs are entitled can vary greatly. In particular, a hypothetical scale once again may be constructed, where, to the extent to which a person can properly claim to be rational with respect to his beliefs, there should be an appropriate correspondence (which need not necessarily be an identity) between his degree of subjective belief that something is the case (as displayed by Figure 2) and the measure of objective evidence in its support (as displayed by Figure 1). Otherwise, such a person does not distribute those degrees of

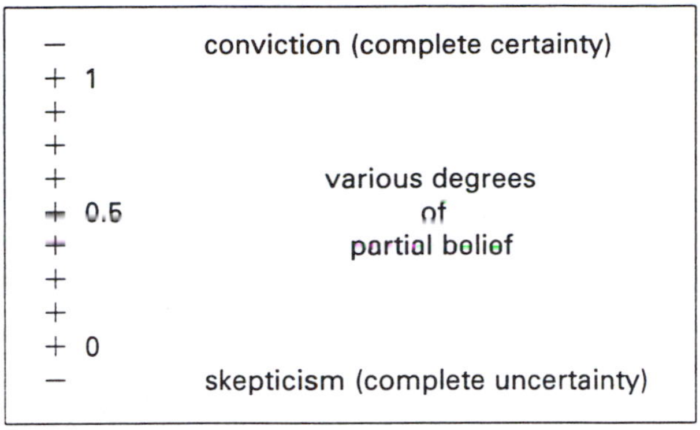

```
  —              conviction (complete certainty)
  + 1
  +
  +
  +              various degrees
  + 0.5              of
  +              partial belief
  +
  +
  + 0
  —              skepticism (complete uncertainty)
```

Fig. 2. A measure of subjective belief.

belief in accordance with the available evidence and is to that extent irrational [11, Ch. 10].

The conception of a program as a causal model suitable for execution by a machine reflects the interpretation of programs as causal factors that interact with other causal factors to bring about a specific output as an effect of the introduction of specific input. As everyone appears willing to admit, the execution of a program qualifies as causally complex, insofar as even a correct program can produce "wildly erratic behavior . . . if only a single bit is changed." The reason the results of executing a program cannot provide deductive support for the evaluation of a program [as Hoare 20, p. 116 acknowledges], moreover is that the behavior displayed by a causal system is an effect of the complete set of relevant factors whose presence or absence made a difference to its production. Indeed, this reflection has an analog with respect to inductive procedure, since it is a fundamental principle of inductive methodology that measures of evidential support should be based upon the complete set of relevant evidence that is currently available, where any finding whose truth or falsity increases or decreases the evidential support for a conclusion is evidentially relevant.[14]

The principle of maximal specificity for causal systems and the principle of total evidence for inductive methodology are mutually reinforcing: reasoning about programs tends to be (a) non-demonstrative, (b) ampliative, and (c) non-additive precisely because the truth of a generalization about a causal system depends upon *its complete specifi-*

cation, which can be very difficult — if not practically impossible — to obtain. In the absence of information of this kind, however, the best knowledge available is uncertain. Indeed, if the knowledge that deductive warrants can provide is said to be 'perfect', then our knowledge of the behavior of causal systems must always be 'imperfect', experimental and tentative (like physics) rather than demonstrative and certain (like mathematics). It is therefore ironic to discover the position advanced by DeMillo, Lipton and Perlis implicitly entails "the fuzzy notion that the world of programming is like the world of Newtonian physics" — not in its subject matter, of course, but in its methodology.

INDUCTIVE TESTING AND COMPUTER PROGRAMS

> Could the God that plays dice trigger a nuclear holocaust by a random error in a military computer?
>
> H. A. Pagels

At least two lines of defense might be advanced against this conclusion, one of which depends upon the possibility of an *ideal* programmer, the other upon the prospects for verification by *machine*. The idea of an ideal programmer is that of a programmer who knows as much about algorithms, programming and computers as there is to know. When this programmer is satisfied with a program, by hypothesis that program is 'correct'. The catch is two-fold. First, how could any programmer possess the knowledge required to be an 'ideal programmer'? Unless this person were God, we may safely assume the knowledge he possesses has been ascertained by means of the usual methods, including (fallible) inductive reasoning about the future behavior of complex systems based upon evidence about their past behavior. Second, even a correct program is but one feature of a complex causal system. The performance of a computer while executing a program depends not only upon the software but also upon the firmware, the hardware, the input/output devices and all the rest. While it would not be mistaken to suggest that, *ceteris paribus*, if these other components perform as they should, the system will perform as it should, such claims are not testable.

The emphasis here is on the word 'should'. Since the outputs that result from various inputs are complex effects of an interacting arrangement of software, firmware, hardware, and so on, the determination that some specific component of such a system functions properly ('as it should') depends upon assumptions concerning the specific states of each of the other, in the absence of which, strictly speaking, no program as such can be subject to test. Even when the specific states of the relevant components have been explicitly specified, the production of output O given input I on one occasion provides no guarantee that output O would be produced by input I on another occasion. Indeed, the type of system created by the interaction of these component parts could be probabilistic rather than deterministic. Repeated tests of any such system can provide only inductive evidence of reliability. Taken together, these considerations suggest that even the idea of an ideal programmer cannot improve the prospects for program verification.[15]

A fascinating example of the kind of difficulty that can be encountered is illustrated by the distinction between 'hard' and 'soft' errors, which occur when quantum phenomena are implicated in situations like these:

In the 1980s a new generation of high-speed computers will appear with switching devices in the electronic components which are so small they are approaching the molecular microworld in size. Old computers were subject to 'hard errors' — a malfunction of a part, like a circuit burning out or a broken wire, which had to be replaced before the computer could work properly. But the new computers are subject to a qualitatively different kind of malfunction called 'soft errors' in which a tiny switch fails during only one operation — the next time it works fine again. Engineers cannot repair computers for this kind of malfunction because nothing is actually broken. [31, p. 125]

It should be clear by now that the difference between proving a theorem and verifying a program does not depend upon the presence or absence of any social process during their production, but rather upon the presence or absence of causal significance. A summary of their parallels is illustrated in Table III. The chart shows the difference in social processes is merely a difference in practice, but the difference in causal significance is a real difference in principle.

The suggestion can also be made that program verification might be performed by higher-level machines that have the capacity to validate proofs that are many orders of magnitude more complex than those that can be mechanically verified today. This possibility implicitly raises issues of mentality concerning whether or not computers have the capacity for semantic interpretation as well as for syntactic manipulation [12]. Even assuming that their powers are limited to string pro-

TABLE III

A final comparison

	Proving theorems	Verifying programs
Syntactic objects of inquiry:	Yes	Yes
Social process of production:	Yes	No
Physical counterparts:	No	Yes
Causal significance:	No	Yes

cessing, this is an intriguing prospect, especially since proofs and programs alike are syntactic entities. There are no special difficulties so long as their intended interpretations are abstract machines. When their intended interpretations are target machines, then we encounter the problem of determining the reliability of the verifying programs themselves ("How do we verify the verifiers?"), which invites a regress of relative verifications of relative verifications. As long as our reasoning is valid, causally significant conclusions can be derived only from causally significant premises.

Tymoczko [36], however, suggests that proof procedures in mathematics have three distinctive features: they are convincing, they are formalizable and they are surveyable. His sense of 'surveyability' can be adequately represented by 'replicability'. Proofs are convincing to mathematicians because they can be formalized and replicated. Insofar as the machine verification of programs has the capacity to satisfy the desiderata of formalizability and of replicability, their successfully replicated results ought to constitute evidence for their correctness.[16] This, of course, does not alter the inductive character of the support thereby attained nor does it increase the range of the potential application of program verification, but it would be foolish to doubt the importance of computers in extending our reasoning capabilities, just as telescopes, microscopes, and all the rest have extended our sensible capacities: verifying programs, after all, could be published (just as proofs are published) in order to be subjected to the criticism of the community — even by means of computer trials! Even machine verifications, however, cannot guarantee the performance that will result from executing a program, which is yet one more form of our dilemma.[17]

COMPLEXITY AND RELIABILITY

> We must therefore come to grips with two
> problems that have occupied engineers for
> many generations: First, people must plunge
> into activities that they do not understand.
> Second, people cannot create perfect mecha-
> nisms.
>
> DeMillo, Lipton and Perlis

From this perspective, the admonitions advanced by DeMillo, Lipton
and Perlis against the pursuit of perfection when perfection cannot be
realized are clearly telling in this era of dependence upon technology.
There is little to be gained and much to be lost through fruitless efforts
to guarantee the reliability of programs when no guarantees are to be
had. When they assess the situation with respect to critical cases (such
as air-traffic control, missile systems, and the like) in which human lives
are at risk, the ominous significance of their position appears to be
overwhelming:

> ... the stakes do not affect our belief in the basic impossibility of verifying any system
> large enough and flexible enough to do any real-world task. No matter how high the
> payoff, no one will ever be able to force himself to read the incredibly long, tedious
> verifications of real-life systems, and, unless they can be read, understood, and refined,
> the verifications are worthless.

Thus, even when allowance is made for the possibility of group collab-
oration, the mistaken assumption that program performance can be
guaranteed could easily engender an untenable conception of the
situation encountered when human lives are placed in jeopardy as in
the case of SDI. If one were to assume the execution of a program
could be anticipated with the mathematical precision that is characteristic of demonstrative domains, then one might more readily suc-
cumb to the temptation to conclude that decisions can be made with
complete confidence in the (possibly unpredictable) operational performance of a complex causal system.

Complex systems like SDI are heterogeneous arrangements of complicated components, many of which combine hardware and software.
They depend upon sensors providing real-time streams of data where,
to attain rapid and compact processing, their avionics portions are
programmed in assembly language — a type of programming that does

not lend itself to the construction of program verifications. Systems like these differ in important respects from, say, brief programs that read an ASCII file in order to count the number of characters or words per line. Any analysis of computer-system reliability that collapses these diverse types of systems and programs into a single catch-all category would be indefensibly oversimplified. Therefore it should be emphasized that, in addition to the difference between absolute and relative verifiability with respect to programs themselves, the reliability of inductive testing — not to mention observation techniques — declines as the complexity of the system increases. As a rule of thumb, the more complex the system, the less likely it is to perform as desired [22]. The operational performance of these complex systems should never be taken for granted and cannot be guaranteed.

The blunder that would be involved in thinking otherwise does not result from the presence or the absence of social processes within this field that might foster the criticism of a community, but emanates from the very nature of these objects of inquiry themselves. The fact that one or more persons of saintly disposition might sacrifice themselves to the tedium of eternal verification of tens of millions of lines of code for the benefit of the human race is beside the point. The limitations involved here are not merely practical: *they are rooted in the very character of causal systems themselves.* From a methodological point of view, it might be said that programs are conjectures, while executions are attempted — and all too frequently successful — refutations (in the spirit of Popper [32, 33]). Indeed, the more serious the consequences that would attend the making of a mistake, the greater the obligation to insure that it is not made. In maintaining that program verification cannot succeed as a generally applicable and completely reliable method for guaranteeing the performance of a program, DeMillo, Lipton and Perlis thus arrived at the right general conclusion for the wrong specific reasons. Still, we are all indebted to them for their efforts to clarify a confusion whose potential consequences — not only for the community of computer science, but for the human race — cannot be overstated and had best be understood.

ACKNOWLEDGEMENTS

The original version of this paper was composed while a Post-Doctoral Fellow in computer science at Wright State University. Special thanks to Henry Davis, David Hemmendinger, Jack Kulas and especially Al Sanders for encouraging a philosopher to poke around in their back-yard. I am also indebted to two very conscientious but anonymous referees for this magazine and to Rob Kling and Chuck Dunlop for their stimulating criticism and penetrating inquiries, which forced me to clarify the basis for my position.

University of Minnesota,
Duluth, U.S.A.

NOTES

[1] Popper advocates the conception of science as an objective process of 'trial and error' whose results are always fallible, while Kuhn emphasizes the social dimension of scientific communities in accepting and rejecting what he calls 'paradigms'. See, for example, [23], [32—33]. A fascinating collection of papers discussing their similarities and differences is presented in [25].

[2] The point is that there appear to be three kinds of evidence that can be advanced in support of the truth of a sentence, two of which occur in the form of other sentences (whose truth may require their own establishment). While descriptions of the data of more-or-less direct experience presupposes causal interactions between language-users and the world, the construction of arguments does not. [11 esp. pp. 18—24]

[3] For an exceptionally lucid discussion of the differences between so-called natural deduction systems and axiomatic formal systems, where the former operate with sets of inference rules in lieu of formal axioms but the latter operates with sets of axioms and as few as a single rule. see [3].

[4] The claim that a proposition has been 'verified', therefore, can mean more than one thing, since some derivations establish that a claim is a theorem (which cannot possibly be false), while other derivations establish that a claim is a conclusion (which cannot be false, so long as its premises are true). Derivations of both types are equally 'valid', of course, but only the former show that their conclusions cannot be false.

[5] This point differs from the previous note. That the valid conclusion of an argument from true premises cannot be false does not mean that we can know, in general. whether or not a valid argument does or does not have true premises. Thus, the difficulty we confront, from an epistemic point of view, is establishing the truth of our premises as well as the validity of our arguments. The importance of this difference is great.

[6] It could be argued, of course, that even these purely syntactical entities may be viewed as having semantical relations to some domain of abstract entities. In the case of pure mathematics, these entities might be variously entertained as Platonic, as Intuitive, or as Conventional. See, for example, the discussions found in [1]. The key issue, however, is not whether there might be some such abstract domain of interpretation but whether there is any such physical domain.

[7] Moreover, differences in degree with respect to measurable magnitudes — such as

heights, weights, and so forth — are not precluded from qualifying as differences in kind. Indeed, to suppose that there cannot be any 'real' difference between two things merely because there are innumerable intermediate degrees of difference between them is known as the fallacy of the continuum. The distinction recommended here is appropriate either way.

[8] A fascinating illustration of this attitude may be found in Holt [21, pp. 24—25], who discusses what he takes to be "the three C's" of formal program specification: clarity, completeness, and consistency. He suggests that the formal verification of program correctness represents an idealization, "(much as certain laws of physics are idealizations of the motion of bodies of mass). This idealization encourages careful, proficient reasoning by programmers, *even if they choose not to carry out the actual mathematical steps in detail.*" Careful, proficient reasoning by programmers, however, is presumably attainable by methods other than program verification procedures.

[9] There are other aspects of specific programs, of course, including heuristics, especially, where the role of heuristics as 'rules of thumb' or as guidelines that allow exceptions but are useful, nonetheless, could be the subject of further inquiry (emphasizing, for example, that discovering heuristics is an inductive enterprise). Here, however, the focus is upon the difference between programs and algorithms as objects of verification.

[10] I am grateful to my colleague, David Cole, for proposing these examples.

[11] The phrase 'causal model', of course, has been bestowed upon entities as diverse as *scientific theories* (such as classical mechanics and relativity theory), *physical apparatus* (such as arrangements of ropes and pulleys), and even *operational definitions* (such as that IQs are what IQ tests test). Different disciplines tend to generate their own special senses. For discussion, see [15, 18, 34].

[12] A different set of five distinctive senses of 'program' is suggested by [30]. Those cited here, however, appear appropriate for our purposes.

[13] On the difference between pure and applied mathematics, see especially Hempel [16, 17] which are as relevant today as they were then.

[14] That every property whose presence or absence makes a difference to the performance of a causal system must be taken into account in order to understand its behavior is known as *the requirement of maximal specificity*; that inductive reasoning must be based upon all the available relevant evidence is known as *the requirement of total evidence* [11].

[15] An alternative position could emphasize the social processing whereby more than one 'very good programmer' might come to accept or to believe in the correctness of a program. As we have already discovered, this will not do. After all, the claim, "This program reflects what programmer z believes are the right commands," could be true, when the sentence, "This program reflects the right commands," happens to be false. The first is a claim about z's *beliefs*, the later about a *program* — even when z is a programming group.

[16] For an intriguing discussion of these questions in relation to the proof-by-computer of the four-color problem, see [9, 35 and 36].

[17] As Cerutti and Davis [5, pp. 903—904], have observed, "For machine proofs, we can (a) run the program several times, (b) inspect the program, (c) invite other people to inspect the program or to write and run similar programs. In this way, if a common

result is repeatedly obtained, one's degree of belief in the theorem goes up". An interesting discussion of their position may be found in [9, esp., pp. 805—807]; but Detlefsen and Luker beg the question in assuming that people are simply a different kind of computer, a crucial question on which they shed no light.

REFERENCES

1. Benacerraf, P. and Putnam, H., (Eds.): 1964, *Philosophy of Mathematics: Selected Readings*. Prentice-Hall, Englewood Cliffs, N.J.
2. Black, M.: 1967, 'Induction', *The Encylopedia of Philosophy* **4**, Edwards, P., Editor-in-Chief. Macmillan, New York, pp. 169—181.
3. Blumberg, A.: 1967, 'Logic, modern', *The Encyclopedia of Philosophy* **5**, Edwards, P., Editor-in-Chief, Macmillian, New York, pp. 12—34.
4. Bochner, S.: 1966, *The Role of Mathematics in the Rise of Science*. Princeton Univ. Press, Princeton, N.J.
5. Cerutti, E. and Davis, P.: 1969, 'Formac meets Pappus', *Am. Math. Monthly* **76**, 895—904.
6. Church, A.: 1959, 'Logistic system', *Dictionary of Philosophy*. Runes, D., (Ed.) Littlefield, Adam & Co., Ames, Iowa, pp. 182—183.
7. Dancy, J.: 1985, *An Introduction to Contemporary Epistemology*. Blackwell, Oxford.
8. DeMillo, R., Lipton, R. and Perlis, A.: 1979, 'Social processes and proofs of theorems and programs', *Commun. ACM 22*, **5**, 271—280.
9. Detlefsen, M. and Luker, M.: 1980, 'The four-color theorem and mathematical proof', *J. Philos. 77*, 12, 803—820.
10. Dijkstra, E. W.: 1976, *A Discipline of Programming*. Prentice-Hall, Englewood Cliffs, N.J.
11. Fetzer, J. H.: 1981, *Scientific Knowledge*. Reidel, Dordrecht, Holland.
12. Fetzer, J. H.: 1988, 'Signs and minds: An introduction to the theory of semiotic systems', in *Aspects of Artificial Intelligence*, Fetzer, J., (Ed.) Kluwer, Dordrecht/Boston/London/Tokyo, pp. 133—161.
13. Glazer, D.: 1979, 'Letter to the editor', *Commun. ACM 22*, 11, 621.
14. Hacking, I.: 1967, 'Slightly more realistic personal probabilities. *Philos. Sci. 34*, 4, 311—325.
15. Heise, D. R.: 1975, *Causal Analysis*. Wiley, New York.
16. Hempel, C. G.: 1949, 'On the nature of mathematical truth', in *Readings in Philosophical Analysis*, Feigl, N. and Sellars, W., (Eds.) Appleton-Century-Crofts, New York, pp. 222—237.
17. Hempel, C. G: 1949, 'Geometry and empirical science', in *Readings in Philosophical Analysis*, Feigl, H. and Sellars, W., (Eds.) Appleton-Century-Crofts, New York, pp. 238—249.
18. Hesse, M.: 1966, *Models and Analogies in Science*, Univ. of Notre Dame Press, Notre Dame, Ind.
19. Hoare, C. A. R.: 1969, 'An axiomatic basis for computer programming', *Commun. ACM 12*, 576—580, 583.

20. Hoare, C. A. R.: 1986, 'Mathematics of programming', *BYTE*, 115—149.
21. Holt, R.: 1986, 'Design goals for the Turing programming language. Technical Report CSRI-187', Computer Systems Research Institute, Univ. of Toronto.
22. Kling, R.: 1987, 'Defining the boundaries of computing across complex organization', in *Critical Issues in Information Systems*, Boland, R. and Hirschheim, R. (Eds.). Wiley, New York.
23. Kuhn, T. S.: 1970, *The Structure of Scientific Revolutions*, 2d ed. Univ. of Chicago Press, Chicago.
24. Lakatos, I.: 1976, *Proofs and Refutations*, Cambridge Univ. Press, Cambridge, U.K.
25. Lakatos, I., and Musgrave, A. (Eds.): 1970, *Criticism and the Growth of Knowledge*, Cambridge Univ. Press, Cambridge, U.K.
26. Lamport, L.: 1979, 'Letter to the editor', *Commun. ACM 22*, 11, 624.
27. Marcotty, M. and Ledgard, H.: 1986, *Programming Language Landscape: Syntax/ Semantics/Implementations*, 2d ed. Science Research Associates, Chicago.
28. Maurer, W. D.: 1979, 'Letter to the editor', *Commun. ACM 22*, 11, 625—629.
29. Michalos, A.: 1969, *Principles of Logic*, Prentice-Hall, Englewood Cliffs, N.J.
30. Moor, J. H.: 1988, 'The pseudorealization fallacy and the Chinese room', in *Aspects of Artificial Intelligence*, Fetzer, J. (Ed.) Kluwer, Dordrecht/Boston/ London/Tokyo, pp. 35—53.
31. Pagels, H.: 1982, *The Cosmic Code*, Simon & Schuster, New York.
32. Popper, K. R.: 1965, *Conjectures and Refutations*, Harper & Row, New York.
33. Popper, K. R.: 1972, *Objective Knowledge*, Clarendon Press, Oxford.
34. Suppe, F. (Ed.): 1977, *The Structure of Scientific Theories*, 2d ed. University of Illinois Press, Urbana, Ill.
35. Teller, P.: 1980, 'Computer proof', *J. Philos. 77*, 12, 797—803.
36. Tymoczko, T.: 1979, 'The four-color theorem and its philosophical significance', *J. Philos. 76*, 2, 57—83.
37. van den Bos, J.: 1979, 'Letter to the editor', *Commun. ACM 22*, 11, 623.

CHAPTER 9

PHILOSOPHICAL ASPECTS OF
PROGRAM VERIFICATION

Not least among the fascinating issues confronted by computer science is the extent to which purely formal methods are sufficient to secure the goals of the discipline. There are those, such as C. A. R. Hoare and Edsgar Dijkstra, who maintain that, in order to attain the standing of a science rather than of a craft, computer science should model itself after mathematics. Others, including Richard DeMillo, Richard Lipton, and Alan Perlis, however, deny that the goals of the discipline can be gained by means of purely formal methods.

Much of the debate between adherents to these diverse positions has revolved about the extent to which purely formal methods can provide a guarantee of computer system performance. Yet the ramifications of this dispute extend beyond the boundaries of the discipline itself. The deeper questions that lie beneath this controversy concern the paradigm most appropriate to computer science. The issue not only influences the way in which agencies disburse funding but also the way in which the public views this discipline.

Some of the most important issues that arise within this context concern questions of a philosophical character. These involve 'ontic' (or ontological) questions about the kinds of things computer and programs are as well as 'epistemic' (or epistemological) questions about the kind of knowledge we can possess about thing of these kinds. They also involve questions about crucial differences between 'pure' and 'applied' mathematics and whether the performance of a system when it executes a program can be guaranteed.

The purpose of this essay is to explore the similarities and differences between mathematical proofs, scientific theories, and computer programs. The argument that emerges here suggests that, although they all have the character of syntactic entities, scientific theories and computer programs possess semantic significance not possessed by mathematical proofs. Moreover, the causal capabilities of computer programs distinguish them from scientific theories, especially with respect to the ways they can be tested.

1. THE FORMAL APPROACH TO PROGRAM VERIFICATION

The phrase 'program verification' occurs in two different senses, one of which is broad, the other narrow. In its broad sense, 'program verification' refers to any methods, techniques, or procedures that can be employed for the purpose of assessing software reliability. These methods include testing programs by attempting to execute them and constructing prototypes of the systems on which they are intended to be run in an attempt to discover possible errors, mistakes, or 'bugs' in those programs that need to be corrected.

In its narrow sense, 'program verification' refers specifically to formal methods, techniques, or procedures that can be employed for the same purpose, especially to 'proofs' of program correctness. This approach seeks to insure software reliability by utilizing the techniques of deductive logic and pure mathematics, where the lines that constitute the text of a program are subjected to formal scrutiny. This approach has inspired many members of the community (cf. Linger *et al.*, 1979; Gries, 1979; and Berg *et al.*, 1982).

Thus, while 'program verification' in its broad sense includes both formal and non-formal methods for evaluating reliability, in its narrow sense 'program verification' is restricted to formal methods exclusively. The use of these methods tends to be driven by the desire to put computer science on a sound footing by means of greater reliance on mathematics in order to "define transformations upon strings of symbols that constitute a program, the result of which will enable us to predict how a given computer would behave when under the control of that program" (Berg *et al.*, 1982, p. 1).

The conception of programming as a mathematical activity has been eloquently championed by Hoare, among others, as the following reflects:

Computer programming is an exact science in that all of the properties of a program and all of the consequences of executing it in any given environment can, in principle, be found out from the text of the program itself by means of purely deductive reasoning. (Hoare 1969, p. 576)

Thus, if this position is well-founded, programming ought to be viewed as a mathematical activity and computer science as a branch of mathematics. If it is not well-founded, however, some other paradigm may be required.

2. COMPUTER PROGRAMS AND FORMAL PROOFS
OF CORRECTNESS

No doubt, the conception that underlies Hoare's position exerts an immense intuitive appeal. A computer M, after all, can be viewed abstractly as a set of transformation functions T for effecting changes in its states S:

(I) $M = \langle T, S \rangle$.

A program P in turn can be viewed as a function that transforms a computer from an initial state si to a final state sf when that program is executed E:

(II) $E\langle P, si \rangle = sf$.

(II) thus represents a 'special purpose' instance of a universal machine (I). (The account in this section follows that of Berg et $al.$, 1982, Ch. 2 and 3.)

Since every program is intended to effect a change of state from an initial state si before execution to a final one sf after execution, Hoare (1969) introduced a notation that is equivalent to '$\{si\}P\{sf\}$', where '$\{si\}$' denotes the state prior to and '$\{sf\}$' the state after the execution of program P (or, in general, to '$\{X\}P\{Y\}$', where 'X' describes some property satisfied by M prior to and 'Y' another property satisfied by M after the execution of P).

As Berg et $al.$ (1982, pp. 20–21) explain, a distinction has to be drawn between $proof$ of $correctness$ and $proofs$ of $partial$ $correctness$, where the difference depends upon whether or not the execution of program P terminates. When P terminates, then a formal proof that $E\langle P, si \rangle = sf$ becomes possible, where $E\langle P, si \rangle = sf$ if and only if $\vdash \{si\}P\{sf\}$ (that is, if and only if $\{si\}P\{sf\}$ is syntactically derivable on the basis of the axioms defining M).

Given a formal specification of the state transformations that are desired of a program P when it is executed in the general form $\{X\}P\{Y\}$, the aim of a (complete) correctness proof is to demonstrate $\vdash \{X\}P\{Y\}$, where:

(III) $\vdash \{X\}P\{Y\}$ if and only if
          $(si)[\vdash X(si) \rightarrow \vdash (P$ terminates$)$ and $\vdash Y(E\langle P, si \rangle)]$,

(employing '$\ldots \rightarrow \_\_$' as the material conditional 'if $\ldots$ then $\_\_$' sign);

and the aim of a (partial) correctness proof is to demonstrate $\vdash \{X\}P\{Y\}$ *if P terminates,* where termination is something that may or may not occur:

(IV) $\vdash \{X\}P\{Y\}^*$ if and only if
           $(si)[\vdash X(si)$ and $\vdash (P$ terminates$) \rightarrow \vdash Y(E\langle P, si\rangle)]$,

where the asterisk "*" attached to $\vdash \{X\}P\{Y\}$ indicates partial correctness. Proofs of correctness are therefore not precluded by the halting problem.

3. THE IMPLIED ANALOGY WITH PURE MATHEMATICS

One need not be a student of the history of mathematics to appreciate the implied analogy with pure mathematics. The model of formal proofs of program correctness immediately brings to mind Euclidean geometry with its formal proofs of geometrical theorems. Indeed, it is a plausible analogy to suppose that formal proofs of program correctness in computer science are precisely analogous to formal proofs of geometrical theorems in Euclid (see Figure 1).

	Mathematics	*Programming*
Objects of Inquiry:	Theorems	Programs
Methods of Inquiry:	Proofs	Verifications

Fig. 1. A plausible analogy.

Thus, by employing deductive reasoning that involves the application of formal rules of inference to the premises of an argument, various assertions could be shown to be valid formulae of Euclidean geometry (that is, their status as theorems could be established). Analogously, by employing deductive reasoning that involves the application of formal rules of inference to the premises of an argument, various assertions might be shown to be valid formulae about computer programs (they could be theorems too!).

Indeed, the realization that programs can be viewed as functions from initial states (or 'input') to final states (or 'outputs'), as (I) and especially (II) above imply, provides an even more persuasive foundation for conceding the force of this comparison. For programs in computer science can be viewed as functions from inputs to outputs and rules of inference in mathematics can be viewed as functions from premises to conclusions (theorems) (see Figure 2).

	Mathematics	*Programming*
Domain:	Premises	Input
Function:	Rules of Inference	Programs
Range:	Theorems	Output

Fig. 2. A more plausible analogy.

As though these analogies were not convincing enough, the use of mathematical demonstrations seems to be warranted on the basis of at least two further benefits that accrue from adopting the mathematical paradigm. One is that the abstract characterization of computing machines represented by (I) and (II) attains a generality that transcends the special characteristics of specific machines. Another is that abstract characterizations also emphasize the propriety of adopting formal methods within formal domains. The use of deductive methodology thus appear appropriate (cf. Berg *et al.*, 1982, p. 9).

4. RECENT ADVOCATES OF PURELY FORMAL METHODS

Hoare has not been alone in a advocating the position that computer programming should model itself after mathematics. A fascinating illustration of a similar perspective has been advanced by William Wulf, who contends:

The *galling* thing about the generally poor quality of much current software is that there is no extrinsic reason for it; perfection is, in principle, possible. Unlike physical devices: (1) There are no natural laws limiting the tolerance to which a program can be manufactured; it can be built *exactly* as specified. (2) There is no Heisenberg uncertainty principle operative; once built, a program will behave exactly as prescribed. And (3) there is no friction or wear; the correctness and performance of a program will not decay with time. (Wulf, 1979, p. 40, original italics)

This conception of perfection in programming where, once built, a program will behave exactly as prescribed, could be called 'Wulfian Perfectionism'.

Similar views have been elaborated more recently by Dijkstra, among others, who has definite views on "the cruelty of really teaching computer science", especially when it is properly taught as a branch of mathematics:

> Finally, in order to drive home the message that this introductory programming course is primarily a course in formal mathematics, we see to it that the programming language in question has *not* been implemented on campus so that students are protected from the temptation to test their programs. (Dijkstra, 1989, p. 1404, original italics)

Hoare (1969), Wulf (1979), and Dijkstra (1989) thus represent several decades of commitment to formal methods by influential computer scientists.

It should come as no surprise, of course, that belief in formal methods tends to go hand in hand with the denigration of testing and prototyping. Consider recent remarks by J. Strother Moore of Computation Logic, Inc., in support of the extension of formal methods to whole computer systems:

> System verification grew out of dissatisfaction with program verification in isolation. Why prove software correct if it is going to be run on unverified systems? In a verified system, one can make the following startling claim: *if the gates behave as formally modeled, then the system behaves as specified.* (Moore, 1989, p. 409, italics added)

This claim is indeed 'startling'. (We shall explore later whether it is true.)

And consider some recent messages sent out by Hal Render on USENET. On 17 January 1990, for example, Render transmitted the following claims:

> The process of proving a program correct should either indicate that there are no errors or should indicate that there are (and often what and where they are). Thus, *successful program proving methods should eliminate the need for testing.* In practice, things are not so straightforward, because verification is tough to do for many kinds of programs, and one still has to contend with erroneous specifications. (Render, 1990a, italics added)

Approximately two weeks later, Render returned to this theme in his response to a USENET critic, whom he dismissed with the following remarks:

> No one (except maybe you) thinks that "proving a program correct" means proving absolutely, positively that there is not a single (no, not even one) error in a program.

Since the specification and the verifications can be in error, there is NO (not even one) way to infallibly prove a program correct. I know this, all informed proponents of verification know this, and you should know this (enough people have told you). (Render 1990b, original emphasis; this was not directed toward me.)

This position thus implies that only inadequate specifications, on the one hand, or mistaken reasoning, on the other, can generate program errors (cf. Smith, 1985). Taken together, there can be little doubt that passages such as these from Hoare, Wulf, Dijkstra, Moore, and Render, represent a coherent position. The question thus becomes whether it can be justified.

5. IS THE ANALOGY WITH MATHEMATICS PROPER?

Arguments by analogy compare two things (or kinds of things) with respect to certain properties, contending that, because they share certain properties in common and one of them has a certain additional property, the other has it too. When there are more differences than similarities or few but crucial differences or these arguments are taken to be conclusive, however, arguments by analogy can go astray. Some analogies are faulty. Perhaps programming and mathematics are very different kinds of things.

There is clearly some foundation for a comparison between mathematics and programming, especially since mathematical theorems and computer programs are both syntactical entities that consist of sequences of lines. Computer programs seem to differ from mathematical theorems, however, insofar as they are intended to possess a semantical significance that mathematical theorems (within pure mathematics) do not possess, a difference arising because programs, unlike theorems, are instructions for machines.

Indeed, a comparison between mathematical theorems and computer programs becomes more striking when scientific theories (classical mechanics, special relativity, quantum mechanics, and so forth) are considered as well. For scientific theories, like computer programs, have semantical significance that mathematical proofs do not possess. The lines that make up a program, like the sentences that make up a theory, after all, tend to stand for other things for the users of those programs and those theories.

The specific commands that constitute a program, for example, stand for corresponding operations by means of computing machines, while the generalizations that constitute a theory stand for lawful properties of the physical world. Yet even scientific theories do not possess the causal capabilities of computer programs, which can affect the performance of those machines when they are loaded and then executed. For a more adequate comparison of their general features see Figure 3.

	Mathematics Proofs:	Scientific Theories:	Computer Programs:
Syntactic Entities	Yes	Yes	Yes
Semantic Significance:	No	Yes	Yes
Causal Capability:	No	No	Yes

Fig. 3. A more general comparison.

The comparison that is reflected by Figure 3 suggests rather strongly that the differences between theorems and programs may outweigh their similarities. Whether a difference should make a difference in relation to an analogical argument, however, depends on how strongly it is weighted. If their existence as syntactical entities is all that matters, then computer programs, scientific theories, and mathematical theorems would appear to be exactly on a par. Why should differences such as these matter at all?

6. ARE OTHER IMPORTANT DIFFERENCES BEING OVERLOOKED?

The sections that follow are intended to explain why differences like these are fundamental to understanding programming as an activity and computer science as a discipline. Before pursuing this objective, however, it should be observed that yet another difference has sometimes been supposed to be the fundamental difference between the construction of proofs in mathematics and the verification of programs in computing. This arises from a difference in dependence upon social processing in these disciplines.

DeMillo, Lipton, and Perlis (1979), in particular, have suggested that the success of mathematics is crucially dependent upon a process of social interaction between various mathematicians. Without this social process, they contend, mathematics could not succeed. Because formal proofs of program correctness are complex and boring, however, they doubt there will ever be a similar process of social interaction between programmers. Such comparisons with mathematics thus depend upon a faulty analogy.

Even advocates of formal methods have been willing to acknowledge the significance of social processes within mathematical contexts. Some have accented the subjective character of mathematical proof procedure:

A mathematical proof is an agenda for a repeatable experiment, just as an experiment in a physics or chemistry laboratory. But the main subject in each experiment is another person instead of physical objects or material. *The intended result of the experimenter is a subjective conviction on the part of the other person that a given logical hypothesis leads to a given logical conclusion.* .... A successful experiment ends in a subjective conviction by a listener or reader that the hypothesis implies the conclusion. (Linger *et al.*, 1979, p. 3, italics added)

While they concede that subjective conviction provides no guarantee of the validity of a proof or the truth of a theorem, Linger *et al.* maintain that this process of social interaction is essential to producing mathematical products.

Since even advocates of formal methods seem to be willing to grant this premise of DeMillo, Lipton, and Perlis' position, the extent to which mathematics is comparable to programming apparently depends on the extent to which programs are like theorems, especially with respect to features that might affect their accessibility to social processing. While these arguments have been highly influential, there are reasons to believe that social interaction should be far more important to mathematics than to programming.

7. ARE SUBJECTIVE 'PROOFS' THE ONLY AVAILABLE EVIDENCE?

The ground on which Linger *et al.* stake their claim to the importance of proof procedures (within programming as well as within mathematics) — in spite of their subjectivity — is the absence of procedural alternatives:

Why bother with mathematics at all, if it only leads to subjective conviction? *Because that is the only kind of reasoned conviction possible,* and because the principal experimental subject who examines your program proofs is yourself! Mathematics provides language and procedure for your own peace of mind. (Linger *et al.*, 1979, p. 4, italics added)

Although this position may initially appear very plausible, it fails to take into account other features that may distinguish programs and theorems.

After all, if computer programs possess a semantical significance and a causal capability that mathematical theorems do not possess, then there would appear to be opportunities for their evaluation of kinds other than social processing. Scientific theories (such as classical mechanics, special relativity, and so on) are suggestive illustrations, because (almost) no one would want to maintain that their acceptability is exclusively a matter of subjective conviction. Science relies upon observations and experiments.

If scientific theories are viewed as conjectures, then observation and experimentation afford nature opportunities for their refutation. The results of these observations and experiments are not mere matters of subjective conviction. There thus appear to be other methods for evaluating scientific theories that go beyond those available for evaluating proofs of theorems in mathematics. If that is the case, however, then there would appear to be kinds of 'reasoned conviction' besides mathematical proofs.

If computer programs possess causal capability as well as semantical significance, then there should also be means for evaluating their correctness going beyond those available for scientific theories. Prototyping and testing offer opportunities for further kinds of experiments that arise from atempting to execute programs by machine: these are prospects over which we have (almost) complete control! But this indicates yet another kind of 'reasoned conviction' going beyond social processing alone.

8. ARE FORMAL PROOFS OF PROGRAM CORRECTNESS NECESSARY?

If these reflections are well-founded, then the position of Linger *et al.* (1979), which suggests that mathematical proofs of program correctness are indispensable, appears to be very difficult to sustain. If those who advocate formal methods for evaluating programs want to insist upon the primacy of this methodology, they need to find better ground for their position. And, indeed, that support appears to arise from at least two quite different directions, one of which is ontic, the other epistemic.

The ontic defense consists in characterizing 'programs' as abstract objects to which physical machines have to conform. Consider Dijkstra:

> What is a program? Several answers are possible. We can view the program as what turns the general-purpose computer into a special-purpose symbol manipulator, and it does so without the need to change a single wire. .... I prefer to describe it the other way around. The program is an abstract symbol manipulator which can be turned into a concrete one by supplying a computer to it. After all, *it is no longer the purpose of programs to instruct our machines; these days, it is the purpose of machines to execute our programs.* (Dijkstra, 1989, p. 1401, italics added)

One of the attractions of this approach, no doubt, is its strong intimation that programming only involves reference to purely abstract machines.

The identification of 'program' with abstract symbol manipulators, however, warrants further contemplation. While 'computers' are sometimes characterized as physical symbol systems — by Alan Newell and Herbert Simon (1976), for example — 'programs' are typically supposed to provide instructions that are executed by machine. When he tacitly transforms 'programs' from instructions into machines, Dijkstra thereby distorts the traditional distinction between 'programs' and 'computers'.

The epistemic defense consists in maintaining that formal methods provide the only access route to the kind of knowledge that is required. The maxim that "testing can be used to show the presence of bugs, but never to show their absence" has been promoted, especially by Dijkstra (1972). Such a position seems to conform to Sir Karl Popper's conception of scientific methodology as a deductive domain, where scientific hypotheses can possibly be shown to be false but can never be shown to be true.

The epistemic defense, however, appears to be far weaker than the ontic defense, not least because it almost certainly cannot be justified. A successful compilation supports the inference that certain kinds of bugs are absent, just as a successful execution supports the inference that certain other kinds of bugs are absent. Even the conception of conjectures and (attempted) refutations, after all, must take into account the positive significance of *unsuccessful* attempted refutations

as well as the negative significance of *successful* attempted refutations
(Fetzer, 1981, esp. Ch. 7).

9. PROGRAMS AS ABSTRACT ENTITIES AND
AS EXECUTABLE CODE

The principal defense of the primacy of formal methods in evaluating
computer programs, therefore, appears to depend upon the adequacy
of the conception of *programs* as "abstract symbol manipulators".
Dijkstra offers several alternative accounts that reinforce the ontic
defense. Thus,

> ... Another way of saying the same thing is the following one. A programming
> language, with its formal syntax and with the proof rules that define its semantics, is a
> formal system for which program execution provides only a model. It is well-known
> that formal systems should be dealt with in their own right and not in terms of a
> specific model. And, again, the corollary is that *we should reason about programs
> without even mentioning their possible "behavior"*. (Dijkstra, 1989, p. 1403, italics
> added)

Observe in particular that Dijkstra translates a claim about formal
systems into a claim about computer programs without justifying this
identification.

Dijkstra further obscures the distinction between 'programs' as
abstract objects and 'programs' as executable entities by asserting the
benefits of working with the definition of a set rather than with its
specific members:

> ... the statement that a given program meets a certain specification amounts to a
> statement about *all* computations that could take place under control of that given
> program. And since this set of computations is defined by the given program, our
> recent moral says: deal with all computations possible under control of a given program
> by ignoring them and working with the program. *We must learn to work with program
> texts while (temporarily) ignoring that they admit the interpretation of executable code.*
> (Dijkstra, 1989, p. 1403, italics added)

The differences between sets and programs, however, are such that
there are several good reasons to doubt that even this position can be
justified.

Consider, for example, that sets are completely extensional entities,
in the sense that two sets are the same when and only when they have
the same members. The set $\{x, y, z\}$, for example, is the same as the set
$\{x, x, y, z, z\}$, precisely because they have all and only the same

elements. Programs, by comparison, are quite different, because two iterations of the same command qualifies as two commands, even if two iterations of the same element qualify as one member of the corresponding set. The principles that govern extensional entities do not govern causal relations.

Thus, although Dijkstra wants to view programs as "abstract symbol manipulators", he thereby obfuscates fundamental differences between things of two different kinds. 'Programs' understood as *abstract entities* (to which individual concrete machines have to conform) and 'programs' as *executable code* (that causally interacts with physical machines) have enormously different properties. Indeed, their differences are sufficiently great as to bring into doubt the adequacy of the mathematical analogy.

10. THE AMBIGUITY OF 'PROGRAM VERIFICATION'

Part of the seductive appeal of formal methods within this context, I surmise, arises from a widespread reliance upon abstract models. These include abstract models that represent the *program specification*, which is the problem to be solved. (A program is shown to be 'correct' when it is shown to satisfy its specification.) They also include abstract models that represent the *programming language*, which is a tool used in solving such a problem. (Pascal, LISP, and other high-level languages simulate the behavior of abstract machines rather than describe those of target machines.)

Enormous benefits accrue from the use of these abstract models. The construction of programs in Pascal, LISP, and so forth, for example, is far easier than the composition of programs in assembly language, where there is a one-to-one correspondence between program instructions and machine behavior. And, as was observed in Section 3, the abstract characterization of computing machines attains a generality that transcends the special characteristics of specific machines. But there is the correlated risk of mistaking properties of the abstract models for properties of the machines themselves.

Some machines, for example, have 8-bit words, while others have 16-bit (32-bit, . . .) words. And while register size makes no difference with respect to many operations, it can affect others [see Tompkins, 1989 and Garland, 1990). The capacity to represent real numbers by numerals obviously depends upon the characteristics of specific machines. While it is clearly possible to construct abstract models that successfully model specific machines, these abstract models no longer possess inherent generality.

The formal approach to program verification thus appears to trade upon an equivocation. While it is indeed possible to construct a formal proof of program correctness with respect to an abstract model of a machine, the significance of that proof depends upon the features of that model. When the model is an abstract model (the axioms of which can be given as stipulations) that does not represent a specific physical machine, a formal proof of correctness can then guarantee that a program will perform as specified (unless mistakes have been made in its construction). Otherwise, it cannot.

11. DISAMBIGUATING 'PROGRAM VERIFICATION'

The differences at stake here can be made explicit by using the term 'PROGRAM' to refer to the operations that can be executed by an abstract machine for which there is no physical counterpart and by using the term "program" to refer to the operations that may be executed by an abstract machine for which there is some physical counterpart. It should then become apparent that, although the properties of abstract machines with no physical counterpart can be stipulated by definition, those of abstract machines with physical counterparts have to be discovered by investigation.

This difference can be illustrated by means of rules of inference such as Hoare has introduced. Consider, for example, the following illustrations:

$$Consequence\ 1:\quad \text{If '}\{X\}P\{Y\}\text{' and '}Y \Rightarrow Z\text{',}$$
$$\text{then infer '}\{X\}P\{Z\}\text{';}$$
$$Consequence\ 2:\quad \text{If '}X \Rightarrow Y\text{' and '}\{Y\}P\{Z\}\text{',}$$
$$\text{then infer '}\{X\}P\{Z\}\text{'; and,}$$
$$Conjunction:\quad \text{If '}\{X\}P\{Y\}\text{' and '}\{X'\}P\{Y'\}\text{',}$$
$$\text{then infer '}\{X\ \&\ X'\}P\{Y\ \&\ Y'\}\text{',}$$

(employing '... $\Rightarrow$ __' as the semantical entailment 'if ... then __' sign) (cf. Marcotty and Ledgard, 1986, p. 118). *Consequence* 1 asserts that, if a line of the form '$\{X\}P\{Y\}$' is true and '$Y \Rightarrow Z$' is true, then a line of the form '$\{X\}P\{Z\}$' will also be true, necessarily. And likewise for *Consequence* 2, etc.

The problem that arises here is how it is possible to know when a line of the form '$\{X\}P\{Y\}$' is true. Even on the assumption that semantic entailments of the form '$Y \Rightarrow Z$' are knowable *a priori* (on the basis of grammar and vocabulary), that does not provide any foundation for ascertaining the truth of lines that describe the state of the machine **M** before and after the execution of program P. There appear to be only two alternatives. If **M** is an abstract machine with no physical counterpart, axioms such as '$\{X\}P\{Y\}$' can be true of **M** as a matter of stipulation, but not if **M** has a counterpart.

When **M** is an abstract machine with a physical counterpart, then the axioms that are true of **M** are only knowable *a posteriori* (on the basis of observation and experiment). But this means that two different kinds of 'program verification' are possible, only one of which can be conclusive:

(D1)   (conclusive) *absolute verification* can guarantee the behavior of an abstract machine, because its axioms are true by definition;

(D2)   (inconclusive) *relative verification* cannot guarantee the behavior of a counterpart, because its axioms are not definitional truths.

Verifications that are conclusive are only significant for abstract machines, while those that are significant for physical machines are never conclusive.

12. THE DISTINCTION BETWEEN 'PURE' AND 'APPLIED' MATHEMATICS

The differences that have been uncovered here are parallel to those between 'pure' and 'applied' mathematics, where theorems of applied mathematics, unlike those of pure mathematics, run the risk of observational and experimental disconfirmation. A theorem about the natural numbers, say.

(a) $2 + 2 = 4$,

for example, cannot possibly be false within the context of that theory, since it follows from axioms that are true by definition. The application of those same numerical relations to physical phenomena, however, might be false.

Sometimes the results of mathematical descriptions of physical phenomena are surprising, indeed. Consider, for example, the following sentence:

(b)   2 units of water + 2 units of alcohol = 4 units of mixture.

This certainly sounds plausible. Yet it turns out that, as an effect of their atomic structure, molecules of water and molecules of alcohol have the capacity to partially occupy the same volume when they are mixed together. This apparently true sentence, therefore, turns out to be empirically false.

Other examples afford equally interesting illustrations of the problem we have discovered. What truth-value should be assigned to these claims:

(c)   2 drops of water + 2 drops of water = 4 drops of water?

(d)   2 lumps of plutonium + 2 lumps of plutonium = 4 lumps of plutonium?

(e)   2 gaggle of geese + 2 gaggle of geese = 4 gaggle of geese?

Even if the assumed behavior of abstract machines can be known with deductive certainty, the real behavior of physical things can only be known with the empirical uncertainty that accompanies scientific investigations.

But surely this is something that we ought to have expected all along. The example of Euclidean geometry affords an instructive illustration; for, when 'points' are locations without extension and 'lines' are the shortest distances between them, their relations can be ascertained deductively on the basis of the axioms that define them. But as soon as 'lines' are identified with the paths of light rays in space and 'points' with their intersection, these relations can only be discovered empirically by means of observation and experimentation. (Space even turns out to be non-Euclidean!)

13. WHAT ABOUT HOARE'S 'FOUR BASIC PRINCIPLES'?

From this point of view, certain contentions whose truth-values may have been unclear tend to become obvious. When Hoare maintains that,

Computer programming is an exact science in that all of the properties of a program and all of the consequences of executing it in any given environment can, in principle, be found out from the text of the program itself by means of purely deductive reasoning. (Hoare, 1969, p. 576)

it should now be apparent that, while this may be true for PRO-GRAMS on abstract machines, it is certainly false for programs on physical machines.

Similarly, when Dijkstra asserts that, "We must learn to work with program texts while (temporarily) ignoring that they admit the inter-pretation of executable code" (Dijkstra, 1989, p. 1403), it should be evident that, while this attitude appears to be appropriate for PRO-GRAMS whose properties can be known by deduction and with certainty, it is not appropriate for programs whose properties can only be known by experience and with uncertainty. Indeed, it should be apparent that the very idea of the mathematical paradigm for computer science trades on ambiguity.

Consider the 'Four Principles' of Hoare (1986), which can be viewed as defining the "mathematical paradigm" in application to this disci-pline:

(1) computers are mathematical machines;
(2) computer programs are mathematical expressions;
(3) a programming language is a mathematical theory; and
(4) programming is a mathematical activity.

Clearly, the structures and entities that satisfy these relations (as Hoare intended them to be understood) are PROGRAMS and abstract machines.

As soon as attention turns to programs and physical machines, it is evident that the proper comparison is with applied mathematics instead:

(1') computers are *applied* mathematical machines;
(2') computer programs are *applied* mathematical expressions;
(3') a programming language is an *applied* mathematical theory; and
(4') programming is an *applied* mathematical activity.

To the extent to which computer science can properly be entertained as a mathematical discipline, it qualifies as an applied rather than a pure one.

14. ANOTHER ARGUMENT FOR THE SAME CONCLUSION

The differences between PROGRAMS and programs that have been elaborated here, however, would never have come to light had we failed to appreciate the differences between mathematical theorems, scientific theories, and computer programs. Advocates of formal methods in computer science tend to overlook these differences, especially because they are drawn toward the position "that the meaning or the semantics of a program are precisely equivalent to what the program causes a machine to do" (Berg *et al.*, 1982, p. 9; for a related discussion of 'procedural semantics', see Fodor, 1978). But an equivocation arises at this juncture.

The differences between the positions outlined in Hoare (1969) and in Fetzer (1988) can be formulated to address this point by distinguishing 'programs-as-texts' (unloaded), which consist of sequences of lines, from 'programs-as-causes' (loaded), which affect machine performance. Formal verification invariably involves the application of deductive techniques to programs-as-texts, where it does not even make sense to talk about the application of techniques of deduction to programs-as-causes (cf. Barwise, 1989, p. 848).

Hoare and I both assume (*) that programs-as-causes are represented by programs-as-texts, except that Hoare contends that verifying a program-as-text guarantees what will happen when a program-as-cause is executed, which I deny. Otherwise, in contending that even a successful verification of a program is never enough to guarantee what will happen when that program is executed, I would have simply changed the subject. In that case, we would not have joined issues and we might both be right.

Indeed, a key difference between Hoare's position and my own can be formulated in terms of different versions of thesis (*). For Hoare maintains,

(*′)   that programs-as-causes are *appropriately* represented by programs-as-texts;

but I assert that all he is entitled to assume is the strikingly weaker thesis,

(*″)   that programs-as-causes are *supposed-to-be* appropriately represented by program-as-texts.

For one of the major points I have sought to convey is that there might be two different ways in which this supposition could be grounded, namely: (a) when the program-as-text concerns an abstract machine for which there is no physical counterpart (where this relation can be true by definition); or, (b) when the program-as-text concerns as abstract machine for which there is a physical counterpart (where this relation must be empirically justified). Hoare's position — which, I believe, is tacitly adopted by the vast majority of those favoring the verificationist position — clearly overlooks this distinction.

15. ARE THERE OTHER ALTERNATIVE POSITIONS?

In their reflections on this debate as it has been carried in pages of the *Communications of the ACM*, John Dobson and Brian Randell (1989) raise an important question namely: Why do many proponents of formal methods in computer science deny that they hold the position that I have attacked? There may be more than one answer to this question, of course, since some of them may simply hold inconsistent positions (perhaps by persisting in the belief that purely formal methods *are* capable of providing guarantees concerning what would happen if a program were executed by a machine).

The situation is also complicated by differences regarding the ultimate importance of social processing as an aspect of computer methodology. If issues concerning social processing that DeMillo, Lipton, and Perlis (1979), among others, have addressed, are left aside, however, then the views of Avra Cohn (1989) on behalf of provers of PROGRAMS and Glenford Myers (1979) on behalf of testers of programs contribute to defining some of the most important alternative positions. The following flow chart (Figure 4) is intended as a summary of the debate's central course without exhausting its details.

Thus, Cohn maintains that formal proofs of correctnesss, even those that involve entire computer systems, cannot possibly guarantee the performance of any real system, even when verified programs are being executed:

Ideally, one would like to prove that a chip such as Viper correctly implements its intended behavior under all circumstances; we could then claim that the chip's behavior was predictable and correct. In reality, neither an actual *device* nor an *intention* is an object to which logical reasoning can be applied. ... In short, verification involves a pair of *models* that bear an uncheckable and possibly imperfect relation to the intended design and to the actual device. (Cohn, 1989, pp. 131–132, original italics)

Hoare (1969): purely deductive methods
\+
content about performance
=
branch of pure mathematics.
|

Fetzer (1988): you cannot have both purely
deductive methods + content
about performance = Hoare's
position cannot be justified.
|

Dobson and Randell (1989): but many others
deny that the view I attack is
their view. I agree that these
alternative views are available:

Cohn (1989): keep the purely   Myers (1979): keep the empirical
deductive methods +   content + give up the
give up the empirical   purely deductive methods
content = still a branch   = now a branch of applied
of pure mathematics.   mathematics.
(Proving PROGRAMS)   (Testing programs)

Fig. 4. The program verification debate.

Indeed, as she hastens to point out, these points "are not merely philosophical quibbles": errors were located even in the models assumed
for Viper!

Strictly speaking, however, although specification models and machine
models are *deductively* 'uncheckable', they are not therefore *inductively*
'uncheckable' as well, where 'induction' relies upon the kinds of
observation and experimentation that computer systems permit. It
would therefore be mistaken to assume that the relationship between a
specification and the world, on the one hand, or an abstract machine
and a counterpart, on the other, are matters about which only subjective opinion is possible. Empirical evidence can even support reasoned
convictions about models.

While Cohn disavows responsibility for what happens when a system
executes a program, Myers embraces a Popperian conception of testing
in which primary emphasis is placed upon and discovery of remaining
errors. In his view, "*Testing is the process of executing a program with*

the intent of finding errors" (Myers, 1979, p. 5). Yet it is no more necessary to suppose that testing can only discover errors than it is to suppose that only formal proofs of programs can establish their absence. These are two widely held but unjustifiable beliefs that qualify as myths of computer science.

16. WULFIAN PERFECTIONISM CANNOT BE SUSTAINED

It should be obvious by now that Wulfian Perfectionism, which maintains that, once written, a program will execute exactly as prescribed, cannot possibly be correct. The problems with which it cannot cope even extend to those of the Intel 80486 microprocessor, which turned out to have a (potentially fatal) flaw. When certain instructions were executed in one sequence, they executed properly, yet in another sequence, they failed to execute properly (Markoff, 1989, p. 39). Although this specific case was fixed, it is impossible to know which other cases remain to be discovered.

It should also be obvious that Moore's optimism in asserting that, if the gates behave as formally modeled, the system behaves as specified, is unwarranted even for the case of fully verified systems (Moore, 1989, p. 409). The verification of an abstract model, even in relation to an entire computer system, cannot guarantee system performance; even if the gates behave as formally modeled, unless there is no more to that system than the gates themselves! Moreover, unless gate performance can be guaranteed, this claim amounts to a promissory note that can never be cashed in.

And it should also be obvious that the conception of computer science as a branch of pure mathematics cannot be sustained. The proper conception is that of computer science as a branch of applied mathematics, where even that position may not go far enough in acknowledging the limitations imposed by physical devices. Remarks like these from Hamilton Richards,

... the conversion of programming from a craft into a mathematical discipline requires an unorthodox type of mathematics in which the traditional distinction between "pure" and "applied" need not appear. (Richards, 1990, p. viii)

should be recognized as nonsense. They are both misleading and untrue.

Perhaps the resolution of these difficulties is to concede a point made by David Parnas in response to Dijkstra's piece on teaching programming:

There is no engineering profession in which testing and mathematical validation are viewed as alternatives. It is universally accepted that they are complementary and that both are required. (Parnas, 1989, p. 1405)

Similar views are endorsed by Berg *et al.* (1982, p. 124) and by others (including Goodenough and Gerhart (1975) and Gerhart and Yelowitz (1976)). Computer science, after all, has both theoretical and experimental dimensions, where both formal methods and empirical procedures have a place.

17. WHAT POSITIONS SHOULD BE DISTINGUISHED?

As I have elsewhere emphasized (Fetzer and Martin, 1990), some of the issues at stake here involve questions of logic, others matters of methodology, and others issues of verifiability, which can be summarized here. In relation to questions of logic, for example, two positions are in dispute:

Positions of LOGIC:
(T1) Formal proofs of program correctness can provide an absolute, conclusive guarantee of program performance;
(T2) Formal proofs of program correctness can provide only relative, inconclusive evidence concerning program performance.
 The purpose of Fetzer (1988) was to establish that (T1) is false but that (T2) is true. I would find it difficult to believe that anyone familiar with the course of this debate could continue to disagree. These are separate from three other positions that arise in relation to questions of methodology:

Positions of METHODOLOGY:
(T3) Formal proofs of program correctness should be the exclusive methodology for assessing software reliability;
(T4) Formal proofs of program correctness should be the principal methodology for assessing software reliability;
(T5) Formal proofs of program correctness should be one among various methodologies for assessing software reliability.
 I maintain (T3) is false and, at the ACM Computer Science Confer-

ence 90, I argued further that (T4) is false, but I have no doubt that (T5) is true. My opponents on that occasion — David Gries and Mark Ardis — did not choose to defend the merits of (T4). In relation to verification in the broad sense, finally,

Positions on VERIFICATION:

(T6) Program verifications always require formal proofs of correctness;
(T7) Program verifications always require proof sketches of correctness;
(T8) Program verifications always require the use of deductive reasoning.

I maintain that (T6) is clearly false and that (T8) is clearly true but that the truth-value of (T7) is subject to debate. Much appears to hang on whether such proof sketches have to be written down, could be merely thought through, or whatever. If the former, (T7) becomes closer to (T6); if the latter, (T7) becomes closer to (T8). Charlie Martin believes 'hand proofs' may be a suitable standard (Fetzer and Martin, 1990). However these matters may ultimately be resolved, (T1) through (T8) seem to reflect the principal distinctions that must be drawn to understand the range of issues at stake.

18. WHAT IS THE APPROPRIATE ATTITUDE TO ADOPT?

To admit that formal methods have a place in computer science is not to grant that they have the capacity to guarantee program performance. If Berg *et al.* and others have appreciated the situation any more clearly than the Hoares, the Wulfs, the Dijkstras, the Moores, the Renders, and the Richards of the world, they are certainly to be commended. But it does not follow that Hoare, Wulf, Dijkstra, Moore, Render, Richards and their followers do not hold inadequate positions. The views they offer cannot be justified.

If the entire debate has brought into the foreground some indefensible assumptions that have been made by some influential figures in the field, then it will have been entirely worthwhile. It should be obvious by now that pure mathematics provides an unsuitable paradigm for computer science. At the very least, the discipline appears to have some characteristics that are more akin to those that distinguish empirical sciences and others indicating that it ought to be viewed as an engineering discipline instead.

Although the issues that have been addressed here concern questions of ontology and of epistemology, the most important implications of this debate are ethical. The greater the seriousness of the consequences that would ensue from making a mistake, the greater our obligation to insure that it is not made. This suggests that the role for prototyping and testing increases dramatically as life-critical tasks come into play (cf. Blum, 1989). We can afford to run a system that has been only formally assessed if the consequences of mistakes are relatively minor, but not if they are serious.

Formal proofs of program correctness provide one variety of assurance that a system will perform properly. Testing supplies another. Constructing prototypes yields a third. When we deal with abstract models, formal methods are available. When we want to know whether or not a physical system will perform as it is intended, however, there are no alternatives to prototyping and testing. The program verification debate has implications that are practical and ethical as well as theoretical and philosophical. And the future of our species may depend upon how well we understand them.

ACKNOWLEDGEMENT

Special thanks to David Nelson and Chuck Dunlop for their helpful criticism.

REFERENCES

Barwise, J.: 1989, 'Mathematical Proofs of Computer System Correctness', *Notices of the AMS* **36**, 844–851.

Berg, H. K. *et al.*: 1982, *Formal Methods of Program Verification and Specification*, Englewood Cliffs, NJ: Prentice-Hall.

Blum, B.: 1989, 'Formalism and Prototyping in the Software Process', RMI-89-011, Applied Physics Laboratory, Johns Hopkins University.

Cohn, A.: 1989, 'The Notion of Proof in Hardware Verification', *Journal of Automated Reasoning* **5**, pp. 127–139.

DeMillo, R., Lipton, R., and Perlis, A.: 1979, 'Social Processes and Proofs of Theorems and Programs', *Communications of the ACM* **22**, 271–280.

Dijkstra, E. W.: 1972, 'Notes on Structured Programming', in: O. Dahl *et al.* (Eds.), *Structured Programming*, New York, NY: Academic Press.

Dijkstra, E. W.: 1989, 'On the Cruelty of Really Teaching Computing Science', *Communications of the ACM* **32**, 1398–1404.

Dobson, J. and Randell, B.: 1989, 'Viewpoint', *Communication of the ACM* **32**, 420–422.

Fetzer, J. H.: 1981, *Scientific Knowledge*, Dordrecht, The Netherlands: D. Reidel.

Fetzer, J. H.: 1988, 'Program Verification: The Very Idea', *Communications of the ACM* **31**, 1048—1063.

Fetzer, J. H. and Martin, C. R.: 1990, ' "The Very Idea", Indeed!', Technical Report, Department of Computer Science, Duke University.

Fodor, J.: 1978, 'Tom Swift and His Procedural Grandmother', *Cognition* **6**, 229—247.

Garland, D.: 1990, 'Technical Correspondence Letter', *Communications of the ACM*, forthcoming.

Gerhart, S. and Yelowitz, L.: 1976, 'Observations of Fallibility in Applications of Modern Programming Methodologies', *IEEE Transactions on Software Engineering* **2**, 195—207.

Goodenough, J. and Gerhart, S.: 1975, 'Toward a Theory of Test Data Selection', *IEEE Transactions on Software Engineering* **1**, 156—173.

Gries, D. (Ed.): 1979, *Programming Methodology*, New York, NY: Springer-Verlag.

Hoare, C. A. R.: 1969, 'An Axiomatic Basis for Computer Programming', *Communications of the ACM* **12**, 576—580, 584.

Hoare, C. A. R.: 1986, 'Mathematics of Programming', *BYTE* (August), 115—149.

Linger, R. C., Mills, H., and Witt, B.: 1979, *Structured Programming: Theory and Practice*, Reading, MA: Addison-Wesley.

Marcotty, M. and Ledgard, H.: 1989, *Programming Language Landscape: Syntax/Semantics/Implementations*, 2nd ed., Chicago, IL: Science Research Associates.

Markoff, J.: 1989, 'Top-of-Line Intel Chip Is Flawed', *The New York Times* (Friday, October 27). pp. 25 and 39.

Moore, J. Strother: 1989, 'System Verification', *Journal of Automated Reasoning* **5**, pp. 409—410.

Myers, G. J.: 1979, *The Art of Software Testing*, New York, NY: John Wiley & Sons.

Newell, A. and Simon, H.: 1976, 'Computer Science as Empirical Inquiry: Symbols and Search', *Communications of the ACM* **19**, 113—126.

Parnas, D.: 1989, 'Colleagues Respond to Dijkstra's Comments', *Communications of the ACM* **32**, 1405—1406.

Render, H.: 1990a, Article 755 (comp.software.eng), USENET, 17 January 1990. 20:01:00 GMT.

Render, H.: 1990b, Article 1413 (comp.software.eng), USENET, 1 February 1990. 01:31:30 GMT.

Richards, H.: 1990, 'Foreword', in E. W. Dijkstra (Ed.), *Formal Development of Programs and Proofs*, Reading, MA: Addison-Wesley, pp. vii—ix.

Smith, B. C.: 1985, 'The Limits of Correctness', *Computers and Society* **14**(4) (Winter), 18—28.

Tompkins, H.: 1989, 'Verifying Feature — Bugs', *Communications of the ACM* **32**, 1130—1131.

Wulf, W. A.: 1979, 'Introduction to Part I: Comments on "Current Practice",' in P. Wegner (Ed.), *Research Directions in Software Technology*, Cambridge, MA: MIT Press, pp. 39—43.

CHAPTER 10

PHILOSOPHY AND COMPUTER SCIENCE
Reflections on the Program Verification Debate

ABSTRACT

In the September 1988 issue of *Communcations of the ACM*, the primary publication of the Association for Computing Machinery, an article appeared in which I advanced an appraisal of the scope and limits of formal methods to guarantee the reliability of computer system performance. Although intended as a philosophical critique, the response thereby generated was not altogether "philosophical". The debate has now moved beyond *CACM* to *Notices of the AMS*, *Minds and Machines*, and other journals and books and shows no signs of abating. The APA Committee on Philosophy and Computers has asked me to discuss my experiences relating philosophy and computer science. I suggest that philosophical distinctions not only make a difference to understanding this domain but that their theoretical adequacy is also thereby tested.

SOME BACKGROUND

During 1986-87, four other philosophers and I participated in a special fifteen-month, post-doctoral program offered by Wright State University for Ph.D.s in linguistics and philosophy who wanted to study computer science and artificial intelligence. The program extended over five quarters, with courses distributed over the first four and thesis work toward an M.S. degree the following summer. Among the courses for the fall quarter was one on programming languages, which was taught by Professor Al Sanders. [1]

The course requirements included a term paper on one or more articles listed in the references for the course text by Michael Marcotty and Henry F. Ledgard, *Programming Language Landscape* (1986). The most intriguing item I noticed was "Social Processes and Proofs of Theorems and Programs" by Richard DeMillo, Richard Lipton and Alan Perlis, which had appeared in *Communications of the ACM* in 1979. It had generated several letters and an authors' response and looked as if it might be of philosophical interest.

When I located the paper itself and had the chance to read it through, I was fairly astonished. The authors were appraising the prospects for using formal methods to enhance our confidence in the reliability of software in computer systems. The advocates of this approach, who are an influential group within computer science, maintain that computer science ought to be modeled on mathematics as its paradigm, a conception that DeMillo, Lipton and Perlis on various grounds were intent to reject as an unattainable ideal.

The analogy embraced by advocates of formal methods takes the following form. In mathematics, proofs begin by identifying the propositions to be proven and proceed by deriving those propositions from premises ("axioms") as conclusions ("theorems") that follow from them by employing exclusively deductive reasoning. In computer science, proofs may begin by identifying the proposition to be proven (in this case, *specifications* of desired program performance), where deductive reasoning applied to the text of a program might show it satisfies those specifications and thereby prove it is "correct".

DEMILLO, LIPTON, AND PERLIS

DeMillo, Lipton and Perlis sought to undermine the force of this analogy by discussing several respects in which "proofs" of mathematical theorems differ from "verifications" of program correctness. Their most important argument focused upon the role of social processes in evaluating proofs of theorems, where mathematicians consult other mathematicians to secure agreement that proofs are valid. In their view, the complexity of program verifications means that no comparable social processing ever takes place.

They found words to express what they wanted to convey in vivid and forceful prose. Supporting their position, for example, they remarked that,

> the verification of even a puny program can run into dozens of pages, and there's not a light moment or a spark of wit on any of those pages. Nobody is going to run into a friend's office with a program verification. Nobody is going to sketch a verification out on a paper napkin. Nobody is going to buttonhole a colleague into listening to a verification. Nobody is ever going to read it. One can feel one's eyes glaze over at the thought. (DeMillo, Lipton, and Perlis 1979, p. 276)

Thus, according to DeMillo, Lipton and Perlis, the absence of social mechanisms in the program-verification community parallel to those found in the theorem-proving community destroys the comparison with mathematics.

As a student in search of a thesis, I had stumbled upon what appeared to be a philosopher's bonanza. While the authors described themselves as appraising the prospects for using formal methods to enhance confidence in the reliability of software, I sensed the aim of program verification was to guarantee the performance of programs when they are executed by machine. Having come of age intellectually in the logical empiricist tradition, I was confident that formal methods alone could not attain that objective.

Since DeMillo, Lipton and Perlis were not very specific on this point, I had some homework to do, which led me to publications by C. A. R. Hoare of Oxford, who was among the leading figures in the program verification movement. Imagine my feelings at finding the following passage in which Hoare had articulated what I had conjectured to be the implicit conception:

> Computer programming is an exact science in that all the properties of a program and all the consequences of executing it in any given environment can, in principle, be found out from the text of the program itself by means of purely deductive reasoning. (Hoare 1969, p. 576)

It was immediately apparent to me that this conception, which asserts that purely formal methods can guarantee the performance of a computer when it executes a program, implies the existence of synthetic *a priori* knowledge.

PROGRAMS VS. ALGORITHMS

Although I was already convinced that the program verification movement was predicated upon a misconception about the scope and limits of formal methods, I was not inclined to argue the case in my paper by denying the existence of synthetic *a priori* knowledge. An approach of this kind would have compelled the introduction of the analytic/synthetic distinction within this context, even though many philosophers reject this framework. And while I was confident that their reasons for its rejection were not well-founded, I was reluctant to base my critique upon such a disputed premise.[2]

As a consequence, I introduced other distinctions that I suspected would be easier to convey to computer scientists and that could not be derailed on the basis of purely philosophical concerns. I therefore argued that a distinction had to be drawn between *algorithms* as effective solutions to problems and *programs* as causal models of those algorithms, where the latter but not the former possess the capacity to exercise causal influence over computers when they execute a program. I emphasized the differences between pure and applied mathematics and between abstract models and causal systems.

Computer programming, of course, is ordinarily conducted by means of (what are called) *high-level* programming languages, such as Pascal, LISP, and Prolog, where there is a one-to-many relationship between commands in programs and instructions executed by a machine. Assembly language, by comparison, provides a *low-level* language, where something closer to a one-to-one relationship between commands obtains. Digital machines operate on the basis of strings of zeros and ones (or of high and low voltage), which would be difficult if not impossible to program directly. The causal connection between programs in high-level languages and target machines is therefore effected by interpreters and compilers, which translate them.

This means that programs are ordinarily written for *virtual machines*, which may or may not have physical counterparts. A mini-language, CORE introduced as a pedagogical device by Marcotty and Ledgard (1986, Ch. 2) to illustrate the elements of programming languages but for which there is no interpreter or compiler afforded a perfect illustration, because "proofs" of program correctness in CORE could be constructed in relation to virtual machines that were guaranteed to execute them as definitional properties of those machines. These machines are abstract models of CORE machines.

VIRTUAL VS. PHYSICAL MACHINES

Mistakes could still be made in programming, of course. Marcotty and Ledgard (1986, pp. 45-46) identified various sources of error, such as un-defined value errors, overflow errors, negative value errors, and so forth, which could lead to the abnormal termination of a program. My point was not that programs written in CORE could never be imperfect, but rather that the performance of computers executing programs written in CORE could not be guaranteed in the sense that, assuming there were no programming errors, there could be no possible failure of a machine to execute a CORE program.

The crucial difference thus becomes that between virtual machines for which there are no physical counterparts and virtual machines for which there are physical counterparts. *Virtual machines* only exist as abstract entities beyond space/time for which definitional properties but no causal relations can obtain. *Physical machines*, by comparison, are causal systems in space/time, which can exert causal influence upon other things in space/time. While it may be possible to prove the correctness of a program using purely deductive reasoning, I urged, those formal methods cannot possibly guarantee what will happen when a target machine executes that program.

The analysis, in other words, was an elaboration of the epistemological ramifications that accompany the ontological difference between abstract entities and causal systems. Thus, I argued that the conclusive verification of a virtual machine was logically possible when it had no physical counterpart, because its behavior could be definitively established on the basis of purely deductive reasoning from stipulated axioms. The behavior of a target machine, however, might deviate arbitrarily from those axioms and, as a consequence, could never be definitively established by purely deductive reasoning. The behavior of causal systems must be established inductively.

The term paper I submitted thus suggested that, in contending that program verification could not guarantee what happens when a computer executes a program, DeMillo, Lipton and Perlis had arrived at the right general conclusion but for the wrong specific reasons. The problem was not rooted in the social processing of proofs but in the causal character of computers. When Al Sanders subsequently returned our papers, a lively discussion ensued, during which he reported that he had found mine to be "fascinating!" This enthusiastic reception moved me to send it to *Communications of the ACM*, which had published the original paper by DeMillo, Lipton and Perlis.

THE EDITORIAL PROCESS.

The paper was submitted 26 November 1986 with the title, "Social Processes and Causal Models of Logical Structures", which led James Maurer, the Executive Editor, to send it to Rob Kling, who was the area editor for social aspects of computing. Over the next 18 months, he would ask me to revise it four times in order to insure that my arguments would be accessible to readers of the magazine. Having published a 500-page book manuscript without having to change even one word (Fetzer 1981), this was not something I expected. Each time that he asked me to make further revisions, I became more and more disenchanted with our progress.

In the meanwhile, I had been hired as full professor by the University of Minnesota in Duluth, and my colleagues were aware of my research on this topic. Sometime between the third and forth drafts, David Cole showed me a list of "I/O Statements" from the IBM PC manual for Microsoft BASIC, which included the following commands and their expected consequences:

Statement	Action
BEEP	Beeps the speaker.
CIRCLE (x, y) r	Draws a circle with center and radius r.
COLOR b, p	In graphics mode, sets background color and palette of foreground
LOCATE row, col	Positions the cursor
PLAY string	Plays music as specified by string.

While David had intended these findings as counterexamples to my thesis, I was euphoric, because they were perfect illustrations: there was no way formal proofs could guarantee *a speaker would beep* or *music would play*!

No doubt in part because I incorporated these examples into the fourth draft of my text, the paper was finally acceptable to Rob Kling, and on 13 June 1988, I received a formal acceptance from James Maurer. Since my discussion was no longer primarily criticism of DeMillo, Lipton and Perlis (1979) but a general critique of the limits of formal methods in computer science, Kling suggested I provide a new title for the paper. I responded with "Program Verification: The Very Idea".[3] Since it had taken so long to reach this point, I was surprised when it came out three months later.

The cover of that issue of *Communications* featured a head extending from an enormous pile of computer printouts crying for help. My greatest fear at this point was that my article had finally appeared but no one would even notice or, worse yet, that it would be greeted with yawns as belaboring the obvious. I was therefore pleasantly surprised when my good friend, Chuck Dunlop, with whom I had participated in the program at Wright State, sent me a copy of a message from the Risks Forum, an electronic bulletin board devoted to issues related to computer reliability.

THE INITIAL RESPONSE

In this posting of 5 October 1988, Brian Randell explained that he had just finished my article "with great interest and enjoyment" and affirmed,

> In my opinion it is a very careful and lucid analysis of the dispute between, e.g., DeMillo, Lipton and Perlis on the one hand, and Hoare on the other, regarding the nature of programming and the significance of program verification. (Randell 5 Oct 88 9:56:39 WET DST)

He included the text of the abstract and ended his message by quoting the last lines of the paper, where I suggest these matters are not only important theoretically for computer science but also practically for the human race.

Chuck advised me that many other messages were now appearing over the nets, which I found reassuring. My worst fears had been allayed: the article was not being ignored, and the initial response had been positive. Shortly thereafter, moreover, I received a letter from Robert Ashenhurst, who edits the Forum for the magazine, dated 1 November 1988. Included were copies of six Letters to the Editor of *Communications*, which Ashenhurst thought were appropriate for publication. He invited me to reply. I agreed with his judgment concerning five and submitted my response.

The letters reflected a variety of attitudes, ranging from a complaint (by James Pleasant) that I had traded upon ambiguity by failing to distinguish exactly what I had in mind by the term "program", to a thoughtful critique (by William Bevier, Michael Smith, and William Young), who suggested that, at the level of logic gates, the difference between abstract entities and causal systems virtually disappears, to additional arguments (by Stephen Savitzky) that supplied further grounds supporting my position in the case of useful programs that are not merely unverifiable but even verifiably incorrect, where the most important requirements of programs may be ones that are not formalizable, etc. (Pleasant, et al. 1989).

Pleasant posed no problem (since I had been entirely explicit on this point); Bevier, Smith and Young could be disarmed (since the difference at stake does not disappear); and Savitzky had come to my defense. The potentially most damaging letter in the set, however, was from Lawrence Paulson, Avra Cohn, and Michael Gordon of Cambridge University, who castigated me for contending that programs must work pefectly, for asserting that verification is useless because it cannot guarantee perfection, and for condemning a subject of which I knew nothing. Since I had not made the claims they attributed to me, I was invulnerable to their criticisms, which were based on drastic oversimplifications of my arguments (Fetzer 1989b). But it was beginning to dawn that I might have touched a sensitive nerve.

LETTERS TO THE EDITOR

The worst was yet to come. In correspondence dated 12 December 1988, Robert Ashenhurst sent along four more letters. Three of these (by Harald Muller, by Christopher Holt, and by Arron Watters) were not unexpected. Muller suggested that I was implicitly drawing a (Platonic) distinction between *the world of the pure* (abstract entities) and *the world of the real* (causal systems), whereas computers (as constructed artefacts) instead fall in between. Holt suggested that the issue was the correctness of the imple-mentation of the language in which a program is written in the hardware, which most verificationists assume as an *axiom*. And Watters maintained that the truly important issues were not those discussed in my article but those previously raised by DeMillo, Lipton and Perlis (Muller et al. 1989).

What I liked about Muller's letter was not his Platonic framework but the introduction of artificially contrived machines. As I explained in reply,

> two modes of operation are available. Either the machine is created in accordance with the design (axioms) or the design (axioms) is created in accordance with the machine. *Either way, however, it is necessary to discover precisely how the machine behaves in order to determine whether or not it is in accordance with the design* (Fetzer 1989c, p. 511; original emphasis)

While it may be possible to determine the properties of virtual machines by stipulation as a matter of definition (for abstract entities), it is only possible to discover the properties of target machines by the use of induction (for causal systems), thereby reasserting the basic elements of my position.

There was much about Holt's letter with which I completely agreed, so I sought to accent the subtle points of disagreement. While we are all entitled to assume whatever we want for the sake of hypothetical reasoning, there is an important difference between *assuming something to be the case* and *its being the case*. President Reagan, I observed, presumably assumed that we could lower taxes, increase spending, and nevertheless balance the budget. The issue is not whether or not assumptions can be made but under what conditions an assumption is justified, warranted or true. Arguments based upon hypothetical "axioms" may be valid but are not therefore also sound.

Since Hoare had made observations that appeared to conform to Holt's conception, I offered an illustration that is by no means unproblematical:

> When the correctness of a program, its compiler, and the hardware of the computer have all been established with mathematical certainty, it will be possible to place great reliance on the results of the program and predict their performance with a confidence limited only by the reliability of the electronics. (Hoare 1969, p. 579)

The catch, I remarked, is that this conditional has an antecedent that maybe incapable of satisfaction, since the correctness of the program, its compiler, and the hardware can *never* be established "with mathematical certainty" unless it happens to be an abstract rather than a physical machine!

THE "GANG OF TEN"

If the first three letters were not surprising, the fourth was something else entirely. A scathing diatribe of the likes of which I had never seen before, this letter not only raked me across the coals for misrepresenting the goals and methods of program verification but damned the editors as well:

> by publishing the ill-informed, irresponsible, and dangerous article by Fetzer, the editors of *Communications* have abrogated their responsibility, to both the ACM membership and to the public at large, to engage in serious enquiry into techniques that may justify the practice of computer science as a socially responsible engineering practice. The article is ill-informed and irresponsible because it attacks a parody of both the intent and the practice of formal verification. It is dangerous because its pretentious and ponderous style may lead the uniformed to take it seriously. (Ardis, Basili, et al. 1989, p. 287)

The letter was signed by ten prominent members of the program verification community. In a handwritten note, Robert Ashenhurst penned that he had just learned that this letter had been forwarded to Peter Denning, the Editor-in-Chief, who planned to respond regarding the review process.

I was stunned. Were this letter, which was receiving special treatment, to appear without a response from me, whether or not I might have forceful and convincing replies to the charges they had raised would not matter: my reputation would have already endured serious, irretrievable damage. In his cover letter, Ashenhurst also mentioned that "the original package" had apparently been "bumped" from January to February. This gave me hope that perhaps something could be done. I called the Executive Editor to plead for the opportunity to provide a response of my own that would appear in *Communications* at the same time as this extraordinary letter.

James Maurer listened patiently as I explained that, while I greatly appreciated the fact that Peter Denning was going to respond on behalf of the editors concerning the review process, it was essential for me to have an opportunity to respond on my own behalf concurrent with the publication of this letter. I observed that it was my name attached to this article and that it was my reputation at stake. I was enormously relieved when, after extensive consultation, the Executive Editor and the Editor-in-Chief decided that I was entitled to respond at the time of its publication. This meant in turn that the "package" would be moved from February to March.

DRAFTING A RESPONSE

Under considerable pressure, I began to systematically disentangle the objections the authors had raised and consider my replies. There appeared to be at least six issues involved here, some of which were far more serious than others. They asserted, for example, that there are no published claims to "conclusive absolute verification", a phrase that I had used; that assembly language programs *are* amenable to verification procedures, a prospect they contended I had denied; and that I seemed to be "totally unaware" of a large body of work applying formal procedures to compilers and hardware, which indicated to me that these authors had apparently not understood my views.

The absence of the phrase "conclusive absolute verification" from the literature, of course, did not mean that the concept was not present, and formal methods could do no more for compilers or for hardware than they could for programs. The point about assembly language was bothersome, but the only sentence supporting their interpretation concerned the control mechanism of missile systems processing real-time streams of data, "where, to attain rapid and compact processing, their avionics portions are programmed in assembly language—a kind of processing that does not lend itself to the construction of program verifications" (Fetzer 1988, p. 1062). Having originally discussed this point with Chuck Dunlop, I thought that I ought to call him once again.

While we were going though the program, Chuck and I had considered many of these issues before, but perhaps never with such beneficial effect. While it was true in the example I used that the programming was done in assembly language and that programs written in assembly language could indeed be subjected to program verifications, the circumstances of this case precluded that, since these missiles were able to reprogram themselves in flight. We speculated about possible conditions under which such programs could be verified and laughed at our thoughts. I slept very well that night.

My published response, which appeared immediately following the letter in the March issue of *Communications*, began by with the observation:

> The ancient practice of killing the messenger when you do not like the message receives
> its latest incarnation in the unfortunate letter from Ardis, Basili, et al. ("The Gang of
> Ten"). The authors allege (a) that I have misrepresented the goal of program verification
> (thereby attacking a "straw man"); (b) that I have misunderstood the role of mathematics
> in any engineering endeavor (especially within computer science); and (c) that my
> conclusion, if it were true, would undermine research in vast areas of computer science
> (including most theoretical work). (Fetzer 1989a, p. 288)

In rebuttal, I observed (a) that, since I was attacking Hoare's position, as I had clearly explained, I was attacking a "straw man" only if Hoare's position was a "straw man"; (b) that the role of mathematics in engineering qualifies as *applied mathematics* when used to describe physical structures and as *pure mathematics* when used to describe abstract structures; and (c) that it was hard to believe these authors could seriously maintain that computer science could benefit from misrepresenting the certainty of its findings.

SOME CRITICAL ARGUMENTS

I remarked that the authors had "misdescribed" my conclusion, since it was not my position that program verification was useless or even harmful because it provides no certainty. My point, on the contrary, was that "since program verification cannot guarantee the performance of any program, it should not be pursued in the false belief that it can—which, indeed, might be entertained in turn as the 'ill-informed, irresponsible and dangerous dogma' that my paper was intended to expose" (Fetzer 1989a, p. 288). My favorite passage, however, was one inspired by my discussion with Chuck.

While acknowledging that the sentence I used in describing assembly-language programming as a type that did not lend itself to program verifications might have been misleading, I reaffirmed the force of my example involving real-time transmission of streams of data from sensors to processors:

the specific avionics example that I was discussing . . . reflects a special type of programming that can be found in cruise missiles and other sophisticated systems with the capacity to reprogram themselves en route to their targets. The only technique that would permit the verification of these programs as they are generated in flight would be procedures permitting the correctness of these programs to be established as they are constructed. Perhaps the authors of this letter could volunteer to accompany these missiles on future flights in order to demonstrate that this is a type of programming that actually does lend itself to the construction of program verifications, after all. (Fetzer 1989a, p. 288)

I find it impossible to reread this passage without smiling even to this day.

Having discovered that the *Journal of Automated Reasoning* was about to publish a new paper by Avra Cohn entitled, "The Notion of Proof in Hardware Verification", in which she acknowledged that verification "involves a pair of *models* that bear an uncheckable and possibly imperfect relation to the intended design and to the actual device" (Cohn 1989, p. 132), I cited it as "display[ing] a great deal of sensitivity to the basic issues at stake in my article", in spite of the fact that "she is one of three Cambridge scholars who reject my analysis on peripheral grounds elsewhere" in this magazine.

I concluded my reply by praising the efforts expended on my behalf by the editors and staff of *Communications*, especially Rob Kling, "in providing sympathetic criticism and in enforcing high standards". I finished with observations about the tone and quality of the letter from the Gang of Ten:

> In its inexcusable intolerance and insufferable self-righteousness, this letter exemplifies the attitudes and behavior ordinarily expected from religious zealots and ideological fanatics, whose degrees of conviction invariably exceed the strength of the evidence. (Fetzer 1989a, p. 289)

I remain enormously indebted to James Maurer and to Peter Denning for granting my plea to publish my response at the same time as their letter.

DOBSON AND RANDELL

The March 1989 issue of *Communications* thus began with that letter, which took up a full-page of the Forum, followed by my reply. Peter Denning, the Editor-in-Chief, true to his word, offered a powerful defense of the editorial process, observing that the paper had been put though four rounds of revision and noting that "the article was subjected to a review more rigorous than is required by ACM policy, and that the review process was fair and professionally sound. I stand fully behind my editors." (Denning 1989, p. 289). The letters from Pleasant, the three Cambridge scholars, et al. appeared with my replies as "Technical Correspondence".

The April 1989 issue published the letters from Muller, Holt, and Watters, which was something that I expected, together with an OP/ED piece entitled, "Program Verification: Public Image and Private Reality", which I had not (Dobson and Randell 1989). The authors were John Dobson and Brian Randell, the same "Brian Randell" who had posted a favorable notice of my article on the Risks Forum. I was therefore somewhat distressed to read that, while their initial opinion had been quite favorable in viewing it as "an interesting, and unusually literate, contribution to the literature on the theoretical limitations of program verification", they had now reached the conclusion that it was "undoubtedly . . . misconceived" but perhaps useful in correcting overselling of their product by the verification community.

Thus, although I was alleged to have "failed to give this topic the careful scrutiny it so clearly needs", they said the program verification community had not done so either. Their principal objections to my analysis of the theoretical limitations of program verification, however, were two in number:

(1) "the (unfortunately justifiable) fear that [my] paper will be misinterpreted by laymen, particularly those involved in funding" (Dobson and Randell 1989, p. 420); and,

(2) their belief that I had mistakenly entertained proofs of program correctness as intended to provide explanatory rather than evidential reasons: *it seems to us that Fetzer thinks the verificationists have been representing their work as providing explanatory reasons for program correctness, whereas they claim their work provides merely evidential reasons* (Dobson and Randell 1989, p. 421, original emphasis).

I was acutely disappointed that an author who had been so positive about my work had now withdrawn his support as I began to draft my response.

EXPLANATION VS. EVIDENCE

Before they raised the issue, I had not considered—even remotely—whether or not an analysis of the scope and limits of formal methods in computer science had any financial ramifications. The "fear" that my paper might be "misinterpreted" by those who fund verification projects and that they might be "persuaded" to reallocate their resources for more promising activities, of course, is a classic example of the informal fallacy known as "the appeal to pity", where the unfortunate consequences that might follow if a certain position were accepted as true are treated as though they counted as evidence that it is false. But this was no reason to suppose I was wrong.

Their first objection, therefore, was simply fallacious, although I could appreciate why those whose profession, promotions, or tenure depend on funding of this kind might have been unsettled by my analysis. In asserting that I had mistaken "evidential" for "explanatory" reasoning, however, they raised issues of a different calibre entirely. Their second objection, which implied that I had attacked a straw man by portraying the function of proofs of program correctness as explanatory in relation to executions when they should be understood as evidential, after all, represented a set of issues which to any philosopher of science would be extremely familiar.

There is in fact a fundamental distinction between *evidential reasoning* and *explanatory reasoning*, as Carl G. Hempel, some time ago, explained by distinguishing "explanation-seeking" questions (such as, "Why is it the case that *p*?") from "reason-seeking" questions (say, "What grounds are there for believing that *p*?"). While adequate answers to explanation-seeking questions also provide potential answers to corresponding reason-seeking questions, the converse is not the case (Hempel 1965, p. 335). To that extent, of course, I thought that Dobson and Randell had drawn a relevant distinction.

It was fascinating to observe them illustrating the difference that they wanted to invoke with two examples regarding the height of a tree, which might be *explained* by considerations such as, "that it is a tree of such-and-such a sort, growing in this sort of climate in this sort of soil, and that under such conditions trees of that type can sustain a height of about 100 feet", on the one hand, or established *evidentially* by considerations such as, "that it casts a shadow of 50 feet at a time of day when a 10-foot pole casts a shadow of 5 feet" (Dobson and Randell 1989, pp. 420-421). The parallel with Sylvain Bromberger's flagpole example was both obvious and remarkable.

THE ROLE OF LOGIC

When Dobson and Randell claimed that mathematical logic provides "explanatory reasons", however, they committed a blunder. Logic specifically and formal methods generally are context independent: they are applicable for deriving conclusions from premises without any concern for the purpose of the arguments thereby constructed. Indeed, the flagpole case—and their own example!—clearly indicate that the ability to deduce a conclusion (about the height of a flagpole, for example) is not the same as the ability to explain that phenomenon (why the flagpole has that height). No student of the symmetry thesis would have been prone to commit this mistake (Fetzer 1974).

Since I had drawn a distinction between *algorithms* as logical structures and *programs* as causal models of those structures, they properly noticed that I focused on the causal contribution of programs to the performance of computers. An important ramification of my position is the claim that the outcome of executing a program "obviously depends upon various different causal factors, including the characteristics of the compiler, the processor, the printer, the paper and every other component whose specific features influence the execution of such a program" (Fetzer 1988, p. 1057).

Since programs are only partial causes of the effects of their execution, if I were taking formal proofs to be explanatory, when their proponents only intend them to be evidential, then I would be holding them at fault for failing to guarantee what a computer will do when it executes a program when their reasoning is merely evidential. This position, however, not only contradicts Dobson and Randell's assumption that formal proofs are always explanatory but also overlooks the consideration that differences between virtual machines and causal systems still remain whether program verifications are viewed as evidential *or* as explanatory reasoning.

Even when we overlook the inconsistency in their position by supposing that program verifications as formal proofs of correctness are merely intended to provide evidential reasons for believing that a computer will perform correctly when that program is executed, the difference between *conclusive* and *inconclusive* evidence for a conclusion still remains. Thus, the fundamental objective of my analysis was to establish that, for target machines as opposed to virtual machines, the kind of evidence which program verifications can appropriately provide is uncertain rather than certain evidence, which not only does not contradict the possibility that program verifications are evidential but even implies it (Fetzer 1989e, p. 920).

When I submitted my response to Dobson and Randell (1989), however, Peter Denning balked. I asked for equal time by having it run as an OP/ED piece, which is technically known there as a "Viewpoint", but he wanted to edit it drastically and to print it as a Letter to the Editor instead. It finally appeared in the August issue (Fetzer 1989e). In the meanwhile, the magazine published a letter in which I extended the distinction between algorithms and programs to the problem of patent and copyright protection in the June issue (Fetzer 1989d) and another set of Letters to the Editor regarding the program verification debate in the July issue (Hill et al. 1989).

THE BARWISE COLUMN

These events were insignificant by contrast with the next development, however, which occurred when Jon Barwise devoted his column in *Notices of the AMS* (American Mathematical Society) to the program verification controversy. He began by discussing the celebrated debates that occurred early in the 20th century over the foundations of mathematics which, after extended deliberations that seemed to generate more heat than light, led to the formulation of various positions about the nature of mathematics, such as Platonism, logicism, formalism and intuitionism, which have contributed to our understanding of the subject and have "kept the wolf from the door".

Barwise drew an explicit comparison between the debates over the foundations of mathematics and the program verification debate, which he described as concerning the relation of mathematics "to the rest of the world":

> Today a similar controversy about the nature of mathematics and its relation to the rest of the world is raging out of sight of most mathematicians in the pages of *CACM*, the *Communications of the Association for Computing Machinery*. The debate is almost as

exciting and at least as acrimonious. . . . The present debate swirls around an article called "Program Verification: The Very Idea", written by the philosopher James Fetzer. (Barwise 1989, p. 844)

Barwise believed that the program verification debate might contribute to our understanding of the nature of *applied* mathematics as the earlier debates contributed to our understanding of the nature of *pure* mathematics.

I was enormously flattered. Barwise followed Bevier, Smith and Young in characterizing my position by means of three key contentions as follow:

(1) The purpose of program verification is to provide a mathematical method for guaranteeing the performance of a program.

(2) This is possible for algorithms, which cannot be executed by a machine, but not possible for programs, which can be executed by a machine.

(3) There is little to be gained and much to be lost though fruitless efforts to guarantee the reliability of programs when no guarantees are to be had. (Barwise 1989, p. 845)

And he reported that I accepted this summary as perfectly reasonable, "so long as the first premise is intended as a reflection of the position that is— implicitly or explicitly—endorsed by the proponents of program verification"

In my estimation, the discussion by Barwise was a valuable contribution to the debate, partially because, in general, he endorsed my position. But I also took exception to some of his arguments in a letter that subsequently appeared in his column. In particular, he alleged that I had committed the Fallacy of Identification by viewing "proofs" as purely syntactical entities, an objection to which I took exception on the grounds that this conception of "proof" was the relevant one within this context; and he claimed that I had failed to sufficiently differentiate "programs" as (abstract) types and "programs" as (causal) instances, a conception fundamental to my position.

I therefore responded to this objection by distinguishing programs-as-texts (unloaded) from programs-as-causes (loaded), where (human) verification involves the application of deductive methods to programs-as-texts:

> Hoare and I both assume that programs-as-causes are represented by programs-as-texts. The difference is that Hoare assumes that programs-as-causes are always *appropriately* represented by programs-as-texts, an assumption that I challenge. (Fetzer 1989f, p. 1353)

Thus, programming languages themselves function as models of (actual or virtual) machines, where the degree of correspondence between them is a matter that, in the case of target machines, unlike that of virtual machines, cannot possibly be ascertained on the basis of purely deductive reasoning.

SUBSEQUENT DEVELOPMENTS

There have been several interesting developments since then. In 1990, for example, the Association for Computing Machinery invited me to participate in a formal debate on the scope and limits of formal methods in software engineering. My opponents were Mark Ardis and David Gries, two of "The Gang of Ten". More significantly, in 1991, I received an invitation to contribute a 10,000 word entry on "program verification" from Allen Kent and James G. Williams, the editors of the *Encyclopedia of Mircoprocessors*, an entry that they also included in their *Encyclopedia of Computer Science and Technology*, both published by Marcel Dekker (Fetzer 1993a and 1994).

In my more recent work on this subject, I have emphasized the differences between formal systems, scientific theories, and computer programs. While mathematical proofs, scientific theories and computer programs qualify as syntactical entities, scientific theories and computer programs have a semantic significance (for the physical world) that proofs (in pure mathematics) do not possess. And computer programs possess a causal capability that even scientific theories do not enjoy, which reflects the fact that each of them can be subjected to different methods of evaluation (Fetzer 1991).

I have also collaborated with Tim Colburn and Terry Rankin in editing a collection of classic and contemporary articles on program verification, which includes papers by John McCarthy, Peter Naur, Robert Floyd, C. A. R. Hoare, William Scherlis and Dana Scott, Bertrand Meyer, Bruce Blum, Christiane Floyd, Brian Smith, and other papers I have discussed (Colburn et al., 1993). In my capacity as the editor of *Minds and Machines*, I have sought to nurture the fledgling field of "the philosophy of computer science", as I think of it, and have had the opportunity to publish several important articles by Colburn (1991) and by David Nelson (1992 and 1994), among others.

Opinions appear to differ over whether or not the program verification debate has had any impact on the computer science community. A book entitled *Fatal Defect* by Ivars Peterson appeared during 1995 (Peterson 1995). He discusses a series of mishaps and accidents involving computer systems and reviews contributions by many experts in the field, including four of "The Gang of Ten". He describes the program verification debate, accurately quoting passages from "Program Verification: The Very Idea":

"The limitations involved here are not merely practical: *they are rooted in the very character of causal systems themselves*", Fetzer emphasized. "From a methodological point of view, it might be said that programs are conjectures, while executions are attempted—and all too frequently successful—refutations." (Peterson 1995, p. 181)

Nevertheless, he concludes that, "In the end, the debate didn't settle much of anything, and Fetzer's arguments did not derail program verification", although its proponents are perhaps "less extravagant" in their claims and "less casual" in their use of the language of "proof" (Peterson 1995, p. 183).

PHILOSOPHY AND COMPUTING

During a visit to England in November 1996, however, I had the pleasure of presenting a lecture at King's College of the University of London, during which I reviewed many of these matters. During the discussion, I was fascinated to learn from a member of the audience that he had been in Japan recently and that, while waiting at a train station outside Tokyo, he had encountered C. A. R. Hoare. He took the opportunity to ask Hoare about something he had heard of but did not then understand, the program verification debate. Hoare almost immediately launched into an explanation of how the use of formal methods may detect problems in programs at an early stage and thereby yield better average performance under statistical controls.[4] [Note added 2000: That warmed my heart.]

Whether or not philosophy has contributed to computer science in this instance, there appears to be an important interaction phenomenon here that deserves to be considered. As I previously explained, I deliberately chose to pursue these issues without appealing to the analytic/synthetic distinction, first, because it would have required explanation for the benefit of computer scientists, and, second, because many philosophers deny it. Even though I myself have never believed there were appropriate grounds for its rejection, I was reluctant to rest my case on such a disputed premise.

The more I have examine these problems, however, the more convinced I have become of the tenability—*and even vitality*—of that distinction. The differences between virtual and physical machines, between abstract entities and causal systems, between algorithms and programs, between pure and applied mathematics and between validity and soundness upon which these crucial issues depend are diverse manifestations of the underlying difference between kinds of knowledge that are analytic and *a priori* and kinds of knowledge that are synthetic and *a posteriori*. To those who remain skeptical of this distinction, I ask you to consider the significance of the program verification debate as a form of vindication of the distinction.

My studies of computer systems have also convinced me that the more serious the consequences of making mistakes, the greater our obligation to insure that they are not made. This obligation in turn implies that purely formal methods must give way to program testing and system prototyping as the degree of seriousness of making mistakes increases, as follows:

Formal Proofs	Program Testing	System Prototyping

a priori   *a posteriori*

◀———————— Degrees of Seriousness of Mistakes ————————▶

lowest   highest

Thus, this appears to me to be one situation in which philosophy makes a (non-trivial) difference to important issues of public policy (Fetzer 1996).

ACKNOWLEDGMENTS

I am deeply indebted to Chuck Dunlop, Al Sanders, Rob Kling, David Cole, David Nelson and Tim Colburn. For further discussion, see Colburn (1993).

NOTES

[1] The program had been inspired by David Hemmendinger, a philosophy Ph.D. who had acquired an M.S. in computer science and had joined the faculty at Wright State. The other participants were Charles E. M. Dunlop, an old friend who convinced me that I should join him in taking advantage of this program while it lasted; Ken Ray, a former student of his and of mine when we were visiting faculty at the University of Cincinnati during 1978-80; Adam Drozdek, who recently received tenure at Duquesne University; and Joe Sartorelli, who was then on leave from Arkansas State University.

[2] My grounds for rejecting Quine's critique of the analytic/synthetic distinction are elaborated, for example, in Fetzer (1990), pp. 105-110, and in Fetzer (1993b), pp. 16-21. Indeed, my first written assignment in graduate school at Indiana University in 1966 was composing a critique of "Two Dogmas". While I disagreed with Quine even then regarding the first "dogma", I agreed with him regarding reductionism; see Fetzer (1993b), pp. 51-55.

[3] If the paper had begun with this title, however, it might not have been published. Years later, I was advised that the area editor for dependable computing, John Rushby, had said that, if it had come to him for editorial review, he would have killed it. Such are the vicissitudes of publication.

[4] The audience member turned out to be the philosopher Donald Gillies, of King's College, London.

REFERENCES

Ardis, M., V. Basili et al. (1989), "Editorial Process Verification", *Communications of the ACM* (March 1989), pp. 287-288.

Barwise, J. (1989), "Mathematical Proofs of Computer System Correctness", *Notices of the AMS* (September 1989), pp. 844-851.

Cohn, A. (1989), "The Notion of Proof in Hardware Verification", *Journal of Automated Reasoning* **5** (1989), pp. 127-139.

Colburn, T. R. (1991), "Program Verification, Defeasible Reasoning, and Two Conceptions of Computer Science", *Minds and Machines* (February 1991), pp. 97-116.

Colburn, T. R. (1993), "Computer Science and Philosophy", in T. R. Colburn, J. H. Fetzer, and T. L. Rankin, eds., *Program Verification* (Dordrecht, The Netherlands: Kluwer Academic Publishers, 1993), pp. 3-31.

Colburn, T. R., J. H. Fetzer, and T. L. Rankin, eds., *Program Verification* (Dordrecht, The Netherlands: Kluwer Academic Publishers, 1993).

DeMillo, R., R. Lipton and A. Perlis (1979), "Social Processes and Proofs of Theorems and Programs", *Communications of the ACM* (May 1979), pp. 271-280.

Denning, P. (1989), "Reply from the Editor in Chief", *Communications of the ACM* (March 1989), pp. 289-290.

Dobson, J. and B. Randell (1989), "Program Verification: Public Image and Private Reality", *Communications of the ACM* (April 1989), pp. 420-422.

Fetzer, J. H. (1974), "Grunbaum's 'Defense' of the Symmetry Thesis", *Philosophical Studies* (April 1974), pp. 173-187.

Fetzer, J. H. (1981), *Scientific Knowledge* (Dordrecht, The Netherlands: D. Reidel, 1981).

Fetzer, J. H. (1988), "Program Verification: The Very Idea", *Communications of the ACM* (September 1988), pp. 1048-1063.

Fetzer, J. H. (1989a), "Response from the Author", *Communications of the ACM* (March 1989), pp. 288-289.

Fetzer, J. H. (1989b), "Program Verification Reprise: The Author's Response", *Communications of the ACM* (March 1989), pp. 377-381.

Fetzer, J. H. (1989c), "Author's Response", *Communications of the ACM* (April 1989), pp. 510-512.

Fetzer, J. H. (1989d), "Patents and Programs", *Communications of the ACM* (June 1989), pp. 675-676.

Fetzer, J. H. (1989e), "Another Point of View", *Communications of the ACM* (August 1989), pp. 920-921.

Fetzer, J. H. (1989f), "Mathematical Proofs of Computer System Correctness: A Response", *Notices of the AMS* (December 1989), pp. 1352-1353.

Fetzer, J. H. (1990), *Artificial Intelligence: Its Scope and Limits* (Dordrecht, The Netherlands: Kluwer Academic Publishers, 1990).

Fetzer, J. H. (1991), "Philosophical Aspects of Program Verification", *Minds and Machines* (May 1991), pp. 197-216.

Fetzer, J. H. (1993a), "Program Verification", *Encyclopedia of Computer Science and Technology*, Vol. 28 (New York, NY: Marcel Dekker, 1993), pp. 237-254.

Fetzer, J. H. (1993b), *Philosophy of Science* (New York, NY: Paragon House Publishers, 1993).

Fetzer, J. H. (1994), "Program Verification", *Encyclopedia of Microprocessors*, Vol. 14 (New York, NY: Marcel Dekker, 1994), pp. 47-64.

Fetzer, J. H. (1996), "Computer Reliability and Public Policy: Limits of Knowledge of Computer-Based Systems", *Social Philosophy & Policy*, Vol. 13 (1996), forthcoming.

Hempel, C. G. (1965), *Aspects of Scientific Explanation* (New York, NY: The Free Press, 1965).

Hill, R., R. Conte et al. (1989), "More on Verification", *Communications of the ACM* (July 1989), pp. 790-792.

Hoare, C. A. R. (1969), "An Axiomatic Basis for Computer Programming", *Communications of the ACM* (October 1969), pp. 576-583.

Marcotty, M and H. E. Ledgard (1986), *Programming Language Landscape*, 2nd ed. (Chicago, IL: Science Research Associates, 1986).

Muller, H., C. Holt, and A. Watters (1989), "More on the Very Idea", *Communications of the ACM* (April 1989), pp. 506-510.

Nelson, D. (1992), "Deductive Program Verification (A Practitioner's Commentary)", *Minds and Machines* (August 1992), pp. 283-307.

Nelson, D. (1994), Discussion Review of Robert S. Boyer and J Strother Moore, *A Computational Handbook*, and J Strother Moore (ed.), "Special Issue on System Verification", *Journal of Automated Reasoning* (December 1989), *Minds and Machines* (February 1994), pp. 93-101.

Peterson, I. (1995), *Fatal Defect: Chasing Killer Computer Bugs* (New York: Random House/Times Books, 1995).

Pleasant, J., L. Paulson et al. (1989), "The Very Idea", *Communications of the ACM* (March 1989), pp. 374-377.

EPILOGUE

CHAPTER 11

COMPUTER RELIABILITY AND PUBLIC POLICY: LIMITS OF KNOWLEDGE OF COMPUTER-BASED SYSTEMS*

I. INTRODUCTION

Perhaps no technological innovation has so dominated the second half of the twentieth century as has the introduction of the programmable computer. It is quite difficult if not impossible to imagine how contemporary affairs—in business and science, communications and transportation, governmental and military activities, for example—could be conducted without the use of computing machines, whose principal contribution has been to relieve us of the necessity for certain kinds of mental exertion. The computer revolution has reduced our mental labors by means of these machines, just as the Industrial Revolution reduced our physical labor by means of other machines.

The public policy problems that accompany this technology are diverse—ranging from matters of liability when safety-critical systems malfunction to issues of patent and copyright protection for software and on to questions of propriety relative to the transmission of pornography via electronic bulletin-boards. Some of these, such as matters of patent and copyright protection, may represent old problems in a new guise, while others, such as those of liability when safety-critical systems malfunction, may go beyond the scope of previous technology and create difficulties that require innovative solutions. The available remedies may simply not be adequate.

Discovering adequate solutions to novel problems presupposes that those problems themselves are well-understood. The purpose of this essay is to contribute toward better understanding the dimensions of these problems by an exploration of the limits of our knowledge about computer systems as *knowledge-based systems*. This notion is typically applied to a branch of computer science known as *expert systems*, which uses the knowledge of experts in producing programs, but it can also be applied to *artificial intelligence*, which incorporates procedures intended to model human minds. Even ordinary computers, however, are knowledge-based in a broad sense.

During the course of this study, distinctions will be drawn between the software and hardware components of computers, on the one hand, and between computers and computer systems, on the other. The first of these

* I am grateful to Tim Colburn, M. M. Lehman, and the editors of this volume for critical comments and valuable suggestions regarding this essay.

is no doubt familiar, but becomes especially important in attempting to elaborate different senses in which computer systems qualify as "knowledge-based." The software component of an expert system, for example, crucially depends upon information provided by an "expert" and transmitted by a "knowledge engineer," where the person who writes the program typically uses the "knowledge" thus supplied at the direction of his project manager.

The function of the program, of course, is to control the performance of a computer when it executes that program. The intended effects that may be brought about thereby, however, extend far beyond symbol processing and number crunching to treating cancer and operating aircraft. Studies of reliability, therefore, need to distinguish between techniques and methods that can be applied to software, to hardware, and to entire "computer systems," where computer systems consist of computers and associated equipment situated in the world. For the approaches that are available for evaluating the reliability of some of these may differ from those available for evaluating the reliability of the others.

The discussion that follows will consider the most general features that distinguish computers and computer systems in order to isolate what seem to be their most important features with respect to issues of public policy: (1) their epistemic origins as various kinds of knowledge-based systems; (2) their ontic character relative to models of three distinct varieties; and (3) the limits of the extent to which their performance can be guaranteed. The considerations that follow suggest that the reliability of these systems—including their correctness—cannot be guaranteed, and that our increasing dependence on computer technology in various dimensions of our personal and social lives raises fundamental ethical questions and related problems of public policy which need to be addressed and may no longer be ignored.

II. Expert Systems

A. Computers as data-processing machines

Computing machines are often described as *data-processing* mechanisms, which take "data" as input and produce "information" as output. One author, for example, has distinguished between Tycho Brahe's observations of the positions of the planets as *data* in relation to Johannes Kepler's calculations of the orbits of the planets as *information*.[1] From a theoretical perspective, however, Brahe's "data" appears to be informative about some issues (such as the locations of certain heavenly bodies at certain dates and times), while Kepler's laws have functioned as "data"

---

[1] William S. Davis, *Fundamental Computer Concepts* (Reading, MA: Addison-Wesley, 1986), p. 2.

relative to other inquiries (such as Isaac Newton's calculation of the laws of motion and universal gravitation).

These reflections suggest that the difference between "data" and "information" must be *pragmatic* in character and determined by what we want to learn ("information") in relation to what we already know ("data"). An alternative conception would place computing machines within a pragmatic context by viewing them as *problem-solving* mechanisms, where the (general purpose) computer becomes a special purpose problem-solver when it has been provided with suitable software. The point of computer science thus becomes that of providing the means to create hardware that can run various kinds of software and software that can solve various kinds of problems.

The kinds of problems that might be solved depend upon the kinds of solutions that are available for solving them. Software commonly comes into existence when *programs* are composed that implement algorithms in specific computer languages (Pascal, Prolog, and so on), where *algorithms* formulate "step-by-step" procedures that provide solutions to specific kinds of problems in a finite number of steps.[2] In those cases in which no algorithm happens to exist or can exist, partial solutions may be available in the form of *asymmetrical procedures* (which provide acceptable solutions, when they provide a solution), or of *heuristics* (as "solutions" that have exceptions).[3]

Programs are thus properly understood as sets of instructions for computers, where the adequacy of those instructions tends to depend on and vary with the sources from which they were derived. A program for processing U.S. income-tax returns, for example, could be based upon current (or dated) information provided by the Internal Revenue Service (or by some other source), where its utility for generating acceptable returns could be enormously variable. Those who compose such programs ("programmers") might or might not be highly competent problem-solvers with respect to the problem-domain (of tax policy, for example) and may depend on guidance provided by others.

Those who are highly competent in devising or in evaluating solutions to problems within a specific problem-domain are usually called "experts." In order for the knowledge possessed by an expert to be available to the programmer, however, it must be secured from that expert in a form that makes it accessible to the programmer, a responsibility that is carried by persons known as "knowledge engineers." The process of obtaining knowledge from an expert and recasting that knowledge into

[2] Stephen C. Kleene, *Mathematical Logic* (New York: John Wiley and Sons, 1967), ch. 5.

[3] Douglas Downing and Michael Covington, *Dictionary of Computer Terms* (Woodbury, NY: Barron's, 1986), p. 117. On the use of the term "heuristics" in the field of artificial intelligence, see Avron Barr and Edward A. Feigenbaum, *The Handbook of Artificial Intelligence*, vol. I (Reading, MA: Addison-Wesley, 1981), pp. 28–30, 58, 109.

the form of a program yields an "expert system."[4] There are various kinds of expert systems, whose properties are by and large well-understood.[5]

B. Expert systems as "knowledge-based"

Expert systems thus reflect one familiar sense in which a computer system can qualify as a "knowledge-based" system. An expert system for the diagnosis of blood diseases known as MYCIN, for example, has been studied extensively.[6] MYCIN employs over five hundred rules that relate the results of tests to diagnose diseases and recommend treatments, where the reliability of the system obviously depends upon the adequacy of the knowledge upon which that system is based. The system of rules that MYCIN employs represents a combination of current scientific knowledge about diseases of the blood with heuristic methods to produce a system that approximates human expertise.

The inference rules that expert systems like MYCIN employ include not only "forward-chaining" rules that permit ordinary deductive inferences to be drawn, but also rules that allow other kinds of inferences to be drawn. MYCIN obtains data about patients through interviews with their doctors; information from these interviews is used to assign values to variables relevant to rendering diagnoses of patients' diseases and prescriptions of recommended treatments. That data in turn is processed by applying conditional rules like the following:

RULE 156

IF: 1) the site of the culture is blood, and

2) the gram stain of the organism is gramneg, and

3) the morphology of the organism is rod, and

4) the portal entry of the organism is urine, and

5) the patient has not had a genito-urinary manipulative procedure, and

6) cystitis is not a problem for which the patient has been treated,

THEN: There is suggestive evidence (.6) that the identity of the organism is *E. coli*.[7]

---

[4] Examples of expert systems may be found in Avron Barr and Edward A. Feigenbaum, *The Handbook of Artificial Intelligence*, vol. II (Reading, MA: Addison-Wesley, 1982).

[5] A discussion of various kinds of expert systems may be found in James H. Fetzer, *Artificial Intelligence: Its Scope and Limits* (Dordrecht, The Netherlands: Kluwer Academic Publishers, 1990), pp. 180–91.

[6] Bruce G. Buchanan and Edward H. Shortliffe, eds., *Rule-based Expert Systems: The MYCIN Experiments of the Stanford Heuristic Programming Project* (Reading, MA: Addison-Wesley, 1984).

[7] *Ibid.*, p. 74. The number ".6" represents a "certainty factor" which, on a scale from −1 to 1, indicates how strongly the claim has been confirmed (CF > 0) or disconfirmed (CF < 0); see also note 34 below.

This specific rule exemplifies "backward chaining," which involves drawing an inference from test results (interpreted as "symptoms") to their most likely causes (as "infections" or as "diseases"). It therefore represents a type of inductive inference from effects to their causes that might best be understood as "inference to the best explanation." An inference of this kind presupposes the availability of a set of alternative possible explanations, some of which may provide more adequate (or "preferable") explanations of the evidence (or "data") than do others. When the available evidence is sufficient, then the most adequate explanation ought to be tentatively adopted.[8]

Because more than one cause (infection or disease) might produce some of the same effects (or symptoms), rules of inference of this kind in MYCIN are qualified by "certainty factors" (or CFs), such as .6 in Rule 156. Thus,

> experience with clinicians had shown that clinicians do not use the information comparable to implemented standard statistical methods [such as ordinary "probabilities" and "likelihoods"]. However, the concept of CFs did appear to fit the clinicians' reasoning patterns— their judgments of how they weighted factors, strong or weak, in decision making.[9]

The domain-specific expertise needed to construct a knowledge-based system such as MYCIN thus extends beyond mere descriptions of symptoms (effects) to the capacity to derive inferences to their causes (infections or diseases).

Thus, in providing a characterization of "expert systems" generally, a distinction is commonly drawn between the *knowledge base* and the *inference engine*. In the case of MYCIN, for example, the knowledge base includes information about causal relations and statistical correlations between the occurrence of infections and diseases and the occurrence of various symptoms, including rules such as Rule 156, while the inference engine applies them to specific cases. When data about a new case is provided as input to a system via its user interface, the application of the inference engine produces the information that is desired as output, as shown in Figure 1.[10]

---

[8] Inference to the best explanation is also known as "abductive inference." See, for example, James H. Fetzer and Robert Almeder, *Glossary of Epistemology/Philosophy of Science* (New York: Paragon House, 1993); and especially Yun Peng and James Reggia, *Abductive Inference Models for Diagnostic Problem-Solving* (New York: Springer-Verlag, 1990).

[9] Barr and Feigenbaum, *The Handbook of Artificial Intelligence*, vol. II, p. 189. The tendency has been toward the use of measures of subjective probability in lieu of CFs; see note 34 below.

[10] Buchanan and Shortliffe, eds., *Rule-based Expert Systems*, p. 4.

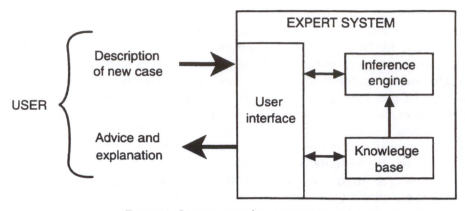

FIGURE 1. Components of an expert system.

C. Expert systems as performance systems

Because MYCIN offers recommendations to doctors with respect to how they should treat their patients, it has sometimes been described as a "performance system" in the sense that it is employed to perform a task.[11] Whether or not this conception successfully differentiates systems such as this one from other systems, however, is not entirely obvious. An income-tax processing system, for example, appears to be employed to perform a task in that very same sense. Indeed, even a pocket calculator might be characterized as a "performance system" insofar as we employ it to perform various arithmetic tasks (of addition, subtraction, division, multiplication, etc.).

Such an approach merely reinforces the notion that programmable computers are best envisioned not simply as "data-processing" devices but rather as "problem-solving" mechanisms. To the extent to which their problem-solving abilities depend upon domain-specific knowledge, however, it should be apparent that computer scientists *as* computer scientists are typically not sources of the domain-specific knowledge which knowledge-based systems require. Sometimes it might happen that an expert on diseases of the blood, for example, happens to program a computer to enable it to diagnose blood diseases, but such circumstances are quite uncommon.

The programmer and the knowledge engineer may sometimes coincide, when both tasks are fulfilled by the same person. This makes individuals who can assume both roles especially valuable, since they not only can interact with experts to acquire domain-specific knowledge but also can codify that knowledge in the form of a program. When this happens, the risk of the introduction of distortion or of the loss of information in going from the expert to the programmer is drastically reduced.

[11] *Ibid.*, p. 5.

Whether or not the knowledge engineer wholly succeeds in understanding the expert, the programmer at least does not risk misunderstanding the knowledge engineer.

As a theoretical possibility, of course, a programmer might become an expert within a specific problem-domain (such as income-tax preparation or blood-disease diagnosis) and thereby position himself to evaluate the information provided to him by knowledge engineers. As a practical necessity, however, this alternative is virtually never available, for all of the obvious reasons motivating divisions of labor. Thus, computer programmers *as* computer programmers are typically not only not the sources of the domain-specific knowledge that expert systems require but also are not appropriately positioned to evaluate the adequacy of that knowledge.

This implies that computer programmers who program expert systems are dependent upon their expert sources in two different ways. First, they must accept those *sources* as appropriate for providing information in the construction of expert systems. Second, they must accept *that information* as suitable for the purpose of programming these systems. Computer programmers are therefore typically dependent upon sources whose competence lies beyond their control, for information the reliability of which they are unable to evaluate. They thus have no alternative but to rely upon "experts" as authorities and cannot assess the quality of the knowledge they are given.

III. KNOWLEDGE AND REASONING

A. "Information" versus "knowledge"

Not all "appeals to authority" are fallacious, of course. When a person who is an authority in one field is cited in another field in which he is *not* an authority, a fallacious appeal to authority occurs. When a person who is an authority is cited in a field in which he *is* an authority, a nonfallacious appeal to authority occurs. (Citing Einstein's views on problems in physics, for example, is clearly nonfallacious, but citing Einstein on world peace is.) The problem is not that knowledge engineers commonly commit fallacious appeals to authority in selecting sources of information for expert systems, but rather that programmers are usually not qualified to tell the difference between fallacious and nonfallacious appeals.

The situation might be alleviated if knowledge engineers were suitably positioned to select appropriate sources of knowledge in their endeavor to secure information for the construction of expert systems. But knowledge engineers are ordinarily directed to rely upon the information provided by specific sources designated by *project managers*, who in turn are responsible to those who have commissioned these systems. It should not be surprising if those who finance the construction of such systems — typically, as products that are intended for military, industrial, or commercial consumption—reserve the right to specify those sources of information to be used.[12]

The appropriate source, of course, depends upon the kind of system under development. An expert system for tax preparation would require an expert on tax preparation; an expert system for the diagnosis of diseases of the blood would require an expert on blood diseases; and an expert system on the behavior of a specific person—such as Joseph Stalin, Adolf Hitler, or Saddam Hussein—would require an expert on Stalin, Hitler, or Hussein. The kind of knowledge required would differ accordingly from case to case: in some cases, it may be easily available, but in other cases, it may be harder to acquire—and in certain other special cases, it may be relatively esoteric.[13]

Perhaps the most important consequence of this is that computer scientists as hardware and software specialists are not well positioned to evaluate whether the information they are provided properly qualifies as "knowledge." They are typically participants in group projects supervised by project managers, and the selection of experts as sources is usually a matter that lies beyond their control. While programmers may be responsible for their programming, responsibility for the construction of the software component of an expert system must be *distributed* between the project manager, the authority selected, the knowledge engineer, and the programmer.

Even when the assumptions are made (a) that no information has been lost in the process of the transmission of information from its source to the programmer by the knowledge engineer, and (b) that no mistakes have been made by the programmer in translating that information into a program by means of a suitable language, it remains possible (c) that the expert system so derived might fail because the information on which it is based is either inaccurate or incomplete. When problems arise with the use of an "expert system" that derive from the content of the program itself, therefore, one possible explanation is that the information provided was not "knowledge."

B. The nature of knowledge

The situation is compounded by the consideration that computer programmers *as* computer programmers need not understand the nature of knowledge itself. The theory of knowledge is a philosophical subject that aims at defining the nature and the scope of human knowledge. Since the theory of knowledge is not a subject in the computer science curriculum,

---

[12] On the project manager, see, for example, Neal Whitten, *Managing Software Development Projects* (New York: John Wiley and Sons, 1989).

[13] Criteria for the selection of domain experts are discussed by D. A. Waterman, *A Guide to Expert Systems* (Reading, MA: Addison-Wesley, 1986).

it is clear that if a computer programmer happened to be familiar with problems in the theory of knowledge, it would not be by virtue of the background and training which he had acquired in the study of computer science but rather by virtue of the background and training which he had acquired in the study of philosophy.

The traditional conception of knowledge defines "knowledge" within the context of sentences of the form "x knows that p" as warranted true belief.[14] That is, a person x possesses knowledge described by the sentence p when x believes that p, x is warranted in that belief, and p is the case (that is, the sentence p is true). Thus, p might describe information for processing tax returns (or information about diseases and infections of the blood, etc.). A person x who was especially knowledgeable about processing tax returns (diseases and infections of the blood, etc.) thus might seem to be an "expert" by virtue of possessing numerous warranted true beliefs about that domain.

What may be most important about "experts" and "knowledge," however, is the presumption that the evidence available that warrants beliefs within this domain is presumed to be warranted in turn. In other words, "experts" are not merely persons who possess *true beliefs* in relation to some problem domain; they are persons who *know how* those beliefs themselves are warranted by means of other beliefs, and, in turn, how those other beliefs are warranted. Thus, the conception of knowledge that characterizes "experts" is not only that their beliefs about problems within their domain are warranted but that the evidence on the basis of which they are warranted is also warranted to the maximum possible extent.

From this perspective, a domain expert is someone who not only possesses knowledge of the *know-that* variety with respect to true beliefs within his domain of expertise, but also possesses knowledge of the *know-how* variety with respect to how those beliefs came to be accepted within that domain.[15] The study of expert systems, however, has had the intriguing side-effect of displaying the difficulty that experts can have in articulating that expertise. There appear to be stages in the acquisition of expertise, where procedures that were initially explicitly rule-governed and self-conscious become habitual. It can be hard for experts to find words that describe what they do.

The knowledge possessed by experts includes (possibly implicit) knowledge of the methods by which that knowledge itself is acquired. Those who pose as "experts" but lack this form of "expertise" may be able to deceive others about themselves but could be exposed by the real thing.

---

[14] The term "traditional" occurs here in contrast to the (far weaker) "artificial intelligence" conception of knowledge, in particular. On the traditional conception, see, for example, Israel Scheffler, *Conditions of Knowledge* (Chicago, IL: University of Chicago Press, 1965). On the use of this term in AI, see especially Fetzer, *Artificial Intelligence*, ch. 5, pp. 127–32.

[15] See James H. Fetzer, *Scientific Knowledge* (Dordrecht, The Netherlands: D. Reidel, 1981), ch. 1.

The principal difference between experts and nonexperts (quacks, frauds, and so on) in relation to a specific problem-domain thus seems to be that while quacks or frauds, especially, may appear to possess domain-specific knowledge, they lack an understanding of the corresponding methods that yield those warrants without which there is no domain-specific knowledge.

C. The analytic-synthetic distinction

The kinds of warrants that are appropriate, however, depend upon and vary with the content of the object of belief. Person x is entitled to believe in the truth of a sentence p whose truth or falsity merely depends upon the language in which it is expressed by appropriate reference to that language. In relation to English, for example, beliefs that bachelors are unmarried, that triangles have three sides, and so on are warranted by *dictionary definitions*, which record the established usage of words within a community. Since their truth follows from definitions, beliefs of this kind are often called "definitional truths," and the sentences that express them are called "analytic."

Sentences whose truth does not follow from definitions alone, however, require other kinds of warrants. The belief that there is a beer in the refrigerator, for example, might be warranted by experience as a description of something x observed. This may be described as a matter of *perceptual inference*, since it involves the use of language to describe the contents of experience. It is important to notice, however, that even perceptual inference does not guarantee the truth of a belief. What x took to be a bottle of beer might turn out to be a new fruit drink that his daughter brought home from the corner store, a drink which comes in bottles that look like bottles for beer.

The conclusions of perceptual inferences depend upon language but are not warranted by language alone. Whether or not there is a bottle of beer in the refrigerator cannot be determined on the basis of the meaning of the words involved. However common an occurrence of an event of this kind may be, the truth of the belief that there is a bottle of beer in the refrigerator is not merely a matter of definition. The meaning of this sentence is compatible with its falsity as well as with its truth. If it should happen to be true, therefore, its truth or falsity depends upon how things are in the world and not merely on the meaning of words. Its truth is not "analytic."

Other beliefs, of course, might be warranted by *deductive inference* or by *inductive inference* from things already known. Inductive reasoning can be applied to draw inferences from the past to the future, from samples to populations, and from the observed to the unobserved—including inference to the best explanation, of course, as a special case. Deductive reasoning can be applied to derive what must be true if something else is true, where that reasoning may or may not be purely hypothetical. Both forms of reasoning are appropriately understood as assuming the form of arguments—where *arguments* are sets of sentences divided into two parts, premises and conclusions, where premises offer warrants for conclusions.

Thus understood, the concept of knowledge has a recursive character, since the premises that warrant deductive or inductive conclusions may require warrants in turn, which might be deductive, inductive, or perceptual in kind. The process of warranting thus continues until premises requiring no further warrant are encountered, such as analytic sentences, warranted by their own meaning, or descriptive sentences, warranted by perception—where the former, unlike the latter, cannot possibly be false. Knowledge that is neither analytic nor warranted by deductive reasoning applied to analytic premises is nonanalytic and is said to be "synthetic."[16]

D. Conclusive versus inconclusive reasoning

The differences between deductive and inductive reasoning are of very great import. Deductive reasoning is *conclusive*, but nevertheless displays two aspects that must be separated. There is an important difference between (deductive) arguments that are *valid* and arguments that are *sound*. An argument is valid when, if its premises were true, then its conclusion could not be false. An argument is sound when it is not only valid but its premises are true. The conclusion of every sound argument, therefore, has to be true and could not possibly be false. An argument with false premises, however, can have a false conclusion, even when it happens to be valid.

Inductive reasoning, by contrast, is *inconclusive*—and once again two aspects must be separated here. There is an important difference between (inductive) arguments that are *proper* and arguments that are *correct*. An argument is proper when, if its premises were true, its conclusion would acquire a degree of evidential support corresponding to the strength of the premises. An argument is correct when it is not only proper but its premises are true. The conclusion of a correct argument, therefore, has acquired a degree of evidential support, but its conclusion may still be false. Thus, inductive arguments remain inconclusive, even when they are as strong as they can be.

[16] The origins of distinctions between analytic and synthetic knowledge can be traced back to the work of eighteenth and nineteenth century philosophers, especially David Hume (1711–1776) and Immanuel Kant (1724–1804). Hume drew a distinction between knowledge of relations between ideas and knowledge of matters of fact, while Kant distinguished between knowledge of conceptual connections and knowledge of the world. While it would not be appropriate to review the history of the distinction here, it should be observed that it has enormous importance in many philosophical contexts. For further discussion, see Robert Ackermann, *Theories of Knowledge* (New York: McGraw-Hill, 1965); Scheffler, *Conditions of Knowledge*; and Fetzer and Almeder, *Glossary*. For a recent defense of the distinction, see Fetzer, *Artificial Intelligence*, pp. 106–9; and especially James H. Fetzer, *Philosophy of Science* (New York: Paragon House, 1993), chs. 1 and 3.

Suitable examples can be used as illustrations. The sentences "All senators are honest" and "Jones is a senator" can serve as the premises of a
deductive argument that provides conclusive support for the conclusion
"Jones is honest"—an argument which is valid and would be sound if its
premises were true. The sentences "Many senators are honest" and "Jones
is a senator," by contrast, can serve as the premises of an inductive argument that provides inconclusive support for the conclusion "Jones is
honest"—an argument which is proper and would be correct if its premises were true. It thus provides a degree of evidential support relative
to the strength of those premises.[17]

The development of a suitable measure of the degree of evidential
support that inductive arguments confer upon their conclusions has proven
to be a difficult task, which remains imperfectly understood. Nevertheless, at least two results have emerged. The first is that every argument
has to satisfy the requirement of a *uniform interpretation*, according to
which the words that occur in an argument must have the same meaning
throughout. The second is that every inductive argument must satisfy the
requirement of *total evidence*, according to which their premises must
reflect all of the available relevant evidence. These conditions inhibit
fallacious reasoning.[18]

Fallacies of ambiguity occur when words have more than one meaning.
They may then appear in premises that are true (under one interpretation)
and in conclusions that are false (under another interpretation). A person
can be *mad* (in the sense of being angry), for example, without also being
mad (in the sense of being insane). To forestall inferences from premises
that describe someone as angry to conclusions describing him as insane,
therefore, the requirement of a uniform interpretation has to be satisfied.
This condition must also be imposed on models and theories as syntactic
structures to ensure that they sustain systematic semantic interpretation.

Other fallacies occur when inductive arguments do not consider all of
the relevant evidence that happens to be available. When coins are bent
(dice are loaded, decks are stacked), that makes a difference to the probability with which various outcomes tend to occur. If we know that a coin
is bent (that the dice are loaded, that the deck is stacked), then we would
commit a fallacy were we to ignore that information. Information that is
relevant is not always available, of course, and information that is available is not always relevant. The requirement of total evidence thus simply

---

[17] Thus, if the "many" who are honest were a large proportion of all the senators, then that
degree of support should be high; if it were only a modest proportion, then it should be low;
and so on. If the percentage were, say, m/n, then the support conferred upon the conclusion
by those premises would presumably equal m/n. See, for example, Fetzer, *Scientific Knowledge*, Part III; Fetzer, *Philosophy of Science*, chs. 4–6; and note 34 below.

[18] On the total-evidence condition, see Carl G. Hempel, *Aspects of Scientific Explanation*
(New York: The Free Press, 1965), pp. 53–79.

insists that whenever relevant evidence happens to be available, it has to be taken into account for inductive reasoning to be proper.[19]

E. Formal science versus empirical science

Perhaps the most important ramification of these considerations within the present context arises from their relations to different kinds of knowledge. A distinction is commonly drawn between the *formal sciences*, such as set theory, various branches of logic (such as sentential, predicate, and modal logic), and various branches of mathematics (such as algebra, geometry, and calculus), on the one hand, and the *empirical sciences* (such as physics [classical mechanics, statistical mechanics, quantum mechanics], chemistry, and biology), on the other—where the empirical sciences aim at the discovery of laws of nature (of physics, of chemistry, of biology).[20]

The disciplines thus classified appear to differ with respect to their content and with respect to their methods. The formal sciences, for example, are typically pursued employing exclusively deductive reasoning, where the consequences of adopting various assumptions are developed into formal theories. These theories tend to assume the form of abstract calculi that might sustain various interpretations, which make them true or false of various—abstract or physical—domains. The empirical sciences, by contrast, are pursued using methods that are deductive and inductive, methods which rely heavily upon focused observation and controlled experiments.

Because the formal sciences are distinguished by methods that do not require data or information from the world around us and can be pursued independently of experience, they may properly be described as "*a priori*" disciplines. Because the empirical sciences are distinguished by methods that do require data or information from the world around us and cannot be pursued independently of experience, they can analogously be described as "*a posteriori*" disciplines. When abstract calculi are provided with abstract interpretations, they are (purely) "formal theories," yet when they are provided with empirical interpretations, they qualify as "empirical theories."[21]

The development of formal theories or of empirical theories presumes the availability of a language consisting of a vocabulary and of a grammar, where the vocabulary can be treated as primitive marks which pos-

---

[19] This is a pragmatic requirement that governs inductive reasoning.

[20] For further discussion, see, for example, Fetzer, *Philosophy of Science*, ch. 1.

[21] See, for example, Carl G. Hempel, "On the Nature of Mathematical Truth" and "Geometry and Empirical Science," both of which are reprinted in Herbert Feigl and Wilfrid Sellars, eds., *Readings in Philosophical Analysis* (New York: Appleton-Century-Crofts, 1949), pp. 222–37 and 238–49.

	A PRIORI METHODS (formal proofs, etc.)	A POSTERIORI METHODS (experimentation, etc.)
ANALYTIC CONTENT	FORMAL SCIENCES	———
SYNTHETIC CONTENT	———	EMPIRICAL SCIENCES

FIGURE 2. Formal versus empirical sciences.

sess no semantic significance. The development of a formal theory thus involves elaboration of the syntactical relations that obtain between the primitives that are postulated by the theory, where the deductive consequences that follow from its primitive assumptions are derived using exclusively formal methods. When these theories are interpreted in relation to abstract domains, therefore, they must be viewed as possessing strictly analytic content.

The situation with respect to the empirical sciences, however, assumes a very different character, since these theories, in relation to the physical world, have to be viewed as possessing synthetic content. Thus, the formal sciences represent the application of *a priori* methods to analytic content, while the empirical sciences represent the application of *a posteriori* methods to synthetic content, as Figure 2 suggests. Moreover, since the methods of formal science are exclusively deductive and their content wholly analytic, these disciplines can acquire a degree of certainty of knowledge about their subjects to which the empirical sciences cannot possibly aspire.[22]

F. Implications for computer science

The most obvious implication for computer science concerns the kind of knowledge that expert systems require. An expert system for blood disease depends upon scientific knowledge of causal relations and statistical correlations between the occurrence of infections and diseases and the occurrence of various symptoms, as elements of its knowledge base. Such knowledge is clearly the synthetic product of observations and ex-

---

[22] Thus, as Einstein observed, to the extent to which the laws of mathematics refer to reality, they are not certain; and to the extent to which they are certain, they do not refer to reality—a point I shall pursue.

periments that provide evidence for inductive and deductive reasoning, where conclusions may be false even when all of their premises are true.

Because scientific knowledge is synthetic and can never be known with certainty, it always remains possible that, no matter how strongly it may be supported by the available evidence, what we take to be true may be false. If we define "knowledge" as warranted true belief, we can never be sure that what we take to be scientific knowledge qualifies as "knowledge." Consequently, we must either *redefine* "scientific knowledge" as warranted belief or *concede* that what we take to be "scientific knowledge" can be false.[23] Either way, even the perfect transmission and the flawless translation of expert knowledge cannot overcome its inherently fallible character.

There are intriguing cases that are more difficult to classify relative to these distinctions. The study of language through empirical inquiries, for example, appears to yield *a posteriori* knowledge that is based upon observations and experiments, but which supplies information about the meaning of words that is analytic. This should really come as no surprise, however, when properly understood, because analytic sentences are those whose truth is guaranteed by their meaning. What specific words mean and which sentences are analytic are matters which depend upon the syntax and semantics of that language. For ordinary languages, those relations must be learned.

This implies that our knowledge of *ordinary language* is synthetic, which means that, in relation to languages in use (English, French, Russian, and so on), the word meanings and analytic sentences that occur in those specific languages have to be discovered. Once we know the dictionary definitions that apply within a specific language, we can derive the conditional consequences that follow from the adoption of that language as a framework, as in the case of "If John is a bachelor, then John is unmarried" within English. That our knowledge of ordinary languages must be synthetic does not destroy the existence of *a priori* knowledge within those specific frameworks. But it does imply that what we take to be analytic within an ordinary language is not a matter about which we can possess knowledge that is certain.

Sometimes circumstances permit a language to be made up as a set of marks and a set of rules for their manipulation—that is, as an *artificial language*, without regard for whether anyone has used the language before. The discoveries of various non-Euclidean geometries qualify as relevant examples. While Euclid codified *axioms* (as unproven assumptions) and *theorems* (that were deducible from them) that were thought to be properties of physical space, Georg Riemann and Nikolai Lobachevski subsequently codified different axioms and derived different theorems as alternative geometries of abstract spaces. What we take to be analytic

---

[23] For further discussion, see, for example, Fetzer, *Scientific Knowledge*, pp. 14–15.

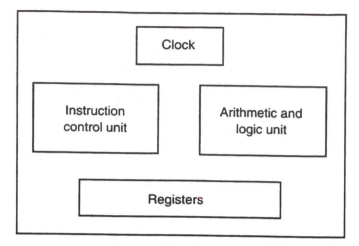

FIGURE 3. The components of a processor.

within an artificial language turns out to be a matter about which we can possess knowledge that is certain, because the definitions which appear in its dictionary are matters of stipulation. The assumptions upon which these definitions are based need no empirical support.[24]

G. The arithmetic and logic unit

Another implication of the analytic-synthetic distinction is somewhat more subtle than its consequences for expert systems. This implication arises from the incorporation of hardware for processing logical and arithmetic operations. Apart from its memory, the most basic component of a computer is its *processor*, which contains the following four important elements: a clock, an instruction control unit, an arithmetic and logic unit, and a set of registers. The function of the registers is to record the operations and the operands that are being operated upon under control of the program. These four components are represented by the diagram provided as Figure 3.[25]

Since knowledge of arithmetic and of logical relations is paradigmatic of analytic knowledge, the arithmetic and logic unit represents analytic knowledge in the form of hardware. Thus, even the construction of the hardware of a computer appears to be "knowledge based" in a broad sense. It may be tempting to assume that knowledge of elementary arithmetic (addition, subtraction, multiplication, division) are matters about which everyone is his or her own "expert." But even when such an assumption is warranted, that knowledge still has to be translated into

---

[24] The differences between stipulative truths and empirical truths are crucial for understanding computer programming.

[25] Davis, *Fundamental Computer Concepts*, p. 20. It should be observed, however, that some consider the clock to be convenient for but not essential to computer operations.

the numerals and registers, voltages and circuits that are the physical embodiment of even elementary mathematics.

The physical limitations that are imposed by the resources available for implementing knowledge of this kind by means of arithmetic and logic units are by no means trivial. The first is that the size of the numerals which can be directly operated upon within a computer is determined by the size of its registers. Computers that operate on the basis of words that are 16 bits in length can represent numbers by 16 zeros and ones in binary arithmetic, of which the largest is 32,767 in decimal—or, in the case of 32-bit processors, by 32 zeros and ones, of which the largest is 2,147,483,647 in decimal. Larger numbers, which exceed register size, may be partially represented by approximations using, for example, what is called "floating-point" notation.[26]

The problems imposed by register size are obvious for infinite numbers, such as pi. The continuum of real numbers must therefore be "replaced" by a finite subset of the rational numbers, whose representations are not uniformly dense and many of whose members are only finite approximations: "The pseudo-arithmetic operations performed by real digital computers do not obey the laws of arithmetic. . . . In fact, each concrete computer is known to violate these laws, even for the integers."[27] As a consequence, algorithms with variables that assume real-number values may be impossible to program correctly, even when those algorithms are demonstrable.

Even more disturbing is the prospect that the hardware itself might not behave in accordance with the principles of arithmetic within the bounds of its own registers. A dramatic illustration has recently occurred in the case of Intel's Pentium microprocessor, whose arithmetic and logic unit has turned out to be flawed with an error whose magnitude can be many times larger than those of comparable microprocessors.[28] Intel executives sought to minimize the seriousness of the error by suggesting that it was a problem that should be encountered only rarely. As one observer remarked, however, "these kinds of statistics are based upon the probability

[26] *Ibid.*, p. 189. There are languages and machines that permit the representation of numbers of arbitrary size through the concatenation of 32-bit words, where limitations are imposed by memory resources.

[27] David Nelson, "Deductive Program Verification (A Practitioner's Commentary)," *Minds and Machines*, vol. 2, no. 3 (August 1992), pp. 283–307; the quote is from p. 289. On this and other grounds, Nelson denies that computers are properly described as "mathematical machines" and asserts that they are better described as "logic machines."

[28] Up to ten billion times as large, according to John Markoff, "Flaw Undermines Accuracy of Pentium Chips," *New York Times*, November 24, 1994, pp. C1–C2. As Markoff illustrates, the difficulty involves division:

Problem:
4,195,835 − [(4,195,835 ÷ 3,145,727) × 3,145,727] = ?
Correct Calculation:
4,195,835 − [(1.3338204) × 3,145,727] = 0
Pentium's Calculation:
4,195,835 − [(1.3337391) × 3,145,727] = 256

of events whose probability we don't know."[29] Depending upon the operation, it could run as high as 100 percent.

H. The question of reliability

The problem with Intel's Pentium is not unique. Intel's chip-models 386 and 486 both had different mathematical errors, and other problems have arisen with other microprocessors.[30] The public response to the Pentium chip, however, appears to have exceeded past concerns by several orders of magnitude. Commentaries have ranged from describing the situation as one involving a "crisis of faith," to describing it as merely "an obscure flaw," and then to humorous asides:[31] Sample question: Why didn't Intel call the Pentium the 586? Answer: Because they added 486 and 100 on the first Pentium and got 585.999983605.

The reasons for concern, moreover, are not difficult to discern. Intel is the leading manufacturer of microprocessors in the world. Thus, it would be expected to implement the highest standards of quality. The flaw in the Pentium involves elementary mathematics—a simple matter of inaccurate division—governed by principles that are familiar and easy to understand. This problem has not been generated by limitations imposed by register size or by difficulties in the operation of "floating-point" notation. If the leading manufacturer could nevertheless produce a product with a flaw of this magnitude, then the prospect of reliable computers seems remote.

The deepest felt concerns were articulated in a commentary that appeared on the op-ed page of the *New York Times*, by an author who plaintively inquired, "On the eve of the 21st century, what basis do we have for knowing if anything on our computer screen is error-free?" His answer is *faith*:

> The complexity of today's machines is far beyond our ability to check them by hand. All the fine points are floating; the only orthodox solution is to have more faith. We must accept on faith that

[29] The remark is attributed to William Kahan of the University of California at Berkeley by Markoff, "Flaw Undermines Accuracy," p. C1. A number of articles discussing the problem have since appeared, including John Markoff, "Error in Chip Still Dogging Intel Officials," *New York Times*, December 6, 1994, p. C4; Laurie Flynn, "A New York Banker Sees Pentium Problems," *New York Times*, December 19, 1994, pp. C1–C2; John Markoff, "In About-Face, Intel Will Swap Flawed Pentium Chip for Buyers," *New York Times*, December 21, 1994, pp. A1 and C6; and John Markoff, "Intel's Crash Course on Consumers," *New York Times*, December 21, 1994, p. C1.

[30] Including a security loophole with Sun Microsystems that was acknowledged in 1991, as Markoff observes in "Flaw Undermines Accuracy," p. C2.

[31] John Hockenberry, "Pentium and Our Crisis of Faith," *New York Times*, December 28, 1994, p. A11; Peter H. Lewis, "From a Tiny Flaw, a Major Lesson," *New York Times*, December 27, 1994, p. B10; and "Cyberscope," *Newsweek*, December 12, 1994. Another example of humor at Intel's expense: Question: What's another name for the "Intel Inside" sticker they put on Pentiums? Answer: A warning label.

our telephone bills are absolutely error-free just as we must accept the integrity inside a microprocessor (even a free replacement chip).[32]

The question, no doubt, is well posed, but the answer leaves something to be desired. Articles of faith, after all, are things we believe, not because they are well supported, but in the absence of evidence or even in spite of it. The question the author raises appears to be rational, but his answer quite clearly is not.

Indeed, there are ample indications that the question is appropriate. We have discovered several grounds for disputing the reliability of our expert-system software: (1) The source of information upon which the system was constructed might be inaccurate or incomplete because the source was not an expert in the domain. (2) The transmission of that information may have introduced distortions or omissions because the "knowledge engineer" was not sufficiently competent. (3) The programmer who translated the information into a program using a programming language may have committed numerous programming errors. Because programmers are almost never experts with regard to the problem, they usually must depend on authorities for the information they program.[33]

Even when the source of information is an authority, the transmission of the knowledge introduces no distortions, and the programmer commits no mistakes—a case in which problems of kinds (1) through (3) do not occur—the inherent uncertainty of scientific knowledge would still remain because (4) even warranted scientific knowledge is still fallible and possibly false. We cannot know which among those warranted beliefs that we accept as true are *true* and which among those warranted beliefs that we accept as true are *false*. If we had direct access to the truth, after all, we would not depend on warrants. The risk of error is the price of scientific knowledge.[34]

Moreover, even leaving these sources of possible error to one side, there appear to be other problems that arise, not with respect to the software, but with regard to hardware components that no computer can function

---

[32] Hockenberry, "Pentium and Our Crisis of Faith," p. A11.

[33] As M. M. Lehman has observed, another—often more basic—problem can arise when changes in the world affect the truth of assumptions on which programs are based—which leads him to separate (what he calls) S-type and E-type systems, where the latter but not the former are subject to revision under the control of feedback. See, for example, M. M. Lehman, "Feedback, Evolution, and Software Technology," *IEEE Software Process Newsletter*, April 1995, for more discussion.

[34] Fetzer, *Scientific Knowledge*, p. 15. Other problems not discussed in the text include determining the precise conditions that must be satisfied for something to properly qualify as "scientific knowledge" (by arbitrating among inductivist, deductivist, and abductivist models, for example), and the appropriate measures that should be employed in determining degrees of evidential support (by accounting for the proper relations between subjective, frequency, and propensity interpretations of probability), a precondition for the proper appraisal of "certainty factors" (CFs), for example. These issues are pursued in Fetzer, *Scientific Knowledge*, and Fetzer, *Philosophy of Science*.

without: (5) every physical machine has inherent limitations with respect to its ability to process binary numbers imposed by the characteristics of its registers; (6) every physical machine has an arithmetic and logic unit that may introduce arbitrary errors, even if it was produced by the leading manufacturer. These difficulties appear to be even more disturbing than those encountered in the construction of knowledge-based software. The fallibility of synthetic knowledge, after all, unlike that of analytic knowledge, comes as no surprise.

IV. Programming Languages, Models, and the World

A. Programming languages and virtual machines

The distinction between natural and artificial languages has important ramifications for understanding computers and their reliability. Ordinary computers, as physical machines, operate on the basis of binary languages consisting of sequences of zeroes and ones. Programming by means of sequences of this kind is not merely extremely tedious but practically impossible. Different levels of programming languages have been developed, the lowest level of which is *assembly language*, where there is (more or less) a one-to-one relationship between computer commands and computer operations. In *higher-level languages*, such as Pascal, Prolog, and so forth, there is a one-to-many relationship between computer commands and operations (that is, a single command can cause the computer to perform a number of operations).

As a consequence, it becomes far easier to program using a higher-level language than it is using assembly language, much less using machine language itself. In effect, students are taught to program in languages that correspond, not to the *target machines* on which their programs are intended to run, but to *virtual machines*—hypothetical computers controlled by those languages. The connection between these higher-level languages and the language of the machine is thus effected by means of compilers or interpreters, which translate programs in higher-level (source) code into machine-level (target) code. *Compilers* translate whole programs into machine code and then execute them, while *interpreters* translate and execute programs line-by-line.[35]

For some programming languages, a compiler or interpreter for translating from source code to target code may not even exist. The language CORE, for example, has been introduced as a pedagogical device to familiarize students with basic principles of programming without confronting them with the necessity to master every detail. CORE thus exemplifies the possibility that there can be source languages for which

---

[35] See, for example, Davis, *Fundamental Computer Concepts*, pp. 110–13.

there are no target machines.[36] It functions as a model of a virtual machine for which there exists no physical counterpart. And it serves as a reminder that there can be differences between programming languages and the machines that execute programs.

The most important difference is that between virtual computers and physical machines. Because virtual computers are hypothetical machines, they exist as abstract entities that are not in space-time. Any connection between (the commands of) programming languages for virtual machines and (the commands of) machine languages for physical machines must be effected by compilers or interpreters, in the absence of which the programs cannot exert causal influence over any physical machine. Indeed, in the absence of a corresponding compiler or interpreter, a programming language has a standing that corresponds to that of an artificial language, for which the axioms and theorems that define machines of this kind are true merely by stipulation. The axioms that define CORE are true as matters of definition.

When virtual computers have physical counterparts in the form of target machines, including the existence of compilers and of interpreters, however, then programs that are written in their source code may exert causal influence upon the performance of those machines. The precise character of that influence depends upon the extent to which operations that are causal counterparts of commands written in those languages have been successfully implemented in the corresponding compilers or interpreters and in machine hardware, such as the arithmetic and logic units, in addition to the presence or absence of other causal factors that influence machine performance.

B. Programming languages and physical machines

The difference between virtual machines and physical machines reflects an *ontological* (or "ontic") difference in the kinds of things that they happen to be, but it is one with significant *epistemological* (or "epistemic") implications for what can be known about them. When a program is written in a programming language for which there exists no physical (target) machine, that programming language may be properly viewed as defining a virtual machine whose behavior corresponds to that of the language as a matter of definition. The programming language defines the corresponding machine as an abstract entity whose behavior necessarily conforms to that language.

In cases of this kind, therefore, the type of knowledge that we can acquire about the performance of that virtual machine is analytic and therefore certain. However, when a program is written in a programming

---

[36] Michael Marcotty and Henry E. Ledgard, *Programming Language Landscape*, 2d ed. (Chicago, IL: Science Research Associates, 1986), ch. 2.

language for which there exists a physical (target) machine, that programming language may no longer be properly viewed as defining a virtual machine whose behavior corresponds to that of the language simply as a matter of definition. For the possibility now presents itself that the behavior of the physical (target) machine might deviate arbitrarily from that of the virtual (source) machine. We cannot merely stipulate that they in fact correspond.

There is an important similarity and an important difference in comparison with alternative geometries. Euclidean and non-Euclidean geometries alike may be viewed as axioms and theorems that are true of corresponding abstract domains of entities and relations that satisfy them as matters of stipulation. Thus, the sum of the interior angles of a triangle turns out to be *greater than* 180 degrees in Riemannian geometry (which is the geometry of the surface of a sphere), *less than* 180 degrees in hyperbolic geometry (the geometry of the surface of a saddle), and *equal to* 180 degrees in Euclidean geometry. And yet, as formal theories of abstract domains, all three geometries are equally analytic!

That certain axioms define an abstract domain and that certain theorems follow from them, however, does not determine whether or not those axioms are true of the physical world. We have already discovered that the study of formal systems for abstract domains can be pursued employing purely *a priori* methods. But when the elements of those systems are subjected to a physical interpretation—where *straight lines* are identified with rays of light and *points* with their intersections, for example—then their truth or falsity is no longer a matter of meaning alone but depends upon the properties of the world. And that is an empirical question that may only be settled by *a posteriori* methods appropriate to claims that are synthetic.

Indeed, while Euclid may have assumed that the axioms of his geometry were those of physical space and did not merely define an abstract domain, the mathematical structure of space within contemporary theories of physics is regarded as non-Euclidean. Thus, when programmers in turn presume that the axioms and theorems of a programming language control the performance of a physical machine, they are making assumptions that are synthetic, that are not determined by stipulation. A program written in a language for which there exists some physical machine has causal capabilities that purely formal systems (as abstract calculi) or even scientific theories (as interpreted formal systems) do not possess.[37]

C. *Programs as causal models of algorithms*

While programs are constructed on the basis of algorithms when an appropriate step-by-step solution for a problem happens to exist, there is

---

[37] See James H. Fetzer, "Philosophical Aspects of Program Verification," *Minds and Machines*, vol. 1, no. 2 (May 1991), pp. 197–216.

an important difference between algorithms and programs. An algorithm can be implemented in different programs by different programmers who utilize different languages. The result is a causal model of that algorithm, by means of which that program can exert an influence on the performance of a physical machine that could not be exerted by the original algorithm.[38] Thus, the problem of determining whether integer n happens to be even or odd can be solved by means of a rather simple algorithm in two steps as follows:

Step 1: Divide n by two.
Step 2: If the remainder is zero then n is even; otherwise, n is odd.

This algorithm, as it stands, can exert no influence on any physical machine because it is formulated in English rather than in some programming language.

When that algorithm is implemented in the form of a program in a programming language for which there exist physical machines, such as Pascal, however, then the situation is completely different:

```
program even_or_odd(input, output);
var n: integer;
begin
   write('Enter an integer: ');
   readln(n);
   if (n mod 2) = 0 then
      writeln('The number is even')
   else
      writeln('The number is odd')
end.
```

This program, **even_or_odd**, takes an integer **n** and calculates whether the result after division by 2 (**mod**) is 0 or not. If the result equals 0, **writeln** ("write line") directs that a message be sent to the screen, "**The number is even**"; otherwise, "**The number is odd.**"

The **writeln** command is among the simplest directions that computers can execute. In Microsoft BASIC, for example, there are commands such as **BEEP** which beeps the speaker; **CIRCLE(x,y)r** which draws a circle with its center at point **x,y** and its radius **r**; **COLORb,p** which sets background color and palette of foreground colors when in graphics mode; **LOCATErow,col** which positions the cursor; and **PLAYstring**, which plays music as specified by **string**.[39] Thus, in all of these cases, the commands that occur in a program possess a causal capability that goes far beyond

---

[38] See *ibid.*, p. 202.
[39] See James H. Fetzer, "Program Verification: The Very Idea," *Communications of the ACM*, vol. 31, no. 9 (September 1988), p. 1057.

that of ordinary formal systems, even when such systems are provided with empirical interpretations.

Precisely which causal capabilities a specific program may possess, however, clearly depends on several different kinds of factors. One is the programming language in which it is written. A program, like **even_or_odd**, that is written in Pascal, for example, might be executed by any computer equipped with a Pascal compiler or interpreter. In contrast, the same algorithm incorporated into a program written in CORE might properly qualify as a set of instructions for a virtual machine, but since there is no interpreter or compiler for CORE, it would not possess any causal capabilities with regard to a physical counterpart. It could not control any actual machine.

D. Smith's analysis of the role of models

Other students of the foundations of computer science have noted that it appears to be heavily dependent on the use of models. As Brian Smith, for example, has observed, the construction of a program usually depends upon a presupposed model of the problem that is to be solved, where that model is supposed to represent some aspect of the real world. Techniques drawn from the field known as "model theory" can then be applied within computer science to determine whether or not our program corresponds to our model of the problem. As Smith remarks, alas, there is a hidden problem: "Unfortunately, model theory does not address the model-world relationship at all. Rather, what model theory does is to tell you how your descriptions, representations, and programs *correspond to your model*."[40] Thus, during the course of his discussion, Smith advances the diagram represented in Figure 4. He then invites us to think of computer systems, programs, descriptions or even thoughts as occupying the left-hand box, which is marked "COMPUTER," while "the very real world," marked "REAL WORLD," is on the right.[41]

Smith's discussion drives home the important point that "models" mediate the relationship between computer systems (computers, programs, and so on) and the world. Smith also emphasizes that models depend upon the essential use of *abstraction and idealization*, at least in the sense that they represent only some but not all of the properties of what they model. He acknowledges that model theory provides for the systematic investigation of the "left-hand" relationship (between models and computers), but asks: "What about the relationship on the right? The answer,

---

[40] Brian C. Smith, "Limits of Correctness in Computers," Center for the Study of Language and Information, Stanford University, Report No. CSLI-85-35 (1985); reprinted in Charles Dunlop and Rob Kling, eds., *Computerization and Controversy* (San Diego, CA: Academic Press, 1991), pp. 632–46. The passage quoted here is found on p. 638 (emphasis in original).

[41] Smith, "Limits," p. 639. As Smith also observes, computers and models themselves are "embedded within the real world," which is why the symbol for "REAL WORLD" is open in relation to the box, which surrounds the elements marked "COMPUTER" and "MODEL."

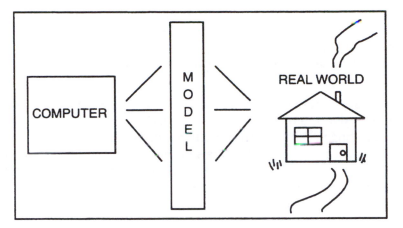

FIGURE 4. Computers, models, and the embedding world.

and one of the main points I hope you will take away from this discussion, is that, at this point in intellectual history, *we have no theory of this right-hand side relationship.*"[42]

At this juncture, however, a distinction needs to be drawn between the the model-world relation, on the one hand, and formulating solutions to specific problems, on the other. It is certainly correct to contend that the the construction of computers, the composition of programs, and the like, depend essentially upon the use of abstract and idealized models. And it is certainly correct to maintain that "model theory" provides resources for investigating the relationship between models of various kinds. But it is a mistake to suggest that, at this point in intellectual history, we do not have a theory of the model-world relationship or the resources to investigate it.

The relationship between models and the world, after all, is the domain of *empirical science.* The goal of empirical science can even be defined as that of constructing *a model of the world,* while the philosophy of science can be defined as having the goal of constructing *a model of science.*[43] The models that scientists construct are usually called "theories," and those that philosophers construct are also called "explications," but they are models in every sense that makes a difference here. The various sciences thus represent a division of labor in the pursuit of knowledge, where physicists seek to develop models of physical phenomena, chemists of chemical phenomena, and so forth. And philosophers of science try to model how this can be done.

Smith's apparent lapse regarding the model-world relation is even more surprising insofar as he explicitly considers the case of physics. He remarks:

[42] Smith, "Limits," p. 638 (emphasis added).
[43] See Fetzer, *Philosophy of Science,* pp. xii–xiii.

How apparently pure mathematical structures could be used to model the material substrate of the universe is a question that has exercised the physical scientists for centuries. But the point is that . . . formal techniques don't themselves address the question of adequacy.[44]

This passage itself appears to suggest where his argument has gone wrong. For the fact that the relations that may obtain between different models can be investigated by purely formal methods does not imply that the relations that obtain between models of the world and the world cannot be investigated by methods that are not purely formal. That the relations between two models are deductively checkable does not preclude the prospect that the relations between models and the world may be inductively checkable.[45]

E. The model-world relationship

The models that are objects of scientific inquiry may be "abstractions" or "idealizations" in the sense that they represent only some but not all of the properties of the phenomena they model, but they are not necessarily therefore either *inaccurate* or *incomplete* with respect to the properties of the phenomena that are causally (as opposed to statistically) relevant to an outcome or attribute of interest. Every instantiation of a physical system x at a specific moment of time t exemplifies an infinite number of properties $F1, F2, \ldots$ with respect to its spatial and temporal relations to other events. Yet that does not mean that each of those properties makes a difference to an outcome or attribute of interest. Most of them turn out to be irrelevant.

Consider diseases of the blood, for example. The expert system MYCIN depends upon laws relating diseases to symptoms and causes, yet many properties of persons who have diseases are not causally relevant to having those diseases or to manifesting specific symptoms. Properties such as *place of birth*, *level of education*, and *sense of humor*, for example, are properties whose presence or absence ordinarily does not contribute to bringing about the presence or absence of *leukemia*. When *being born near*

---

[44] Smith, "Limits," p. 639.

[45] Indeed, on the deductivist model of scientific inquiry, which has been advocated especially by Karl R. Popper, even the adequacy of scientific theories is deductively checkable by comparing deduced consequences with descriptions of the results of observations and experiments, which are warranted by perceptual inference. This process is not a symmetrical decision procedure, since it can lead to the rejection of theories in science but not to their acceptance. The failure to reject on the basis of severe tests, however, counts in favor of a theory. See Karl R. Popper, *Conjectures and Refutations* (New York: Harper and Row, 1968). On the deductivist model, see Fetzer, *Philosophy of Science*. The construction of proofs in formal sciences, incidentally, is also an asymmetrical procedure, since the failure to discover a proof does not establish that it does not exist.

a toxic waste dump, having a Ph.D., and so on, make a difference to the propensity of members of a reference class (such as *adult white females*) to acquire an attribute such as *leukemia*, then they qualify as causally relevant to that attribute, but otherwise not.[46]

The use of the term "propensity" is crucial within this context, however, since it refers to the *strength of the causal tendency* for an outcome of kind K (such as leukemia) to be brought about under conditions of kind $C1$ through Cn (such as adult white female born near a toxic waste dump). The criterion of *causal relevance* must therefore be separated from a counterpart criterion of *statistical relevance*, according to which any property whose presence or absence makes a difference to the frequency with which an attribute is manifested by the members of a reference class is statistically relevant to that attribute, but otherwise not.[47] The distinction is one between causation and correlation. Causal relations imply statistical correlations, but not conversely.[48]

That the difference between causal relations and statistical correlations is enormously important is widely acknowledged but is not therefore necessarily well understood. Virtually any two properties—shapes and sizes, or colors and textures, or heights and weights—stand in relations of statistical correlation, whether or not they are causally connected. The isolation and identification of properties that are not merely statistically correlated but causally related, by comparison, tends to depend upon systematic observation and controlled experimentation. The truth of a causal law requires that its formulation take into account the presence or absence of every property whose presence or absence makes a difference to its outcome.

This condition, which applies to laws themselves and is known as *the requirement of maximal specificity*, has a counterpart which applies to the application of laws for the purpose of explanation known as *the requirement of strict maximal specificity*.[49] While the former demands that every

---

[46] The use of the term "propensity" is crucial here, since it refers to the strength of the causal tendency. The general standard being employed may be referred to as the *propensity criterion of causal relevance*. See, for example, Fetzer, *Scientific Knowledge*, and Fetzer, *Philosophy of Science*, for technical elaboration.

[47] The use of the term "frequency" is crucial here, since it refers to the relative frequency of an attribute. The general standard being employed may be referred to as *the frequency criterion of statistical relevance*. See, for example, Wesley C. Salmon, *Statistical Explanation and Statistical Relevance* (Pittsburgh, PA: University of Pittsburgh Press, 1971). But Salmon mistakes statistical relevance for explanatory relevance.

[48] Strictly speaking, in the case of propensities, causal relations and relative frequencies are related probabilistically. See, for example, Fetzer, *Scientific Knowledge*, and Fetzer, *Philosophy of Science*.

[49] Even when the chemical composition, the manner of striking, and the dryness of a match are causally relevant to its lighting, that outcome may be predicted with deductive certainty (when the relationship is deterministic) or with probabilistic confidence (when the relationship is indeterministic) *only if* no other relevant properties, such as the presence or absence of oxygen, have been overlooked. For discussion, see, for example, James H. Fetzer, "The Frame Problem: Artificial Intelligence Meets David Hume," *International Journal of*

relevant property be included in the formulation of a law, the latter demands that every irrelevant property be excluded from a properly formulated explanation. When the laws of nature or relative frequencies that
obtain within a problem domain are known, they can function as *natural
algorithms* or as *heuristic guidelines* in formulating possible solutions to
problems as distinct kinds of models of the domain.[50]

F. The importance of specifications

Thus, in the case of an expert system such as MYCIN, for example, we
have discovered that information about causal connections and statistical
correlations between the occurrence of infections and diseases and the
occurrence of various symptoms represents the kind of knowledge that
science can provide. An expert system for predicting the behavior of a
certain person, moreover, would presumably apply scientific knowledge
concerning (normal or abnormal) human behavior to the features of that
specific case. An expert system for income-tax preparation, of course,
might not require scientific knowledge, but it certainly does not appear to
pose any problems for modeling that could not be overcome by fashion-
ing suitable algorithms.

While he is wrong to overlook the role of science with respect to right-
hand relations between models and the world, Smith is right to sense that
the *conception* of possible solutions to problems and their *formalization* as
"specifications" appears to be a creative process controlled by imagination and conjecture—an art rather than a science.[51] He thus distinguishes
between *specifications* as formal descriptions—typically in some canonical
language—in which the behavior that is desired of the system is described (where the specifications are normally motivated by a model of
the world), and *programs* as sets of instructions to govern the behavior of
that system. The specification thus describes what proper behavior should
be, while the program is a step-by-step characterization of exactly how
that behavior would be achieved by such a system.[52]

Other authors have introduced a somewhat different conception of
specifications. In a work on the management of software projects, for
example, Neil Whitten advances a definition of "product specifications"

Expert Systems, vol. 3, no. 3 (1990), pp. 219–32; and James H. Fetzer, "Artificial Intelligence Meets David Hume: A Response to Pat Hayes," *International Journal of Expert Systems,*
vol. 3, no. 3 (1990), pp. 239–47.

[50] Laws of nature are nature's algorithms. See Fetzer, "Artificial Intelligence Meets David
Hume," p. 239. A complete theory of the relations between models of the world and the
world would include a defense of the abductivist model of science as "inference to the best
explanation." [Note added 2000: But see p. 178, n. 27, above.]

[51] Smith thus appears to have committed a fallacy of equivocation by his ambiguous use
of the phrase "theory of the model-world relationship."

[52] Smith, "Limits," p. 640.

as a detailed description of *the externals of the product*, in the sense of a description of every feature accessible to system users: "Every function, command, screen, prompt, and so on must be documented here so that all the participants involved in the product development cycle will know the product they are to build, test, document, and support."[53] The appearance of tension between their views on specifications, however, can be resolved by observing that Whitten's specifications are external-model "counterparts" to Smith's internal-model specifications.

An expansive interpretation of this "external model" would encompass the manner in which the system should interact with its users in the real world. Thus, it should not be limited to such outcomes as, say, a series of warning alarms appearing on the screen in response to commands sent by the program to the system; it would also include the behavioral response that the system users would be expected to display in turn as measures to cope with the situation thus encountered. The kinds of situations and the kinds of responses that may be required of system users, therefore, ought to be inventoried or catalogued with suitable explanations and notation in a *user's manual* that enables users to operate the system in the real world.

The failure to find problems with computer systems has sometimes had deadly consequences. For example, the Therac-25 was a computer-controlled radiation machine manufactured by Atomic Energy of Canada, Ltd., that was used during the 1980s for the treatment of cancer. The system allowed radiation to be applied at two levels—an X-ray diagnostic mode and a mild treatment mode—where the intensity of exposure in the X-ray mode could be one hundred times as great as in the treatment mode. If an operator happened to select the X-ray mode by mistake *and then corrected it using the proper controls within an eight second interval*, a patient would be exposed to the full dosage without protection. The result was three deaths due to software.[54]

G. The models used in computer science

The Therac-25 therapy fiasco was further compounded by inadequate specifications in relation to the user's manual and the conditions encountered in the real world. Different warnings were flashed on its control screen identifying malfunctions by number (such as "Malfunction 54"), but they did not indicate the seriousness of the problems they represented. Whether its beam intensity was off merely a little or a lot, the warning looked the same. Moreover, the staff was so confident that their computerized system could not possibly harm their patients that they

[53] Whitten, *Managing Software Development Projects*, p. 13.
[54] Jonathan Jacky, "Safety-Critical Computing: Hazards, Practices, Standards, and Regulations," *The Sciences*, September/October 1989; reprinted in Dunlop and Kling, *Computerization and Controversy*, pp. 612–31.

ignored their complaints. When one patient objected, "You burned me!," the operator replied, "I'm sorry, but that's not possible, it's just not possible." The patient was severely injured.[55]

These considerations suggest that at least three kinds of models may be involved in the design, development, and utilization of reliable computerized products. The first is the *specification* itself as a model of the problem to be solved. When the problem is abstract or an algorithm exists that can solve it, the specification may have a deductive warrant; when it concerns causal relations and statistical correlations that have been subjected to scientific investigation, the specification may have an inductive warrant; but when warrants of neither kind happen to be available, a specification may have no more status than that of a conjecture regarding a possible solution.[56]

The second is the *program* itself as a model of the solution to that problem within a programming language. This component involves "modeling" of two different kinds. The more obvious of the two is that the program is the implementation of a solution to a problem, where that solution is represented by the specification. In this sense, a program is a model intended to satisfy another model, namely, a model of the problem solution in the form of its specification, which may have been proposed or imposed by another source. The less obvious sense in which the program involves modeling is that it is written in a programming language, which itself functions as a model for a virtual or physical machine. The adequacy of that model requires a warrant of its own.

The third kind of model is a model of the *computer system* consisting of a computer and its associated equipment situated in the world. Even in the case of a simple program such as **even_or_odd**, there is the presumption that the program software that implements an algorithmic solution to the problem is an integrated component of a larger system that includes, for example, an arithmetic and logic unit and a screen to which messages may be sent. In Microsoft BASIC, the system presumably includes speakers that can be beeped, background and foreground colors that can be set, and music that can be played. In the case of the Therac-25, the system includes radiation equipment with diagnostic and treatment capacities, a user-interface, etc.

These three kinds of models are obviously not independent. External specifications, for example, are presumably derived from a model of the system that is intended to employ them, and internal specifications are presumably derived from a model of external specifications. The program, in turn, is designed as an implementation of those internal speci-

---

[55] *Ibid.*, p. 617.
[56] As M. M. Lehman has observed (in personal communication with the author), specifications are frequently merely *partial* models of the problem to be solved.

fications by providing a set of instructions which, if it were executed by the hardware component of a computer system, would bring about behavior of that system in conformity with the original system model. Given our discoveries about many ways in which these systems can go wrong, the problem becomes whether computer system reliability can be assured. To what extent, if any, can we know when we can depend on the performance of a system?

V. The Reliability of Computer Systems

A. The limits of formal methods

From the perspective of the theory of knowledge, there appear to be three access routes toward the acquisition of knowledge of computer system reliability: deductive reasoning, inductive reasoning, and perceptual inference. The use of formal methods has been directed toward establishing that programs satisfy their specifications, where proofs of program correctness in this sense are known as *program verifications*. Among the foremost proponents of these formal methods is C. A. R. Hoare, who claims:

> Computer programming is an exact science in that all the properties of a program and all the consequences of executing it in any given environment can, in principle, be found out from the text of the program itself by means of purely deductive reasoning.[57]

This implies that certainty of knowledge about the performance of a computer might be obtainable, after all, by employing purely formal methods.

However, as Smith has remarked, a formal proof that the text of a program satisfies its specification has the character of a *relative consistency proof*, which might establish that the program would perform as desired on the assumption that the specification successfully defines the desired performance.[58] Thus, a distinction is commonly drawn between securing suitable specifications ("Getting the right system!") and writing a program which satisfies those specifications ("Getting the system right!").[59]

[57] C. A. R. Hoare, "An Axiomatic Basis for Computer Programming," *Communications of the ACM*, vol. 12, no. 10 (October 1969), pp. 576–80 and 583; the quotation may be found on p. 576.

[58] Smith, "Limits," pp. 639–43. Other authors have concurred. See, for example, Alan Borning, "Computer System Reliability and Nuclear War," *Communications of the ACM*, vol. 30, no. 2 (February 1987), pp. 112–31; reprinted in Dunlop and Kling, *Computerization and Controversy.*

[59] For further discussion, see, for example, B. W. Boehm, *Software Engineering Economics* (New York: Prentice-Hall, 1981).

Even the successful construction of a formal proof that a program satisfies its specifications could have limited import for securing the right outcome, because the specification model might actually be hopelessly inadequate.

However, the situation seems to be even more problematic than Smith suggests, because there are no built-in guarantees that a computer will properly execute a program, even when that program has been proven to satisfy its specifications—unless that computer is a virtual machine rather than a physical one.[60] The function of a program verification is therefore relatively restricted in relation to ultimate computer system performance, because the program itself is only one factor that contributes toward the behavior of a complex causal system. A proof of correctness can establish that a program conforms to its specifications, but cannot demonstrate that those specifications are suitable, or tell us what would happen were it executed.[61]

Hoare has sought to defend the use of formal methods by encompassing proofs of compiler and even hardware correctness within their scope:

> When the correctness of a program, its compiler, and the hardware of the computer have all been established with mathematical certainty, it will be possible to place great reliance on the results of the program and predict their properties with a confidence limited only by the reliability of the electronics.[62]

The problem now, however, has simply been compounded: the performance of compilers and hardware is no more amenable to formal proof in the case of physical machines than is the performance of programs. The situation that Hoare describes—in which the correctness of the program, its compiler, and its hardware have all been proven correct—can provide no guarantee that the execution of that software by means of that hardware would produce the performance desired using a physical machine.

The possibility that the model-world relationship may be the wrong one means that a proof that a program is valid does not establish that it is also sound. Its specifications might be mistaken because the model it represents does not conform to the world. In that case, getting the program right would not guarantee getting the right program. But there is a deeper problem because, *even if its specifications were correct*, a proof that a program is sound still could not guarantee computer performance. Getting the program right and getting the right program can insure what

[60] See Fetzer, "Program Verification," pp. 1056–57.

[61] See James H. Fetzer, "Author's Response," *Communications of the ACM*, vol. 32, no. 4 (April 1989), p. 512.

[62] Hoare, "An Axiomatic Basis for Computer Programming," p. 579.

would happen if that program were executed only on the assumption that the hardware, the software, and everything else behaves as expected.

B. The limits of empirical methods

The success of program verification as a generally applicable and completely reliable method to guarantee the performance of a computer when a program is executed is not even a theoretical possibility.[63] As Avra Cohn, one of the leading proponents of formal methods, has now acknowledged,

> neither an actual *device* nor an *intention* is an object to which logical reasoning can be applied. . . . In short, verification involves a pair of *models* that bear an uncheckable and possibly imperfect relation to the intended design and to the actual device.[64]

Formal methods applied to the text of a program cannot possibly guarantee the performance of a computer when it executes that program, because the causal capabilities of a program cannot be ascertained by purely deductive reasoning. Hoare's claim to possess certain knowledge of program performance on the basis of formal methods alone thus appears to be rooted in a misconception. It could only exist as a form of synthetic *a priori* knowledge.

The methods available for evaluating the reliability of computer systems, however, are not confined to purely formal methods. *Program testing*, for example, involves running a program, observing its behavior, and removing bugs as they are discovered. As Bev Littlewood and Lorenzo Strigini have observed, however, fixing a program or a device by attempting to remove its bugs runs the risk of introducing new ones: "Because nothing would be known about the new bug, its effects on the reliability of the system would be unbounded. In particular, the system might not even be as reliable as it was before the bug was found."[65] Debugging thus supplies no guarantees.

The three remedies that Littlewood and Strigini recommend, moreover, appear inadequate to the task. The first is to treat design failures as "nonquantifiable" and thereby avoid specifying performance requirements, an approach that they report is "now in fairly wide use." (We might call this "the ostrich policy.") The second, which they prefer over the first, is to impose limitations upon system requirements "so the role

[63] See Fetzer, "Program Verification."

[64] Avra Cohn, "The Notion of Proof in Hardware Verification," *Journal of Automated Reasoning*, vol. 5, no. 2 (June 1989), p. 132.

[65] Bev Littlewood and Lorenzo Strigini, "The Risks of Software," *Scientific American*, November 1992, p. 65.

of software is not too critical." (Call this "the reduced-role policy.") The third is to passively accept the risks involved in relying upon these systems. After all, "[s]ociety sometimes demands extremely high safety for what may be irrational reasons. Medical systems are a good example." (Call this "the blind policy.")[66]

Hardware testing, if anything, fares even worse. As David Shepherd and Greg Wilson have observed, a powerful microprocessor, such as the Inmos T800, which integrates a central processing unit with four communications links and four kilobytes of memory in a single device, turns out to have more possible combinations of input, memory, and output states than there are particles in the universe.[67] Exhaustive testing of an Inmos T800 is not even remotely a practical possibility. As a consequence, it must be tested using a modest subset of possible cases that the chip's designers hope qualifies as a representative sample that would support an inductive inference.

In fact, because the device has not yet been produced, its designers use programs running on other computers to simulate the T800's behavior. It turns out that the number of test results is so large that it is impossible to review each of them individually. As a consequence, designers compare a sample of the output of this new device against the output of a computer simulation or of an existing device already on the market. The problem that still remains, however, is that they cannot tell whether the standard of comparison they are employing might itself turn out to be incorrect.[68] It is not very reassuring when Shepherd and Wilson conclude: "The formal methods that Inmos is developing replace this design-and-test method with [formal] techniques guaranteeing that the final chip will behave correctly."[69]

C. The uncertainty of reliability

If the choice among the three policies proposed by Littlewood and Strigini (the ostrich policy, the reduced-role policy, and the blind policy) is "rather disappointing," as they themselves concede,[70] then how should we proceed? At first blush, the situation would not seem to have to be this disappointing. The same methods of observation and experimentation that apply in the empirical sciences in general ought to apply here, where the laws of computer science are counterparts of the laws of physics, chemistry, and biology. We may even assume that these laws concern the

---

[66] *Ibid.*, pp. 65–66 and 75.
[67] David Shepherd and Greg Wilson, "Making Chips That Work," *New Scientist*, May 13, 1989, pp. 61–64.
[68] *Ibid.*, p. 62.
[69] *Ibid.*
[70] Littlewood and Strigini, "The Risks of Software," p. 75.

behavior displayed by computer systems under various conditions, given maximally specific descriptions.

At least two problems arise with this conception, however plausible it might initially appear. The first problem is that of specifying the complete sets of causally relevant factors involved here. As Hoare observes:

> I find digital computers of the present day to be very complicated and rather poorly defined. As a result, it is usually impractical to reason logically about their behavior. Sometimes, the only way of finding out what they will do is by experiment. Such experiments are certainly not mathematics. Unfortunately, they are not even science, beause it is impossible to generalize from their results or to publish them for the benefit of other scientists.[71]

The complexity of computer systems that combine software, hardware, and associated equipment to operate aircraft, treat cancer, and the like may be such that maximally specific descriptions are practically impossible to secure. Those laws no doubt exist, but they remain largely unknown.

The second problem is that software systems appear to be extremely sensitive to initial conditions, so that even small changes in system software can produce large changes in performance. As David Parnas once remarked, "[t]he thing that makes software so difficult is that we're dealing with highly irregular, discontinuous systems with many states and few, if any, exploitable regularities."[72] Indeed, the sensitivity of these systems is so acute that a single misplaced comma in the specification of a control program for an Atlas rocket carrying Mariner 1, the first U.S. interplanetary spacecraft, caused the vehicle to veer off course and have to be destroyed, perhaps the most costly grammatical error in history.[73]

These considerations raise the possibility that computer systems may be *chaotic systems*, in which the least change in initial conditions can cause enormous and unexpected changes in outcome performance.[74] Chaotic systems are not indeterministic systems, in which one or another outcome within a fixed class of outcomes occurs, not in every case but with a specific probability—but rather are deterministic systems, in which the same outcome occurs in every case under the same conditions. What makes chaotic systems difficult to understand and practically impossible

[71] C. A. R. Hoare, "Mathematics of Programming," *BYTE*, August 1986, p. 116.

[72] David Parnas, quoted in William E. Suydam, "Approaches to Software Testing Embroiled in Debate," *Computer Design*, vol. 24, no. 21 (November 15, 1986), p. 50.

[73] Littlewood and Strigini, "The Risks of Software," p. 63.

[74] For an introduction to chaos theory, see James Gleick, *Chaos: Making a New Science* (New York: Penguin Books, 1988).

to predict is that the minuteness of the changes to which these systems are sensitive makes them very hard to replicate and investigate.

If computer systems are sufficiently complex that it is practically impossible to provide them with maximally specific descriptions, and if they are immensely sensitive to initial conditions (as chaotic systems are), then the prospects for the formulation of laws of behavior for these systems are not encouraging. In the absence of knowledge of the laws of systems of these kinds, it appears altogether likely that the best we may be able to discover are statistical correlations that relate partial and incomplete descriptions of the causal factors that affect system performance to system performance. Given ignorance of system laws, information about correlations may have to serve as a fallible warrant for statistical predictions.[75]

VI. IMPLICATIONS FOR PUBLIC POLICY

Strictly speaking, the reliability of a computer system should be understood as the propensity of that system to produce the effects that its users expect. A system's specifications may not be the best evidence of what users should expect.[76] If those systems could be given maximally specific descriptions and be subjected to controlled experiments across large numbers of trial repetitions, then it would be possible, in principle, to draw inferences from the relative frequencies of system success and failure to the reliability of those systems—characterized as system propensities.[77] The difficulties that confront this conception, however, are rather imposing.

The conclusion that emerges from these considerations has been expressed by M. M. Lehman, who has advanced the following formulation as (what he calls) the "Uncertainty Principle for Computer Application": *"In the real world, the outcome of software system operation is inherently uncertain with the precise area of uncertainty also not knowable."*[78] Provided we embrace a conception of morality that emphasizes respect for persons and their rights, this principle supports the inference that computer systems ought to be employed for safety-critical purposes where human lives are placed in jeopardy only when appropriate attention is devoted to an assessment of dangers and risks.

[75] See Fetzer, "The Frame Problem," pp. 228–29. Predictions based upon partial and incomplete descriptions of chaotic systems are obviously fallible—their reliability would appear to be unknowable.

[76] Sometimes unverifiable or incorrect programs can even be preferred; see Stephen Savitzky, "Technical Correspondence," *Communications of the ACM,* vol. 32, no. 3 (March 1989), p. 377. These include cases where a verifiably incorrect program yields a better performance than a verifiably correct program as a solution to a problem—where the most important features of a successful solution may involve properties that are difficult or impossible to formalize—and other kinds of situations.

[77] For further discussion, see Fetzer, *Scientific Knowledge,* and Fetzer, *Philosophy of Science.*

[78] M. M. Lehman, "Uncertainty in Computer Application," *Communications of the ACM,* vol. 33, no. 5 (May 1990), p. 585 (emphasis added).

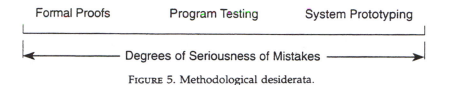

FIGURE 5. Methodological desiderata.

The most promising approach toward promoting health and safety arises from *system prototyping*, which involves testing entire computer systems within the environments for which they are intended. If the Therac-25 radiation machine had been subjected to severe tests deliberately designed to reveal potential inadequacies, that might have made a difference, but there are no guarantees. As David Nelson observes, system prototyping supports a different paradigm for computer science than that supported by the use of formal methods, since formal methods emphasize elegance and economy in programming, while prototyping and reliability testing emphasize safety-system redundancy and explanatory documentation.[79]

These results imply that statistical measures of the reliability of computer system performance should be employed as procedures intended to improve quality control. The use of formal proofs might even be statistically justifiable as a process that can contribute to improving the performance of computer systems when their performance is subjected to reliability tests.[80] In safety-critical situations, the point is not whether formal proofs may be useful but that prototype testing is indispensable.[81]

Other methods that can contribute toward the development of more reliable computer systems include the adoption of *software engineering standards*, which require programming projects to be conducted in specific stages with evaluations at each stage, and of a process of *certification and regulation* of competence in programming, enforced by requirements and periodic examinations.[82] Moreover, when systems fail, which they almost inevitably will, victims and survivors ought to be entitled to legal compensation by way of *liability protection*, which may take many forms, depending upon whether software is viewed as a service or as a product.[83]

[79] Nelson, "Deductive Program Verification" (*supra* note 27), p. 292.

[80] Donald Gillies has informed me that Hoare now advocates this position.

[81] The prospect of having to conduct statistical tests of nuclear weapons, space shuttle launches, etc., suggests the dimensions of the problem.

[82] See, for example, Jacky, "Safety-Critical Computing," pp. 622–27.

[83] *Ibid.*, p. 627. An excellent and accessible discussion of problems involving computer systems that affect many important areas of life is Ivars Peterson, *Fatal Defect: Chasing Killer Computer Bugs* (New York: Random House/Times Books, 1995).

Ultimately, the methods that should be employed for evaluating the reliability of computer systems tend to depend upon and vary with the seriousness of the consequences of making mistakes, as shown in Figure 5. Thus, no matter what solutions a society might adopt to enable its citizens to better cope with computer systems, such as software standards and liability protection, the full dimensions of the problem must be understood. Our confidence in this technology should not be merely an article of faith.

Philosophy, University of Minnesota, Duluth

INDEX OF NAMES

INDEX OF SUBJECTS

STUDIES IN COGNITIVE SYSTEMS

1. J.H. Fetzer (ed.): *Aspects of Artificial Intelligence.* 1988
    ISBN 1-55608-037-9; Pb 1-55608-038-7
2. J. Kulas, J.H. Fetzer and T.L. Rankin (eds.): *Philosophy, Language, and Artificial Intelligence.* Resources for Processing Natural Language. 1988   ISBN 1-55608-073-5
3. D.J. Cole, J.H. Fetzer and T.L. Rankin (eds.): *Philosophy, Mind and Cognitive Inquiry.* Resources for Understanding Mental Processes. 1990   ISBN 0-7923-0427-6
4. J.H. Fetzer: *Artificial Intelligence: Its Scope and Limits.* 1990
    ISBN 0-7923-0505-1; Pb 0-7923-0548-5
5. H.E. Kyburg, Jr., R.P. Loui and G.N. Carlson (eds.): *Knowledge Representation and Defeasible Reasoning.* 1990   ISBN 0-7923-0677-5
6. J.H. Fetzer (ed.): *pistemology and Cognition.* 1991   ISBN 0-7923-0892-1
7. E.C. Way: *Knowledge Representation and Metaphor.* 1991   ISBN 0-7923-1005-5
8. J. Dinsmore: *Partitioned Representations.* A Study in Mental Representation, Language Understanding and Linguistic Structure. 1991   ISBN 0-7923-1348-8
9. T. Horgan and J. Tienson (eds.): *Connectionism and the Philosophy of Mind.* 1991
    ISBN 0-7923-1482-4
10. J.A. Michon and A. Akyürek (eds.): *Soar: A Cognitive Architecture in Perspective.* 1992
    ISBN 0-7923-1660-6
11. S.C. Coval and P.G. Campbell: *Agency in Action.* The Practical Rational Agency Machine. 1992   ISBN 0-7923-1661-4
12. S. Bringsjord: *What Robots Can and Can't Be.* 1992   ISBN 0-7923-1662-2
13. B. Indurkhya: *Metaphor and Cognition.* An Interactionist Approach. 1992
    ISBN 0-7923-1687-8
14. T.R. Colburn, J.H. Fetzer and T.L. Rankin (eds.): *Program Verification.* Fundamental Issues in Computer Science. 1993   ISBN 0-7923-1965-6
15. M. Kamppinen (ed.): *Consciousness, Cognitive Schemata, and Relativism.* Multidisciplinary Explorations in Cognitive Science. 1993   ISBN 0-7923-2275-4
16. T.L. Smith: *Behavior and its Causes.* Philosophical Foundations of Operant Psychology. 1994
    ISBN 0-7923-2815-9
17. T. Dartnall (ed.): *Artificial Intelligence and Creativity.* An Interdisciplinary Approach. 1994
    ISBN 0-7923-3061-7
18. P. Naur: *Knowing and the Mystique of Logic and Rules.* 1995   ISBN 0-7923-3680-1
19. P. Novak: *Mental Symbols.* A Defence of the Classical Theory of Mind. 1997
    ISBN 0-7923-4370-0
20. G.R. Mulhauser: *Mind Out of Matter.* Topics in the Physical Foundations of Consciousness and Cognition. 1998   ISBN 0-7923-5103-7
21. K.L. Butler: *Internal Affairs.* Making Room for Psychosemantic Internalism. 1998
    ISBN 0-7923-5261-0
22. B.A. Thyer (ed.): *The Philosophical Legacy of Behaviorism.* 1999   ISBN 0-7923-5736-1
23. D. Livingstone Smith. *Freud's Philosophy of the Unconscious.* 1999   ISBN 0-7923-5882-1
24. M. Perlman: *Conceptual Flux.* Mental Representation, Misrepresentation, and Concept Change. 2000   ISBN 0-7923-6215-2
25. J.H. Fetzer: *Computers and Cognition: Why Minds are Not Machines.* 2001
    ISBN 0-7923-6615-8

STUDIES IN COGNITIVE SYSTEMS

26. H. Cruse, J. Dean and H. Ritter (eds.): *Prerational Intelligence: Adaptive Behavior and Intelligent Systems Without Symbols and Logic, Volume 1*. 2000   ISBN 0-7923-6665-4
H. Ritter, H. Cruse and J. Dean (eds.): *Prerational Intelligence: Adaptive Behavior and Intelligent Systems Without Symbols and Logic, Volume 2*. 2000   ISBN 0-7923-6670-0
J. Dean, H. Ritter and H. Cruse (eds.): *Prerational Intelligence: Interdisciplinary Perspectives on the Behavior of Natural and Artificial Systems*. 2000   ISBN 0-7923-6669-7
ISBN Indivisible Set 0-7923-6666-2

KLUWER ACADEMIC PUBLISHERS – DORDRECHT / BOSTON / LONDON